A BUSINESS HISTORY *of* ALBERTA

Henry C. Klassen

University of Calgary Press

University of Calgary Press
2500 University Drive N.W.
Calgary, Alberta, Canada T2N 1N4

Canadian Cataloguing in Publication Data

Klassen, Henry C. (Henry Cornelius), 1931-
    A business history of Alberta

    Includes bibliographical references and index.
    ISBN 1-55238-022-X (bound) — ISBN 1-55238-009-2 (pbk.)

    1. Alberta–Commerce–History. I. Title.
    HF3229.A5K32 1999   338.097123   C99-910550-7

Canada We acknowledge the financial support of the Government of Canada through the Book Publishing Industry Development Program (BPIDP) for our publishing activities.

COMMITTED TO THE DEVELOPMENT OF CULTURE AND THE ARTS

Publication and promotion of this book has been made possible by financial assistance from the Alberta Foundation for the Arts.

Printed and bound in Canada by Veilleux Impression à Demande Inc.

∞ This book is printed on acid-free paper.

Cover and book design: Glitch Graphics.
Cover photographs:
    Calgary skyline, detail from photo of Standen's, courtesy of Standen's.
    Jasper Avenue, Edmonton, view east from 1st Street, 1913. Provincial Archives of Alberta, A5372.
    Oil rig at Leduc, 1947, courtesy of Imperial Oil.
    A. E. Cross' A7 Ranch in the late 1890s. Glenbow Archives, NA-857-1.

FOREWORD

Dr. Henry Klassen's *A Business History of Alberta* chronicles a rich history of people and enterprise – an enduring spirit of entrepreneurship, and an evolution of economic foundations – from pioneer outposts to sophisticated global players. It is with pride and pleasure that the Certified Management Accountants of Alberta support the publication of this work.

Our own history, as a profession with a focused and specialized area of practice inside organizations, has evolved with the business history of this province. The demand for CMAs, and the popularity of the designation has grown tremendously alongside the Alberta economy and its ever-expanding industry base.

The origins of the CMA designation are interesting. Although the history of accounting dates back about 5000 years, it is only in the last 150 years that accounting has emerged as an organized profession. Originally, the role of professional accountants was primarily in the attest function. During World War I, accounting talents and skills found expression in a wide range of administrative capacities, such as managers, cost accountants and cost investigators – largely to settle contract disputes between government and industry. From this experience, the importance of cost accounting, and its implications on controlling expenditure, eliminating waste and measuring profits became a mainstay of the manufacturing industry. The search to improve profitability in business had found a champion.

In the mid 1920s, a management-oriented accounting profession, with a dedicated body of knowledge, and a focus on the planning and control function, took root in eastern Canada. The first official Alberta charter was established in 1939 in Edmonton. In 1944, legislation was enacted to establish the Society of Industrial Accountants of Alberta, and the right to award the RIA (Registered Industrial Accountant) designation – later to become the Certified Management Accountants of Alberta, and CMA.

From a foundation of 63 members led by insightful businessmen and educators like J. Alvin Tupper, and Francis Winspear, our membership now approaches 6000. Today's CMAs reflect the fabric and diversity of the economy – and enjoy a much broader role, providing financial and strategic leadership to industry, government and education throughout Alberta, and around the world. Our members, and our contributions, both past and future, are interwoven in the success of Alberta's enterprises. It has been a privilege to play a role in its rich history.

CMA CANADA | CERTIFIED MANAGEMENT ACCOUNTANTS OF ALBERTA
Shaping the Future

This book is dedicated with love to my family.

Henry C. Klassen

CONTENTS

PART TWO:
BUSINESS DEVELOPMENT IN THE NEW PROVINCE
(Continued)

PREFACE

I have written this book not only for students in various disciplines but also for the general public. The work provides a look at the maturing of businesses in Alberta as they faced opportunity, depression, and the challenge of confronting the necessity for change. The main themes that underlie the history of Alberta business — the development of the business firm and the development of business-government relations — are at the heart of this study. I explore the history of business over two hundred years of Alberta history, from the late eighteenth century to the present. Albertans directed their entrepreneurial talents into firms that contributed enormously to the transformation and enrichment of Alberta. In my view, business history is more than the examination of the firm. The context of the culture and the political system in which it functions is of central importance in understanding the firm and the firm, at the same time, has an impact on that context. In one way or another, the firm reacts to the social and political environments in which it operates. In the democratic society that exists in Alberta and Canada, the broader political setting in which the firm has evolved is another aspect of its history. The stories of business and government have always been closely intertwined in Alberta.

Both the political setting and the firm have changed significantly over the years and in the process, Alberta's business system has been reshaped. As Albertans continue to reshape their business system in the 1990s, the historical experience of earlier generations active in similar developments becomes more pertinent. Possessing knowledge of that experience does not necessarily provide solutions to contemporary problems, for every age faces unique challenges. Still, it is helpful to know something about the evolution of business. In addition to providing a sense of the development of Alberta's business system, such an understanding can foster a feeling of confidence, alerting a new generation to a common heritage it shares with previous generations in a province with long traditions of coming to grips with economic difficulties.

Restructuring the business system as Albertans inch toward the end of the twentieth century is not the first such reshaping in the provincial experience. Over the last two centuries, Albertans have responded to economic, technological, and political pressures, trying to reorganize their business institutions and change them for the better. This was as evident before World War II as after that conflict and took place in Alberta about once each generation, just as elsewhere in Canada. Marked by dramatic ups and downs in the business cycle and shattered hopes for expansion, the process was frequently painful. In a democratic society such as Alberta and Canada, the process of reshaping the business system was especially complex given the unpopularity of explicit national or provincial or local planning. At all levels, governments usually shied away from publishing detailed plans in which goals were clearly spelled out. They also did not provide rigid regulatory machinery to implement the many details required by the extensive plans put into the hands of bureaucrats and experts by legislative action. Such rigid machinery, Albertans and Canadians believed, might be acceptable in a totalitarian regime, but not in a democracy. Even those who favoured planning did not want inflexible regulatory mechanisms.

In Alberta and Canada, the reshaping of the business system has been achieved through a complex process of co-ordination. This has meant reliance on pragmatism open to all kinds of institutional experiments, in which there has been close interaction between government agencies and private business enterprise. From this interaction emerged public policy, reflecting an imperfect consensus on business goals and on the most desirable way for their realization. Without a clear sense of direction, such planning in a democracy has often been baffling, has not always proved economically efficient, and has still been accepted by many Albertans and Canadians as part of the price to be paid for the maintenance of political freedom, together with a workable business system.

In tracing the evolution of Alberta's business system, I have employed a historical approach that focusses on individuals, on the people who were involved in shaping business firms and public policy. This book describes and analyzes the contributions men and women have made to the development of Alberta's business system over the years. I have not tried to write an economic history, a comprehensive account of all economic and social developments, or to assess the importance of real estate activity and tourism. My method of analysis does not rule out other approaches that could be effectively applied to the subject. Nor have I attempted an exhaustive treatment of the history of business enterprise in Alberta. A number of significant topics, such as labour relations and consumerism, have been dealt with in a meaningful way but are not covered intensively in this book. My aim has been to make an initial foray into a previously little known field and to raise points others may desire to explore more fully or from different perspectives.

For business historians, the field of business enterprise in Alberta history promises to be a fertile one. Much work remains to be done and possible avenues for future research on business in Alberta can be identified. For instance, we need to understand the historical evolution of small firms and their contributions to the economic development of Alberta. As well, we need to know more about the rise of big business and changes the development of big business brought to Alberta's business system.

My scholarly life as a business historian has been enriched by this project. An opportunity to undertake the time-consuming study of a large subject, my research for the book has involved me deeply in the history of business in Alberta. Besides representing a culmination of my quest to chart the evolution of business enterprise in the province, it has allowed me to enjoy stimulating conversations with businesspeople. While at the University of Calgary I have taught business history. Finishing this project has provided me with many ideas and examples to use in my classes.

INTRODUCTION

When I began this book, I was struck by the widespread and growing interest in the story of Alberta business enterprise in the past and present. A subject rich in human action and ideas, business in Alberta merits concentrated attention. Within the province, the successful operation of business has played a central role in the creation and maintenance of communities. The significance of business to the lives of Albertans makes it important to explore the historical development of business in Alberta.

Business has exerted a powerful and continuing influence on Alberta society, and this book focuses on business as a basic theme of Alberta history from the 1790s to the present. Business history is a valuable key to understanding the past, and studying Alberta offers a chance to investigate the development of business in a western Canadian province. In a broad sense, business here means the organization of the production and distribution of goods and services. Citizens have long recognized that business has created opportunities for Alberta. My study examines some of the institutions, practices, and views that have developed within business over two centuries. I address two major themes in Alberta business history: the evolution of the business firm and the development of business-government relations. Although the theme of the development of the firm dominates my book, the theme of business-government relations is also present.

Over the years, Albertans funnelled their entrepreneurial drive and energies into firms that have done a great deal to build Alberta. The first main theme of the history of business in Alberta is the evolution of the firm. In business history, however, there is a need to go beyond a look at the firm. It is also helpful to see the history of the firm in relation to the environment — politics and culture — in which business enterprise evolved. In particular, the changing relationships between business and government constitute the second principal theme of this book.

Analyzing the development of the firm in Alberta provides a fascinating challenge to a business historian. Business firms can properly be called institutions and, as is the case for other human institutions, have changed over time. This study explores the changes in the Alberta business firm; it records ways the firm first appeared and notes the conditions that brought about alterations as well as their impact on Alberta society. Business firms are developed and managed by entrepreneurs. The personality of any entrepreneur makes an imprint on the firm he or she is developing. Entrepreneurs are innovators who alter the established routines of production and distribution by

seizing profitable opportunities, taking risks, creating new products and services, developing new markets, and finding new ways of organizing a firm.
While there is a close connection between the entrepreneur and the firm, not
every firm, or every individual active in business, is creative and innovative.
Throughout Alberta history, some people have conducted essential business
operations in a routine manner and have commonly been referred to as businesswomen or businessmen. At the same time, some of these very men and
women legitimately belong to the entrepreneurial group, because they have
been willing to risk their money and labour in an attempt to achieve greater
wealth for themselves and their children.

Business historians exploring the institutional development of the firm
can benefit from economic historians' understanding of the bigger forces —
like economic booms and contractions — that affect the accumulation of
wealth. Such larger forces are the arenas in which business firms begin,
develop, and fade. Business historians pay heed to individual firms and
their development patterns. These patterns and the interrelationship of
firms make up the business system. Firms are parts of industries, such as the
agricultural or oil industries, and industries are components of the entire
economy. In their analysis of the evolution of firms and the relationships
between firms, business historians need a command of the history of the
whole economy, including the larger picture of economic expansions and
depressions. An awareness of the bigger picture of economic upturns and
downturns is essential for comprehending the history of the business firm.
Readers will find in these pages a brief discussion of the economic settings
in which Albertans have become involved in business activities.

An understanding of government-business relations — the second
major theme of the history of business in Alberta — helps provide a political perspective on the development of the firm. Business firms carry on
operations within environments created in part by law and politics.
Entrepreneurs and businesspeople have always tried to influence public
policy in Alberta, attempting to shape the legal and political environments
in which firms operate. The opportunities and difficulties surrounding business owners' efforts to make effective use of law and government are
significant features in Alberta life. Politicians have often been active in
business promotion. In short, business and politics have been closely interwoven throughout Alberta history. Government leaders and business firms,
though they often worked together in a spirit of co-operation, frequently
disagreed in their views of what was desirable or possible. Business continued, however, to have strong, enduring ties to government.

The investigation of government-business relations and the development of the firm permits deeper probes into the overall picture of the
Alberta business system, which is much different now from the business system first established in Alberta by entrepreneurs and businesspeople in the

late eighteenth century. At that time, the rise of big business was still in the future. This book assesses the rise of the big firm and how big firms contributed to Alberta's evolving business system. By examining changes and differences in business firms and government policies over time, we obtain information essential to understanding larger historical developments in Alberta, especially how alterations in the business system in the pre-World War II period laid the foundations for the business system of the post-World War II era.

I offer, then, a look at the principal themes of Alberta business history, and I draw attention as well to the important aspects of the broader evolution of Alberta's economy and society. For two centuries, Albertans have made use of natural resources, purchased and sold goods and services, adopted and refined technological devices, and worked through government officials to develop their economy. Alberta's business system, like its firms, has not been a static phenomenon. Instead, its history has been one of continuity and change. Dominant in the history of business in Alberta is the story of entrepreneurs who took advantage of new opportunities and, in the process, shaped and reshaped the institution of the firm and the way it carried on its operations.

At the core of business history is the firm, and the history of the Alberta firm encompasses several distinct but overlapping stages. In the first stage, the fur trade era in the century before 1870, fur companies organized their operations around networks of fur trading posts. The companies commanded wealth that could be invested profitably in just one major economic activity, and so investments flowed in one main direction, the fur trade.

In the second stage, the territorial period before 1905 when Alberta was a district in the Canadian North-West Territories, the most prominent firms, those of general merchant, farmer, and rancher, were personally owned and managed, and provided leadership in Alberta's economic activity as well as in its political and social life. The general merchant, rancher, and farmer, at times called all-purpose business firms, participated in a wide range of economic activities. For example, the general merchant or farmer or rancher might have been simultaneously involved in producing, distributing, and marketing goods. Because of their broad functions, these business firms stood at the heart of the territorial business world.

Throughout the territorial period in Alberta, the general merchant, rancher, and farmer found themselves operating alongside small firms that specialized in only one line of business. In the third stage, which started soon after Alberta became a province in 1905, these small, specialized but still personally owned and managed firms multiplied rapidly in a provincial economy of growing opportunities and markets. During this third stage of specialized business firms, which marked business history in the early decades of the new province, opportunities expanded enough to allow even general merchants, ranchers, and farmers to become specialized, and the all-purpose firm declined.

The third stage in the history of the business firm in Alberta lasted until about World War II, by which time new types of business institutions had started to emerge. Even by World War I, some firms grew large and came to be seen as big businesses, signalling the beginning of the fourth stage in the history of the Alberta firm. In contrast to the small, personally managed specialized firms that dominated business life in the previous stage, these new big businesses developed bureaucratic management. The tremendous increase in size and complexity of the big firms made it impossible for any one person to manage them. Personal management gave way to bureaucratic organization, and management became separated from ownership in big businesses in Alberta.

Small firms did not, however, disappear from the Alberta business scene. Despite the rise of big business in the fourth stage, many small personally owned and managed enterprises co-existed with big firms. To avoid direct competition with big businesses, small firms in Alberta developed specialty products or services for niche markets.

The fifth stage in the history of the business firm in Alberta is diversification and decentralization. After World War II, some big businesses grew larger and set up decentralized management structures, especially as they diversified their products and services across a range of markets in different geographical areas. Older institutional forms of business did not vanish from the Alberta business system. Rather, the big diversified, decentralized firms supplemented the big centralized firms and small personally owned and managed enterprises.

With the stages in the history of the firm in Alberta came several phases in the development of distribution, or marketing. In the first phase, during the century before 1870, the firms' participation in the collection of furs for foreign markets was the prime engine of economic growth. Throughout this period, the North Saskatchewan River and the Atlantic Ocean connected Alberta to overseas markets.

In the second phase, from about 1870 to 1905, the Alberta market was fragmented among many localities. Most business firms, especially general merchants and farmers, were small and had little control over the market. Local and regional markets became the primary focus of their efforts. Many products sold by general merchants were generic, unbranded goods. Their main business strategy was profits through high prices. Although firms advertised their names, the turnover of stock was generally slow.

During the third phase, starting around 1905 and continuing to the present time, a national mass market for some Alberta goods developed in an integrated national economy. By emphasizing low prices, large manufacturing firms came to exercise great impact on the market. The principal business strategy of these firms was profit through volume and rapidly turning stock. Generic goods gave way to name-brand products.

The fourth phase in the history of marketing in Alberta, which began for some goods after World War II, was characterized by segmented, specialized markets. With rising prosperity, consumer preferences became more segmented. Big, successful firms responded to the demand for more specialized, less standardized goods by focussing on particular consumer preferences.

Business-government relations, like the business firm itself, developed in stages in Alberta. In the first stage, during the century before 1870, British subjects lived and worked under a system known as mercantilism, government direction of business activity intended to increase the British crown's power. The second stage, in the territorial period before 1905, was developmental. Albertans used local, territorial, and federal governments to create and develop business opportunities. Individuals in Alberta may have had their doubts about engaging in manufacturing, but some looked to its potentialities. In 1879, John A. Macdonald's Conservative government established a tariff system designed to protect Canadian manufacturers from competition abroad, providing private citizens, including Albertans, with greater opportunities to invest their capital in manufacturing firms. This developmental tradition grew in the early twentieth century and continues in Alberta at the present time.

Regulation, the third stage of business-government relations, added to the developmental tradition established in the late nineteenth century. From the early days in Alberta, through personal participation in urban politics, businesspeople helped regulate the local environment in an effort to promote business, as well as encourage the economic growth of the community. For instance, they became involved in planning fire-protection facilities. Their actions grew from the conviction that government intervention could be an important factor in the development of business firms.

The new regulation — the fourth stage of business-government relations — arose in the 1960s out of the need for all Alberta citizens to live and work in a healthful environment. Traditional developmental and regulatory arrangements remained important to the business system and the larger society. In the last third of the twentieth century, however, the new regulation exerted a steady pressure on business firms in Alberta to help create good health and safety conditions at the workplace. Blended with the customary goals of promoting business and fostering economic growth was a powerful new concern for the health and welfare of Albertans.

As a work in business history, my book analyzes the historical development of Alberta's business system. Part One looks at the founding of Rupert's Land as a business enterprise, addresses the development of the early Alberta business system, and, by concentrating on the political economy, examines changes that occurred in that business system as part of the growth of capitalism in Canada. Capitalism, best understood as an economic order characterized by private ownership and control of the means of production, permitted Canada to develop a thriving economy, an economy dominated by business firms that invested capital in anticipation of profits. I begin my history of Alberta business with an exploration of business activity in medieval Europe. When Europeans first came to Alberta in the eighteenth and early nineteenth centuries, they brought with them their capitalist business institutions and practices. In this way, the Alberta business system had its origins in European business institutions. Part Two, besides tracing the expansion of business and the growth of specialized business firms in Alberta arising from new opportunities springing up in the early and mid-twentieth century, discusses the role government authorities played in creating these opportunities. Part Three delves into the rise of big business, how the evolution of big business changed business-government relations, and the development of diversified, decentralized corporations. Finally, small business, new kinds of governmental promotion and regulation of business, along with the still-developing business firm are the main topics of Part Four.

MAP of ALBERTA

■ ∙ ▪ Towns & Cities

❶ The Edmonton, Dunvegan & British Columbia Railway

❷ The Alberta & Great Waterways Railway

❸ The Canadian National Railway

❹ The Pembina Valley Railway

❺ The Canadian Pacific Railway

Rivers & Lakes

National Parks

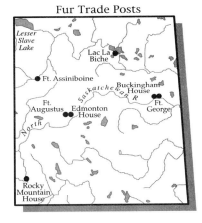

Fur Trade Posts

Lesser Slave Lake

Lac La Biche

Ft. Assiniboine

Buckingham House

Ft. Augustus Edmonton House

Ft. George

Saskatchewan R

North

Rocky Mountain House

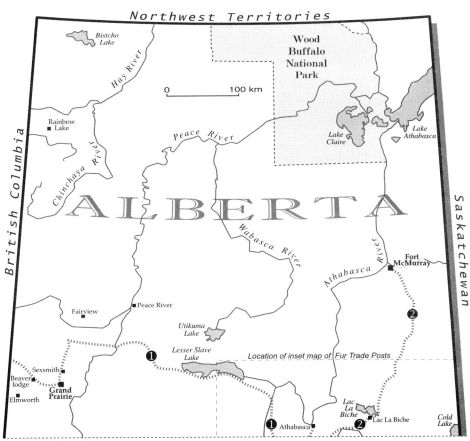

Northwest Territories

Bistcho Lake

Hay River

Wood Buffalo National Park

0   100 km

Rainbow Lake

Peace River

Lake Claire

Lake Athabasca

British Columbia

Chinchaya River

ALBERTA

Saskatchewan

Wabasca River

Athabasca River

Fort McMurray

Fairview

Peace River

Utikuma Lake

❷

Lesser Slave Lake

Location of inset map of Fur Trade Posts

❶

Sexsmith

Beaver lodge

Grand Prairie

Elmworth

❶ Athabasca

Lac La Biche

❷ Lac La Biche

Cold Lake

Peace River
Grande Cache
Athabasca River
Westlock
Redwater
Beaver River
Cold Lake
Saskatchewan River
St. Paul
St. Albert
Stony Plain
EDMONTON
Edson
Hinton
Vegreville
Tofield
Vermilion
Lloyd-minster
North
Leduc
Bruce
River
Jasper Nat. Park
Wetaskiwin
Camrose
Sedge-wick
Wainwright
Killam
Ponoka
Bashaw
British Columbia
Nordegg
Eckville
Lacombe
Battle
Provost
Benalto
Rocky Mountain House
Sylvan Lake
Red Deer
Stettler
Castor
Cadogan
Innisfail
Coronation
Trochu
Olds
Three Hills
Banff Nat. Park
Didsbury
Hanna
Youngstown
Carbon
Acme
Drumheller
Airdrie
Banff
Bow
Cochrane
Canmore
Calgary
Strathmore
Red Deer River
Gleichen
Rosemary
Turner Valley
Okotoks
River
Brooks
South Saskatchewan R
High River
Blackie
Cayley
Vulcan
Nanton
Champion
Stavely
Redcliff
Oldman
Claresholm
Medicine Hat
Granum
Nobleford
River
Bow Island
Crowsnest Pass
Coleman
Frank
Taber
Fort Macleod
Lethbridge
Stirling
Lundbreck
Pincher Creek
Raymond
Manyberries
Waterton Nat. Park
St. Mary R
Cardston
Milk River
Milk River
Coutts
Montana
Saskatchewan
1
2
3
4
5
Fort McMurray
Grand Prairie
EDMONTON
Red Deer
Calgary
Medicine Hat
Lethbridge
Roadways of ALBERTA
Index map of ALBERTA

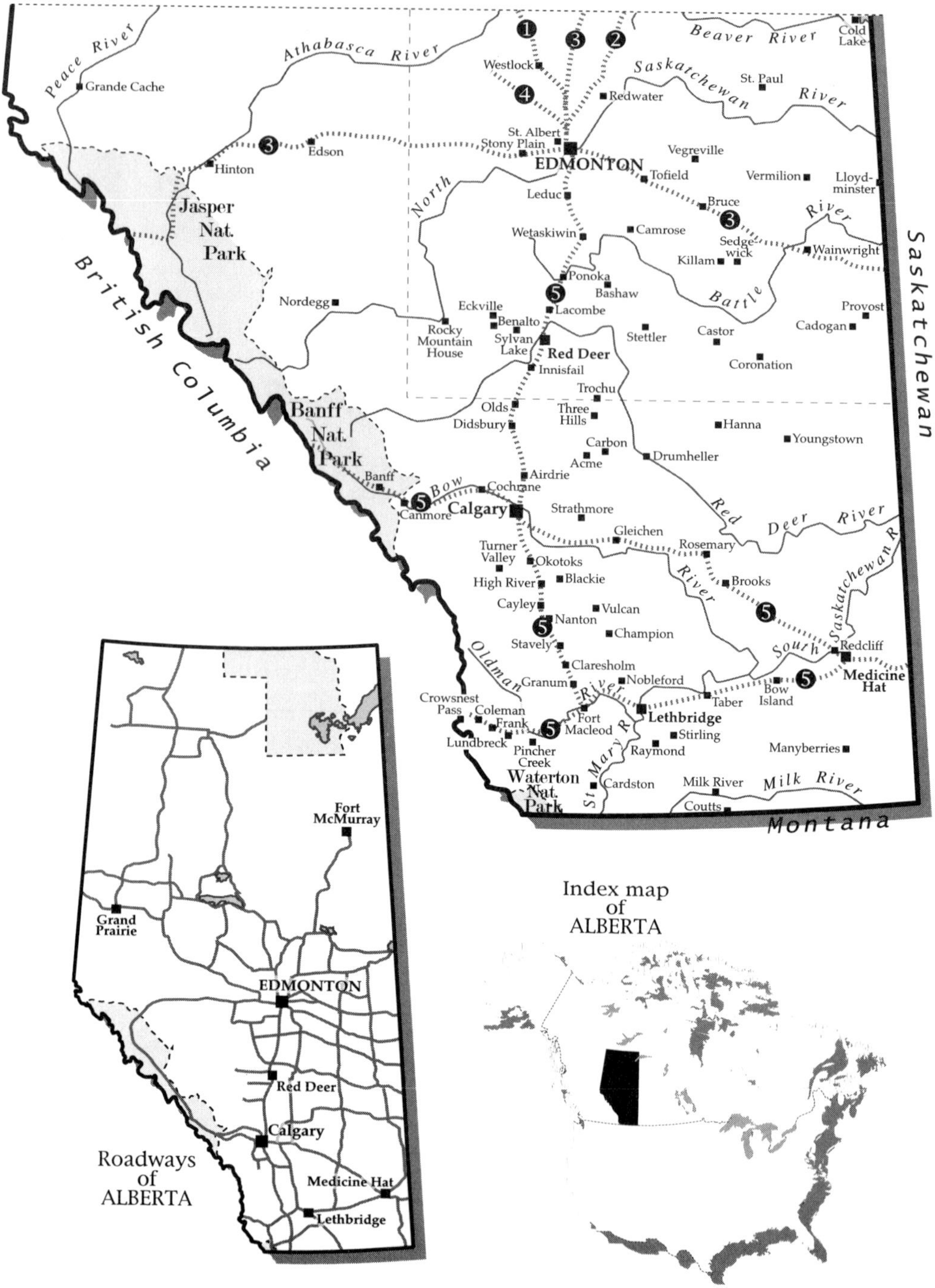

ACKNOWLEDGEMENTS

I would like to thank the many people who gave me valuable help in writing this book. My colleagues in Canadian history at the University of Calgary — David Bercuson, Pat Brennan, Sarah Carter, Warren Elofson, Doug Francis, Herman Ganzevoort, Louis Knafla, David Marshall, Tony Rasporich, and Don Smith — have been supportive, often sharing with me their thoughts on Canadian development. I am grateful as well to Debra Isaac, Wendy Amero, Linda Toth, Carol Murray, Kelly Morris, and Dorothy Harty for superb typing. My thanks also to Michael Bliss at the University of Toronto for encouraging me in my study of business in Canada over many years.

It is a pleasure to express my gratitude for the generous financial support provided by the Canada Council in the initial stages of my work on this project and for the indispensable assistance I received from archivists and librarians at many repositories. Information and collections of manuscripts at a number of institutions were vital to this book, and I thank the staff for their help: Alberta Corporate Registry, University of Calgary Library, Glenbow-Alberta Institute Archives, Alberta Economic Development and Tourism Library, Provincial Archives of Alberta, City of Edmonton Archives, Alberta Municipal Affairs Archives, Red Deer and District Museum and Archives, Alberta Treasury Branches Head Office Library, Calgary Land Titles Office, and the court houses in Fort Macleod, Calgary, and Lethbridge.

I would like to extend my gratitude to numerous people in the business world. Executives and their staff in big firms and small businesses gave cheerful assistance whenever I needed it. The list of people I interviewed is a long one, and I have included it in the bibliography. In each case, interviewees played a significant role in my research by sharing their expertise. Without their help, this book would not have been possible, and I heartily thank all the men and women whose memories of their business careers have added to my own knowledge. To Max Foran and two anonymous readers I owe thanks; their knowledge and careful reading of the manuscript are deeply appreciated. Thanks are also due to Shirley Onn, Walter Hildebrandt, Linda Reynolds, John King, Maureen Ranson, and Joan Barton at the University of Calgary Press for invaluable editorial assistance. I am also grateful to Ed Wiens for designing the book, to Robin Poitras for the preparation of the map, and to Annabelle Moore for her work on the index. Finally, I offer lively thanks to my family for their unwavering support and inspiration.

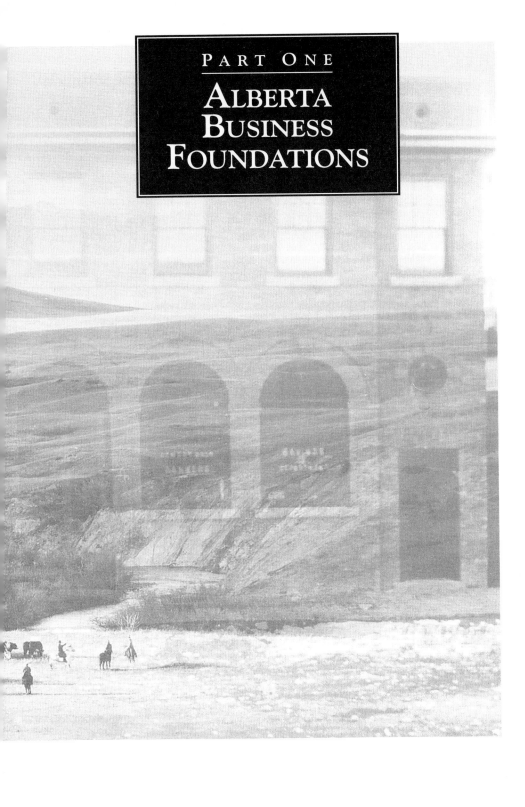

PART ONE

ALBERTA BUSINESS FOUNDATIONS

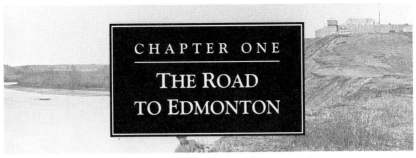

CHAPTER ONE

THE ROAD
TO EDMONTON

On 5 October 1795, a handful of fur traders began constructing Edmonton House, a Hudson's Bay Company post, at the junction of the North Saskatchewan and Sturgeon rivers in the area known as Rupert's Land. Schoolchildren know the subsequent story of Edmonton, the first permanent British settlement in Alberta. Wracked by shortages of building materials, cold winters, insufficient medical supplies, and fire, the tiny community struggled to survive. Traders continued to search for furs and to depend in part on sturgeon for food. Writing in his journal after the settlement's third winter, Peter Fidler observed that three North West Company canoes had arrived at the company's nearby trading post, and there would "be a great competition for trade" at Edmonton House.[1] Everyone was an employee of either the British Hudson's Bay Company or the Canadian North West Company and, while both companies lasted, was involved in fierce competition.

At Edmonton, and in Alberta, the fortunes of the North West Company and the Hudson's Bay Company waxed and waned over the next few decades, fluctuating with changing economic conditions and the politics of business. Whether based in the British world or the Canadian, a business enterprise in Alberta faced many problems. Both the Hudson's Bay Company and the North West Company in Alberta were part of growing regional fur trading networks that remained tied to their Old World heritages through business traditions and practices. To understand this, and the evolution of the business firm in Alberta, we must return to Europe – and the golden age of medieval business.

The history of Alberta business reveals many continuities, including the survival of capitalist business practices of medieval Europe.[2] In Venice during the Middle Ages, merchants did business on wooden benches in the town square in the heart of the business community. Creditors followed standard practice when they put a merchant, who could not pay his debts, out of business by breaking his bench. From the Italian phrase *banca rotta*, "broken bench," and this medieval practice comes the English word bankruptcy. Italian capitalist demand for repayment of debts was intense, and Alberta business techniques are rooted deeply in European capitalism.

In fact, the first Alberta entrepreneurs still relied on capitalist techniques invented and perfected by merchants of medieval Europe. Business

The early stages of settlement at Edmonton on the North Saskatchewan River, the first permanent British settlement in Alberta. The first British settlers were strongly linked to the sea, for ships and canoes brought manufactured goods and supplies to them from England and carried back profitable furs.

(Courtesy of Glenbow Archives, NA-282-3).

York Factory on Hudson Bay. (Courtesy of Glenbow Archives, NA-1041-7).

practices created at that time were brought to colonial Canada by French immigrants in the seventeenth and early eighteenth centuries, by British fur traders following the creation of the Hudson's Bay Company in 1670, and by British immigrants after the British conquest of Canada in 1760. Albertans inherited these practices. From earliest times, Alberta traders and merchants used the business techniques first developed by northern Italian merchants during the Middle Ages.

■

Northern Italian Merchants

In the fourteenth century, northern Italian towns, such as Venice, witnessed the beginnings of capitalism and new business practices. Venetian and other Italian merchants responded to the growth of markets by creating a new business organization — the partnership. At the same time, the important Italian travelling merchants became sedentary or resident merchants. These changes in business organization did not completely sweep away an earlier form of transacting business associated with peddlers who moved from one place to another with their goods. Merchants who stayed in one city, however, frequently worked together through partnership agreements, which as time passed became standardized. Such Italian entrepreneurs often carried on a large share of their trade beyond local markets through reliance on relatives and trusted friends, taking advantage of business opportunities throughout Europe and the Near East. They engaged in business to make profits and measured their success in financial terms. Italian merchants retained their profits to provide adequate capital for business expansion and broadened investments.

New business practices, which marked the golden age of medieval business, helped Italian merchants meet the needs of their growing trade. By devising double-entry bookkeeping, for instance, they gained an accurate view of the financial situation of their businesses. Prior to the appearance of this organizational innovation, they merely listed their transactions, each in a single entry. In double-entry bookkeeping, however, they recorded each transaction in the ledger twice, in one account as a credit and in another account as a debit. In the sale of cloth for one hundred ducats in cash, for example, the cloth account was credited one hundred ducats and the cash account was debited the same sum of money. To determine the state of their finances, merchants balanced their accounts from time to time. Merchants also developed the promissory note, a financial instrument used to do business with each other. They were often paid, not in cash, but in promissory notes which formed part of the credit system. A promissory note was a written promise to pay a sum to a particular individual at a fixed time. Italian entrepreneurs with the largest resources, through extending credit to others, became the most influential merchants of the day.

By the sixteenth century, the traditions, skills, and techniques of Italian merchants had moved, from the Mediterranean to parts of north-western Europe including France and Great Britain. French and British entrepreneurs made use of partnerships and promissory notes, as well as double-entry bookkeeping, learned from printed manuals.

■

French Mercantilism, Canadian Business, and French Canada

Many French entrepreneurs shared the view of the French government that the purpose of the business system was to enlarge the wealth of the state and enhance the power of the crown, not the individual. A strong central government in France brought more security, the spread of trade, the growth of capitalism, and new business opportunities. As capitalism grew, mercantilism encouraged the expansion of French power through the establishment of colonies, such as Canada.

According to mercantilist philosophy, the goal in setting up businesses in Canada was to promote the interests of the French crown.[3] Mercantilists saw Canada as a source of raw materials not available in the mother country, and as a market for its manufactured goods. To ensure that France benefited from business opportunities at home and in the colony, they stressed close government regulation of these opportunities.

Mercantilists who wanted to see France expand overseas naturally became a factor behind the important exploratory voyages of the sixteenth century that led French people to the shores of Canada. Thus, Jacques Cartier, funded by the French crown, began his exploration of Canada in 1534, searching for a trade route to Asia.

The French crown continued to encourage overseas expeditions, and French mercantilism, which through the French explorer and colonizer Samuel de Champlain resulted in the settlement of Quebec in 1608, assumed a special business form. By the late 1620s, the Paris government had chartered a quasi joint-stock company, the Company of New France, to get private individuals to put capital into the Canadian business venture and thereby help increase French power.[4] This company was a business with mercantilist ambitions in which French merchants, with the support of their government, sought opportunities to trade in furs on Canadian soil. The Company of New France, though it did little to carry out its responsibility for colonizing Canada, helped maintain French power in the colony in the long run despite the fact that the British Kirke brothers succeeded in controlling Quebec for a few years during the early 1630s.

Eventually, however, the Company of New France, unable to attract new capital investments, failed after operating in Canada for more than three decades. The fundamental problem of developing profitable enterprises in the colony remained difficult to solve. Yet, some merchants who operated in Canada as members of partnerships or as single-owner proprietors had considerable success. For instance, in Quebec during 1743, François Havy and Jean Lefebvre formed a partnership, and this firm became a prolific contributor to business in the colony. It engaged in general mercantile activity, importing and exporting, and entered the fur trade and shipbuilding industries. In its counting house, it carefully recorded its transactions, using the Italian double-entry method. The partnership lasted with the support of the French government until the 1750s, exploiting Canada's natural resources, especially furs.[5]

■

British Mercantilism, Canadian Business, and British Canada

The failure of the Company of New France and the success of Havy and Lefebvre symbolize the importance of business in the development of Canada's economy and society, and the story of British settlement in Canada started another theme of Canadian business history — the evolution of the firm in the colony within the British mercantilist system.

Under the doctrine of mercantilism, the London government encouraged colonization, and, stimulated by the requirement of trade with Great Britain, capitalism flourished in Canada. As new settlers became involved in doing business with the French-Canadian people and learned how to cope with their new environment, the colonial Canadian economy expanded and, with that expansion, business opportunities grew especially among English-speaking but also among French-speaking Canadians.[6] The new settlers proved able to attract substantial, new capital investments.

The merchants, manufacturers, and farmers of colonial Canada were, however, not entirely free to pursue all business opportunities. A number of British laws aimed at providing benefits for British entrepreneurs somewhat abridged the economic freedom of Canadian entrepreneurs; at the same time, these very laws often promoted the growth of the Canadian business system.[7] Beginning in 1760, the British government, through the Navigation Laws, tried to regulate business in Canada for the benefit of Great Britain, in keeping with the mercantilist philosophy. These laws helped shape business opportunities for colonial Canadians. The Navigation Laws provided that no goods could be either imported into Canada or exported from the colony except in British or colonial ships. The considerable use of colonial ships in this trade stimulated Canada's shipbuilding industry. Then, too, starting in 1810, Canadian timber enjoyed a substantial tariff preference in Great Britain; the result was a boom in Canada's lumber industry. Finally, between 1815 and the mid-1840s, the British Corn Laws spurred the growth of Canada's wheat industry by giving protection to Canadian wheat in British markets.

As part of the British mercantilist system, colonial Canadian entrepreneurs thus enjoyed many advantages. Even after the disappearance of the Corn Laws, the protective tariff on timber, and the Navigation Laws and the coming of free trade in the British Empire in the late 1840s and early 1850s, colonial Canadian merchants, farmers and manufacturers continued to find and take advantage of many business opportunities, partly through Canada's ongoing political and economic ties with Great Britain, and partly through freer trade with the United States under the Reciprocity Treaty of 1854.[8] Numerous colonial Canadian entrepreneurs operated and prospered as single-owner proprietors, members of partnerships, and investors in joint-stock companies.

But, for many farmers, manufacturers, and merchants in colonial Canada the opportunities to transform effort into reward were few. Business was adversely affected by depressions in the mid-1830s, in the late 1840s, and in 1857-58, as well as by the Upper and Lower Canadian Rebellions in 1837-38 and the cholera epidemics in the mid-nineteenth century. Most beginning businesses went bankrupt within a few years of their founding in colonial Canada.

The British mercantilist system nonetheless provided essential support for the development of the Hudson's Bay Company in the western interior of British North America after 1670. By this time, British mercantilism had taken a special business form, a new institutional shape. Ever since the mid-sixteenth century, with the widening of British commercial horizons, the London government had been chartering joint-stock companies.[9] Designed to encourage private citizens to invest in transport and supplies for overseas business ventures in order to increase British power, these joint-stock companies were enterprises in which individual merchants pooled their capital and spread their risk by sharing ownership. London merchants became the most important investors, and England's overseas trade was centred in London. English merchants as investors purchased shares in the joint-stock companies and hoped to earn dividends on the shares they held. Rather than continuing to bring in eastern goods through middlemen in Antwerp and Lisbon, English merchants began to use longer trade routes to get to the sources of supply themselves. Set up by London merchants, the Moscovy Company was the first British joint-stock company, and its goal was to go directly to eastern countries to tap their riches. The company financed profitable voyages to Russia. Exporting a variety of English products to Russia, it imported Russian goods such as furs and hemp. Eastward expansion grew in importance as the Moscovy Company was followed by the Levant Company in 1581 and the East India Company in 1600. The principal aim of the Levant Company was to return from the Levant to England with items such as spices and silks to meet the growing demand for luxuries among the wealthy. During the years of the reign of Elizabeth I,

1558 to 1603, it was imports more than exports that lay behind the commercial expansion.

It is clear, however, that the London government believed the interests of the home country would be served by trade that produced a balance in favour of England. Joint-stock companies, Englishmen thought, should always be careful to sell more to foreigners than buy from them. Products made at home would not only put their own people to work but would also bring outside goods into the country. Englishmen increasingly came to accept the view that an empire in the West, the possession of colonies in North America, would enhance the country's wealth and security in the future. Besides serving as markets for the home country's manufactured products, such colonies would make England less dependent on foreigners for valuable goods. Chartered in 1610, the London and Bristol Company was a joint-stock company established for the colonization of the Avalon peninsula of Newfoundland which, along with several others in New England, the London government expected would promote British interests in North America and at home. But the expectations of the investors in Newfoundland proved unrealistic; the climate of Newfoundland was unreceptive to the cultivation of crops and the London and Bristol Company failed.[10]

The story of the British in Rupert's Land began another theme of Canadian business history: the struggle within the western interior of British North America to reconcile the competing interests of the fur trade and colonization. The Hudson's Bay Company was a joint-stock venture chartered in 1670 to allow a group of British investors including Charles II's cousin, Prince Rupert, to seek profits through the fur trade and colonization in Rupert's Land.[11] But the hopes of the investors favouring colonization soon came into conflict with the ambitions of those whose interest was entirely in the profit potential of the fur trade. Disagreements between the two parties led, by the end of 1670s, to the withdrawal of the investors who supported colonization. Winning profits from trade in furs became the sole objective of the Hudson's Bay Company. Seen from a larger perspective, the next two centuries defined the classic age of mercantilism in Rupert's Land, a period in which a corporate charter conferred monopoly rights of trade in furs in the region upon the Hudson's Bay Company and delegated sovereign powers of government to the company as well. Indeed, in keeping with an important aspect of mercantilist practice, England provided public support for a private enterprise in Rupert's Land.

■

Early Growth of Edmonton House

By the late eighteenth century, under mercantilist philosophy, the British government was encouraging the fur trade industry in what later became Alberta, and, spurred by the need for trade with the mother country, capitalism thrived. The availability of abundant furs in north-central and northern Alberta helped to undermine attempts to end the Hudson's Bay Company's monopoly. In October 1795, the company set up a fur trading post, Edmonton House, on the North Saskatchewan River. As the fur traders overcame the early trials of their new environment, the Edmonton economy began to prosper, and with this prosperity, business opportunities grew.

Edmonton's initial growth occurred against a background of significant developments in the fur trade industry in Rupert's Land. The Hudson's Bay Company had received the monopoly right to pursue the trade in furs within the entire drainage basin of Hudson Bay, but for over a century, from 1670 to the early 1770s, the company confined its overseas operations to Hudson Bay coast posts: York Factory, Moose Factory, Fort Albany, Severn House, and Fort Churchill in particular. With its head office in London, the small company sent a few ships across the Atlantic each year and carried on barter trade at the bayside posts. The salaried post masters or chief factors exchanged European goods for the furs Native people brought them. The post masters faced intense competition from French traders. The Hudson's Bay Company did not get off to a quick, profitable start. Leading a tenuous and unstable life, the company was losing money until the early 1680s. A large sale of coat beaver came in 1684, allowing the enterprise to pay dividends to the shareholders for the first time. But the fundamental problem of developing a profitable company remained unsolved, as competition continued year after year. Markets and war between England and France during the War of the Spanish Succession were other perennial difficulties.[12]

The development of the fur trade required time, with most of the Hudson's Bay Company's growth taking place after 1713, when the French withdrew from the Bay under the terms of the Peace of Utrecht. The company was earning profits, an average of thirty percent on an annual outlay of £27,000 between 1739 and 1749. Competition nonetheless bit into the company's profits between the late 1720s and early 1750s, as Pierre de La Verendrye collected furs from Native people in the western interior by building a line of French fur trading posts from Lake Superior to the lower Saskatchewan River. The British Conquest of New France in 1760 had significant repercussions in the Hudson's Bay Company business world. Montreal's new business leaders, such as Alexander Henry the Elder, were members of a generation that challenged the Hudson's Bay Company's trade monopoly and established an economy that promoted the Canadian fur trade in the western interior.[13] This competition hurt the Hudson's Bay Company and, in 1774, the company's management opened Cumberland House on the main lower Saskatchewan River in hopes of solving their problems.

Abandoning its long-standing strategy of relying on Native people to bring their furs to the bayside posts and embarking on western expansion to Cumberland House, the Hudson's Bay Company committed itself to constructing other posts in the interior as well. There was consensus that business opportunity deep in the West was desirable, even necessary, for the survival of the company. The establishment of Manchester House (1786), Buckingham House (1792), and Edmonton House (1795) on the North Saskatchewan was as important for the creation of business opportunity in the near future as for the economy the company eventually developed.

The founding of Edmonton House as a major business enterprise was a sign of the importance business was to have in the history of Alberta society. In terms of natural resources, the Edmonton region was among the richest areas in Rupert's Land. At Edmonton House, the Hudson's Bay Company successfully exploited both the Edmonton area's natural resources — furs, navigable waterways, and fertile land — and the benefits of being part of the British Empire to achieve wealth. Although Edmonton residents did not live near the seacoast, the significance of ocean commerce between Edmonton and Great Britain reverberated throughout the Edmonton community's economy. Overseas trade stimulated opportunities for the Hudson's Bay company to prosper from its labour and investments. Company-owned ships sailing the Atlantic and its canoes navigating the North Saskatchewan and other inland waters linked the old and new worlds. Edmonton residents grasped the chance to enlarge the production of furs for sale in the markets of Great Britain and Europe.

At Edmonton House, William Tomison became the first chief factor in 1795. Born in 1739 on South Ronaldsay, one of the Orkney Islands, Scotland, Tomison began with the Hudson's Bay Company in 1760 as a labourer.[14] By 1767, he had become an important company trader at Severn House. To combat competition from Montreal traders, Tomison mounted a trade excursion to try to keep the furs of the interior flowing down to the bayside posts rather than by canoe to Montreal. By 1777, he was serving as chief factor at Cumberland House and, in time, won much of the trade in furs that had previously travelled to Montreal for shipment to British and European markets. In 1786, Tomison was made chief factor at York Factory with authority to supply inland posts with men and goods.[15] He used his power to penetrate far west into the interior and, in the process, set up new posts such as Manchester House on the North Saskatchewan. By 1792, Tomison himself had moved farther upriver to take command of the newly opened Buckingham House.

Seeing an opportunity to make his mark on Edmonton and on the Hudson's Bay Company, Tomison supervised the building of Edmonton House on the north bank of the North Saskatchewan in the fall of 1795. Edmonton House, the new headquarters of the company on the

Saskatchewan River, was extremely important in the development of the company's business. It acted as a catalyst, eventually transforming north-central Alberta into a network of fur trading communities like Rocky Mountain House and Fort Assiniboine. As chief factor, Tomison combined his fur-trading skills with his desire to provide his men and himself with suitable accommodation and adequate supplies of food. In addition to Tomison, the Hudson's Bay Company employed thirty-one men at Edmonton House, including carpenters, a blacksmith, canoemen, canoe builders, and a tailor. Like Tomison, most of his men were Orcadians.[16] Lacking a natural growth of trees to construct the trading room and other buildings such as a blacksmith shop, a warehouse, and cabins, Tomison's men cut logs some distance upstream and floated them down to the site. They covered the roofs with turf. Finally, they surrounded the establishment with a stockade. A substantial part of the diet for everyone consisted of fresh buffalo and deer meat and fresh sturgeon, as well as pemmican made by Tomison's men.

To encourage Native people to bring in furs during their visits to Edmonton House in the winter months, Tomison offered them warm clothing made by the tailor. In their trade with Tomison, Native people also obtained guns, ammunition, tobacco, brandy, copper kettles, hatchets, and ice chisels in exchange especially for beaver skins but also for wolf pelts, fox skins, and buffalo robes, as well as birch bark from which Tomison's men made canoes. Tomison traded with several tribes, particularly the Cree, Assiniboine, and Blackfoot Confederacy. Mutual gift giving and complex negotiations played important roles in these exchanges, which Native people controlled as much as Tomison did.[17] This was only the beginning of Native peoples' visits to Edmonton House, for over the next several decades they would return year after year, the Assiniboine coming from the southeast, the Blackfoot Confederacy tribes from the south, and the Cree from the northeast.

Tomison began to expand the range of operations of Edmonton House, offering his Native customers trade goods on credit. Native hunters often needed a variety of goods on credit to tide them over several months during the winter hunt. Tomison understood their circumstances and was willing to make advances to them. Like other chief factors, Tomison usually based his credit policies on the individual's track record in bringing in furs to pay off debts. He found it necessary to maintain complete accounts based on double-entry bookkeeping. But the mercantile credit Tomison provided was informal and unsecured. Never did he receive from Native hunters promissory notes, business instruments which in England formed the basis of a large volume of business and could be discounted at banks or commercial houses. Instead, Tomison had his customers' word of honour, which was usually enough. He also kept in mind the character of Native hunters, relying on the soundness of his assessment. More often than not, his appraisal was on the mark. With the passage of time, he became increasingly confident in sizing up a particular business situation. Thus Tomison wrote in his journal, "trusted several Indians a little debt." On another occasion, he noted that a Native hunter "arrived and paid a credit of nineteen beaver." Sometimes, however, debtors were slow in meeting their obligations. "At noon an Indian arrived that had thirty beaver in credit last autumn and has brought no more than one small otter," observed Tomison one day in May 1796.[18]

At Edmonton House, Tomison also faced other problems. Flawed trade goods scared away new commerce. One of the Hudson's Bay Company's English suppliers had not perfected the art of manufacturing guns. Tomison complained about "the badness of guns" he had to use in the fur trade. "Many of the guns the Indians have brought back that they had in credit, some of which have not been more than once fired out of, being split two inches from the breech; several Indians were disabled last season by their hands being shot away. This with other circumstances will reduce the trade very much," warned Tomison. Other unfavourable circumstances included the shortage of trade goods, because York Factory's management had underestimated Tomison's opportunities to trade with Native people at Edmonton House. As head of the Hudson's Bay Company's operations in the Saskatchewan River region, Tomison developed important links with the post masters at Buckingham House, Carlton House, and Cumberland House, but from their poorly stocked posts, they could offer Edmonton House only a few trade goods. Tomison's efforts to obtain badly needed goods from them were often fruitless. The lack of sufficient trade items at Edmonton House poorly befitted an organization established for the fur trade. Reported Tomison:

> There is no orris lace come up here, nor half so many shirts as I used last year to dress the Indians with, not a bit of duffle of any kind has been sent up and only nineteen yards of red blaize, not one small blanket. I have no more than 168 lbs. of Low India shot. I have been much distressed for want of kegs [for brandy]. There being no cooper here has been the means of many skins going past this house.[19]

In December 1795, Tomison summarized the picture: "The trade here is very little as yet. I am obliged to do here as a poor pedlar does in England, lay by and get a skin now and then, not being able to bid up for them, my stock of goods being too small."[20] Initially, Edmonton House clearly operated under a considerable disadvantage.

During the winter of 1795-96, business activity at Edmonton House lagged because competition from the nearby North West Company's trading post, Fort Augustus, hurt Tomison's important trade with the Native people. Angus Shaw was in charge of Fort Augustus. "My neighbour," wrote

Tomison, "trades brandy and gives powder and shot for nothing, which I am not able to do. The tobacco is little and a great part of it rotten, so that the aforementioned circumstances will be the loss of trade."[21] The lack of men with a knowledge of Native languages complicated Tomison's situation. "Our neighbours," he emphasized, "are now sending out liquor to every Indian they know of, but I cannot do so, for I have not a man fit to send out to an Indian."[22] Tomison, however, also put rum into the hands of Native people. Conflict, especially between the Cree and the Blackfoot, was nothing new, but Hudson's Bay Company rum, like North West Company rum, generated new levels of violence that destroyed some of Tomison's business.

The furs Tomison obtained in his trade with Native people at Edmonton House by the spring of 1796 came to 8,226 "made beaver," the unit established by the Hudson's Bay Company to measure the value of the furs as well as the British goods used for the trade.[23] After packing the furs into bundles at his fur press, Tomison headed for Buckingham House, taking some bundles down the North Saskatchewan on canoes and others overland on pack horses. Picking up additional bundles of furs at Buckingham House, Carlton House, and Cumberland House, all of which operated under his supervision, Tomison reached York Factory by canoe with furs totalling 12,978 made beaver for the Saskatchewan River trade on 11 August. Then he left on a Hudson's Bay Company ship laden with furs for London, spending part of a year's leave there and the rest in his native South Ronaldsay.

The westward expansion of the Hudson's Bay Company's operations to Edmonton House helped bring prosperity to the company in the last half of the 1790s. Although the fur returns for the Saskatchewan River region for 1795-96 were lower than for the previous year because of the shortage of trade goods, the company remained profitable. It also continued to use its traditional sales system. As before, the company's head office salesmen mailed advertisements to potential customers in the London market, especially those who might be interested in beaver pelts. Some of these customers were from continental Europe. In particular, the salesmen sent out brochures proclaiming the merits of their company's furs. Fur sales were successful. But the great war between England and revolutionary and Napoleonic France, which had begun in 1793, made it increasingly difficult for the company to obtain trade goods and threatened its profits. It proved impossible to secure French brandy. The Hudson's Bay Company also groaned under the war-related increase in prices for trade goods, which added to the cost of doing business at Edmonton House and other posts. Despite these problems, the modest profitability of the company in 1795-96 allowed its London officers to pay out a small dividend of six percent.[24]

Improvements begun by Tomison at Edmonton House continued after he went on leave. In the summer of 1796, he was replaced by George Sutherland, who assumed direct supervision of the post's daily operations. Born in about 1754 in Wick, Caithness, Scotland, Sutherland began with the Hudson's Bay Company in 1774 as a servant to chief factor Thomas Hutchins at Fort Albany. Over the next two decades, besides compiling "A Short Vocabulary of the most useful and common words in the Northern Indian Language," Sutherland gained much experience in the inland fur trade.[25] As chief factor at Edmonton House, Sutherland enlarged the post's yard and garden. He led the Hudson's Bay Company at the post into a year of substantial growth. By the spring of 1797, at the close of its second full year of operations, Edmonton House had collected furs from the Blackfoot, Cree, and Assiniboine amounting to 12,500 made beaver.[26]

The growth of Edmonton House occurred as part of the general development of the Hudson's Bay Company's fur trade in the Saskatchewan River region. As headquarters for the company's business in this area, Edmonton House continued to control a system of smaller posts: Buckingham House, Carlton House, and Cumberland House. Co-ordinating the work at headquarters with that at the other posts, Sutherland was concerned about maintaining an adequate volume of trade goods at each place, especially at Edmonton House, where the demand was the greatest. The Hudson's Bay Company's sizable investment in Edmonton House required a substantial supply of trade goods for efficient operation. On 3 October 1796, Sutherland arrived at Edmonton House with a number of pack horses carrying dry goods, and the next day came his brigade of six canoes loaded with brandy, guns, powder, and other items. Assisted by thirty-four men at the post, thirty-two of whom were Orkneymen, Sutherland immediately launched a vigorous trade with Native people, exchanging British goods for furs. Within three weeks, he had collected more than 1,000 beaver skins from Native people. Unfortunately, some of the beaver skins were "of a very indifferent quality."[27]

The large trade so early in the season had Sutherland sending four men on 13 December with ten pack horses down to Peter Fidler, chief factor at Buckingham House, for additional trade goods. Arriving at Edmonton House two weeks later, the goods included ten blankets, five ice chisels, twenty-four hatchets, twenty-eight guns, eleven dozen knives, forty-seven kettles, six pairs of stockings, two rolls of Brazil tobacco, three bags of ball, and two bags of shot.[28] Long-range planning was one of the secrets of Sutherland's success. Already back in October, he had sent a letter to James Bird, chief factor at Carlton House, asking for any trade goods and men he could spare as soon as the ice disappeared from the North Saskatchewan in the following spring. On Christmas Day, Bird's reply, written on 28 November, reached Edmonton House by pack horse: "You may depend upon my sending up all the men and goods that can possibly be spared from this place (and Cumberland House if the season will permit) early in the spring if I can be supplied with a steersman. The two who are here will at that time be employed building canoes."[29] With this positive response from Bird, Sutherland continued to coax Native people to bring their furs to Edmonton House. By early January 1797, Sutherland could report excellent results. "Trade at this place," he wrote to Bird," is great at this season, being about 6,000 beaver."[30]

As the Hudson's Bay Company's operations at Edmonton House grew in size and complexity, so did the firm's relationships with its nearby competitor, Fort Augustus, the North West Company post, just a mile and a half away on the same side of the North Saskatchewan. The fur trade became increasingly competitive. In fact, stiff competition in the fur industry would grow even more pronounced in the early 1800s. In 1796-97, Sutherland tried to limit that competition to protect his company's earnings. Instead of enlarging Edmonton House, which might have permitted him to compete more effectively with the North West Company, Sutherland sought to stop price cuts by his competitor through co-operation. This tactic succeeded only to some degree.

George Sutherland and Angus Shaw, the master of Fort Augustus, sometimes worked together in an informal way. They divided markets, shared price information, and tried to standardize the practice of extending credit to the Assiniboine, Cree, and Blackfoot. Through his co-operative work, Sutherland was able partially to protect the profits of the Hudson's Bay Company. Writing to James Bird at Carlton House about the competition he faced from the North West Company at that post, Sutherland noted:

I am glad to hear that a good understanding subsists between you and James Finlay. It's also the case here, Mr. Shaw being an excellent neighbour; by this means we bring the natives to terms. A contrary conduct I am well convinced answers no end to either party. It makes the natives impertinent and by that means creates unnecessary expense to our employers.[31]

The winter of 1796-97 was one of prosperity and growth for the Hudson's Bay Company at Edmonton House. The made beaver Sutherland collected from Native people rose significantly to 12,500 by the spring of 1797. Nonetheless, Sutherland had a hard time keeping up with his counterpart at the neighbouring North West Company post.

In the fall of 1797, William Tomison replaced George Sutherland to become chief factor at Edmonton House again. The management change at Edmonton House brought a change in the approach this Hudson's Bay Company post took to competition. Competition continued to plague Edmonton House, but Tomison never seriously considered co-operating with his counterpart in the North West Company. Unlike Sutherland, Tomison did not look to co-operation as a way to stabilize his business.

Tomison and Sutherland were sharply divided on the issue at this time. Most likely, Tomison thought he could do better on his own. On 6 October, Tomison reached Edmonton House with thirty-six men and two large canoes carrying trade "goods equal to forty men in canoes." Eagerly awaiting Tomison's arrival, many of the Hudson's Bay Company's traditional Native customers were already at the post. "Gave all our trading Indians some tobacco and a general drink," reported Tomison. But not all of them were ready to ask for credit on trade goods and willing to commit themselves to bring back furs. Only "some of the Indians taken debt and part going away," wrote Tomison in his journal.[32]

Over the next seven months, however, many Assiniboine, Cree, and Blackfoot obtained trade goods on credit from Tomison at Edmonton House and in time returned with furs to pay off some of their debt. In mid-March 1798, Tomison reported that his men had "finished tying up the skins now brought, the quantity as follows viz. whole parchment beaver 20, wolves 940, foxes red 22, grey 3,212, badgers 12, wolverines 6, bears old grizzly 2, cubs 2."[33] Yet, the unimpressive number of beaver pelts Tomison had received so far from Native people presented a basic business problem, one that did not really go away. Many were unable to meet their obligations. More than a month later, Tomison noted in his journal: "At 4 p.m. three Indians arrived, brought a few furs but could not pay half their credits; these used to bring 100 beaver each and now the three have brought only seventy-five made beaver in all. Gave them a supply and they went away again." Tomison nourished hopes of doing better business, but soon he was disappointed once more. "At one p.m.," he wrote, "an Indian man and family arrived, brought about four made beaver in furs and had seventy-four beaver in credit last autumn; this man [used to bring not] less than 200 beaver in a season."[34] This Native hunter tried to repay as much of his debt as he could. But others took most of their beaver pelts to the nearby North West Company post. Obviously, competition from the Canadian company was hurting Edmonton House. The furs Tomison collected at Edmonton House from Native people during the 1797-98 season dropped to 10,755 made beaver.

In the 1798-99 season, Tomison again rejected the idea of limiting competition by co-operating with the North West Company. Instead, at Edmonton House he promoted the concept of making the best of a difficult situation. In an attempt to keep traditional Native customers loyal to the Hudson's Bay Company, Tomison built on an earlier program. He continued to offer the Blackfoot, Assiniboine, and Cree trade goods on credit. On 25 September 1798, a week and half after he arrived at Edmonton House with his men and canoes loaded with trade goods, Tomison wrote in his journal: "Gave a supply to several Indians and put them across the river."[35] Tomison's efforts had a strong psychological impact on many Native hunters, who developed a sense of operating in a trading partnership with the Hudson's Bay Company. The personal contact between Tomison and the hunters in trading sometimes fostered a mutual understanding that could be valuable for both the Hudson's Bay Company and Native people. "In the evening received sixty made beaver from [an] Indian, forty of which was credit," reported Tomison one day in the spring of 1799, as the Hudson's Bay Company's share of the fur trade increased a little.[36] During the 1798-99 season, the market share of Edmonton House rose to 10,889 made beaver.

■

North West Company and the Rise of Fort Augustus

Fort Augustus, the nearby North West Company post, developed simultaneously with the growth of Edmonton House. A Canadian business, the North West Company was not a latecomer to the business scene in this area; its evolution was an essential part of the growth of the business system of Edmonton and Alberta. The North West Company became increasingly important to the Edmonton economy from the mid-1790s onward.

The North West Company's growth at Fort Augustus took place against a background of developments in commerce in Montreal, where the company established its head office. A number of Montreal merchants were able to take advantage of business opportunities during the American Revolution, and, with the coming of peace in 1783, a new business system appeared. American independence meant that Canadian merchants were excluded by the peace treaty from trading with Native people southwest of the Great Lakes for furs. This exclusion hurt many Montreal fur traders in the short term. But in the long term, it forced fur traders to develop new business activities northwest of the Great Lakes, many of which turned out to be quite profitable. For example, Montreal merchants began shipping furs from the Northwest to British markets and earned a good return on their investment. Adopting the British as well as the Canadian practice, Simon McTavish and other Montreal traders built on previous partnerships and entered into a new partnership, the North West Company, in 1783.[37]

The history of the North West Company, Montreal's main fur-trading enterprise, represents a unique chapter in the annals of Canadian fur trading because of the firm's record of expansion and the duration of its success. Initially, this partnership operated under the disadvantage of instability. Over the years, however, Simon McTavish and his partners brought to the firm some degree of stability through their considerable wealth and business connections with other local merchants, Native people of the western interior, and entrepreneurs in London, England. The use of the partnership form of business organization quickly became widespread in Canada, as the colonial government encouraged the formation of partnerships to achieve

Simon McTavish, a leading Montreal merchant, became one of the founders of the North West Company. His commitment and devotion to the company helped create a fur trade civilization in Alberta and the prairie West.

(Courtesy of Glenbow Archives, NA-1194-10).

public goals. Partnerships were firms created to bring private individuals together for a particular purpose. Unlike corporations, partnerships did not enjoy the great advantage of limited liability, and this placed a large constraint on their ability to raise the capital needed for expansion. To invest in a firm, a person had to become a partner, and all partners took big risks because they were liable for the firm's debts to the full extent of their resources. Despite these limitations, partnerships attracted investors who were willing to combine their capital and talents in joint ventures which promised to allow them to seize new business opportunities. In return for this advantage, the Canadian public generally expected partnerships to serve not only the interests of their private partners but also the public interest. To augment the general prosperity, it was necessary, many Canadians believed, to encourage business growth and permit individual merchants to reap substantial rewards in developing Canada's economy.

The development of the North West Company spurred the economic growth of Canada. In the late 1780s and early 1790s, the company's fur shipments across the Atlantic to London significantly increased the Canadian export trade. Reflecting the process of economic growth, the company developed an elaborate transportation system, improving the road between Lake Ontario and Georgian Bay, launching sailing vessels on the upper Great Lakes, and sending canoe brigades from Montreal to the company's inland headquarters (first at Grand Portage and, from 1803 onward, at Fort William on Lake Superior) and its posts on the Saskatchewan River and beyond in the Athabasca country. By integrating Montreal and its rich northwestern hinterland replete with potential Native customers, this transportation system facilitated the rise of local businesses.

Fort Augustus rapidly became the North West Company's preeminent trading post on the Saskatchewan River. Possessing a good site on the North Saskatchewan, Fort Augustus had well-established connections with other company posts on the river. The early growth of Fort Augustus occurred against a background of developments at Fort George, another North West Company post in Alberta, about 130 miles downstream on the North Saskatchewan.

Angus Shaw set up Fort George in the fall of 1792. Born in Scotland, Shaw began in the North West Company as a clerk in the late 1780s. In 1789, he came to Alberta to build a post for the company at Moose Hill Lake.[38] After trading with Native people for furs there for three years, Shaw established Fort George on the North Saskatchewan, which consisted of several rough log shacks surrounded by a stockade. He also joined the North West Company as a wintering partner and contributed a modest sum of money to the partnership. Shaw led the North West Company at Fort George into a period of significant growth. Like other North West Company post masters, Shaw kept records of his financial transactions using the double-entry system. By the fall of 1794, at the beginning of its third season of operations, Fort George had 110 men, 16 canoes, and 375 pieces of trade goods.[39] Shaw faced a competitor in the fur trade business, the nearby Hudson's Bay Company post, Buckingham House, but this post could not keep up with Fort George. At this time, Buckingham House had 35 men, 114 pieces of trade goods, and 9 canoes.

As head of Fort George, Angus Shaw supervised the post's operations, assisted by his clerk Duncan McGillivray. Born around the early 1770s in Inverness-shire, Scotland, McGillivray was a nephew of Simon McTavish.[40] McGillivray got along well with Shaw and recorded the developments at Fort George during the 1794-95 season in his journal. On a daily basis, power rested with Shaw, who was in charge of carrying on trade with the Cree, Blackfoot, and Assiniboine for furs. Usually Shaw provided Native people with gifts before he obtained furs from them in exchange for goods like rum, guns, blankets, and tobacco.

Writing in his journal, McGillivray noted,

when a band of Indians approach near the Fort, it is customary for the chiefs to send a few young men before them to announce their arrival, and to procure a few articles which they are accustomed to receive on these occasions, such as powder, a piece of tobacco, and a little paint to besmear their faces, an operation which they seldom fail to perform previous to their presenting themselves before white people. On entering the house they are disarmed, and treated with a few drams and a bit of tobacco. When their lodges are erected by the women they receive a present of rum proportioned to the nation & quality of the chiefs and the whole band drink during 24 hours and sometimes much longer. When the drinking match has subsided, they begin to trade. They obtain the large keg at 30 beavers, long guns at 14, blankets at 6, and tobacco at 3 beaver. In short, they procure the goods at cheaper rates here than in most other places in this country.[41]

In the exchange between Shaw and Native hunters, the individual beaver skin was used as the unit to measure the value of the trade goods. Native hunters exercised as much control over the negotiations as Angus Shaw did.

At Fort George, there was also gift giving on the part of Native hunters from time to time. For instance, a chief brought special gifts on his first visit to the North West Company post. "He made a present of his favorite horse and feather war bonnet to Mr. Shaw, two invaluable articles in the estimation of an Indian," observed McGillivray.[42] In their trade with the North West Company, many Native hunters sought luxury goods rather than more practical items such as ammunition because they had independent means of harvesting the bountiful resources of the prairie West in order to earn a livelihood. McGillivray noted that

the inhabitants of the Plains are so advantageously situated that they could live very happily independent of our assistance. They are surrounded with innumerable herds of various kinds of animals, whose flesh affords them excellent nourishment and whose skins defend them from the inclemency of the weather, and they have invented so many methods of the destruction of animals, that they stand in no need of ammunition to provide a sufficiency for these purposes. It is then our luxuries that attract them to the Fort and make us so necessary to their happiness. The love of rum is their first inducement to industry; they undergo every hardship and fatigue to procure a skinful of this delicious beverage, and when a Nation becomes addicted to drinking, it affords a strong presumption that they will soon become excellent hunters. Tobacco is another article of as great demand as it is unnecessary.[43]

Angus Shaw typically provided Native hunters with trade goods on credit and, in making their choices, they certainly sometimes placed more emphasis on rum and tobacco than on guns, ammunition, and blankets. Violence among Native hunters increased as they consumed more and more North West Company rum. In their desire for rum, Native hunters were not alone. Most of Shaw's own men also found rum irresistible.[44] Tempers flared under its influence. On St. Andrew's day, for example, Shaw "gave them 6 gallons of rum to divert themselves, which they did with a vengeance, for one bottle succeeded another so quick that scarcely a man in the Fort escaped a black eye," wrote McGillivray.[45] Shaw and his men nonetheless remained committed to trying to take advantage of the commercial opportunities at Fort George and the surrounding area.

Overall, the North West Company enjoyed a successful trade effort at Fort George during the 1794-95 season. In gathering furs such as beaver skins and wolf pelts, Shaw was ahead of his counterpart at the Hudson's Bay Company's Buckingham House. Shaw's large workforce allowed him to make arrangements for fifteen of his men to leave Fort George for several months during the winter to kill beavers wherever they could find them in the prairies. Their work alone resulted in the addition of 2,000 beaver skins to the total at Fort George. By the spring of 1795, Shaw had collected 22,750 skins of all kinds, tied together in 325 packs of 90 pounds each, in addition to producing 300 bags of pemmican.[46] This edge gave the North West Company a competitive commercial advantage.

Shaw, however, did not make the classic mistake of concluding that where he was promoting the North West Company was the best place to do so. By mid-May 1795, he was thinking of putting someone else in charge of Fort George and moving on, upstream to the confluence of the North Saskatchewan and Sturgeon rivers, where he wanted to construct a new fur trading post named Fort Augustus. Fort George was gradually slipping out of the mainstream of the fur trade because of the exhaustion of the beaver supply around the post. Observing the North West Company scene, McGillivray noted,

Mr. Shaw has projected a plan of erecting a House farther up the [North Saskatchewan] in the course of the summer. For this purpose James Hughes has received directions to build, 12 or 14 days march from [Fort George] by water, on a spot called the Forks, being the termination of an extensive plain contained between two branches of this river. This is described to be a rich and plentiful country, abounding with all kinds of animals especially beavers & otters, which are said to be so numerous that the women & children kill them with sticks and hatchets. The country around Fort George is now entirely ruined. The Natives have already killed all the beavers, to such a distance that they lose much time in coming to the House, during the hunting season.[47]

While James Hughes was building Fort Augustus, Shaw and McGillivray guided their canoes laden with the season's furs on the long annual spring trip down the North Saskatchewan and along other interior waterways to Grand Portage on Lake Superior, the North West Company's inland headquarters. From Grand Portage the furs were shipped by canoe to Montreal, and then by sailing vessel to England, where the North West Company's London house of McTavish, Fraser & Co. provided indispensable services selling the furs. At the same time, McTavish, Fraser & Co. purchased manufactured trade goods in London and sent them to Grand Portage via Montreal.[48]

Shaw and McGillivray took trade goods back with them on their canoe trip from Grand Portage to Fort Augustus, arriving on 29 September 1795 with nineteen large canoes carrying 450 pieces of trade goods, each piece

Members of the Peigan tribe of the Blackfoot Confederacy and the Hudson's Bay company chief factor at Rocky Mountain House. In Alberta, chief factors operating from their fur trading posts traded with Native people, exchanging British manufactured goods for furs. (Courtesy of Glenbow Archives, NA-575-1).

weighing ninety pounds.[49] Altogether, there were now 105 men at the post. James Hughes had finished much of the construction of Fort Augustus on the north bank of the North Saskatchewan. The post consisted of a few log shacks arranged in a square, but as yet there was no stockade surrounding them for protection. Nonetheless, Fort Augustus possessed a key asset, a large workforce eager to attract Native hunters.

When William Tomison arrived at the junction of the North Saskatchewan and Sturgeon rivers on 5 October 1795 to start building Edmonton House for the Hudson's Bay Company, Angus Shaw was already revelling in the role of big shot, Fort Augustus having emerged as a powerful fur trading post. Compared to Tomison's relatively small workforce of thirty-one men, Shaw's large one was indeed impressive. Tomison had come with only eight canoes loaded with ninety-six pieces of "goods of inferior weight," as he described them.[50] With a quantity of trade goods more than four times as large at hand, Shaw was obviously in a much stronger position.

Problems surfaced, however. The greatest difficulty lay in fierce competition from Tomison, who fought hard to increase his trade with Native people. To lessen competition, Shaw and McGillivray showed interest in co-operating with Tomison. They entered into an agreement with him to have Fort Augustus and Edmonton House protected by a common stockade. The stockade was built with both the North West Company post and the Hudson's Bay Company post inside it.[51] In November 1797, McGillivray also sought to work with Tomison informally to gain the respect of Native hunters. "Let us then," McGillivray wrote to Tomison, "cast away old prejudices & begin a new score. We will find it to be ultimately for the good of both parties, and the interests of the country in general."[52] But Tomison rejected the idea of such a co-operative effort.

A continuing commitment to co-operation was, however, part of the picture at Fort Augustus. James Hughes played an important role in co-operation, becoming master at Fort Augustus around 1799. Born in 1772 in Montreal, Hughes began with the North West Company as a clerk in 1791.[53] By the turn of the century, he had become one of the company's wintering partners. Hughes possessed the imagination to keep the North West Company moving ahead and, in early September 1799, participated in opening Rocky Mountain House on the upper North Saskatchewan to attract the furs that the Kootenay were gathering. In expanding up the North Saskatchewan, the North West Company was hardly alone. Within a few weeks, James Bird, the new chief factor at Edmonton House, provided competition by sending a number of his men upstream to construct Acton House beside Rocky Mountain House for the Hudson's Bay Company.[54] Although the North West Company thus faced ongoing competition as it pushed upstream, co-operation remained part of its strategy.

As it developed, the North West Company's Fort Augustus both competed and co-operated with the Hudson's Bay Company's Edmonton House. During the first decade or so of the nineteenth century, James Hughes and James Bird often worked together to try to stabilize their businesses. The two posts continued to operate within the same stockade. Even as both Fort Augustus and Edmonton House moved upstream to Edmonton's present site in 1802, and then downstream to the confluence of the North Saskatchewan and White Earth Creek in 1810, and finally back again to the present site of Edmonton in 1813, they used a common stockade as a defence against possible attacks by Native people.[55]

In its main operations, trading with the Native people for furs, Fort Augustus faced the challenge of working in an increasingly competitive industry. Led by James Hughes, the response of Fort Augustus to this situation proved adequate for the most part. While co-operation was a deliberate strategy, part of an effort to lessen the impact of competition, aggressive investments in North West Company trading networks were not eschewed. For instance, at Fort Augustus Hughes put money into additional trade goods, canoes, and food supplies for use in promoting the trading post the North West Company had opened on Lac La Biche in 1798.[56] Underlying

Hughes's move was the company's long-established policy of expansion. Through the development of its post on Lac La Biche, the company hoped to increase its share of the fur trade in northern Alberta. Greenwich House, the post the Hudson's Bay Company had set up at Lac La Biche in 1799, cut into the trade of the North West Company's post, but it continued to be an important venture, one that remained closely tied to the growing business at Fort Augustus. In the first decade and a half of the nineteenth century, the Hudson's Bay Company's Edmonton House enjoyed some prosperity, but continued to trail Fort Augustus in performance.

In running Fort Augustus, Hughes was sometimes joined by Alexander Henry the Younger. Born around 1765 in New Brunswick, Middlesex County, New Jersey, Henry began working for the North West Company in 1791. By 1802, Henry had become a partner in the company. When Henry first came to Fort Augustus in 1809, he played an important role in assisting Hughes in the post's management. Hughes and Henry were planning for an expansionary future. Fort Augustus had by no means exhausted its possibilities. Anticipating good times, the North West Company reinvested some of its earnings in a new Fort Augustus at the junction of the North Saskatchewan and White Earth Creek in 1810. While Hughes took the season's furs down to Fort William, the company's new inland headquarters since 1803, Henry supervised the building of the new post. One aspect of Henry's task was to work with James Bird in erecting a common stockade for the new Fort Augustus and the Hudson's Bay Company's new Edmonton House.[57]

In addition to seeking security through a stockade, Henry tried to rely partially on a new garden to solve the food problems his men faced at Fort Augustus. The usual fresh deer and buffalo meat and pemmican were not enough to keep everyone happy. Eager to enjoy a more comfortable life, the men wanted fresh garden produce. Under Henry's guidance, potatoes, turnips, radishes, and other crops were planted in the garden. However, the results were disappointing. Henry wrote in his journal on 26 August 1810:

Whether it proceeds from the nature of the soil or that our gardens were not properly cultivated and taken care of this spring, by the ground not being well broken up, I cannot say, but to appearance nothing will come to perfection this season. The barley is still green, the potatoes very small and not even blossomed. The turnips have run into leaves only, and all other garden stuff has remained in a stunted state.[58]

Much more successful was Henry's attempt to provide the men with wild strawberries, raspberries, and cherries.

Henry's efforts to collect furs from the Cree, Blackfoot, and Assiniboine also met with considerable success at Fort Augustus. Native people proved willing traders, keen to exchange their beaver skins, marten pelts, and other furs, as well as dried meat for tobacco, rum, guns, ammunition, axes, beads, and awls. To help keep Native people loyal to the North West Company, Henry built on earlier practices. One of the most attractive inducements he offered to get the furs he wanted was to provide Native people with trade goods on credit. As early as the end of July 1810, Henry had obtained a substantial number of furs, including 292 beaver skins, 70 marten pelts, 12 muskrat skins, 3 grizzly bear pelts, 4 otter skins, and 1 buffalo robe.[59] By the spring of 1811, Fort Augustus had collected many more furs and continued to outstrip Edmonton House in the business.

By this time, James Hughes had once more taken sole command of Fort Augustus. When the confluence of the North Saskatchewan and White Earth Creek proved inadequate in 1813, both the North West Company's Fort Augustus and the Hudson's Bay Company's Edmonton House moved back to the present site of Edmonton, again inside a common stockade. Over the next six years, however, Hughes mounted a spirited attack against growing competition from Edmonton House. For all its activity in the fur trade, Edmonton House was not a pacesetter, and it grew less rapidly than Fort Augustus. Even so, intensifying competition hurt both posts, and in 1819 this led James Hughes and Francis Heron, the new chief factor at Edmonton House, to attempt to sustain the co-operation that had begun much earlier. Indeed, in that year Hughes and Heron agreed to limit competition.[60] However, the co-operation between Fort Augustus and Edmonton House was always filled with tension until 1821, when the two posts united to become Edmonton House, as the Hudson's Bay Company and the North West Company merged into a reorganized Hudson's Bay Company. The two companies had to merge to survive, for both were teetering on the verge of bankruptcy. In fact, fierce competition came close to killing both of them. Acutely conscious of the need to address the looming catastrophe, the two fur trading firms in the end sought preservation in a merger.

■

Hudson's Bay Company and the Development of Edmonton House

The reorganized Hudson's Bay Company, a corporation which was granted exclusive trading rights in the western interior including Alberta by the British Parliament in 1821, formulated a special policy to reward and motivate the leading members of its workforce, especially the chief factors and chief traders at the fur trading posts. In large part, this policy was a response to pressure from former North West Company wintering partners, who hoped that the opportunity to become partners in the reorganized Hudson's Bay Company would prove a powerful enough incentive to co-operate in order to overcome the pre-1821 antagonisms between the North West Company and Hudson's Bay Company people. The policy, combined with a continuing barrage of loyalty pressures from top corporate executives, was generally successful.

John Rowand, who benefited from the policy, served as chief factor at Edmonton House for much of the period from 1821 to the mid-1850s. Born around 1787 in Montreal, Rowand was the son of John Rowand, a medical doctor.[61] After attending a local school, John Rowand went at the age of sixteen to become an apprentice clerk in the North West Company at Fort Augustus. As events would show, the move to Fort Augustus in 1803 brought Rowand luck, landing him at the right place at the right time for the kind of business he hoped to develop. Becoming an expert horseman, he served capably as a buffalo hunter. Optimistic about his future, Rowand married Lisette Humphraville of the North Saskatchewan country, a prominent Metis woman, around 1810, thus solidifying his social and economic position in the Metis and Native communities. The two had met at Fort Augustus when Rowand was serving as a clerk at the post. Probably most important to Rowand before they were married, Lisette had nursed him back to health after he broke his leg in a tumble from his horse while hunting buffalo. Before long, Rowand rose in the ranks at Fort Augustus, becoming a wintering partner in the North West Company by 1820.

In 1821, John Rowand became a chief trader for the Hudson's Bay Company at the enlarged Edmonton House, which embraced the two former posts: Fort Augustus and Edmonton House.[62] At the same time, Rowand joined the company as a partner. As chief trader, he was paid a regular annual salary and, as a partner, received a relatively small share of company profits. In 1826, Rowand was promoted to chief factor and assigned the general supervision and charge of all the affairs and business of the Hudson's Bay Company at Edmonton House, the company's prairie headquarters, and the Saskatchewan country, a position he held for most of the years until his death in 1854.

Rowand helped lead Edmonton House into a period of significant growth and prosperity. By 1824, Edmonton House and its prairie outposts, such as Fort Carlton, at the close of their third year of operations, posted handsome profits.[63] By the mid-1840s, the population of Edmonton House had grown to about 130 men, women, and children, many of the men being either former North West Company or former Hudson's Bay Company employees. Observing the Edmonton scene on 26 September 1846, the Canadian painter and social commentator Paul Kane noted:

> Edmonton is a large establishment, with forty or fifty men with their wives and children, amounting to about 130, who all live within the pickets of the fort. Their employment consists chiefly in building boats for the trade, sawing timber, most of which they raft down the river from ninety miles higher up, cutting up the small poplar which abounds on the margin of the river for firewood, 800 cords of which are consumed every winter, to supply the numerous fires in the

The fur trade attracted John Rowand early in life. First, he was employed by the North West Company, eventually joining the company as a wintering partner. In 1821, he joined the Hudson's Bay Company as a chief trader. Soon promoted to chief factor, Rowand took charge of Edmonton House for many years. (Courtesy of Glenbow Archives, NA-1747-1).

establishment. The employment of the women, who are all, without a single exception, either squaws or half-breeds, consists in making moccasins and clothing for the men, and converting dried meat into pemmican.[64]

The British and Canadians at Edmonton House had clearly formed relationships with the Assiniboine, Blackfoot, and Cree. Over the years, Canadian and British men and Native women had established familial bonds that played an important part in the conduct of the fur trade as well as in the creation of a unique society that came to depend on the business. From the beginning, the co-operation between former Hudson's Bay Company and North West Company employees contained relatively little tension. Despite their separation from Canada for the next half century because of the Hudson's Bay Company's decision to bring in all trade goods and supplies and send out all furs through Hudson Bay rather than through Montreal, and the consequent disruption of their business ties with Montreal, former North West Company employees usually left acrimonious disputes behind them and worked peacefully with former Hudson's Bay Company employees. John Rowand had a key role in this development, sending continuing messages imploring full co-operation at Edmonton House. The legacy of co-operation among the men augured well for Edmonton House's ability to maintain its fur-trade operations. The Blackfoot, Cree, and Assiniboine were assured that they would receive good prices for their furs, about twenty-five percent more than they had been paid for them before 1821.[65] How many Native people obtained better prices in the next half century is unknown, but they continued to bring their beaver skins and other furs to Edmonton House in large numbers.

Edmonton House experienced mixed success from the mid-1850s to the late 1860s. The Hudson's Bay Company at Edmonton House was, by any measure, a successful business during its new period of monopoly in the prairie West after 1821. A major thrust of expansion in the fur trade at Edmonton House came in 1858, reflecting the relative aggressiveness of the post's new leader, William J. Christie. Born in 1824 in Fort Albany, Ontario, Christie was the son of Ann Thomas and Alexander Christie, a Hudson's Bay Company chief factor.[66] Educated in Aberdeen, Scotland, William Christie began working for the Hudson's Bay Company in the early 1840s. By the mid-1840s, he had become an apprentice clerk at Rocky Mountain House. The position was instrumental in Christie's advancement, for it brought him into contact with top management, including George Simpson, governor of Rupert's Land. Christie's work eventually took him to Fort Churchill as a clerk in 1848 and to Edmonton House as chief trader in 1858. He was promoted to chief factor at Edmonton House two years later, a position he held until 1872.

Christie saw profits from trading with Native people for furs sustain Edmonton House in the spring of 1858. Fascinated by what he witnessed at Edmonton House at this time, C.A. Loveland, a miner from Wisconsin, observed:

> A band of about 3,000 Blackfeet Indians arrived from the south to trade at the fort. The first morning after their arrival a chief came down in full dress accompanied by 50 or 100 of his followers, bringing a present for the H.B. Co.'s chief trader. When the present had been made the cannons of the fort fired a salute, which was answered by the Indians firing their guns. Then the chief retired and another came, and the ceremony was repeated, until all had greeted the trader. Then trading commenced. The Indians got considerable rum and had a carousal. When the trading was ended the six sober Indians were taken into the fort and treated to drink and the best of what was going. The party remained about three or four days and then returned south.[67]

Trade goods on credit from Christie allowed the Blackfoot to continue their hunt for furs.

In 1858, the Hudson's Bay Company still held an almost complete monopoly in the Edmonton House region. Here and there, small individual free traders from the Red River Settlement, Manitoba were doing business, but no other major supplier of trade goods had appeared.[68] Observing the operations at Edmonton House in May 1859, James Hector of John Palliser's British North American Expedition noted:

The fort was now very lively, as all were busy preparing for the great annual voyage to the coast of Hudson Bay, which occupies the whole summer. The repacking of their furs, the launching and loading of the boats, and all the necessary preparation, gave the inside of the fort an air of business and mercantile activity that looked more civilized than anything we had before seen in the Saskatchewan.[69]

Edmonton House enjoyed prosperity in the spring of 1859, and Christie sought to ensure that he had essential trade goods at reasonable prices. Although bringing in trade goods from York Factory was a time-consuming job, he succeeded in preparing Edmonton House for the approaching season.

By the end of 1859, however, Christie realized that there was little prospect of the Hudson's Bay Company at Edmonton House earning the solid profits of earlier times. In that year, the British government permitted the Hudson's Bay Company's licence for exclusive trade in Rupert's Land to expire. By the mid-1860s, Edmonton House faced growing competition from American free traders, who brought trade goods, especially whiskey, to Native people in the prairies from Fort Benton, Montana, in exchange for their furs. As the halcyon days of expansion in the fur trade at Edmonton House in the 1840s gave way to rising competition and violence, the profits the Hudson's Bay Company earned began to dwindle. By the late 1860s, Edmonton House was reporting annual losses as high as £4,000 as American free traders increased their market share in furs in Alberta.[70] By offering Alberta Native people an alternative source of trade goods, the Americans were making serious inroads into Christie's business.

Christie wrestled with the challenge of devising a plan to secure more furs from the Cree, Assiniboine, and Blackfoot. As he struggled to deal with his problems, the need to provide Native hunters with trade goods on credit necessarily occupied much of his attention. Christie continued to advance rum, guns, ammunition, and a substantial stock of other supplies on credit for the hunters and their families through the winter, all of which was to be paid in furs with the advent of spring. Christie's trading efforts bore mixed results. The fur trade remained important to Edmonton House, as well as to the Hudson's Bay Company as a whole. At the end of the season, however, the winter's catch sometimes did not cover the credit the hunters obtained. When the hunters remained in debt, Christie lost ground in the fur market to American free traders, and this hurt his business at Edmonton House.

In spite of this unstable business environment, the forces of competition did not prove too powerful for Edmonton House. Like many British businesses, the Hudson's Bay Company sought to solve its economic problems through co-operative action involving the British government. To overcome its difficulties, the company also worked with Canadian government officials. Negotiations between the Hudson's Bay Company and the

British and Canadian governments led to the transfer of Rupert's Land to the new Dominion of Canada in 1870, with Edmonton House remaining the company's most important fur-trading post in Alberta, and achieving new strength by gaining control of 3,000 acres of land around it on the north bank of the North Saskatchewan.[71] The era when the great canoe or boat brigades climbed from York Factory through the rivers and lakes to Edmonton House was not completely over. A stream of British trade goods destined for Edmonton House still poured through the waterways. The returning wave of beaver pelts and other furs continued to go eastward via Lake Winnipeg and Hudson Bay.

Dramatic alterations were about to occur in the last third of the nineteenth century, however, as the business environment in which the Hudson's Bay Company operated in Alberta changed. At Edmonton House, the company was already a complex blend of tradition and transformation. True to its tradition of investing capital in the fur trade, the company remained a fur-trade enterprise. It was also becoming a transformed company that had decided to enter the agricultural industry to produce food for its workforce at Edmonton House. Observing the Edmonton sphere of activity in 1870, by which time the fur-trade society at Edmonton House had increased to about 150, Canadian soldier and author William F. Butler noted:

> Edmonton, the headquarters of the Hudson's Bay Company's Saskatchewan trade, and the residence of a chief factor of the corporation, is a large five-sided fort with the usual flanking bastions and high stockades. It has within these stockades many commodious and well-built wooden houses, and differs in the cleanliness and order of its arrangements from the general run of trading forts in the Indian country. Farming operations, boat-building, and flour-milling are carried on extensively at the fort, and a blacksmith's forge is also kept going.[72]

Although the traditional pursuit of the fur trade was still the main influence in the lives of the residents of Edmonton House, they also supported the policy of investment in the development of agricultural products such as flour, the kind of investment that would eventually become more significant in building up the Edmonton community. A long tradition had developed in the Hudson's Bay Company at Edmonton House of relying on the British government for support. Even as Rupert's Land was being transferred to Canada in 1870, the British government played an important role, providing opportunities for the company at Edmonton House to continue to invest in the fur trade as well as in agriculture.

Much of the expansion of Canada's commerce northwest of Lake Superior and the new directions this trade took between the 1870s and 1905 was also the result of the actions of the British government. The British government was a major factor behind the union of Canada with the other British North American colonies in 1867, as well as in the development of the new Dominion of Canada in the post-confederation period. Although trade abroad was the most powerful engine of Canadian business, developments in the Canadian Northwest Territories were becoming important by the 1880s. Marketing networks were reaching out from Toronto and Montreal to Edmonton, Calgary, and other trading centres as well as to ranches and farms in Alberta. The rich natural resources of Alberta, especially fertile land, timber stands, coal deposits, and rivers capable of generating large quantities of power, encouraged the spread of settlement and stimulated the development of business. Ranchers and farmers were sending their produce via middlemen to central Canadian cities for sale in domestic and international markets.

From the beginning, there was a commercial outlook among the individuals who came to live and work in Alberta after 1870. For many Albertans — an increasing proportion as time passed — the ways they made a living were the ways of the market. They invested capital in a variety of ventures and embraced risk in a commercial community in hope of reward. Although the market dominated the forces playing upon business enterprise, the acts of government were also influential.

NOTES TO CHAPTER ONE

1. *Saskatchewan Journals and Correspondence, Edmonton House, 1795-1800, Chesterfield House, 1800-1802.* Alice M. Johnson (London: The Hudson's Bay Company Record Society, 1967), 144.

2. For an overview of the economic development of Europe in the Middle Ages, see Robert-Henri Bautier, *The Economic Development of Medieval Europe* (New York: Harcourt, Brace, Jovanovich, 1971).

3. Christopher Moore, "Colonization and Conflict: New France and its Rivals 1600-1760," in Craig Brown, ed., *The Illustrated History of Canada* (Toronto: Lester Publishing Limited, 1991), 122-124.

4. Graham D. Taylor and Peter A. Baskerville, *A Concise History of Business in Canada* (Toronto: Oxford University Press, 1994), 24.

5. Dale Miquelon, *Dugard of Rouen: French Trade to Canada and the West Indies, 1729-1770* (Montreal-Kingston: McGill-Queen's University Press, 1978), 136-137.

6. Graeme Wynn, "On the Margins of Empire (1760-1840)," in Brown, ed., *The Illustrated History of Canada*, 262-265.

7. W. L. Morton, *The Kingdom of Canada. A General History From Earliest Times*, Second Edition, (Toronto: McClelland & Stewart, 1969), 220-221.

8. Michael Bliss, *Northern Enterprise: Five Centuries of Canadian Business* (Toronto: McClelland & Stewart, 1990), 159.

9. W. T. Easterbrook and Hugh G. J. Aitken, *Canadian Economic History* (Toronto: Macmillan of Canada, 1967), 82-83.

10. Bliss, *Northern Enterprise*, 26-28.

11. Ibid., 80-81.

12. Morton, *The Kingdom of Canada*, 91-94.

13. *The Journal of Alexander Henry the Younger 1799-1814.* Barry M. Gough, Volume I (Toronto: The Champlain Society, 1988), xxii.

14. John Nicks, "William Tomison," *Dictionary of Canadian Biography*, Volume VI 1821-1835 (Toronto: University of Toronto Press, 1987), 775-777.

15. E. E. Rich, *The Fur Trade and the Northwest to 1857* (McClelland and Stewart, 1967), 177.

16. *Saskatchewan Journals and Correspondence*, xxxi.

17. Ibid., 28, 34; See also Arthur J. Ray and Donald Freeman, *Give Us Good Measure: An Economic Analysis of Relations between the Indians and the Hudson's Bay Company before 1763* (Toronto: University of Toronto Press, 1978), 54-75, and Arthur J. Ray, *I Have Lived Here Since the World Began: An Illustrated History of Canada's Native People* (Toronto: Lester Publishing and Key Porter Books, 1996), 84-85.

18. *Saskatchewan Journals and Correspondence*, 14, 33, 36.

19. Ibid., 48-49, Edmonton House, 12 November 1795, William Tomison to James Spence.

20. Ibid., 52-53, Edmonton House, 20 December 1795, William Tomison to James Swain.

21. Ibid., 51, Edmonton House, 20 December 1795, William Tomison to George Sutherland.

22. Ibid., 54-55, Edmonton House, 11 February 1796, William Tomison to James Bird.

23. Ibid., xxxv.

24. Ibid., xcv.

25. Ibid., xiv.

26. Ibid., 93.

27. Ibid., 67-68, Edmonton House, 20 October 1796, George Sutherland to James Bird.

28. Ibid., 79, Buckingham House, 20 December 1796, Peter Fidler to George Sutherland.

29. Ibid., 77-78, Carlton House, 28 November 1796, James Bird to George Sutherland.

30. Ibid., 80-81, Edmonton House, 3 January 1797, George Sutherland to James Bird.

31. Ibid., 80-81, Edmonton House, 3 January 1797, George Sutherland to James Bird.

32. Ibid., 100.

33. Ibid., 113.

34. Ibid., 117.

35. Ibid., 145.

36. Ibid., 166.

37. Bliss, *Northern Enterprise*, 92-97.

38. Gratien Allaire, "Angus Shaw," *Dictionary of Canadian Biography*, Volume VI 1821 to 1835 (Toronto: University of Toronto Press, 1987), 704-705.

39. *Saskatchewan Journals and Correspondence*, xxv.

40. Sylvia Van Kirk and Jennifer S. H. Brown, "Duncan McGillivray," *Dictionary of Canadian Biography*, Volume V 1801 to 1820 (Toronto: University of Toronto Press, 1983), 530-532.

41. *The Journal of Duncan McGillivray of the North West Company at Fort George on the Saskatchewan 1794-95*, introduction, by Arthur S. Morton (Toronto: Macmillan of Canada, 1929), 30-31. See also Lynda Gullason, "No less than 7 different nations: Ethnicity and cultural contact at Fort George-Buckingham House," in Jennifer S. H. Brown, W. J. Eccles, and Donald P. Heldman, eds., *The Fur Trade Revisited Selected Papers of the Sixth North American Fur Trade Conference, Mackinac Island, Michigan, 1991* (East Lansing: Michigan State University Press, 1994), 139.

42. *The Journal of Duncan McGillivray*, 43.

43. Ibid., 47.

44. See also Bliss, *Northern Enterprise*, 97.

45. *The Journal of Duncan McGillivray*, 48.

46. Ibid., 77.

47. Ibid.

48. *Saskatchewan Journals and Correspondence*, lxxxix.

49. Ibid., 12.

50. Ibid.

51. J. G. MacGregor, *Edmonton: A History* (Edmonton: M.G. Hurtig Publishers, 1967), 21.

52. *Saskatchewan Journals and Correspondence*, xlv-xlvi, Fort Augustus, 8 November 1797, Duncan McGillivray to William Tomison.

53. *Documents Relating to the North West Company*, edited with introduction, notes, and appendices by W. Stewart Wallace (Toronto: The Champlain Society, 1934), 458-459.

54. *Saskatchewan Journals and Correspondence*, lxxi-lxxii.

55. MacGregor, *Edmonton*, 23-24, 29, 31.

56. *The Journal of Alexander Henry the Younger 1799-1814* edited by Barry M. Gough, Volume II, The Saskatchewan and Columbia Rivers (Toronto: University of Toronto: 1992), 463.

57. *The Journal of Alexander Henry the Younger*, Volume II, 449, 462.

58. Ibid., 465.

59. Ibid., 460.

60. J. G. MacGregor, *John Rowand: Czar of the Prairies* (Saskatoon: Western Producer Prairie Books, 1978), 37.

61. Sylvia Van Kirk, "John Rowand," *Dictionary of Canadian Biography*, Volume VIII 1851 to 1860 (Toronto: University of Toronto Press, 1985), 779-781.

62. MacGregor, *John Rowand*, 42.

63. Ibid., 62.

64. Quoted in MacGregor, *Edmonton*, 48.

65. MacGregor, *John Rowand*, 41.

66. Irene M. Spry, "William Joseph Christie," *Dictionary of Canadian Biography*, Volume XII 1891 to 1900 (Toronto: University of Toronto Press, 1990), 194-195.

67. Quoted in MacGregor, *Edmonton*, 59.

68. Gerhard J. Ens, *Homeland to Hinterland: The Changing Worlds of the Red River Metis in the Nineteenth Century* (Toronto: University of Toronto Press, 1996), 90-91.

69. Quoted in Irene M. Spry, *The Palliser Expedition: An Account of John Palliser's British North American Expedition 1857-1860* (Toronto: Macmillan of Canada, 1963), 205.

70. MacGregor, *Edmonton*, 77.

71 H. John Selwood and Evelyn Baril, "The Hudson's Bay Company and Prairie Town Development, 1870-1888, in Alan F. J. Artibise, ed., *Town and City Aspects of Western Canadian Urban Development* (Regina: University of Regina, Canadian Plains Research Center, 1981), 63.

72. *The Great Lone Land: A Narrative of Travel and Adventure in the North-West of America by William Francis Butler*, introduction by Edward McCourt (Edmonton: M. G. Hurtig, 1968), 258.

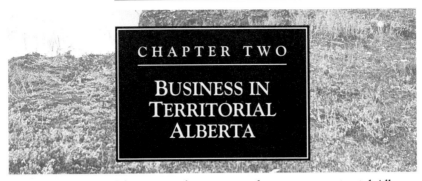

CHAPTER TWO

BUSINESS IN TERRITORIAL ALBERTA

Most of the principal investors in business in territorial Alberta were from central Canada. Indeed, many of the earliest Alberta entrepreneurs were central Canadians whose firms had links with the Ontario and Quebec business system. Until 1905, numerous businesspeople living in the territorial district that became the province of Alberta saw themselves as Ontarians or Quebecers. Some of them first came to Alberta from Ontario or Quebec in the early 1870s, uprooting themselves and taking the risk of looking for business opportunities in their new surroundings. Business activity gradually grew in Alberta as the population increased.

In the territorial Alberta experience, certain aspects of business development stand out. Business opportunities arose out of Albertans' willingness to exploit the great natural resources of Alberta, particularly the rich land. The abundance of fertile soil in Alberta made agriculture an inviting prospect. Business opportunities for Albertans increased as the population grew and the economy expanded. In taking advantage of economic opportunities, Albertans followed central Canadian traditions and business practices that hardly changed in the territorial years. For the most part, business remained a family enterprise. Family firms invested in a variety of business activities and accumulated wealth.

Throughout Canada, economic, social, and political developments have always been interconnected. As in the past, business today does not exist in a vacuum. Business has a life of its own, however, its growth and health have always been influenced by its environment. Examining the development of business in territorial Alberta requires first a look at the political and economic settings of this district, settings that had a positive impact on business development.

■

Political Setting

In 1882, Alberta became a district of the Northwest Territories under the lieutenant-governor in Regina, the territorial capital.[1] The British North America Act of 1867 — the Canadian constitution — provided for a strong federal government. The Northwest Territories Act of 1875 gave the territorial government limited powers, reflecting the federal government's determination to control the Northwest Territories in the interest of national development.

For the federal government to play that role in Alberta, the land had first to be reordered, a process that affected the Native Canadian population of the region. For centuries, Native people had been using the land in Alberta. In the Calgary area, they allowed the earliest settlers to use their land right away. The Native people and nature provided settlers with their initial means of agricultural production. The combination of Native land and settlers' farming business created the beginnings of Alberta agriculture and provided the necessary basis for its eventual development.

By the mid-1870s, there were signs that the end of this world might come quickly. One sign was the growth of interest in large-scale settlement in Alberta on the part of the federal government and private citizens willing and able to invest in the transportation and supply costs that such settlement would necessarily involve. A second sign was the great pride in national identity and achievement that people associated with the age of John A. Macdonald, Alexander Mackenzie, and the birth of the North-West Mounted Police.[2] When the Mounted Police force was established in 1873, and indeed throughout the previous half dozen years, furs and buffalo robes were by far the most important commodities exported from southwestern Alberta. Exports went in one principal direction: to Fort Benton, Montana, and from there eastward to large American cities such as Chicago and New York. Roaming especially through southwestern Alberta were small-scale Fort Benton merchants known as whiskey traders. Carrying their trade goods in small wagons or on packhorses, they joined Fort Benton with the Canadian prairies. Bartering whiskey and other trade goods for buffalo robes and furs wherever they went among Native people, the traders provided commercial ties between southwestern Alberta and Fort Benton, giving this part of Alberta an important link to midwestern and eastern American markets. Many Native people in Alberta suffered from the whiskey trade, experiencing whiskey-related violence and decimation of their opportunities to secure the goods they needed, such as flour and blankets.

Violence among Fort Benton merchants and Native people in Alberta as a result of the whiskey trade had significant repercussions in the Canadian political sphere. Federal political leaders fashioned a Mounted Police force capable of dealing with the whiskey traders and shaping new business opportunities for settlers in Alberta. The founding fathers of Canada believed that government should safeguard freedom and that the purpose of the business system was to broaden the material and social well-being of Canadians, not enrich whiskey traders or their backers. In their opinion, democracy and the success of the new Dominion of Canada depended on law-abiding citizens who enjoyed business opportunities and were concerned about the general welfare of the people.

With the advent of the Mounted Police in 1874 and the creation of police posts at Fort Macleod and Fort Saskatchewan near Edmonton in the winter of 1874-75 and at Fort Calgary in the summer of 1875, a new business system emerged. Calgary, Fort Macleod, and Fort Saskatchewan became polyglot worlds of Canadian, Native, and American cultures linked to a large trading network that was as much Native Canadian as it was Canadian and American. While the Hudson's Bay Company at Edmonton, as well as at its new trading post in Calgary, continued to trade with the Native people of Alberta for furs and buffalo robes and then exchanged them in London for British manufactured trade goods, Montana and Canadian merchants at Calgary and Fort Macleod exported buffalo robes and furs from southwestern Alberta to Fort Benton in exchange for Canadian and American goods.[3] A dramatic new opportunity at Fort Macleod and Calgary was the Canadian trade. From 1876 onward, after Montana merchants in Calgary and Fort Macleod obtained permits from the U.S. government to purchase and sell goods in bond in Canadian cities like Montreal or Toronto to avoid customs duties, the Canadian trade in southwestern Alberta flourished.

The opening of the Canadian trade and the indirect export of furs and buffalo robes especially to Montreal were the most spectacular examples of fresh business opportunities, but there were also others, particularly in Alberta. There were more than one hundred mounted policemen in Alberta, all of whom needed supplies, thus encouraging some entrepreneurs to bring in goods especially for them. Already in the mid-1870s, merchants in Alberta supplied the mounted policemen with clothing, groceries, saddles, guns, and ammunition. The federal government helped these merchants prosper by giving them contracts to provide the Mounted Police force with goods over the next two decades and beyond.

The federal government also gave these same merchants contracts to supply Native people in Alberta with goods, including beef, flour, clothing, and farm implements. Federal political leaders wanted Native people to engage in farming, creating reserves for them and justifying their attempt to make these tracts of land into Native communities. Native people were everywhere in territorial Alberta. But the new Canadian nation, committed to expansion, could not accept Alberta as Native Canadian country. For Native people, the significance of the creation of Alberta was that it eventually unleashed onto their lands a flood of settlers. Increasingly, settlers viewed the future as one with Native people on reserves. Settlers, supported by the federal government, established a new business culture, one in which Native people did not have equal opportunity. Native people held no political authority over the emerging political and economic system, which was largely governed from Ottawa and Regina.

Contention over Native lands in Canada was an old theme by the mid-1870s, but the coming of settlers made the acquisition of Native lands in Alberta part of national policy. In 1870, when Alberta was transferred to Canada, it was all still in the hands of Native people, but a new age had started. By the end of that decade the buffalo, long an important source of food for Native people as well as fur traders, had vanished from Alberta.[4] In the early nineteenth century, Alberta had been home to thousands of buffalo. But the huge market in buffalo robes that sprang up in the eastern United States and in central Canada after the American Civil War encouraged fur traders and Native people in Alberta to view the buffalo less as a source of food than of trade. In the process, the great herds of buffalo in Alberta were rapidly slaughtered. Canada's political leaders thought that the once-numerous buffalo on Alberta's grasslands should be replaced by livestock and grain crops on Native reserves. Responding to general pressure, they moved to take control of Native territory in Alberta by treaty.

In 1876, Canada concluded Treaty Number Six with the Cree and Assiniboine tribes of north-central Alberta and Saskatchewan.[5] Native people dropped their claims to their lands in return for relatively small reserves, agricultural implements, seed grain, a few oxen and cows, instruction in farming, and annual treaty payments. But the pressure on other Native lands in Alberta continued with no letup. At the Treaty Number Seven conference held at Blackfoot Crossing on the Bow River in southern Alberta in 1877 between the federal government and the Siksika, Blood, Peigan, Tsuu Tina, and Stoney, these tribes surrendered their claims to their lands.[6] They were promised all that was offered by the government in Treaty Number Six, but the main thread of the Blackfoot Crossing story now shifted to livestock raising and became closely entwined with that of cattle ranching in southwestern Alberta.

The Native reserves did not always restrict Native people to local activities. Instead, Native people and settlers became interconnected with business. Some Native people won the admiration of new ranchers in Alberta for their traditional skills as horsemen and new skills as cowboys. Some ranchers lived around Native reserves and exercised much influence as culture brokers. For instance, Roderick Macleay, a rancher in the High River and Nanton region, earned a reputation as culture broker that gave him far-reaching influence in the Stoney community in the early twentieth century. "One of his great solicitudes over a period of years was concern for the Stoney Indians who had left the Morley reserve because of impoverished conditions and were leading a nomadic life in the foothills. He had sympathy and understanding with Indian problems, held their trust, and was looked upon by them as a true friend and adviser," observed the *High River Times*.[7]

Many Native people in Alberta, however, were uneasy about the treaties their chiefs had signed. As their traditional economy was disrupted and the fur and buffalo robe trades declined, they found it hard to share the hopes of political leaders who sought to encourage them to venture down new paths on their reserves. The forces of change produced confusion in Native communities. Even Native people who still actively participated in the fur trade in the Edmonton area wrestled with the challenge of transformation in the late 1870s and 1880s. Richard Hardisty, a mixed-blood chief factor for the Hudson's Bay Company at Edmonton, could not help but notice "the unsettled state in the Indian mind since the treaties with the Canadian government."[8]

Not infrequently, traders found that they achieved the greatest success in doing business with Native people when they married into kinship networks of Native communities. Some time before Treaty Number Seven was signed, Montana trader Charles E. Conrad married the daughter of an Alberta Blackfoot chief. By that time, Conrad had had long and varied contact with Alberta Native people. The couple had a son, Charles E. Conrad, Junior. For a while, the elder Conrad lived closely with the Alberta Blackfoot, acquiring from them furs and buffalo robes in exchange for American goods and prospering as time passed. Conrad's ties to John A. Macdonald, before and after the signing of Treaty Number Seven, immensely strengthened his position as a supplier of goods to Native people in Alberta. Although his wife left him within a few years, Conrad agreed to educate their son largely according to her wishes.[9] He sent him to a good school in Montreal, where he received a fine education. But "that certain half-breed Indian known as Charles E. Conrad, Junior," as Conrad described him in his will, in which he provided generously for him, suffered psychological stress in Montreal as he faced racial conflicts which brought back memories of his Alberta childhood.[10]

Conflict between Native people and settlers sometimes increased, as the pressure on Native lands undermined previous patterns of coexistence. Howell Harris, manager of the Conrad Circle Cattle Co. in the Fort Macleod area, faced hostility from nearby Native people in the 1880s and 1890s. Writing about the cattle in the Conrad herd that had been killed in its first year in Alberta, especially during the severe winter of 1886-87, Harris noted: "I don't know how many died that first winter and what the Indians killed that first year. They killed a good many of them when they were yearlings."[11] A huge prairie fire in November 1889 complicated the situation in the ranching community, leading Harris to speculate that the big Cochrane Ranche would likely drive its cattle onto the Blood reserve for free grass without Blood consent. "A big part of the Cochrane Range has been burnt off," observed Harris, "and they will shove their cattle down on that part of the Indian reserve that has not been burnt off."[12] Commenting on the Conrad herd in December 1893, Harris reported that "the cattle look fine but the Indians are killing some this fall again and the wolves are thicker than they were last year."[13] Settlers and Native people in Alberta who diverted their labour into conflict often felt the repercussions in lost cattle, disrupted social relationships, and political instability.

In territorial times, Alberta was nonetheless generally characterized by political stability, which helped assure economic growth and the development of business. Political stability in Alberta was enhanced by the presence of the North West Mounted Police.[14] The Saskatchewan Rebellion, however, shattered this political stability in 1885. This major conflict had both cultural and political origins, pitting rebel leader Louis Riel against the federal government and French-Canadian Metis against English Canadians. The struggle was a short but bloody conflict that sorely divided Canadians. The arrival of General Frederick D. Middleton's militia battalions in Saskatchewan and Alberta in April 1885 soon ended the actual fighting, but political tension continued.[15] Never again would the prairie West be divided by civil war. After the rebellion, the Metis felt the renewed attempt of the federal government to assimilate them into the larger society. The federal government restored the political stability of the Northwest Territories, including Alberta.

The federal government indirectly encouraged economic development in Alberta by providing a stable political framework for national and regional economic growth. Albertans, especially merchants and other businessmen, came to believe that the territorial government was too weak and that its lack of strength was hindering development of their business enterprises. Merchants wanted a strong territorial government to help build up the territorial economy. Partly as a result of this desire, the Canadian Parliament established a legislative assembly in the Northwest Territories in 1888 and responsible government there in 1897.[16]

As well, the territorial government obtained greater powers to tax, using taxes to aid, among other things, the building of roads and bridges. Early business life in Alberta was built around the wagon. Steamboats were almost non-existent, and any used on the North Saskatchewan, Oldman, and South Saskatchewan rivers often found themselves in shallow and unnavigable waters. Wagons on trails and dirt roads were the usual means of moving goods. Improvements in road transportation created growing business opportunities for Albertans despite the fact that overland travel on roads was slow.

As significant as roads were, the realization of Prime Minister John A. Macdonald's dream of a railway linking central Canada with the Pacific coast was a much more dramatic development.[17] Calgary first enjoyed the benefit of rapid east-west commerce when the Canadian Pacific Railway, carrying goods purchased in central Canada, arrived from Winnipeg on 11

August 1883. Macdonald's federal government gave a great deal of financial assistance to this pathbreaking railway, which, by the end of 1885, connected Calgary to Montreal as well as to Vancouver. The federal government also funded construction of several Canadian Pacific branch lines in Alberta — the Calgary-Edmonton and the Calgary-Fort Macleod in the early 1890s and the Medicine Hat-Lethbridge and the Lethbridge-Crowsnest Pass in the late 1890s.

Alberta business was also aided by Frederick Haultain, who from the late 1880s to the mid-1890s was responsible for the broad policy of the territorial government and who served as premier in this government between 1897 and 1905.[18] Born in Woolwich, England in 1858, Haultain was called to the Ontario Bar in 1882. After practising in Kingston, Ontario for two years, the young lawyer settled in Fort Macleod in 1884, where he established a successful practice and was elected to the territorial legislative assembly in 1888. One of the main purposes of government, Haultain believed, was to provide a legal structure for the expansion of business. To this end, for example, in 1893 he pushed an ordinance to amend the law regarding partnerships through the assembly.[19] The new ordinance brought Northwest Territories legislation on the subject in line with federal law and thus ensured equal opportunity for this territorial business institution. Partnerships were essential to the growth of Alberta business.

By 1905, territorial Alberta had achieved a large measure of political stability, which had significant economic consequences for Alberta. Most important, political stability provided an environment conducive to economic growth and business development.

■

Economic Setting

A distinctive feature of Alberta's territorial economy was its commercial nature. In Alberta, people lived by purchasing and selling goods, not in a subsistence economy in which individuals simply made goods or produced crops and livestock mainly for their own consumption. The abundance of good land and the generally long growing season in Alberta attracted many settlers. Between 1901 and 1906, the population increased more than twofold, rising from 73,000 to 185,000.[20]

Several elements characterized Alberta's commercial or market economy in the territorial period. Agriculture was market-oriented, and this orientation became more pronounced in the late nineteenth and early twentieth centuries. Trade at local, regional, national, and international levels was expanding with the help of regional specialization in commercial agriculture. Urbanization, the growth of cities and towns, was advancing. All these characteristics were related to political stability, which spurred the growth of the commercial economy in territorial Alberta.

From the beginning, agriculture was commercialized in Alberta. Territorial Alberta ranchers and farmers raised some food for their own use, but sold most of their livestock and crops in the markets. Ranchers eagerly grasped opportunities to increase the production of cattle, horses, and sheep. Farmers soon expanded the production of wheat, barley, and oats, as well as livestock.

The provisions for 160-acre homesteads in the Dominion Lands Act of 1872 served the interests of farm families. Alberta homesteaders had to live on their 160-acre farms for six months of each year for three years and, during this period, break thirty acres and put twenty acres into crop.[21] Barbed wire fencing enabled homesteaders to protect their farms from the grazing herds of ranchers. Farmers also needed access to water. But the largesse of nature did not fall evenly throughout Alberta. In central, north-central, and northern Alberta, rainfall was usually adequate. In semi-arid southern Alberta, it was meager and spasmodic, and farmers relied on dry farming, a technique for producing crops with relatively little rainfall, as well as on irrigation, using ditches with water from the St. Mary and Bow rivers.

Like farmers, ranchers grazing their herds in Alberta needed access to water. Ranchers usually selected a ranch site along a river or stream, which gave them control of the surrounding area. Possessing rich grasslands and numerous rivers and creeks, Albertans could look to ranching to prosper. The foundation of the livestock-raising industry in Alberta lay in the lease system created by John A. Macdonald's Conservative government by an order-in-council in 1881, in which the federal government could grant ranchers leases closed to settlement of up to 100,000 acres for a term of twenty-one years at the rate of one cent per acre per year. The importance of raising livestock on the open range reverberated throughout the Alberta economy.

Between the early 1880s and mid-1890s, however, in southern Alberta ranchers contested more and more bitterly with farmers for access to grass on the open range. Ranchers built up huge herds of cattle on their large leases. Growth in demand for beef kept up with growth in supply. The number of cattle exported from southern Alberta increased from 19,000 in 1899 to 34,000 in 1904.[22] During the same period, farming in southern Alberta also grew rapidly. Between 1900 and 1906, the number of farms in all of Alberta rose from 9,433 to 30,286.[23] Growth in the development of farming was intimately related to the federal government's decision in 1896 to end the system of ranching leases that were closed to settlement. Open grazing leases — land which could be transformed into farms — replaced the closed leases. The cattle kingdom in southern Alberta declined, but the federal government soon provided new encouragement for the development of ranching.

In Alberta, commercial agriculture evolved along the lines of regional specialization, noticeable as early as the period from the 1870s to 1905, which helped Alberta's economy become more productive and efficient, and contributed to a rising standard of living for its citizens. Southwestern and southeastern Alberta became famous for cattle, the area around Vulcan for wheat, central and north-central Alberta for mixed farming, and the Lethbridge area for sugar beets, trends which continue to the present.

The growth of trade allowed regional specialization in territorial agriculture and was, in turn, spurred by it. Albertans learned what kinds of crops and livestock their regions grew most effectively and produced them for sale in both internal and external markets. The commodities for trade within Alberta included cattle, horses, wheat, barley, oats, milk, cream, and eggs. Cattle and wheat emerged as the most important exports. Other parts of Canada and Great Britain took most of the exports of territorial Alberta.

As the years passed, Alberta's internal commerce and external trade increased. The development of roads was slow, but the appearance of some new roads stimulated internal transportation of goods. Transportation improvements resulting from the spread of the Canadian Pacific Railway network to Alberta and across the nation invigorated internal as well as external trade.

Urbanization was a final characteristic of Alberta's territorial economy. Cities and towns grew in importance before 1905. The expansion of cities and towns was important, for together they provided substantial markets for agricultural produce, thereby stimulating the commercialization of agriculture and growth of trade. Significantly, Alberta as a whole was becoming more urbanized. People living in towns and cities made up twenty-six percent of Alberta's population in 1901, but thirty-one percent five years later.[24] By 1901, Calgary, the only city at that time, had 4,000 inhabitants and the town of Edmonton 2,600. There were three other towns with a population over 1,000: Lethbridge with a population of 2,000, Strathcona 1,500, and Medicine Hat 1,500. By 1904, Edmonton had become a city.[25]

Developments that linked the urban and rural worlds were becoming significant by the eve of the formation of Alberta as a province in 1905. Marketing networks were stretching out from Edmonton and Calgary to nearby towns and homesteads. Many homesteaders were moving their products to towns and cities for sale in territorial and national markets. These networks, in business terms, were made up of hundreds of small firms. Buying and selling within a commercial economy was the way of life for numerous territorial Albertans.

In this setting, new arrivals showed a willingness to take new risks. Many, upon arriving in Alberta, went to partially settled areas where they became involved in farming, ranching, merchandising, manufacturing, and service industries. The fertility of the land and the business opportunities in territorial Alberta produced a commercial and agricultural society that by 1905 had a fairly high standard of living. The commercial outlook of farmers and ranchers as well as merchants and manufacturers was a stimulant to economic development.

■

Territorial Enterprises as Small Family Businesses

Although inadequacies in transportation and communications limited the distribution of goods and constraints in technology hampered the production of manufactured items, many business enterprises flourished in territorial Alberta. Like most central Canadian businesses, territorial Alberta businesses were relatively small family affairs. In running their businesses, Alberta merchants, farmers, ranchers, and manufacturers relied on their own efforts and on their family members, making bonds of marriage and blood ties vital in the territorial business system.

In all of these ventures, women's roles were influenced by territorial views of the family, which were generally advanced. Husbands and wives were partners in family enterprises and often thought of themselves as joint owners even though only the husband's name appeared on the title to the business property. For the most part, husbands depended heavily upon their wives, who served as clerks in the family store, worked in the family manufacturing establishment, and attended to the cooking, garden, dairy cattle, and poultry on the family farm and the family ranch.

Wives frequently became sole owners of family business upon the death of their husbands. For instance, in 1901, Emma Berry of Pincher Creek became the owner of the family hardware store following the death of her husband William, in accordance with his will.[26] Elsewhere, widows continued family enterprises in general merchandising, farming, ranching, the lumber trade, and the grocery business.

There were five main types of small family business in territorial Alberta. In towns and cities, entrepreneurs became involved in general mercantile activity, service industries, and manufacturing. In the country, in addition to farmers who produced and sold grain, cattle, milk, butter, and eggs, there were ranchers who raised and marketed livestock. Before 1905, and even up to World War II, small family businesses were the norm in most fields of enterprise, with non-bureaucratic firms sprinkling the Alberta landscape. Only after World War II was the dominance of small family business seriously challenged by the rise of big business in Alberta. Even so, small family businesses did not disappear.

■

The General Merchant

To territorial Albertans, a "general merchant" usually meant a person who carried a wide variety of merchandise; the business was called a general store. The cities of Calgary and Edmonton and the towns of Medicine Hat, Pincher Creek, and Lethbridge were the homes of the leading general merchants: the Bakers, Hatfields, Nolans, McDougalls, Secords, Revillons, Marshalls, Lebels, and Hills, among others. Usually territorial merchants operated as single-owner proprietors or as members of partnerships. Most partnerships were short-lived, limited to a few years, while some had longer lives, continuing for one or more generations. Like their central Canadian counterparts, some territorial Alberta merchants organized joint-stock companies.

The general store was the centre for business activities of the territorial merchant. Even the most prominent merchants employed only a few clerks, however. Traditional business techniques passed down from medieval Europe through central Canada remained significant: the use of single- and sometimes double-entry bookkeeping as well as promissory notes. General merchants operated retail stores, supplying urban and rural customers with goods and periodically travelling to large cities such as Toronto and Montreal in central Canada and Winnipeg in the West to select their wares.

Some merchants went beyond trading goods, carrying out a number of basic commercial functions essential to the territorial business system. Many acted as financiers, providing short-term credit to customers in towns and cities and in the countryside. Besides being retailers, they were wholesalers, importers, and exporters. They had interests in utility companies and supplied capital for other local enterprises. They became members of urban boards of trade and of town and city councils. Many became involved in real estate projects, making money through speculation and rents. Merchants were a key element in holding the business system of territorial Alberta together.

■

John A. McDougall: a General Merchant

John A. McDougall, one of the most important territorial merchants, illustrates the connections between family and business so significant in the territorial period. A late nineteenth- and early twentieth-century Edmonton merchant, McDougall relied heavily on family and friends in carrying out his numerous business ventures.

Born in the village of Oakwood, Ontario in 1854, McDougall was the son of Alexander J. McDougall, an impoverished but well-regarded carpenter, who had migrated there from Scotland.[27] Trained as a general merchant and grocer in Woodville and Cannington, Ontario, John A. McDougall entered the grocery trade as a small businessman in Winnipeg in 1874 at the age of twenty, using money earned in clerking as his initial capital. From the beginning, McDougall moved in the commercial society

John A. McDougall's general store in Edmonton as a young business, the nerve centre for the business activities of the territorial merchant. Even the principal merchants employed only a few clerks.

(Courtesy of City of Edmonton Archives and Edmonton Bulletin).

of Winnipeg and quickly made the personal contacts essential for success in business. Competition in Winnipeg's grocery trade greatly increased in the mid-1870s, and McDougall soon left this trade to become a travelling fur trader in the prairie West. Over the next few years, he brought his merchandise to Native Canadians at places such as Edmonton to exchange it for furs. In 1878, McDougall married Lovisa Jane Amey of United Empire Loyalist stock in Cannington, Ontario, enhancing his social position.

Using his savings, McDougall opened a general store in Edmonton in 1879 and in the process successfully transferred the general store pattern from Ontario to Alberta. With Lovisa's help, he sold $2,000 worth of goods during the first month.[28] He also continued his involvement in the fur trade. To assist him in building up his business, McDougall took Lovisa with him on his trading trips for some years. Needing capital for further growth, he formed a partnership, John A. McDougall & Co., in 1882, with Winnipeg entrepreneurs Charles Stewart and Hugh Bannerman.[29] Only a little of the anticipated expansion occurred, however. "Our first great disappointment was the change of route of the CPR which carried the line 200 miles south of Edmonton" through Calgary, McDougall later told Edmontonians. "This was a severe and what many considered a knock-out blow for Edmonton. Although we were badly hit we were not discouraged – we came to stay and stay we would. After this our growth was slower still."[30] McDougall was viewed as a man with endurance, an ability to persevere in difficult times.

McDougall was successful and used the earnings from the general store and the fur trade to diversify. He became an investor in a number of enterprises; a colonization company and a coal company, among others. Most important, however, was McDougall's general store, the backbone of his business. He kept fairly complete records based on single-entry bookkeeping. The accounts were arranged by customer in his ledger and were settled only once a year, in April.

McDougall also used a stock book, which showed the variety of goods in which he dealt.[31] He opened his store early and closed late, but stock turnover was slow. Page four from his book for the period from 1 April 1884 to 1 April 1885 shows dry goods — grey cotton, white cotton, white blankets, grey blankets, horse blankets, umbrellas, wadded quilts, cotton batting, wadding, and wool scarves. Page 56 shows his stock on hand on 31 March 1885:

ready made clothing	$1,915.68
hats and caps	701.89
toys	181.16
crockery	184.84
boots and shoes	1,674.58
harness	151.77
groceries	801.53
dry goods	4,892.01
hardware	2,016.31
shop furniture	463.42
total	12,983.19

McDougall purchased most of his goods from wholesalers in Winnipeg, including the James H. Ashdown Hardware Company, G. F. & J. Galt (groceries), Ames Holden & Co. (shoes, branch office of Ames, Holden & Co., Montreal), and James O'Brien & Co. (clothing, branch office of James O'Brien and Co., Montreal).[32] Because of his good credit rating, McDougall was able to build up a strong position in the Winnipeg market. He also bought some items from firms in Edmonton, such as the local Hudson's Bay Company store.

From his Edmonton general store, McDougall resold goods brought in from Winnipeg, as well goods purchased locally, to Edmonton citizens and farmers in the surrounding countryside. He had to offer liberal credit terms, especially to farmers, often up to a full year, for they could pay their bills only after they had harvested their crops. McDougall also had to accept farmers' products, such as grain, in payment for their debts to him.

On the withdrawal of Stewart and Bannerman from John A. McDougall & Co. at the end of July 1886, McDougall became sole owner, and the firm was reorganized as John A. McDougall. He then made a trip to purchase goods from wholesalers in Toronto and Montreal.[33] For McDougall, this buying trip was arduous, requiring more than six weeks to complete. The goods travelled by rail from Montreal and Toronto to Calgary, and then by Red River cart to Edmonton.

To help him develop his general store business upon his return, McDougall hired Ontario-born Richard Secord, a former Edmonton schoolteacher, as a sales clerk.[34] Personal ties came to link McDougall to Secord. He taught Secord merchandising during the day, and he and Lovisa often included him when they invited people to their home for a social gathering in the evening.[35] Later, in 1897, McDougall and Secord formed a partnership known as McDougall & Secord, which sold all types of products at retail and wholesale and handled a substantial part of the fur trade in northern Alberta. As a wholesaler, the firm was especially active in supplying country stores in the Edmonton region with goods.

McDougall also used his ties to Edmonton's business community to create a favorable environment for his general store trade. He was active in town boosterism and the work of business organizations. McDougall helped organize the Edmonton Board of Trade in 1889 and, as one of its leading members and president in 1895, sought to attract new farmers to the surrounding region. "We were all in business," he recalled later, "and realized that it was the settlement of the country by a good class of industrious farmers that would do more than anything else to build up the town."[36] McDougall invested in the newly organized Edmonton Light and Power Company and thus helped give the town its first electric light system in 1891.

McDougall's involvement in government was also important to the development of his general store business. He became an alderman of the town of Edmonton in 1894 and its mayor in 1897. As mayor, he provided a bold initiative for co-operation between the town and the federal government, building the Low Level Bridge from Strathcona, which had obtained Canadian Pacific Railway service in 1891, over the North Saskatchewan River to Edmonton. When the bridge was finally completed in 1902, it enhanced Edmonton's position as a distribution centre, contributing to the growth of McDougall's general store.

McDougall continued to take part in other business activities as well, for example, investing in real estate in Edmonton. He was also heavily involved in commercial, industrial, and residential mortgage lending in the city. McDougall's various activities, especially his general store trade, made him one of Edmonton's leading merchants. Around 1900, his son

John C. began to help him in his work. Nine years later, in 1909, John A. McDougall, his son, and Secord forsook the general store trade and reorganized McDougall & Secord as McDougall & Secord Ltd., a corporate venture that operated primarily as a financial and mortgage house.[37]

In territorial times, John A. McDougall was a general merchant, a jack-of-all trades who was involved in a broad range of business enterprises. Many of the most prominent merchants of territorial Alberta, like him, were general merchants. Markets were not large enough and too widely separated by inadequate transportation to permit merchants to make substantial profits from specialized business ventures. Nonetheless, by the end of the territorial period, specialization was starting to appear in the distribution of goods in the cities and larger towns. By 1905, the spread of commercial agriculture and the expansion in the size of markets was encouraging merchants to begin to specialize in particular lines of trade. This development clearly stimulated the growth of the Alberta business system.

■

The Manufacturer

Most manufactured goods in territorial Alberta came from central Canada, but there were still opportunities for small-scale manufacturers in territorial cities and towns to meet some of the needs of local markets. The cities of Edmonton and Calgary had flourmills, sawmills, foundries, and harness- and saddle-making establishments. As the growing population widened markets in the late territorial period, some manufacturing ventures acquired regional importance. By 1905, breweries in Calgary, Edmonton, and Lethbridge produced thousands of gallons of beer, much of which was consumed in these centres and surrounding areas. In Edmonton, Calgary, Medicine Hat, and Strathcona, flourmills helped satisfy local and regional markets. Alberta had coal reserves of unusual richness, which made the district one of great promise for coal-mining activity. Coal, produced at coal mines in centres such as Lethbridge, Canmore, Frank, and Edmonton, became an important source of energy for railways and manufacturers.[38]

In both towns and cities, manufacturers, investing relatively small amounts of money in tools, worked as gunsmiths, carpenters, bricklayers, and tinsmiths. Milliners, such as Mrs. H. H. McCully in Lacombe, designed and made hats.[39] In Lethbridge, E. T. Saunders, a printer and publisher, produced a newspaper, pamphlets, and cards. Such opportunities increased in Alberta cities and towns before 1905 as the territorial business system flourished, often with technologies transferred from central Canada to Alberta.

David Suitor: an Iron Founder

A good example of successful technology transfer is the career of David Suitor, whose foundry in Calgary in the late nineteenth and early twentieth centuries was a transfer of Quebec technology.

Born in St. Sylvester, Quebec in 1859, Suitor was the son of David Suitor, a farmer and native of Ireland. Beginning as an apprentice in an iron foundry in St. Sylvester, young David Suitor struck out on his own in Calgary in 1883, using funds he had earned back home to establish a small iron foundry. At first he had no help in the foundry and did all the work himself, making farm tools, machines, cattle branding irons, and horse-shoes, as well as shoeing horses and repairing carriages.[40] A skilled artisan, Suitor understood and personally took all the steps involved in making his products. On 4 January 1893, he married Frances Mabel Black, the daughter of John Black, a farmer at Shepard, and she assisted him in keeping the books.[41]

The foundry was badly damaged by fire,[42] and when he rebuilt it in 1893, Suitor also expanded and moved from handicraft to industrial production. He changed the making of machines and tools from a craft to an industrial operation by building a larger establishment that employed thirty-six workmen by 1911.[43] Within the foundry, by 1905, Suitor divided work into several different departments, each involving a single step in making machines. Until 1905, however, his firm remained a small family business, which he continued to own and manage.

Like other small manufacturers in territorial Alberta, Suitor adopted the technique of internally generated growth. He ploughed the family firm's earnings back into the enterprise. The growth of the iron foundry required more capital than retained earnings could supply. To expand his business, Suitor also relied on funds from financial institutions and friends. In the early 1890s, he borrowed $500 from the Yorkshire Guarantee Company.[44] As his foundry grew, however, he needed more money, and, in 1905, obtained a $2,500 loan at eight percent interest from John Hume of Port Hope, Ontario, a grain merchant.[45]

By 1906, he was producing iron columns, pile-driving hammers, and stone derricks, among other things. Suitor broadened the financial base of his foundry by reorganizing it as Calgary Iron Works, a corporate venture in which some of his local friends invested, including especially prominent Calgary entrepreneur Peter A. Prince of the Eau Claire and Bow River Lumber Company, the largest lumber manufacturer in the city.[46] In the process, Suitor yielded control of his family firm to outsiders, although he still had a large interest and continued to manage the business.

Service Businesses

The growth of manufacturing and commercial activities caused important changes in the Alberta firm in the territorial period. By 1905, a complex web of business transactions had developed, which presented numerous opportunities for providing specialized business services such as commercial banking for Alberta's expanding economy. The impact of these services on Alberta business did not become fully apparent until after 1905, but they did start to make themselves felt before that year.

Commercial banking existed in an informal manner in the territorial period, as mercantile firms such as I. G. Baker & Co., a Fort Benton, Montana enterprise with branches in Fort Macleod, Calgary, and Lethbridge, loaned funds to other businesses in these Alberta communities.[47]

Most territorial banks, however, functioned as formally organized chartered banks. In territorial Alberta, branches of central Canada's large federally chartered banks began to appear as early as the mid-1880s, to engage in commercial banking. By 1905, some chartered banks, such as the Bank of Montreal, were active, especially in Edmonton and Calgary, while others, like the Toronto-based Canadian Bank of Commerce, besides operating in the cities, were becoming increasingly visible in towns, Ponoka and Nanton for example. These and other chartered banks, all of which were regulated by the federal government, provided the bulk of the bank credit to territorial businesses. As the Alberta economy evolved in the twentieth century, the chartered banks became increasingly important.

An additional form of commercial banking closely tied to economic development in territorial Alberta was the private bank. Unlike the chartered bank, the private bank disappeared from the Alberta business scene at the end of this period. In the cities and in some towns, local merchants and other businesspeople sometimes entered commercial banking as unregulated private bankers. When the capital available to territorial businesses was not enough to finance their growth, they did not hesitate to seek funds from private bankers, who played a significant role in providing commercial banking services for Alberta's growing economy before 1905.

■

Cowdry Brothers: a Private Banking Firm

Starting as a small private bank at Fort Macleod in 1886, Cowdry Brothers lasted until 1905.[48] A family affair from the beginning, the bank was organized as a partnership by Nathaniel Cowdry and his younger brother John to provide local and regional commercial banking services. The relatively slow growth of the federally chartered banks in Alberta in this decade encouraged the opening of this institution.

Cowdry Brothers became one of the best-known private banks in territorial Alberta. Operating in Fort Macleod, this bank was owned by Nathaniel and John Cowdry, and its credit served as part of Alberta's money supply, thereby easing business transactions. (Courtesy of Main Street Office, Fort Macleod).

Among the many transfers of important central Canadian business developments to Alberta was commercial banking. Former Ontarians, Nathaniel and John Cowdry, the sons of Thomas Cowdry, a Toronto physician and surgeon, transferred their commercial banking experience in federally chartered banks from Ontario to Alberta. Born in Torrington in Devon, England in 1849 and educated at Upper Canada College in Toronto, Nathaniel began as a clerk first in the Royal Canadian Bank in Toronto and then in the Toronto branch of the Dominion Bank. John, born in Toronto in 1857 and also educated at Upper Canada College, started his business career as a clerk at the Toronto branch of the Merchants Bank of Canada.

Using savings they had accumulated as Ontario chartered bank employees before 1882 and as homesteaders in the Regina area during the next four years, the Cowdry brothers opened their private bank in Fort Macleod in October 1886. In contrast to a chartered bank, their private bank was unincorporated and much smaller, had no note issuing privileges, was not required by the federal government to provide it with financial statements, was unaffected by legislative control of capitalization, reserve funds, and interest rates, and was at liberty to take land to secure loans. Like chartered banks, Cowdry Brothers made loans to local and regional merchants, ranchers, and farmers, who used livestock, crops, personal promissory notes, and business securities as collateral. John and Nathaniel Cowdry, though they enjoyed considerable success for many years, yielded to the growing power of chartered banks in Alberta by selling their private bank to the Canadian Bank of Commerce in 1905.

Ranching Businesses

From the beginning, ranching in territorial Alberta was commercial agriculture. Ranchers were market-minded, a way of thinking that heightened in the 1880s, 1890s and early years of the twentieth century. Many ranchers operated their ranches as small family businesses. Large ranching establishments existed in two main areas — southwestern and southeastern Alberta. By 1905, however, small to medium-sized ranches, not huge spreads, were the most common units of livestock production throughout southern and central Alberta.

At first, from the 1870s to the 1890s, large incorporated ranching ventures dominated the agricultural business system of southern territorial Alberta. The rural population was dispersed along rivers and streams, and most agricultural business activity centred on big ranches, usually located at a desirable site along a waterway. Small cattle ranchers, many of whom were retired North-West Mounted Policemen from central Canada, appeared after 1876 and helped organize the production of beef for sale in Alberta and in the national and British markets. But by the mid-1880s, following the advent of leases of up to 100,000 acres in 1881, large central Canadian-owned ranches such as the Cochrane Ranche and the Northwest Cattle Company, and British-owned ranches, such as the Oxley Ranche and the Walrond Ranche, dominated the Alberta ranching industry.[49]

With the advance of the settlement frontier in territorial Alberta, however, the small to medium-sized, owner-occupied family ranch became the typical unit of livestock production by 1905. Often some 600 to 2,000 acres in size, the ranches had about 200 to 1,000 cattle. Among such ranchers were Richard and A. H. Lynch-Staunton of Pincher Creek, Walter C. Skrine of Nanton, James Hargrave of Medicine Hat, and Frank Collicutt of Wetaskiwin. Most of these territorial ranchers engaged in diversified ranching, raising some food for their own personal needs but always producing primarily for markets, in Alberta, other parts of Canada, Great Britain, and the United States. Market production of cattle was particularly common and horses and sheep were also raised for sale in various markets.

■

A. E. Cross: a Cattle Rancher

The growth of A. E. Cross's A7 Ranch at Nanton reveals the importance of small to medium-sized family businesses in ranching across Alberta during the territorial period.[50] Formed as a partnership in 1886, the A7 Ranch was initially simply one of dozens of businesses producing cattle for the local market in southwestern Alberta. The A7 Ranch lacked a good location or any other advantage over its competitors and was in great difficulty during the hard winter of 1886-87. Through personal ties, however,

Cowboys and a growing herd of cattle on A. E. Cross' A7 Ranch by the late 1890s. Cross was known for his willingness to experiment with several types of cattle, including Shorthorns, Herefords, and Galloways, and for his approach to breeding innovation. Historically, the A7 Ranch was closely associated with the development of the Alberta livestock industry and is still owned by the Cross family and continues to operate in the foothills of the Canadian Rockies.

(Courtesy of Glenbow Archives, NA-857-1).

the A7 Ranch's founders, A. E. Cross and his brothers William and Edmund, were able to obtain financial assistance, especially from their father and the Bank of Montreal. The individual most responsible for making effective use of this aid and helping the ranch to hold its own was A. E. Cross.

A. E. Cross saved the A7 Ranch. The story of how he did so indicates some of the ways small ranching businesses were able to co-exist with their larger counterparts in territorial Alberta. Born in Montreal in 1861, Cross was the son of Alexander Selkirk Cross, a wealthy judge and native of Scotland. A. E. Cross attended Bryant and Stratton Montreal Business College, where he developed his interest in business management, and went on to Ontario Agricultural College in Guelph, from which he graduated as a veterinary surgeon in 1884, shortly before he began working on the Cochrane Ranche near Calgary as assistant manager, bookkeeper, and veterinary surgeon. Subsequently, in 1886, he played a leading role in founding the A7 Ranch.[51] Cross saw a close relationship between his education in Quebec and Ontario and business achievement in Alberta.

Cross's most outstanding attribute as a rancher was a clear understanding that excellence in management was the prerequisite for success in the ranching business during the open-range herding period. Like other Alberta free-rangers in the late nineteenth and early twentieth centuries, Cross wintered his herd of cattle on leased and unfenced rangeland. When the A7 Ranch ran into serious trouble in the winter of 1886-87 as extremely heavy snowstorms and deep drifts covered the grass on the range, he favoured ranch relocation and better feeding methods as a solution. Cross moved the A7 Ranch westward into the rolling foothills of the Rockies, along what came to be called Cross Creek and Ranch Creek. Gorgeous valleys with superb grass, springs of water, and wooded hills surrounded these creeks and gave the A7 Ranch control of valuable waterfronts and grasslands. Besides continuing to keep down production costs by grazing his high-quality cattle on the unfenced range, Cross put up a great deal of hay to handfeed the animals whenever it was necessary.[52]

Cross thus embodied the virtues of the best Alberta ranchers and, in 1899, several years after his brothers had withdrawn from the A7 Ranch, he brought additional strength to this family business by marrying Helen Macleod, who gave him her full support. Seeking investment outlets for ranching profits, Cross had been rewarded for diversifying into brewing in Calgary in 1892. In choosing to grow through diversification, he found himself devoting time and energy to his brewery as well as his A7 Ranch, yet he did not neglect the ranch. Rather, Cross expanded his ranching operations, so that, by the turn of the century, the A7 herd had grown to 1,000 head of cattle.

Cattle ranching, however, was a very competitive business, and Cross and his rivals found themselves battling fiercely over local, national, and British markets for beef products. The A7 Ranch was nevertheless able to prosper by producing excellent beef.[53] Both the federal and territorial governments promoted the ranching business. Even after the pro-ranching federal Conservatives lost power to the pro-farming federal Liberals in 1896, federal government policies fostering business opportunities in ranching in Alberta continued.

■

Farming Businesses

Like ranching, farming in territorial Alberta was commercial agriculture from the start. Farmers were market-oriented, and this outlook became more apparent as the years passed. Relying on both male and female skills, most farmers ran their farms as small family businesses. In the territorial period, large farm establishments did not exist. Throughout Alberta, the owner-occupied family homestead was the typical unit of farm production. Obtaining credit from relatives, friends, and merchant connections, many homesteaders assumed fairly high levels of indebtedness as they developed their farms.

Frequently 160 acres in size, fully developed farms in the semi-arid areas of southern Alberta had about 80 to 110 acres of planted crops, the rest in fallow land and pastures; in central and north-central Alberta such farms had about 60 to 100 acres in crops, the balance in pasture, fallow land, and forest. Most territorial farmers engaged in diversified or mixed agriculture, growing enough food for their own use but producing mainly for markets, in Alberta, other parts of Canada, and Great Britain. In the central and north-central as well as the southern parts of Alberta, the market production of wheat, barley, and oats was especially evident. Farmers in all three areas also produced surpluses of livestock, hogs, and eggs for sale.

Most territorial farmers were entrepreneurially motivated. Still, the majority of them aimed for profits more for their families than for themselves as individuals. They placed more emphasis on the daily needs of their families and the long-term security of their farms than on quick economic gain, but they usually also sought to increase their property and wealth. They tried to get ahead by breaking new land, constructing houses, barns, and fences, and gradually raising more cattle and hogs and producing more cream and eggs for eventual sale. Alberta farmers gave careful consideration to the most favourable markets where they could sell their products, sometimes travelling considerable distances to get the best prices. The majority of tenant farmers also had an entrepreneurial outlook. Many saw tenancy as a first stage in their farming business before they used their income to purchase their own farms.

Developments abroad and within Alberta and Canada fueled farm development and reinforced the profit orientation of Alberta farm families in the territorial period. A rising British demand for Alberta wheat spurred the expansion of Alberta farming and brought more farmers into market production. Fertile soil permitted wheat to prosper and grow into an important export soon after settlement. The growth of urban markets in Alberta, as well as in central Canada, further stimulated the production of commercial wheat. As the density of the rural population grew, the price of land rose. When the price of wheat increased, additional land was purchased, as farmers tried to maximize their earnings. By 1905, many were raising substantial food surpluses for sale in Alberta and Canadian towns and cities as well as overseas. Numerous farmers also sought gain through involvement in land speculation.

The small family farm lay at the heart of territorial farming in Alberta. The growth in farming, like the expansion of general store trade, was based on family businesses. The family farm and the family general store spread across Alberta together. Farming wedded to the principle of agricultural diversity but centred especially on wheat, barley, and oats spurred the development of small family farms. Among territorial family farms that produced foodstuffs and cash crops for local consumption and long-distance trade were farms operated by James Jones of Tofield, Robert Findlay of High River, Louis Hammer of Olds, and Conrad Anderson of Shepard. These and other farmers made conscious choices about how to run their farms efficiently and profitably. While security for themselves and their families through owning their own farms motivated many Alberta farmers, the quest for profits remained particularly important.

■

Thomas Hoskin: a Farmer

The evolution of the farm of energetic homesteader Thomas Hoskin is a classic case study in the development of small family farming businesses in territorial Alberta.

Born in Cornwall, England in 1845, Thomas Hoskin emigrated to Toronto when he was young. In the 1860s, he married Mary Fieldhouse; and some time later opened a confectionery store on Yonge Street in Toronto. It was the start of an interesting business career.

Hoskin and his wife Mary made and sold choice jams, jellies, and candy in their store.[54] In their back yard, they kept a cow, which gave them milk for their own use as well as for sale. Carrying their milk in a small wagon, they peddled it in their neighbourhood. The most substantial part of their business, however, was their confectionery trade.

With the competition in Yonge Street's confectionery business becoming intense, the Hoskins embarked on a new conquest. In 1892, they sold their store and moved to the Red Deer area, where they began developing their new 160-acre homestead, using funds from the sale of their store.[55] They treasured the rolling, well-watered land and the rich black topsoil on their homestead. It was a time and a place propitious for the small farmer.

Despite his lack of experience in farming, Thomas Hoskin managed to create a valuable farm. In the swift change from running a store to opening a homestead, he took ideas developed in retailing in Toronto and applied them to farming. As in retailing, he immersed himself in the details of the farming business, carefully considering risks and acting to minimize them.[56]

With the help of his two sons, Hoskin broke five acres of virgin land a day, using a team of horses and a one-furrow walking plough. Oats, barley, wheat, and timothy grass were seeded by the broadcast method. Hoskin produced more barley and oats than wheat. The wheat was sold to Red Deer grain dealers, and most of the oats and barley was fed to the cattle and hogs to fatten them for sale in local and regional markets. For Hoskin, his wife Mary, and their sons, work on the farm included raising dairy cattle and chickens to sell cream and eggs in Red Deer. The search for security through diversification led Hoskin to move into producing ducks for sale.

As time passed and money became available from the sale of produce,

Hoskin added to his few implements a seed drill, a two-furrow plough, harrows, a cultivator, a binder, a mower, and a hayrake. He replaced the log house that provided initial shelter for his family with a frame house, improved the barn, and erected better barbed wire fences.

Like most small farm businesses in territorial times, the Hoskin farm had to finance these improvements internally through retained earnings.[57] Sources outside the farm provided relatively little in the way of funding for the farm's growth. Mary Hoskin took an active part in running the farm, both in planning its long-term development and carrying out day-to-day operations.[58] Thomas and Mary Hoskin were partners, and together they made the family farm work.

■

Close of the Territorial Period

At the close of the territorial period in 1905, prosperous farms and ranches and bustling towns and cities dotted the Alberta landscape. Thousands of people had contributed by building different types of businesses in urban and rural communities. Everywhere the capitalist mentality and entrepreneurial spirit of individuals was evident. A great variety of business activities had enhanced the economic well-being of Alberta society.

Alberta turned out to be a friendly environment for the growth of businesses. Geography and plentiful natural resources were significant factors in the territorial period, as they were to be after the formation of Alberta as a province. Territorial Albertans were aided by land capable of supporting diversified agriculture, rivers and streams supplying water for people and animals, and forests providing lumber for buildings. Such natural advantages played an important role in the development of Alberta's business system. Territorial Albertans also benefited from being part of a young but vibrant Canadian nation and a global economy that was expanding and creating new entrepreneurial opportunities. By 1905, the Canadian political system was, by and large, conducive to business development.

By 1905, Alberta's business system was coming out of its infancy, its heart in flourishing farms and ranches, with merchant establishments acting as channels for marketing their products. Trade connections linking Alberta to other parts of the world were fairly well established. Still, the business system of Alberta was far from mature, even in late territorial times. Despite the arrival of the Canadian Pacific Railway and the building of some roads, the lack of a fully developed transportation system hindered regional trade and specialization in business. Manufacturers, while important, were to become a more significant part of the economy in the future. A business infrastructure of banks, insurance companies, and shipping services was only in the beginning stages.

With the development of their economy, many Albertans living in the 1880s, 1890s, and the early years of the twentieth century came to see the need to create a new province, primarily as a political event, not a business occurrence. In the formation of the province of Alberta, however, views emerged about the political economy that helped unleash a flurry of new business opportunities.

NOTES TO CHAPTER TWO

1. Lewis H. Thomas, *The North-West Territories 1870-1905*. The Canadian Historical Association Historical Booklet No. 26 (Ottawa: The Canadian Historical Association, 1970), 3-5.

2. S. W. Horrall, *The Pictorial History of the Royal Canadian Mounted Police* (Toronto: McGraw-Hill Ryerson, 1973), 11-12.

3. Henry C. Klassen, "The Hudson's Bay Company in Southwestern Alberta, 1874-1905," in Jennifer S. H. Brown, W. J. Eccles, and Donald P. Heldman, eds., *The Fur Trade Revisited Selected Papers of the Sixth North American Fur Trade Conference*, Mackinac Island, Michigan, 1991 (East Lansing: Michigan State University Press, 1994), 395-398.

4. Gerald Friesen, *The Canadian Prairies: A History* (Toronto: University of Toronto Press, 1984), 149-150.

5. R. Douglas Francis, Richard Jones, and Donald B. Smith, *Destinies: Canadian History Since Confederation,* Third Edition (Toronto: Harcourt Brace & Company Canada, 1996), 59-62; Sarah Carter, *Lost Harvests: Prairie Indian Reserve Farmers and Government Policy* (Montreal: McGill-Queen's University Press, 1990).

6. *The True Spirit and Original Intent of Treaty 7: Treaty 7 Elders and Tribal Council* with Walter Hildebrandt, Sarah Carter, and Dorothy First Rider (Montreal: McGill-Queen's University Press, 1996). Arthur J. Ray, *I Have Lived Here Since the World Began: An Illustrated History of Canada's Native People* (Toronto: Lester Publishing Key Porter Books, 1996), 248-259.

7. *High River Times*, 5 November 1953.

8. Provincial Archives of Manitoba, Hudson's Bay Company Archives, D20/18, ff. 264-266, Edmonton, 25 February 1881, Richard Hardisty to James A. Grahame.

9. James E. Murphy, *The Story of the Conrad Mansion* (Kalispell: James E. Murphy, 1976).

10. Flathead County, Kalispell, Montana, Clerk of the District Court, Estate of Charles E. Conrad file, 3 December 1902.

11. John Harris Papers, Marjorie Gray collection, Highwood, Montana, Lethbridge, 10 January 1889, Howell Harris to John Harris.

12. Ibid., 2 November 1889, Howell Harris to John Harris.

13. Ibid., 8 December, 1893, Howell Harris to John Harris.

14. R. C. Macleod, *The North-West Mounted Police and Law Enforcement, 1873-1905* (Toronto: University of Toronto Press, 1976).

15. Desmond Morton, *Ministers and Generals: Politics and the Canadian Militia, 1868-1904* (Toronto: University of Toronto Press, 1970), 73-84.

16. Thomas, *The Northwest Territories*, 10, 16-17.

17. Pierre Berton, *The National Dream: The Great Railway, 1871-1881* (Toronto: McClelland & Stewart, 1970), and *The Last Spike: The Great Railway, 1881-1885* (Toronto: McClelland & Stewart, 1971); Hugh A. Dempsey, ed., *The CPR West: The Iron Road and the Making of a Nation* (Vancouver: Douglas & McIntyre, 1984).

18. Grant MacEwan, *Frederick Haultain: Frontier Statesman of the Canadian*

Northwest (Saskatoon: Western Producer Prairie Books, 1985), 105; Howard Palmer with Tamara Palmer, *Alberta: A New History* (Edmonton: Hurtig Publishers, 1990), 66.

19. Northwest Territories, Legislative Assembly, *Debates*, 23 August 1893, 4, 6.

20. *Census of the Northwest Provinces*, 1906, 101.

21. Kirk N. Lambrecht, *The Administration of Dominion Lands, 1870-1930* (Regina: Great Plains Research Center, 1991), 22-24.

22. David H. Breen, *The Canadian Prairie West and the Ranching Frontier, 1874-1924* (Toronto: University of Toronto Press, 1983), 132.

23. *Census of the Northwest Provinces*, 1906, 105.

24. Ibid., 101.

25. *Census of Canada, 1931*, 190.

26. Fort Macleod Court House, estate of William Berry file, 4 July 1901.

27. *Edmonton Bulletin*, 17 December 1928.

28. James G. MacGregor, *Edmonton Trader: The Story of John A. McDougall* (Toronto: McClelland & Stewart, 1963), 123.

29. *Edmonton Journal*, 17 December 1928.

30. Quoted in MacGregor, *Edmonton Trader*, 156.

31. City of Edmonton Archives, John A. McDougall & Co., Stock Book, 1 April 1884 - 1 April 1885.

32. John A. McDougall & Co., Stock Book, 1 April 1884 - 1 April 1885.

33. MacGregor, *Edmonton Trader*, 196-197.

34. David Leonard, John E. McIsaac, and Sheilagh Jameson, *A Builder of the Northwest: The Life and Times of Richard Secord, 1860-1935* (Edmonton: Richard Y. Secord, 1981), 17-18.

35. City of Edmonton Archives, Richard Secord Papers, Daily Journal for 1891, 7 January 1891.

36. Quoted in MacGregor, *Edmonton Trader*, 202.

37. Alberta Corporate Registry, Edmonton, McDougall & Secord Ltd. file.

38. A. A. den Otter, *Civilizing the West: The Galts and Development of Western Canada* (Edmonton: University of Alberta Press, 1982), 118-124; Geoff Ironside, "Slopes and Shafts," in Bob Hesketh and Frances Swyripa, eds., *Edmonton: The Life of a City* (Edmonton: NeWest Publishers, 1995), 193-202.

39. See also Donald G. Wetherell and Irene R. A. Kmet, *Town Life: Main Street and the Evolution of Small Town Alberta, 1880-1947* (Edmonton: University of Alberta Press, 1995), 118-119.

40. Interview by the author with William E. Suitor, 22 April 1975; *Calgary Herald*, 25 July 1888.

41. Suitor interview, 22 April 1975; Ruth Suitor Miller, *Some Suitor Families of Canada and the United States of America* (Asheville, North Carolina: Ward Publishing Company, 1987), 45-46, 58-59.

42. Glenbow-Alberta Institute Archives (hereafter cited as GAIA), Wesley F. Orr letterpress book, vol. 3, Calgary, 4 January 1893, Wesley F. Orr to R. G. Dun & Co.

43. *Calgary Alberta Merchants and Manufacturers Record: The Manufacturing, Jobbing and Commercial Center of the Canadian West* (Calgary: Jennings Publishing Company, 1911), 48.

44. Wesley F. Orr letterpress book, vol. 3, Calgary, 4 January 1893, Wesley F. Orr to R. G. Dun & Co.

45. Calgary Land Titles Office, mortgage records, 1905.

46. Alberta Corporate Registry, Calgary Iron Works Ltd. file.

47. Henry C. Klassen, "I. G. Baker and Company in Calgary, 1875-1884," *Montana. The Magazine of Western History* 35 (Summer 1985), 46-47; GAIA, Godsal Family Papers, Reel A 1610, Fort Macleod, 19 July 1883, F. W. Godsal to P. W. Godsal.

48. Henry C. Klassen, "Cowdry Brothers: Private Bankers in Southwestern Alberta, 1886-1905," *Alberta History* 37 (Winter 1989), 9-22; Henry C. Klassen, "Private Banking in the West," *Canadian Banker* 97 (September-October 1990), 52-56.

49. Breen, *The Canadian Prairie West and the Ranching Frontier*, 3-69.

50. Henry C. Klassen, "Entrepreneurship in the Canadian West: The Enterprises of A. E. Cross, 1886-1920," *Western Historical Quarterly* 22 (August 1991), 313-333.

51. Ibid.

52. Ibid.

53. Ibid.; Interview by the author with Mary Dover, 29 October 1973.

54. Interview by the author with Tom Hoskin, 17 May 1996.

55. Ibid.

56. Ibid.

57. Ibid.

58. Ibid.

PART TWO

BUSINESS DEVELOPMENT IN THE NEW PROVINCE

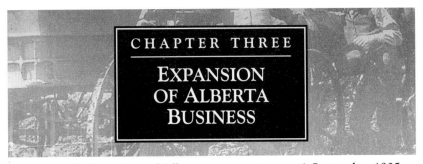

CHAPTER THREE

EXPANSION OF ALBERTA BUSINESS

The formation of Alberta as a province on 1 September 1905 as a result of federal legislation had important repercussions in the business realm. Alberta businessmen, besides assisting in the birth of the province as political leaders, helped create a provincial political structure capable of increasing and shaping entrepreneurial opportunities. The Alberta leaders belonged to a generation that had rejected territorial status, and they built in its place a new political economy that did more to promote business. They believed that the purpose of the business system was to foster the material well-being of the Alberta people. In their eyes, the success of the new province depended on individuals who were property owners and took advantage of entrepreneurial opportunities.

In the decade after 1905, there was disagreement over the best ways to provide opportunity and over what types of business to encourage, but at the same time there was a great deal of consensus that entrepreneurial opportunity was essential for the growth of Alberta and the general welfare of its people. The very formation of Alberta as a province was as important for the evolution of business opportunity as the new political economy that leaders eventually fashioned.

Alberta was already known for its abundant natural resources by 1905. These resources, Albertans emphasized, included fertile soils, waterpower sites, forests of commercial timber, coal fields, and oil and natural gas reserves. Entrepreneurs successfully exploited both Alberta's natural resources and the benefits of being part of Canada. Provincial status, of course, did not bring the benefit of control of natural resources within Alberta; but, although the federal government retained control of natural resources until 1930, it allowed Albertans to use them and continued to provide other benefits to the province as well. Alberta entrepreneurs could still operate over a large free-trade area whose peoples, by and large, spoke the same language. Continuing political stability and political freedom also meant that the freedom to choose an occupation remained intact. Political stability, occupational freedom, and plentiful natural resources helped create a society with growing business opportunities.

Some businessmen and lawyers, conscious of the economic potential of the new province, were among the most significant politicians in Alberta. They did not know, however, how provincial status would affect their business enterprises. They had to establish government policies for the development of business, a task that severely tried the new Alberta government and led to conflict between two leading politicians, Alexander C. Rutherford and R. B. Bennett.

■

Developing the Tradition of Government–Business Relations

On 2 September 1905, George H. V. Bulyea, lieutenant-governor of Alberta, called on Alexander Rutherford as leader of the Liberal party to form the first government. It was done within four days, and the new Liberal government included several members important to the development of business.[1] Premier Rutherford, a Strathcona lawyer, also became provincial treasurer and minister of education. C. W. Cross, an Edmonton lawyer, joined the government as attorney-general. W. H. Cushing, a Calgary sash and door manufacturer, became minister of public works. The other businessman in the government was W. T. Finlay, a lumber merchant and rancher from Medicine Hat who was minister of agriculture and provincial secretary. Rutherford, Cross, Finlay, and Cushing all sought to enlarge business opportunities in Alberta. On 9 November, there was an overwhelming victory for Rutherford's government in the provincial election.[2] Twenty-three Liberals and only two Conservatives took their seats in the legislative assembly in Edmonton.

The Liberal victory, however, left many questions unanswered. Inevitably, as events would show, there were differences of judgment between the Liberals and Conservatives concerning provincial economic policy, differences that sprang from conflicting political views and varying business interests. By 1910, these differences focussed on the personalities of Alexander Rutherford and the Conservative R. B. Bennett.

■

Alexander Rutherford and Alberta Business

The views and leadership of Alexander Rutherford led to the first major dispute over government-business relations in the new province of Alberta. Born on a farm near Ottawa in 1857, Rutherford completed a Bachelor of Arts degree and a Civil Law degree at McGill University after teaching school for a year.[3] In 1881, he began a legal apprenticeship in the Ottawa law office of Scott, McTavish and McCracken. Rutherford practised law in Ottawa, from his call to the Ontario bar in 1885 until he moved to Strathcona in 1895.

Rutherford developed a flourishing practice as a prominent citizen of Strathcona, in part through legal work involving the local branch of the Imperial Bank of Canada and other Strathcona businesses. In 1899, he and Frederick C. Jamieson formed a legal partnership, the firm Rutherford &

Jamieson. Growing demand to provide legal services to local businesses encouraged the firm to add a partner within the next seven years, A. T. Mode.[4]

While law remained important to Rutherford, he also began to take an active interest in politics. A Liberal, Rutherford represented the riding of Strathcona in the territorial legislative assembly from 1902 to 1905. He was very influential in the Liberal Party, and in 1905, it was logical for him to become the first premier of Alberta.

As premier, Rutherford provided significant initiatives for the provincial political economy, initiatives that triggered much political controversy by 1910. Conflicts over his policies helped confirm the division of Albertans into their first two political parties – Liberals and Conservatives.

Rutherford wanted to build up Alberta through co-operation between government and business. As premier, he felt compelled to promote business development. To him business was an essential element in expanding the wealth of the province. Rutherford, therefore, sought to stimulate the growth of Alberta through close ties with business enterprises, believing he was acting in the public interest.

From the outset, Rutherford clearly saw the connection between business and political situations and political stability. His program reflected co-operation between the public and private sectors. He aided Alberta ranching businesses by pushing a measure for the registration of brands through the legislative assembly in 1906.[5] He also devoted a considerable part of his time and energy to bolstering farming businesses by establishing provincially owned and run creameries. Private investors were unwilling to support the risky undertaking of establishing and maintaining an adequate number of creamery businesses. "There were quite a number of creameries in the province," Rutherford told assemblymen on 19 March 1906, "and it was expected the government would take these over and carry on their operation so long as it was conducive to the good of the country."[6] In the fall of 1905, Alberta had twelve provincially owned creameries and thirteen private creameries. By the spring of 1907, there were eighteen provincially owned creameries, and twenty-four private creamery firms. As a result of this expansion, the value of butter output increased by more than $100,000.[7]

To encourage the development of sugar beet farms in southern Alberta, Rutherford provided them with a total bonus of $250,000 in 1906. In the same year, he created the province-wide Alberta Government Telephone system, which soon absorbed the Alberta arm of the Bell Telephone Company, thus giving business advantages not only to merchants and manufacturers but also to farmers and ranchers. By 1913, there were 16,350 miles of telephone service in operation in the province.[8] Rutherford was interested in establishing a political economy favourable to commerce, agricultural development, and manufacturing.

Rutherford also proposed aid to railways in Alberta. Under his plan, which the legislative assembly adopted in 1909, his government supported a great deal of railway construction.[9] The Canadian Northern Railway and the Grand Trunk Pacific Railway asked for provincial help in constructing branch lines in the province, and Rutherford responded by guaranteeing the interest on the bonded debt for these branch lines. The Canadian Northern branch lines included a line from Edmonton to the Peace River and a line from Morinville to Athabasca Landing.[10] Rutherford also guaranteed the interest on the bonded debt of the newly organized Alberta and Great Waterways Railway, a private road that was to extend from Edmonton to Fort McMurray.

Rutherford's support of the Alberta and Great Waterways Railway, like his backing of the northernmost Canadian Northern branch lines, reflected his appreciation of the need to provide new settlers immediately north of Edmonton as well as all the way to the Peace River region with railway service.[11] He believed that the Alberta and Great Waterways Railway was very important "to the development of the north country, and the province at large."[12] The future exploitation of the oil sands at Fort McMurray could become rewarding for Alberta as a whole. Rutherford, therefore, asked Albertans "to stand shoulder to shoulder to make Alberta the banner province."[13]

Rutherford's Alberta and Great Waterways Railway policy proved highly controversial. Details of a high-cost contract the Rutherford government had signed with William Clarke, a Kansas City railway construction contractor, to construct the railway became public knowledge in March 1910.[14] Calls for an inquiry into the alleged financial abuses of the government in connection with the contract intensified. Rutherford appointed a royal commission to investigate the government's relations with Clarke. Rutherford was not opposed to testifying and not disturbed by having to talk about the basis of his conduct.[15] The investigation, though it revealed confusion and incompetence in the government, did not disclose wrongdoing on the part of Rutherford or any other member of the cabinet.[16]

Disaster rained down on Rutherford from all sides. First Cushing and then Cross resigned, although Cross soon re-entered the cabinet. A significant minority of Liberals in the assembly turned against Rutherford.[17] Finally, on 26 May 1910, Rutherford himself resigned as premier. By 1 June, Arthur L. Sifton, former chief justice of Alberta and a Calgary lawyer, had formed a new Liberal government.

Rutherford's idea of using the provincial government to assist railways throughout Alberta continued in Sifton's new Liberal regime from 1910 to 1917, as well as in the Liberal administration of Charles Stewart, a Killam farmer who governed Alberta from 1917 to 1921. Although Rutherford advocated a political economy favourable to all parts of Alberta, a myth arose portraying him as a great champion of Edmonton and northern development. The principles underlying his program from 1905 to 1910 were supportive of strong provincial government intervention in the economic system to aid the expansion of business everywhere in Alberta. However, some Albertans who were most interested in developing the southern part of the province began to oppose Rutherford politically. They turned to Rutherford's main opponent, R. B. Bennett, to provide leadership to increase business opportunities for the development of southern Alberta.

■

R. B. Bennett and Alberta Business

In some ways Bennett's background was similar to Rutherford's. Bennett was born in 1870 in New Brunswick, where his father was a struggling shipbuilder at Hopewell Cape. After teaching school for several years and graduating from Dalhousie Law School with an LL.B. degree, Bennett was admitted to the New Brunswick bar and became a full-time lawyer in the Chatham law office of Lemuel Tweedie in 1893, where he had articled.[18] Bennett practised law with Tweedie for four years, and his excellent work helped propel him forward, so that in 1897 he moved to Calgary to become the junior partner of the well-known lawyer James Lougheed in the firm of Lougheed and Bennett.[19]

Bennett's upward march was reflected in his association with Lougheed, who had arrived in Calgary from Ontario in 1883. Lougheed had immediately become the Canadian Pacific Railway's solicitor in Calgary. In 1889, John A. Macdonald had made him a member of the Canadian Senate. Lougheed's professional prominence and political activities had given his fledgling law firm high standing in Calgary and Alberta.

As a young Calgary lawyer, Bennett soon built a thriving practice, partly by taking over much of Lougheed's work and acting as solicitor for the Canadian Pacific Railway and other businesses in Calgary. But the lure of politics in the Northwest Territories also drew him to Regina. A Conservative since his New Brunswick days, he represented Calgary West in the territorial legislative assembly from 1898 to 1905.[20] His seven-year stint in the assembly served to enhance his reputation, as well as that of the firm of Lougheed and Bennett.

By the autumn of 1905, when Alberta became a province, Bennett had already made a name for himself in Calgary as an expert in corporate law. His courtroom skills helped him develop a strong, ongoing relationship not only with the Canadian Pacific Railway, but also with other corporations such as the Bank of Montreal, the Royal Bank of Canada, the Great West Life Assurance Company, and the Massey-Harris Company.[21] By 1911, Lougheed and Bennett had brought in four additional partners including

William H. McLaws, which greatly aided Bennett in meeting the growing legal needs of corporate businesses.[22]

The successful lawyer also had ambitions as a Conservative politician. In the summer of 1905, Bennett became leader of the Conservative Party in Alberta. He knew that Albertans would go to the polls on 9 November in the first provincial election. As Conservative leader, Bennett gave prominence in the election campaign to the need for Alberta to control its resources for the benefit of all Albertans, but emotionally he remained rooted in the business of the Canadian Pacific Railway and other corporations in Calgary from which he made his living. He was first and foremost a corporate lawyer and served his numerous corporate clients in Calgary well. At the same time, his Liberal opponents took advantage of his image among farmers and many Calgarians as solicitor of a monopolistic and high-freight-rate Canadian Pacific in the hope of winning the election. Seriously hurt by this negative image, Bennett lost in the Calgary riding to W. H. Cushing by thirty-seven votes.[23] After the election, Bennett stepped down as leader of the Conservative Party.

Bennett was elected in what had become a two-member Calgary riding along with Cushing in the next provincial election on 22 March 1909. The legislative assembly opened on 10 February 1910, and Bennett, as the real but not the avowed leader of the three Conservatives in a forty-one-seat house, was given the task of leading the attack on Rutherford's Alberta and Great Waterways Railway policy. Bennett stressed the incompetence of the government especially in connection with its contract with William Clarke and eventually helped drive Rutherford out of the premier's office.

During the debate in the assembly, Bennett portrayed the Alberta and Great Waterways Railway project as unnecessary and a waste of provincial government funds. He said, for instance, that the railway "was traversing a country which the Dominion government had said was not good enough to survey."[24] The passenger traffic, Bennett stated, would be "a mere bagatelle."[25]

Bennett showed little understanding for the need to open the Peace River country for settlement and to exploit the northern forest and the Fort McMurray oil sands through the creation of a railway network north of Edmonton. Bennett's preference was for a corporate society organized around the Canadian Pacific and Calgary. This did not mean that he believed corporations in Calgary to be the source of all wealth but, instead, that they were very important to Alberta's economy. Bennett was appalled by what he saw as Rutherford's favouring Edmonton not only by funding the Alberta and Great Waterways Railway, but also by giving Edmonton the University of Alberta after it had already become the capital of the province.

The two men clearly held different views on significant questions of provincial economic policy. Bennett's ideas embodied especially corporate values that contrasted with Rutherford's broader outlook. As a politician, Bennett attracted the support of those Albertans who sought the growth of Calgary and southern Alberta. As premier, Rutherford also recognized that corporations had a positive impact on Alberta society. He showed his practical side by furthering the interests of Edmonton and northern Alberta as well as those of the rest of the province.

■

Conflict between Bennett and Rutherford

Bennett's disagreement with Rutherford became more bitter as time passed, especially their dispute over the Canadian Pacific Railway. To Bennett, the Canadian Pacific was an essential factor in the development of southern Alberta, and he wanted to encourage the growth of this part of the province through the economic ties with the railway that had already been established. Further, he sought to maintain the Canadian Pacific's exemption from taxes.

Rutherford, on the other hand, wanted to tax the Canadian Pacific in Alberta just as he wanted to tax other railways in the province. His goal was local and provincial development; his means toward this goal was provincial legislation in 1906 that imposed taxes on all railways. Through its solicitor, Bennett, the Canadian Pacific fought this legislation in the courts. In 1911, the judicial committee of the Privy Council in London, England ruled in favour of the Canadian Pacific, at least with respect to its main line in Alberta.[26]

■

Legacy of the Rutherford and Bennett Generation

The death of Rutherford's railway tax and Bennett's response to the issue of northern railway development may seem to have closed a chapter in the history of the Alberta political economy, with one side winning the battle against the other. From one viewpoint, this was true, but from another, more important historical viewpoint, it was not. On the surface, the disagreement between Rutherford and Bennett was a dispute between clashing personalities, but more basically it involved ongoing questions of provincial economic policy.

The views underlying Rutherford's program appeared in subsequent discussions regarding Alberta's political economy. Although Rutherford left the legislative assembly in 1913 and died in 1941, his idea of using the provincial government to develop the natural resources of Alberta and employing public funds to assist a wide variety of businesses continued in later generations. Enduring as well was his belief that the provincial government could help resolve economic problems not only by promoting the interests of major private corporations, but also by working for the economic and social advancement of small farmers, ranchers, and merchants.

Rutherford thus assimilated a particular kind of political economy into his vision of Alberta. In reaction to this vision, Bennett remained in the corporate orbit. He felt most comfortable as an advocate of the Canadian Pacific and other corporations in southern Alberta. Although he withdrew from the legislative assembly to enter the House of Commons in 1911, through his law practice he continued to connect Alberta's development primarily to the establishment and maintenance of corporate ventures. His notion that corporate power could play an important role in making Alberta strong economically persisted in debates on behalf of corporations in later decades.

If the generation of Rutherford and Bennett left a legacy of disagreement in the Alberta political economy, it also left institutions fundamental to the future evolution of the Alberta business system. The most significant result for Alberta business of Alberta becoming a province was the gradual development of an important internal market. In 1905, Alberta was already a wealthy province by Canadian standards, but unlike some provinces it covered a large geographical area. At the beginning of the twentieth century, the internal market, still underpopulated and largely unreachable, existed mostly as a dream to be realized in the future.

Another legacy of the Rutherford and Bennett generation was the development of a political system that encouraged private investment. Albertans were free to invest in business enterprise. Under the law, individuals could hold property to increase its value. The fundamental aspects of capitalism were safeguarded by the same political system that helped bring into being a substantial market.

A further legacy of Rutherford and Bennett's generation was the creation of a legal system that gave legal life to various forms of business organization. The Alberta government, for example, passed laws that established hundreds of business corporations in the four decades after 1905, thus stimulating corporate development. A corporation was a legal entity created to bring people together for a particular purpose. Under law, a corporation had a life of its own, apart from that of its owners who held shares of stock in it. As well, incorporating granted limited liability to investors in a business enterprise. Like corporations, the many partnerships and single-owner proprietorships in Alberta looked to the legal system to adjudicate and enforce claims and obligations growing out of promissory notes, contracts and other aspects of private business transactions. Certainly, all this facilitated the development of markets within Alberta and beyond.

Finally, occupational freedom was another legacy of the Rutherford and Bennett generation. Albertans were free to move from one occupation to another. However, it was apparent from the beginning that Native Canadians in Alberta had limited occupational freedom. The many Albertans who could move freely from one occupation to the next greatly aided the conduct of business in the province by providing fluid human resources.

Later generations of Albertans often took for granted the gifts left by Rutherford and Bennett's generation. The ability to influence provincial government policy through democratic institutions, the geographically large and rich internal market, and the efforts to secure property rights provided a setting for Alberta business institutions to change, for entrepreneurs to seize fresh opportunities, and for wealth to grow over the next century.

Besides, as Rutherford, Bennett, and others debated the basic features of the new provincial political economy, important changes were starting to take place that would trigger new entrepreneurial opportunities and significantly affect the Alberta business system. Among these features were the development of the transportation network, the expansion of agricultural enterprise, and the beginnings of industrialization.

■

Economic Growth

In May 1906, Alexander Rutherford concluded his first budget speech in the new province of Alberta with a reference "to the bright future before the province, to the optimism of the citizens, and to the immigrants, who he hoped would come in their millions to find homes in Alberta."[27] Like many other leaders of his generation, Rutherford foresaw the internal development of Alberta and, as early as 1896, began buying land in Strathcona and the surrounding region.[28] Now, as premier, he sought not just to enrich himself, but to provide business opportunities for other investors as well.

Besides serving as the new province's first premier, Rutherford lived to see some of his hoped-for developments in Alberta. At his death in 1941, many Albertans continued to look inward at the great prospect of developing business within Alberta. Numerous entrepreneurs also continued to look outward, toward other parts of Canada and the world, for business opportunities.

Between 1906 and 1941, the Alberta economy developed rapidly, and with this development came several significant changes. Economic growth brought transportation, communication, agricultural, and industrial changes of lasting importance. Alberta capitalism flourished in the early twentieth century, and Albertans worked and prospered as seldom before. Entrepreneurs increasingly invested in business opportunities. Also, the provincial government continued to become involved in business activity by developing commercial, agrarian, and industrial opportunities, believing that developmental opportunities aided the whole province.

The growth of Alberta was remarkable. When Rutherford made his first budget speech in 1906, the new province had about 185,000 inhabitants. By 1921, that figure had expanded to 588,000 and by 1941 had reached 796,000.[29] This dramatic growth of population caused an equally dramatic expansion of the internal market, which in turn created an ever-increasing number of entrepreneurial opportunities.

Without heavy immigration — especially before World War I and during the 1920s — such dramatic changes could not have occurred in such a relatively short period of time. With assistance from east central European countries, Great Britain, and the United States, which permitted Alberta to drain off their excess populations, the provincial leaders were able to fill much of the large province by 1941. Transportation, agricultural, and industrial developments resulted in important expansion in entrepreneurial opportunities, and each of these developments stimulated growth in Alberta's wealth. The expansion in material wealth was not always smooth; there were major downturns in the business cycle in 1913, in the early 1920s, and during the Great Depression in the 1930s. Overall, however, the period from 1906 to 1941 was one of energy and development. Alberta business success helped earn the province one of the highest standards of living in Canada.

■

Developing the Transportation Network

At the start of the twentieth century, overland transportation in Alberta was still difficult. Arthur Sifton, Alberta's second premier, a lawyer and a businessman, was among the provincial leaders who understood that overcoming the barriers to overland transportation was essential for the growth of the internal market. Sifton and other entrepreneurs sought to lower transportation costs through internal improvements.

■

Railways

The construction of railways was one of the first internal improvements Albertans made in the early twentieth century. The major advantage railways offered was speed of passage. When J. D. Harrison, sheriff of Edmonton, travelled to Calgary in 1883, he left Edmonton on a democrat. The 200-mile trip to Calgary on the Edmonton and Calgary trail took one week.[30] Seventeen years later, in 1901, a correspondent for the Toronto *Mail and Empire* made the trip from Calgary to Edmonton by rail in thirteen and a half hours.[31]

These two trips illustrate why Alberta entrepreneurs preferred the

Transportation improvements helped speed business development and economic growth in Alberta during the early twentieth century. Trains running through Edmonton connected the city to other areas in Alberta and in Canada.

(Courtesy of Glenbow Archives, NA-1529-9).

railway for overland transportation. They recognized that the railway offered potential advantages of speed and all-season reliability over road transportation. By the end of Sifton's tenure as premier in 1917, Albertans had invested tens of thousands of dollars in railways. The next three years, when Charles Stewart served as Alberta's premier, would see additional investment in the construction of an eventual total of thousands of miles of track.[32]

By 1920, the railway network had spread to most parts of Alberta. Lines radiating northward from Edmonton, including the Edmonton, Dunvegan and British Columbia Railway and the Alberta and Great Waterways Railway, connected that city with Grande Prairie, Peace River, Athabasca Landing, Lac La Biche, and St. Paul des Metis. In central Alberta, the network of lines was more dense than that north of Edmonton. The Canadian Northern and the Grand Trunk Pacific had been combined to form the Canadian National Railways system, which tied Edmonton to Toronto and Vancouver, as well as to Vermilion, Edson, Camrose, Stettler, Drumheller, Calgary, and Nordegg within Alberta. In southern Alberta, growth was more moderate, although Canadian Pacific branch lines connected Calgary to Empress, Manyberries, Lethbridge, Cardston, and Vulcan.[33] The development of the railway network spurred the rise of hundreds of villages and towns, stimulating the expansion of Alberta business.

The depression that began in 1919 and continued until 1923, however, made it impossible for the Alberta and Great Waterways Railway and the Edmonton, Dunvegan and British Columbia Railway to survive. With the continuing movement of population northward beyond Edmonton to all parts of the North but especially to the Peace River country, the need to maintain overland transportation links was clear. In 1920, the Liberal government under Stewart took over the Alberta and Great Waterways Railway and funded its operations. Herbert Greenfield, a Westlock farmer who served in the premier's office from 1921 to 1925, was the first of the United Farmers of Alberta premiers to support provincial government ownership of northern railways and, in 1926, his successor, Calgary lawyer J. E. Brownlee, convinced his government to take control of the Edmonton, Dunvegan and British Columbia Railway.[34]

Operating losses, however, prompted Brownlee to sell these and other provincially owned northern railways as the Northern Alberta Railways Company to the federally owned Canadian National Railways and the Canadian Pacific in 1929.[35] Thus, provincial support for northern railways was no more. In its place was a mix of federal and Canadian Pacific action. The need for railway development in northern Alberta remained, and the federal government and the Canadian Pacific together commanded enough financial resources to help fund it. This support for northern railways in turn spurred the growth of Alberta business enterprises.

■

Roads

As significant as railways were, the realization of Arthur Sifton's dream of roads linking cities, towns, and villages across Alberta was also important.[36] Most of Alberta's original roads were almost impassable. Sifton's road-building program was a long, costly process. His perceptive forecasting of better roads in Alberta rested on the province's great human and natural resources, its rich and expanding market, and a provincial government policy supportive of private business.

Sifton's clear view of business-government relations surfaced in his decision in 1913 to establish a highways branch within the Department of Public Works. Building on the work of his predecessor, Alexander Rutherford, Sifton pushed ahead with the construction of highways. From 1905 to 1917, the provincial government spent $8 million on roads, bridges, and ferries.[37] In the next few years, Premier Stewart also made an impressive contribution to the highway network in Alberta.

By 1920, considerable work had been done on several main highways.[38] Most important was the road from Athabasca Landing through Edmonton, Calgary, and Lethbridge to Coutts. There were the Walsh-Medicine Hat-Lethbridge-Crowsnest Pass road, the Lloydminster-Edmonton road, the

In early provincial times, roads were primitive. Stagecoach on the Calgary and Edmonton Trail. (Courtesy of Glenbow Archives, NA-1162-3).

Lacombe-Compeer road, and the Medicine Hat-Calgary-Banff road, among others. The roads, however, were still primitive. In general, the provincial government relied on horse-drawn scrapers to turn a dirt surface into a road.[39] Despite the primitive highway technology, roads speeded travel and the movement of goods somewhat, stimulating the growth of business enterprise.

The road situation changed in 1923, when the United Farmers of Alberta government under Herbert Greenfield began using a mixture of gravel and Fort McMurray oil sands to hard-surface the Edmonton-St. Albert road.[40] The use of this new technology remained limited for a number of years, but the government clearly saw the advantage of employing it on some of the principal highways in the province, for the cost of moving goods over such hard-surfaced roads decreased. The next year, in 1924, Greenfield secured federal government help in developing Alberta's main highways.[41] Provincial and federal government aid continued to be instrumental in expanding and improving Alberta's road network after Brownlee became premier of the province in 1925.[42] This was also the case when William Aberhart, a Calgary high school teacher, became Alberta's premier at the head of a Social Credit government ten years later.[43] In the years 1936 and 1937, Aberhart expanded the road program by spending $405,000 on the construction and maintenance of district highways and local roads.[44]

Travel was still fairly expensive for most farmers and small-town merchants, who continued to depend on gravel-surfaced and especially dirt roads, but sections of main highways that were hard-surfaced provided economical transportation. Overall, road improvements permitted merchants, manufacturers, and farmers along Alberta's roads and highways to reach their customers more profitably.

■

Age of the Car and Truck

At the same time, Alberta began changing from a railway-dominated to a car-and truck-oriented society, a shift that continued after World War II. Patterns of travel and moving goods changed. In 1907, there were only fifty-five motor vehicles in Alberta. This figure soared to 38,000 in 1920, and to 121,000 twenty years later.[45] Albertans now transported a much greater proportion of their goods by truck and car than ever before. Trucks made it possible to move goods at a cost only slightly above railway charges. Automobiles became much more than luxuries for Albertans, and were increasingly seen as necessities.

The use of cars and trucks came to affect most aspects of life in Alberta, including business. By giving Albertans more mobility, automobiles and trucks connected farms and ranches to towns and cities. Relatively cheap small-scale transportation helped preserve small businesses and enlarge their markets.

■

Communications

Substantial improvements in the transportation network permitted corresponding improvements in Alberta's communications system. Better communication was an important factor in the snowballing volume of business in the province's cities and towns. In 1875, there was only a handful of post offices serving Albertans. Although the first railway mail car came to Alberta in 1883, most mail was still carried by wagon or sleigh. Mail service remained slow and costly. The situation began to change in the 1890s, and by 1910, there were 695 post offices serving the province.[46] This figure rose to 1,191 in 1920, and to 1,267 twenty years later.[47] It was the transportation improvements resulting from extensive railway and highway networks that allowed significant improvements in the speed and quality of mail service. This, in turn, helped decrease information costs for businesspeople.

The telegraph was a second major development in communications. As railways spread across Alberta, so too did the telegraph. Appearing in towns and cities as soon as they got the railway, the telegraph provided rapid communication between these centres as well as between them and

*The telegraph line — such as the line near Beaverlodge in the Peace River
country around 1915 — became a symbol of communication success
in Alberta.* (Courtesy of Glenbow Archives, NA-493-8).

railway centres in other parts of Canada. The telegraph, though it was
important to all Albertans, was particularly significant for business enterprise. Alberta businesses frequently needed to send and receive messages
fast, and the telegraph helped speed the distribution of vital information.

A third important development in communications was the telephone.
In 1912, there were 15,800 telephones in Alberta.[48] By 1920, this figure
had jumped to 54,500, and to 73,400 twenty years later.[49] Employed at first
mostly for local conversations, telephones became increasingly used for
long-distance calls as Alberta Government Telephones developed long-distance telephone lines. Businesspeople wanted to confer often with outside
agencies, and telephones allowed them to do this. As Alberta Government
Telephones developed across Alberta, business owners' grasp became as
firm over long distances as in their own building.

■

Agricultural Development

The growth of the transportation network opened up Alberta and contributed significantly to the development of the agricultural sector of its
economy. Beginning in the early years of territorial settlement, entrepreneurs invested in opportunities to harvest Alberta's agricultural resources.
Opportunities favourable to the profitable sale of grain and livestock in
local, national and international markets during the territorial period con-

tinued to appeal to Alberta farmers and ranchers. Alexander Rutherford wanted to open railway and highway routes to new agricultural areas. The first shipments by road and rail to towns and cities within the new province were agricultural products. Clearly, rural Alberta was a resource awaiting development.

Commercially minded Alberta farmers soon tapped the rich resources of fresh agricultural areas. To increase their wealth, they made great efforts to break new acres. The general drives of Alberta culture gradually led to the expansion of land ownership. Many farmers, besides ploughing most of their profits back into their farms, saved money to purchase more land. In Alberta, with the population growing rapidly, the demand for land was immense. All over the province, including the Peace River country, market opportunities for farmers grew, so that by the 1930s a market-oriented agriculture, in which farmers saw themselves primarily as small business owners selling farm produce for manufactured items, characterized the progress of farming. The high general competence of Alberta farmers contributed to the development of a lively business system.

Between 1911 and 1941, improved farm land in Alberta rose from four million acres to twenty million acres. During the same period, the number of farms increased from 61,000 to 100,000.[50]

■

Charles S. Noble, the Noble Blade Cultivator, and Farming

Alberta inventions bore the stamp of regional culture and physical environment. Practical advances on the frontier of early agrarian development in the province owed much to an inventor-entrepreneur named Charles S. Noble. Born in State Center, Iowa in 1873, Noble opened a 160-acre homestead near Claresholm in 1903. An inspired and versatile man, Noble shifted first to selling real estate and then back to farming north of Lethbridge at Nobleford.[51] He did well, with bumper wheat yields of forty-five to fifty-four bushels per acre as well as bumper oats yields of one hundred to one hundred and thirty bushels per acre and, by 1917, was involved in bonanza farming on a 33,000-acre farm.[52] Large-scale farming operations of this kind were unusual in Alberta at this time, but Noble anticipated the big agribusinesses of the post-World War II period. He employed machinery extensively to operate his farm. Yet, by 1922 the giant farm had collapsed, destroyed by six years of severe droughts.

Noble's creditors, however, allowed him to continue farming, and by 1927 he was beginning to recover from the blow. The terrible drought and dust storms during the Great Depression of the 1930s threatened to drive Noble out of business again and gave him an incentive to turn to new technology in farming. In the mid-1930s, in his blacksmith shop at Nobleford, Noble invented a straight blade cultivator, a tractor-drawn device to create

In his blacksmith shop, Charles S. Noble developed the Noble Blade cultivator to produce stubble mulch or trash cover to prevent wind-driven soil erosion on his farm. His successful machine and system of manufacturing and marketing cultivators allowed farmers in Alberta and, later, elsewhere in the Canadian prairies, as well as in the United States to reduce greatly the risk of soil erosion and to increase their chances of growing grain profitably.

(Courtesy of Glenbow Archives, NA-4884-29).

stubble mulch or trash cover in stubble fields and thus prevent wind-driven soil erosion. Many Alberta farmers saw his cultivator in action, and their testimonials aroused great interest. Later, Noble returned to his blacksmith shop to improve his cultivator by making a v-shaped blade.[53] The machine was very effective, especially when its work was combined with strip farming.

As early as the late 1930s, Noble exhibited a knowledge of manufacturing as well as an understanding of the market for his product and began producing and marketing his Noble Blade cultivator. By 1941, he felt that he had a machine good enough to capture a fairly large share of the market. In that year, Noble built a factory at Nobleford and, in 1942, made and sold 125 cultivators. Production soared to nearly 1,000 machines just four years later.[54] Over time, Noble's successful device and his system of producing and marketing cultivators helped farmers in Alberta, the rest of the Canadian prairies, and the Great Plains of the United States improve and expand their farms. Noble's skill as both inventor and entrepreneur earned him a small fortune.

The growth of the grain trade, already well under way before the Noble

Blade cultivator was developed, created new business opportunities in Alberta. Flour millers in Edmonton, Calgary, Lethbridge, Medicine Hat, and Red Deer expanded their operations. Providing the farm economy with merchandise and credit as well as transportation and marketing services became important areas of enterprise for many Alberta businesspeople. For example, the grain elevator business became a major industry in Alberta. By the end of the 1920s, the Alberta Wheat Pool, established by the United Farmers of Alberta in 1923 and backed by the provincial government and the large chartered banks, had emerged as the biggest grain handling and marketing enterprise in the province.[55]

The provincial government played a positive role in the development of farming businesses by promoting the application of science to agriculture at small colleges. By the early 1920s, provincial agricultural colleges at Olds, Raymond, Gleichen, Vermilion, Claresholm, and Youngstown, with a total of 254 students, were securely in place.[56] As well, the provincial government had opened demonstration farms at Athabasca Landing, Stony Plain, Olds, Claresholm, Sedgewick, Vermilion, and Medicine Hat.[57] Besides providing assistance in funding these demonstration farms and colleges, the federal government had established experimental farms at Lethbridge, Lacombe, Beaverlodge, and Peace River by this time. Better-trained farmers with more capital meant a growing internal market for manufactured goods, and entrepreneurs trying to satisfy this market contributed significantly to the maturing of Alberta industry.

■

Maturing of Alberta Industry

Between 1905 and World War II, the industrial sector became an increasingly important part of the Alberta economy. Although the economy of the province remained primarily agricultural and commercial during this period, considerable capital was invested in Alberta industry. New technologies for producing goods provided important new business opportunities in these years. Opportunities to establish industrial enterprises encouraged merchants to put money into new types of factories. Most Albertans continued to earn their livelihood in small-scale farming, and entrepreneurs advanced the process of industrialization by making goods in new ways.

The process of industrialization did not await the formation of the province of Alberta in 1905 before starting to evolve. The Alberta economy began to move along the road of industrialization as early as the 1890s. That decade saw the rise of small industrial enterprises.

The availability of new means of transportation and communication in the early twentieth century, combined with the simultaneous development of new markets arising from the growth of agriculture, led to the fairly rapid adoption of mechanical means of production. But while Alberta industrialized, craft and small shop work persisted alongside the new factories.

The successful transition to industrialization has often been associated with the processing of raw materials. Among Alberta entrepreneurs who chose to organize industrial production were those involved in processing agricultural products. These products included flour and beer, but meat handled by Pat Burns probably provides the best example.

■

Pat Burns, Cattle, and Meat Packing

Burns became the first important meat packer in Alberta because he was the first to create his own integrated and province-wide organization for purchasing cattle, sheep, and hogs, slaughtering them, and then distributing the meat to consumers. He did not, however, build this enterprise overnight.

Born in Kirkfield, Ontario in 1855, Burns went to work for a lumber merchant who, unable to pay him, gave him two oxen. Burns ventured out on his own, slaughtering the oxen himself, and then peddling the cut meat from door to door in the community.[58] By the 1890s, Burns had become a prominent cattle dealer, butcher, and salesman of dressed meat in Calgary.[59] Growing sales soon required an increase in supply, so Burns also became involved in raising cattle on his ranch in Alberta to add to those he purchased for his packing plant in the city.

By the end of the first decade of the twentieth century, Burns had developed a major vertically integrated organization, with substantial departments for purchasing, processing, and marketing, and with the whole concern built around a network of branch houses controlled from the head office in Calgary.[60] The branches were located in Alberta centres such as Edmonton, Wetaskiwin, and Lethbridge and outside centres such as Vancouver, Nelson, and Victoria. Like the head office, each branch included refrigerated storage space and a sales staff to carry on wholesale and retail trade.[61]

■

John Gainer and Meat Packing

Other meat packers recognized that, in order to compete effectively with Burns in the Alberta market, they must build up similar integrated organizations. By 1912, the year the cities of Edmonton and Strathcona united to become the city of Edmonton, John Gainer of Edmonton had started on a path leading to this kind of enterprise.

Little is known of Gainer's background, apart from the fact that he was born in St. Mary's, Ontario in 1858 and that both his father and mother died when he was a child.[62] As a boy, he lived with his uncle, before leaving at the age of nine and eventually going to Emerson, Manitoba to open his own cartage and transfer business.

In 1891, already married to Amy Crawford of New Brunswick, Gainer settled with his wife and several children in Strathcona, where he started his own butchering firm, John Gainer. Its capital grew slowly from an initial $250 to between $1,000 and $2,000 by 1899.[63] The butcher shop was located at the front of the Gainers' modest home on Railway Street (later 103 Street). Gainer killed and dressed cattle, sheep, and hogs and sold the meat in his shop, and also in the community from his horse-drawn wagon, frequently trading his products for more animals. For cold storage space, he relied on an ice-cooled building in his back yard.[64] Besides assisting him in selling meat in the shop, Amy added a bakery to the family business, offering customers bread and cakes as well.[65]

Once the market for meat was assured, Gainer had to enlarge his production facilities to meet growing demand. In 1892, he built a two-storey, brick store on Whyte Avenue. In addition to the Strathcona retail store, he set up retail outlets in Edmonton and Wetaskiwin. Gainer soon supplemented the local and regional meat trade with shipments of live cattle and hogs by rail to outside centres such as Vancouver. In 1904, Gainer built a new packing plant near Mill Creek in Strathcona, and then erected corrals and purchased cattle, sheep, and hogs from farmers.[66]

Improved transportation encouraged Gainer to enter the local and regional wholesale market. In 1909, he sold his retail stores and began to concentrate on the wholesale meat trade. Two years later, in 1911, he incorporated his firm as Gainers Limited which employed thirty workers.[67] By 1915, Gainer's older sons Arthur, Clifford, and Chester had become his partners in the firm, participating in its management.[68] His two youngest sons, Herbert and Lloyd, had begun to learn the family business but were killed in action overseas during World War I.[69]

By the time John Gainer died in 1937, Gainers, still a family affair, had emerged as a major integrated meat packing firm, in which Clifford Gainer, the managing director, co-ordinated the flow of meat from the purchasing of livestock through the slaughtering process and through distribution to consumers in Alberta and beyond.[70]

In 1940, despite an impressive start in manufacturing, Alberta still lagged behind Ontario and Quebec in industrial output. Nonetheless, significant progress had been made in the manufacturing sector of Alberta's economy. By the end of the 1930s, much of Alberta's output was the product of incorporated business enterprises. Small to medium-sized, family-owned and -operated firms distinguished industry in Alberta. Edmonton and Calgary had emerged as the dominant manufacturing centres. Visible as well in Alberta were other important locations of industry, such as Lethbridge, Medicine Hat, and Red Deer.

The maturing of industry was not a threat to the social order in the province. In general, Albertans greeted the machines and factories of the age with enthusiasm. Newspaper publishers and editors incorporated technological advances into their vision of a prosperous Alberta. The reorganization of production in the workshop led to a more impersonal business environment.

Another sign of the times was the beginning of formal training for businesspeople in Alberta. In 1907, Frederick G. Garbutt, who had taught in the Shaw Business School in Toronto, established Garbutt Business College in Calgary, and by the following year student enrollment stood at 165.[71] Around the same time, Alberta Business College was opened in Edmonton. By the end of the 1920s, Garbutt Business College had set up branches in Lloydminster, Drumheller, Red Deer, and Medicine Hat. Alberta Business College and Garbutt Business College were founded against the backdrop of provincial debates about the need for business education. Most successful in imparting technical skills, these pioneers in business education offered courses for young women and men in shorthand, typewriting, bookkeeping, and penmanship.[72] This type of education and training helped graduates obtain office jobs and, in turn, aided the firms that employed them to take advantage of business opportunities.

NOTES TO CHAPTER THREE

1. *Edmonton Journal*, 17 March 1906.

2. L. G. Thomas, *The Liberal Party in Alberta: A History of Politics in the Province of Alberta, 1905-1921* (Toronto: University of Toronto Press, 1959), 21-33.

3. D. R. Babcock, *A Gentleman of Strathcona: Alexander Cameron Rutherford* (Calgary: University of Calgary Press, 1989), 1; *Edmonton Journal*, 17 March 1906.

4. Babcock, *A Gentleman of Strathcona*, 48.

5. *Edmonton Journal*, 15 March 1906.

6. Ibid., 21 March 1906.

7. *Edmonton Bulletin*, 13 March 1907.

8. Ibid., 13 February 1913.

9. Ibid., 15 March 1909.

10. T. D. Regehr, *The Canadian Northern Railway: Pioneer Road of the Northern Prairies, 1895-1918* (Toronto: MacMillan of Canada, 1976), 201-202; Thomas, *The Liberal Party in Alberta*, 62.

11. *Edmonton Bulletin*, 26 November 1908.

12. *Edmonton Journal*, 3 March 1910.

13. Ibid.

14. *Edmonton Bulletin*, 1 March 1910.

15. Ibid., 18 May 1910.

16. Ibid., 11 November 1910.

17. Ibid., 4 March 1910.

18. P. B. Waite, *The Loner: Three Sketches of the Personal Life and Ideas of R. B. Bennett, 1870-1947* (Toronto: University of Toronto Press, 1992), 3-22.

19. Ibid., 23-24.

20. James H. Gray, *R. B. Bennett: The Calgary Years* (Toronto: University of Toronto Press, 1991), 46-69.

21. Louis A. Knafla, "Richard Bonfire Bennett: The Legal Practice of a Prairie Corporate Lawyer, 1898 to 1913," in Carol Wilton, ed., *Beyond the Law: Lawyers and Business in Canada 1830 to 1930* (Toronto: The Osgoode Society, 1990), 328-329; Gray, *R.B. Bennett*, 76-77.

22. *Henderson's Calgary City Directory for 1911*, 4, 472.

23. Stanley Bruce Gordon, "R. B. Bennett, M.L.A., 1897-1905: The Years of Apprenticeship," (unpublished MA thesis, University of Calgary, 1975), 161-176.

24. *Edmonton Bulletin*, 3 March 1910.

25. Ibid.

26. Thomas, *The Liberal Party in Alberta*, 42; MacGregor, *A History of Alberta*, 193-194.

27. *Edmonton Journal*, 8 May 1906.

28. Babcock, *A Gentleman of Strathcona*, 16.

29. Census of Canada, 1941, 46.

30. James G. MacGregor, *Edmonton Trader: The Story of John A. McDougall* (Toronto: McClelland & Stewart, 1963), 158.

31. Ted Byfield, ed., *The Birth of the Province, 1900-1910: Alberta in the Twentieth Century*, Volume 2 (Edmonton: United Western Communications, 1992), 180-181.

32. Ted Byfield, ed., *The Great War and its Consequences, 1914-1920: Alberta in the Twentieth Century*, Volume 4 (Edmonton: United Western Communications, 1994), map of Alberta's railway system, circa 1920, on page opposite inside front cover.

33. Ibid.

34. Ena Schneider, *Ribbons of Steel: The Story of Northern Alberta Railways* (Calgary: Detselig Enterprises, 1989), 113-136.

35. Ibid., 145-146.

36. *Edmonton Bulletin*, 7 December 1911.

37. *Canadian Annual Review for 1917*, 803.

38. *Canadian Annual Review for 1920*, 792.

39. Ted Byfield, ed., *The Boom and the Bust, 1910-1914: Alberta in the Twentieth Century*, Volume 3 (Edmonton: United Western Communications, 1994), 48.

40. *Canadian Annual Review for 1924-25*, 435.

41. *Canadian Annual Review for 1925-26*, 501.

42. *Canadian Annual Review for 1934*, 310.

43. *Canadian Annual Review for 1935-36*, 363.

44. *Canadian Annual Review for 1937-38*, 491.

45. *Canada Year Book for 1921*, 552; *Canada Year Book for 1942*, 606.

46. *Canada Year Book for 1910*, 315.

47. *Canada Year Book for 1921*, 592; *Canada Year Book for 1942*, 662.

48. *Canada Year Book for 1912*, 341.

49. *Canada Year Book for 1921*, 589; Canada Year Book for 1942, 648.

50. *Census of Canada for 1941*, 921.

51. Palmer, Howard with Tamara Palmer, *Alberta: A New History*, Edmonton: Hurtig Publishers, 1990, 253.

52. Grant MacEwan, *Charles Noble: Guardian of the Soil* (Saskatoon: Western Producer Books, 1983), 43-90.

53. Ibid., 150-169.

54. Ibid., 170.

55. Palmer, *Alberta*, 211-212.

56. *Canadian Annual Review for 1921*, 815.

57. *Strathcona Plaindealer*, 11 May 1911.

58. Grant MacEwan, *Pat Burns: Cattle King* (Saskatoon: Western Producer Prairie Books, 1979), 19.

59. *Calgary Herald*, 22 November 1899.

60. Alberta Corporate Registry, Edmonton, P. Burns & Company Ltd. file.

61. *Calgary Herald*, 10 May 1928.

62. City of Edmonton Archives, Gainers clipping file, A. M. Macdonald, "An All-Alberta Company, 1891-1961," in pamphlet, 10.

63. MacDonald, "An All-Alberta Company," 10; University of Calgary Library, *Dun & Bradstreet Reference Book*, March 1899, 375.

64. Gainers clipping file, Tony Cashman, "Edmonton Story: That Local Flavor," *The Edmontonian*, July 1964, 33.

65. MacDonald, "An All-Alberta Company," 10.

66. Cashman, "Edmonton Story," 33.

67. *Strathcona Plaindealer*, 13 October 1911.

68. Alberta Corporate Registry, Gainers Ltd. file.

69. MacDonald, "An All-Alberta Company," 11.

70. Alberta Corporate Registry, Gainers Ltd. file.

71. *Albertan*, 1 March 1909.

72. *Edmonton Bulletin*, 30 June 1910.

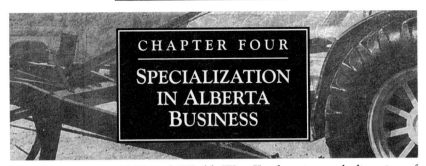

CHAPTER FOUR

SPECIALIZATION IN ALBERTA BUSINESS

Between 1905 and World War II, the size and diversity of Alberta's resources, combined with the growing population and the expanding internal market and transportation system, opened up extensive opportunities for specialization in business. Pouring into the province, thronging onto trains, and often beating their way over Native Canadian trails and rough roads, Albertans continued a process of settlement which drove the frontier northward. It is difficult to exaggerate the importance of the northward movement and of the great stretches of accessible, rich land that sustained it. Settlements spread north from the southern boundary of Alberta until they covered most of the southern, central, and north-central portions as well as much of the Peace River country. Entrepreneurs invested heavily in specialized opportunities and contributed to the creation of a new Alberta business system. During this period, there was tremendous growth in the number of specialized business firms.

Before 1905, specialization was already starting to appear in the distribution of goods in Edmonton and Calgary, as well as in many towns and villages. Distinctions between general merchants and specialized businesspeople were becoming clear. Some merchants were beginning to specialize in particular lines of trade such as drugs, jewellery, and boots and shoes. Well before 1905, specialization was also coming in manufacturing — for example, in harness, tin, and clothing. The growth of specialization in business was much swifter after 1905 than in territorial times. After 1905, hundreds of specialized business firms made their appearance in Alberta, as Alberta and Canadian economies became more integrated as a result of the establishment of improved systems of transportation, distribution, and banking.

■

Urban Growth and Specialization in Business

The rapid development of specialized business firms after 1905 began in the cities and then spread to other areas of Alberta where urbanization was becoming a marked trend. A growing urban centre was a major advantage for a specialized firm, providing a large enough market to justify the firm's existence. The amount of city growth was impressive. From a small city of 11,000 residents in 1906, Edmonton became a large centre of 94,000 in 1941. In the same period, Calgary went from 12,000 to 89,000.[1] It was in these two cities that specialization in business started and advanced most rapidly. By 1941, the population of Lethbridge had reached 15,000; Medicine Hat 11,000; Red Deer 3,000; Drumheller 3,000; and Wetaskiwin 2,000.[2] Specialization in business occurred in the smaller cities as well, proceeding at a slower pace than in Calgary and Edmonton, but the progress was still significant.

The specialized business firm was also a common theme in the development of Alberta's towns. By 1941, the population of Camrose had risen to 2,600; Pincher Creek to 2,000; Raymond to 2,000; Fort Macleod to 1,900; Coleman to 1,900; Cardston to 1,900; Grande Prairie to 1,700; and Vegreville to 1,700.[3] By the same year, the urban component of Alberta's population had expanded to forty-five percent.[4] Urban growth and increasing specialization in business went hand in hand.

The development of cities and towns and the growth of specialization combined with increased agricultural and industrial production to create more individual wealth. In the process, individual wealth flowed to many Albertans, mostly to men but only a few women, who found themselves unable to participate fully in Alberta's business opportunities. Social customs kept all but a small number of women from advancing to management positions. Only occasionally did women emerge as business entrepreneurs in their own right, running grocery stores, millinery shops, and hotels, for instance. In Medicine Hat, Mrs. I. Brougham owned a grocery store in 1906. By 1921, A. E. Mollison was running a hotel in Calgary. At the same time, many Alberta women became vital participants in family businesses.

■

Specialization in Commerce

In commerce from 1905 onward, special kinds of business became increasingly separated from the broad functions of earlier general merchants. Because these activities had been aspects of the merchant role, the new businesses were often developed by individuals from the mercantile ranks. The rapidly mounting volume of agricultural trade helped make Edmonton and Calgary the leading cities in the province and sparked the decline of the general merchant. Within the growing complexity of these city economies, there developed a need for specialized business firms. Essentially Calgary and Edmonton became a series of markets, providing ever greater opportunities to specialize. Businesspeople set up retail outlets for groceries, hardware, dry goods, clothing, boots and shoes, drugs, books, and jewellery, among other things. With the appearance of these special types of enterprise, general merchants became but one part of a diversified commercial community. Although general merchants did not disappear, they were often replaced by specialized firms serving the local and regional economies.

Edmonton and Calgary grew from trade with their hinterlands, and as backcountry populations expanded and transportation improved, intra-regional commerce became increasingly significant. Business is an interconnected network, and wholesalers in Calgary and Edmonton quickly developed ties with small city and small town merchants in their surrounding regions. Wholesalers handled the flow of manufactured goods out of central Canada to Edmonton and Calgary and their trading areas. The importance of Edmonton and Calgary as transshipping centres grew in the process. In small cities, towns and villages, specialized firms in items such as clothing, hardware, jewellery, and drugs often appeared alongside the general merchants, all of whom had links to Calgary and Edmonton wholesalers. The role of the general merchant remained more important in small towns than in cities, but even small towns to some extent became devoted to, and reliant upon, specialized businesses.

■

Hardware Businesses

By 1939, hardware stores had appeared in significant numbers in Alberta. In Edmonton, there were twenty retail and seven wholesale hardware stores. In Calgary, there were twenty retail and six wholesale hardware outlets.[5] Three or four retail hardware stores could be found in smaller cities such as Lethbridge and Medicine Hat. Drumheller had only one retail hardware outlet.[6] The wholesale hardware enterprises provided a great deal of credit so essential in the financing of the retail hardware trade.

Many small towns and villages with one retail hardware store dotted the Alberta landscape, including the villages of Westlock, Sexsmith, Provost, Bruce, Rocky Mountain House, Champion, Acme, Cadogan, Mundare, Cochrane, Turner Valley, and Cayley and the towns of Leduc, Castor, Edson, Okotoks, Three Hills, Olds, Wainwright, Ponoka, and Bow Island. By contrast, the town of Grande Prairie possessed three retail hardware outlets.[7]

Entrepreneurs seeking to satisfy city, town, and village markets as well as those of the surrounding areas initiated the rise of these hardware stores, both retail and wholesale. A good example is Ross Bros. of Edmonton.

■

Ross Bros. Hardware

In 1883, two Toronto-born brothers, James and Frederick Ross, arrived in Edmonton, eager to enter the retail hardware business. The Ross brothers were harbingers of the coming of specialization in business to Alberta. Their arrival in Edmonton was a significant event in Alberta business history because they were knowledgeable in the techniques of tinsmithing and hardware distribution that Toronto entrepreneurs had developed in the second half of the nineteenth century.

Beginning as apprentices in Toronto tinsmithing establishments, James and Frederick Ross struck out on their own in Edmonton in 1883.[8] Their partnership, known as Ross Bros., was the first hardware firm in Alberta. One of their suppliers was the J. H. Ashdown Hardware Company of Winnipeg, a company that had employed James for several years before he came to Edmonton.

An unincorporated partnership, Ross Bros. retailed hardware as well as goods they made from sheet metal. In 1902, the brothers incorporated their business with authorized capital of $250,000.[9] With Frederick Ross serving as president and general manager and his brother James as vice-president, the firm brought two new relatively small investors into the picture: John C. Dowsett, as its secretary-treasurer and accountant, and James R. Harper, as one of its clerks. The firm, however, remained a family enterprise.

Emboldened by their success, the Ross brothers decided to diversify into wholesaling hardware around 1906.[10] Between 1907 and 1908, the firm's paid-in capital increased from $216,500 to $238,000. Its stockholders boosted its authorized capitalization to $750,000 in 1910. By 1912, Ross Bros. owned a large business block in Edmonton, with both retail and wholesale departments.[11]

In that year Ross Bros. found it increasingly difficult to meet the challenge of competition and sold out to the Marshall-Wells Company, an American hardware wholesaler with headquarters in Duluth, Minnesota and one of Ross Bros.' major suppliers and creditors.[12] The Marshall-Wells firm in Edmonton eventually phased out the retail side of the business and concentrated on wholesaling. All this bred caution instead of boldness among potential hardware merchants.

■

George L. Chesney Hardware

As in Edmonton, the wholesale hardware business in Calgary fell increasingly into the hands of large wholesalers such as J. H. Ashdown Hardware Company. Like its counterpart in Edmonton, the retail hardware field in Calgary was left largely to small firms such as George L. Chesney.

Born in York, England in 1887, Chesney began his career as an apprentice in a hardware store in Seaforth, Ontario after graduating from Seaforth high school. Following a four-year apprenticeship, he became a partner in this store before moving to Calgary in 1912.[13]

Chesney started in a small way in Calgary and survived as an enduring and important presence. Making the personal contacts necessary for

George L. Chesney, the chief personality at his hardware store in Calgary from 1912 almost until his death in 1957. Chesney's strategy was founded upon his belief in high-quality products and excellent service.

(Courtesy of Olga Chesney).

business success, he relied on family and friends in his hardware venture. He married Edna Pickard, the daughter of a prominent men's ready-to-wear merchant, solidifying his economic position in Calgary. In 1912, Chesney borrowed money from his father-in-law to launch his family hardware and tin shop on Sixteenth Avenue on the North Hill.[14]

Chesney's initial offerings were the two carloads of goods he had brought with him by rail from Seaforth.[15] These goods included paints, screen doors, stoves, stove pipes, saws, hammers, screws, nails, bicycles, buggy accessories, and sleigh bells. Chesney sold almost every product that was being retailed by hardware merchants at this time and maintained an ample supply of merchandise by purchasing new goods from local wholesalers such as Ashdown's.

From the beginning, Chesney exploited the demand for hardware in Calgary. His firm found a niche for hardware products in the city market and grew modestly. But during the depression of 1913 and its aftermath, Chesney found the going tough. To stay afloat, he borrowed money from the Standard Bank to buy an old Model T Ford truck to carry his hardware trade into the surrounding countryside.[16] Applying for the bank loan, Chesney took the approach that farmers in the process of building a house or barn would buy his high-quality and reasonably priced products. At the core of his argument was the thesis that the economies of Calgary and its region were intertwined. It was a golden opportunity, and Chesney had the enterprise to translate his faith in hardware products into practical results.

Farmers did, indeed, purchase his goods, which helped his hardware business get through the depression of 1913 and the World War I years.[17]

In the 1920s and 1930s, Chesney continued to show an acute understanding of where his hardware store's fundamental long-term interests lay — excellent service to his city and rural customers in terms of offering top-quality goods at reasonable prices. To help him provide such service, he hired competent and knowledgeable people, a store manager, a bookkeeper, and several clerks. This left Chesney free to oversee the business as a whole, make business calls, interview travelling salesmen, and prepare advertisements that appeared every Friday in the *Calgary Herald*.[18] He advertised galvanized pails, door locks, thermos bottles, gas ranges and heaters, Norton door closers, window glass, wheelbarrows, lawn fence and gates, garden tools, Brockville lawn mowers, garden seeds, bicycles, screen doors, Bapco paints, Sunoco auto oil, C.C.M. skates, hockey sticks, children's sleighs, and alarm clocks, among other things.[19]

Chesney worked diligently, against the backdrop of the Great Depression in the 1930s, to dodge pitfalls and keep his hardware business alive. He continued to be sensitive to his customers' needs. His financial planning included a successful attempt to maintain his high credit rating at the bank of Nova Scotia, where he obtained funds essential to his operation.[20] While Chesney's retail trade remained crucial, he diversified by moving into wholesaling in the 1930s, supplying major house builders in Calgary with hardware goods.[21]

Chesney shaped important policies in his roles as overseer and planner, such as making provision for family continuity in his hardware store by bringing his oldest son Art into the business.[22] After graduating from Crescent Heights High School as well as from Garbutt Business College, where he learned to read financial statements, file documents, and type at a speed of sixty words per minute, Art became an employee in his father's hardware store in 1932. As a high school student in the late 1920s, Art had already worked in the store after school and on Saturdays, cleaning front windows, helping in the tin shop, serving customers, and sweeping floors after closing. At that time and into the 1930s, Art's thoughtful attention readily commanded his father's respect. Following service with the Canadian Army overseas during World War II, Art became the store manager and, in 1957, at the time of his father's death, took over the family hardware business on the North Hill with his brother Doug.[23]

■

High River Hardware Company

Although the hardware trade was especially concentrated in Alberta's larger cities in the early twentieth century, hardware businesses also emerged elsewhere. Small town merchants were able to organize hardware firms because they could profitably supply hardware goods. The great emphasis on settlement and the development of farming in Alberta after 1905 led small-town merchants to become more specialized than those of territorial days. In a sense, the High River Hardware Company, another family enterprise, did for the town of High River and its surrounding area what George Chesney did for Calgary and its region.

The High River Hardware Company was the brainchild of Charles A. Farquharson. Born in Charlottetown, Prince Edward Island in 1880, Farquharson was the son of former Prince Edward Island premier Donald Farquharson.[24] A well-known engineer, Charles was active as a bridge builder in Charlottetown before he came to High River in 1908.[25] In the autumn of that year, he began organizing the High River Hardware Company by purchasing the hardware component of the High River Trading Company, a grocery, hardware, and clothing concern.[26]

The purchase of this hardware business proved to be a good bargain for Charles Farquharson. To satisfy his need for more capital, he brought in his brother-in-law, Frederick D. Blake, as a partner in 1910, heightening the firm's family character.[27] Blake was married to Charles's sister Loretta Farquharson. Earlier, Blake had worked in his parents' meat-processing business in Charlottetown. In 1911, the partners expanded their hardware business by opening a branch store in Blackie with Blake in charge, but Blake's illness made this branch a short-lived venture.[28] The partners closed the Blackie branch in 1912 before Blake returned to High River to help Charles Farquharson build up their hardware trade in that town and its region. By the end of that year, their High River hardware business was flourishing.[29]

By 1921, their small firm, the High River Hardware Company, was worth $20,000 to $35,000, according to the R. G. Dun & Co. credit reporter.[30] The company cultivated the High River and rural markets with considerable success. By the end of that decade, annual sales had risen to $20,000.[31] Throughout the 1920s and 1930s, the High River Hardware Company steadily exploited the potential of its wide line of products, such as saws, nails, axes, hammers, pliers, Stephens paints, toys and games, Edison light bulbs, General Electric washing machines and radios, Hoover vacuum cleaners, Johnson's wax, Simmons beds and couches, lawn mowers, grass catchers, edgers, coal, Plymouth binder twine, and gopher poison.[32]

Family continuity in the High River Hardware Company was important to Charles Farquharson and Frederick Blake. They persuaded Blake's son Donald, who had shown early interest and promise in their hardware business, to work in the store after school and on Saturdays during his high school years in High River. In 1942, during World War II, after Donald had served with the Canadian Army for several years, the partners chose him to learn the hardware trade in the store, with the idea that he would eventually inherit it. After working as a clerk for six years, Donald became manager of the High River Hardware Company in 1948 and its owner fifteen years later, following the death of his father and his uncle Charles.[33]

Until around World War II, the hardware trade in Alberta was still a very personal world full of relatively small family-owned and -managed businesses. Family connections and personal ties remained paramount in these specialized concerns. The founders of family enterprises still trained their heirs in their own firms, passing their business skills and tradition from one generation to the next.

■

Drugstores

Specialization also occurred in the selling of prescription drugs, packaged pills, and other goods distributed by drugstores between 1905 and World War II. Druggists in Alberta's cities and towns were involved in retailing, and they served as crucial links joining the sources of their goods and consumers. The main sources of goods were wholesalers such as the Alberta National Drug Company, the Stevens Alberta Company, and Parke, Davis & Company, a large American pharmaceutical firm. The wholesalers' business became increasingly that of granting credit to retail druggists.

A check of the Edmonton and Calgary city directories emphasizes how important specialized retail druggists had become by the 1930s. *Henderson's Edmonton Directory for 1939* shows that Edmonton had forty-eight retail druggists, while *Henderson's Calgary Directory for 1939* reveals that Calgary had thirty-six retail druggists.[34] Taken together, the smaller cities and the small towns also had many merchants in the retail drugstore field. William Dunlap of Stettler was among those in small-town Alberta who turned to the retail side of the drugstore business.

■

Dunlap Drug Company

Born on a farm near Truro, Nova Scotia in 1880, William Dunlap opened a drugstore in Stettler in 1904.[35] He was not a pharmacist, but he went into partnership with Walter Hart, a pharmacist who also came from Nova Scotia. In 1906, however, the partnership was dissolved as Hart left the firm to start his own drugstore business in Stettler.[36] Consequently, Dunlap hired another pharmacist.[37] Over the next two years the drugstore gradually prospered, and in 1908, Dunlap incorporated the business as the Dunlap Drug Company. In the same year, he married Blanche Hunt of Blackfalds, who became actively involved as the company's secretary in developing the business.[38]

Capitalized at $10,000, the Dunlap Drug Company was financed largely by ploughing profits back into the business. As was true of many drugstore owners in Alberta in these years, Dunlap had close personal and business ties with the Stettler business community. He became a charter member of the Stettler Board of Trade in 1905 and later joined the local Rotary Club.[39] A founder of the town of Stettler in 1906, Dunlap became a member of the first town council and served as its mayor for a short time in its early years.[40] Through his active support of W. F. Puffer, a Liberal and the local representative in the legislative assembly, he showed an interest in working with Rutherford's government to create opportunities for business.[41]

As a drugstore owner, Dunlap attracted many customers from the town and the surrounding region. The sale of prescription drugs and packaged pills was important for the development of his business, but he relied especially on the sale of items at the front end of the store, including stationery, perfumes, battery-operated radios, and guns.[42] In 1916, Dunlap diversified into the gopher poison business by manufacturing gopher poison and selling it mostly to rural municipalities for distribution to farmers.[43] This was a very popular product, particularly during the depression of the early 1920s and the Great Depression of the 1930s, when hordes of gophers combined with droughts to make life extremely difficult for farmers trying to save their precious grain crops. Also, it was comforting to Dunlap to know that most farmers who received credit from him to purchase other goods from his store would eventually pay their bills, if not in cash then in farm products such as chickens and butter.[44]

Dunlap was concerned enough about family continuity in his drugstore to bring first his son Jack, a pharmacy graduate from the University of Alberta, into the business as a salaried clerk in the late 1930s before he went overseas with the Canadian Army during World War II, and then his son Stuart, also a University of Alberta pharmacy graduate, as a salaried clerk in 1941. Later, in 1953, when William Dunlap died, Stuart took over the family drugstore in Stettler, thus allowing the small enterprise to continue to participate in the community's business opportunities.[45]

■

Stokes Drug Company

Another noteworthy example of the drugstore business in Alberta was the Stokes Drug Company. Founded in Lethbridge in 1918 by Ernest B. Stokes, the Stokes Drug Company was a small family-owned and -run business. Born in Windsor, Ontario in 1881, Stokes graduated from the Ontario College of Pharmacy in 1903 and moved to Calgary three years later, where he soon became a clerk in Wendell McLean's drugstore.[46] For several years between 1910 and 1917, Stokes served as manager of the Empire Hotel

The Stokes Drug Company provided a wide variety of goods to its customers.
In the drugstore in Lethbridge around 1921 are company staff Martha
McDonald and Agnes Stafford on the left and majority owner Ernest B. Stokes
on the extreme right. (Courtesy of Jack E. Stokes).

owned by his brother, W. J. Stokes.[47] In 1909, Ernest Stokes married Emma
O. Radke, and in 1918, he moved with his wife and infant son Jack to
Lethbridge, where he purchased the Kenny & Allin Company drugstore at
314 Fifth Street South.[48]

The store's operations were generally satisfactory and in 1920, Stokes
incorporated it as the Stokes Drug Company.[49] Stokes owned most of the
company stock. William Oliver, the owner of the drugstore building, was a
relatively small stockholder for about a decade, during which time he was
associated with the company as a director.[50] In 1921, the R. G. Dun correspondent reported that the company was worth from $10,000 to $20,000
and that it enjoyed a high credit rating.[51] Stokes was a remarkably good
credit risk. He understood the needs of his customers in Lethbridge and its
region very well. In the 1920s and 1930s, he successfully sold prescription
drugs, packaged pills, and other goods such as cards, straw hats, chocolates,
shampoo, toothpaste, and Kodak cameras, among other items.[52] All the
goods in the showcases and on the shelves, as a photograph of the store's
interior reveals, were carefully and attractively arranged.[53]

In a business faced by great danger during the depression of the early
1920s and the Great Depression in the next decade, Stokes strove constantly to maintain a sense of order in his drugstore. He had to be extremely

cautious in its finances. His good understanding of accounting and his great human relations skills contributed significantly to the drugstore's success. Stokes knew how to operate within the context of his financial resources. He always looked forward, using mostly retained earnings but also a small line of bank credit and credit from his suppliers, such as the Alberta National Drug Company and the L. E. Waterman Company to expand his business. By 1944, when he had a heart attack, sales had reached $30,000.[54]

At this point, Stokes stepped away from major responsibilities in his drugstore and asked his only son Jack, who was serving Canada with the Royal Canadian Air Force, to come home and take over the management of the business.[55] A 1939 pharmacy graduate of the University of Alberta with three years of experience as a clerk in the family drugstore, Jack managed it until his father's death in 1947 and, with his mother, inherited it under his father's will.[56] Always a good planner, Ernest thus saw to it that his son had the opportunity to provide leadership in the business for many more years.

■

Jewellery Stores

The rise of specialized business firms in Alberta after 1905 to handle prescription drugs, packaged pills, and other drugstore goods was parallelled by the emergence of comparable specialization in the jewellery field. Alberta's expanding economy increased the demand for jewellery that was often produced in central Canada, the United States, and Great Britain. General merchants increasingly gave way to specialized enterprises, including Edmonton and Calgary wholesale jewellery firms, which brought jewellery into these cities and thence to Alberta's smaller cities and small towns.

By 1939, two wholesale jewellery firms — McGeachie & Holdsworth and Peoples Credit Jewelers — had appeared in Calgary, and one — the Dominion Laurier Company — in Edmonton. By this time, there were thirty-six retail jewellery stores in Edmonton and twenty-six in Calgary.[57] Collectively, Alberta's smaller cities and small towns also had many retail jewellery stores.

■

Alexander B. Mitchell: Jeweller

The experience of Alexander B. Mitchell of Red Deer illustrates the operations of the small city retail jeweller in Alberta. Born and reared in Auchinblae, Scotland, where he also served a seven-year apprenticeship in business as a jeweller and watchmaker in a jewellery store, Mitchell came to Red Deer in 1908.[58] He began there as a salaried watchmaker in Harold

J. Snell's Jewellery Store. Snell was not only a jeweller but also an optometrist. Mitchell ran the store in World War I between 1914 and 1918 during Snell's service overseas with the Canadian Army.

In 1919, after Snell's release from the Army, Mitchell purchased the jewellery part of the store from Snell, who continued his optometry business by himself.[59] Thus, the firm of A. B. Mitchell came into being.

With resolute single-mindedness, Mitchell maintained a sharp focus in his jewellery and watchmaking business from the beginning. He devoted a considerable portion of his energies to other time-consuming tasks in Red Deer, including town council activities and family life with his wife Alma.[60] Alexander Mitchell's marriage earlier to Canadian-born Alma Hewson made it possible for him to develop a jewellery business that attracted many customers from Red Deer and its region during the 1920s and 1930s and beyond. Alma was an outgoing women, extremely popular with a wide variety of customers. While Alexander immersed himself in the details of watch and jewellery repairs at the back of their small family store, Alma concentrated on the front end, selling their goods and helping their business take off.[61]

Sales did not skyrocket, but grew gradually. Mitchell's advertisements in the *Red Deer Advocate* stressed that in his offerings — Gruen watches, cut glass, silverware, rings, pearls, belt buckles, pins, brooches, cuff links, china, and Columbia records — customers would "find a price for every purse, and an item for every eye." [62] To stave off serious trouble in November 1932, in the depths of the Great Depression, Mitchell held a Dollar Day sale designed to lead to greater sales of dollar items such as salad servers, tea spoons, and china dishes, as well as the sale of watches at half price.[63]

Despite the trying times, Alexander and Alma turned their jewellery store into a force to be reckoned with and, in 1938, moved the family business into their new building.[64] The new structure, along with the substantial mahogany showcases they acquired at this time, reflected their commitment to the jewellery business. Eleven years later, in 1949, they brought in Robert M. Jewell as a partner.[65] As the years passed, Mitchell & Jewell became a flourishing enterprise.

■

Godley's Jewellery

Like Alberta's cities, its small towns also attracted important jewellers, as the example of George M. Godley of Claresholm shows. Born in Sarnia, Ontario around 1884, Godley served an apprenticeship as a jeweller there and then learned watchmaking and engraving in Woodstock before coming to Claresholm in 1912.[66] He immediately purchased the jewellery store of George Farrer, who had been in business in Claresholm for six years.[67]

Godley's jewellery store grew slowly, and in April 1914, in the first issue of the *Claresholm Advertiser*, he described it as "the shop where you can buy the best goods at fair prices."[68] The most popular offerings included Regina, Hamilton, and Illinois watches, Waterbury clocks, Standard Silver Company's holloware, diamond rings, gold and pearl goods, lockets, bracelets, and tie clips. Godley followed the policy of accurate descriptions of items advertised with money-back guarantees if the customers were not satisfied.[69]

Godley had many charge accounts, giving credit to about fifty percent of his customers.[70] He usually sold goods to his other customers on a cash basis. With relatively small and irregular incoming cash flows, Godley bought from wholesalers on credit. The wholesalers who provided Godley with goods included McGeachie & Holdsworth of Calgary, A. Fremes (rings) of Toronto, Western Wholesale Jewellers of Vancouver, Rolex Watch Company of Toronto, G. R. L'Esperance of Montreal, Eversharp International of Toronto, Mitchell Distributing Company of Montreal, and General Western Supply of Winnipeg.[71]

One of the greatest challenges for Godley was to create a purchasing system. His objective was to ensure profits by buying goods that had the best chance of selling from commercial travellers representing wholesalers. Godley's venture in Claresholm succeeded between 1912 and World War II. While watch and jewellery repairs were significant in the development of his store, selling his goods to townspeople and especially to ranchers and farmers in the surrounding region became increasingly important to Godley's prosperity and profits.[72]

Until his death in 1946, George Godley was the sole owner of his jewellery store. He had planned for succession, and by his will his second wife Lily (his first wife Maude had died in 1930) inherited the family store.[73] Maude and Lily in turn had assisted George in developing the business by selling goods. After George's death, Geoffrey Godley, George's son by his first wife, and Lily ran the business for many years, in accordance with George's plans. With his father's encouragement, Geoffrey had started to work in the store in 1936.[74] By the time of his father's death, he had completed his apprenticeship as a jeweller and watchmaker in the store and was well prepared to join Lily in managing it.

Because Lily recognized Geoffrey's value to the business, she included him in her succession plans, and when she died in 1977, he took over the family jewellery store.[75] Thus, the role of family relationships in this small business was significant at all stages in its development.

Specialization in Manufacturing

As in commerce, specialization had considerable impact on manufacturing in Alberta between 1905 and World War II. Many small, specialized business firms arose in Edmonton and Calgary and in smaller cities, as well as in small towns, to produce particular goods. A remarkable array of products poured from the workshops and factories of the urban centres, including harnesses, saddles, tools, machines, bricks and tiles, lumber, furniture, tailored wear, plain garments, hats, and dresses.

The advantage of specialized production lay in Alberta manufacturers' ability to compete with large manufacturers in central Canada and elsewhere. Instead of producing standardized goods, many manufacturers in Alberta profited by turning to specialized or local markets. The small scale of their operations provided a flexibility that permitted them to move into fresh product lines with market alterations.

Specialization not only in products but also in operations was an important feature of Alberta's urban manufacturing system. Separate firms for specific products emerged as the pattern in production. In clothing, for instance, independent manufacturers engaged in making women's wear or men's wear. Often urban firms flourished by manufacturing small-batch custom goods to the specifications of their customers.

Another significant feature of urban industrialization was the small family-owned and -managed business. The average worker laboured in a production unit of less than thirty employees. While a number of firms adopted the corporate form of ownership, manufacturers in Alberta frequently organized as unincorporated single-owner proprietorships or partnerships.

■

Thomas Hutchinson: Harness and Saddle Manufacturer

Among Alberta manufacturers who started as single-owner proprietors was Thomas Hutchinson of Medicine Hat. Born in Ontario, where he apprenticed as a harness and saddle maker, Hutchinson came to Medicine Hat in 1893 to open a harness and saddlery shop.[76] He was a highly skilled craftsman. With the settlement of ranchers and farmers in the Medicine Hat area, the time was ripe for the production of saddles and harnesses. Hutchinson received important orders from farmers and ranchers, and before long his harnesses and saddles became well known in the community.

In 1911, Hutchinson built a substantial business block — the Hutchinson Block which contained a workshop — in Medicine Hat to increase his output of harnesses and saddles.[77] Growing demand, especially for harnesses, from farmers served as the impetus for this move to invest more capital in manufacturing. Hutchinson installed machines to manufacture harnesses and saddles in his shop but did not replace his apprentices with unskilled machine tenders. Machines did not preclude manufacture by hand. Hand-crafted products, along with machine produced goods, continued to flow out of Hutchinson's shop to the market.[78]

By 1913, Hutchinson was specializing in the production of harnesses for strong working horses.[79] In addition, he purchased and sold blankets, robes, whips, and other stable and horse equipment, as well as trunks and handbags required by travellers. He had expanded further by selling his goods not only at retail but also at wholesale.

To finance all this expansion, Hutchinson was soon borrowing large sums from one of his major suppliers, the Winnipeg-based Great West Saddlery Company with branches in Calgary and Edmonton. These loans proved to be a heavy burden. By 1913, Great West Saddlery had gained control of Hutchinson's harness and saddle business in Medicine Hat.[80] Great West Saddlery incorporated the Hutchinson firm as the T. Hutchinson Company Ltd.[81] Thomas Hutchinson became a director of the company, for it could ill afford to lose his unquestioned expertise. He brought to his position, which he continued to hold through the World War I years and the 1920s and 1930s, an extraordinarily good understanding of the manufacture of harnesses and other leather goods.[82] During the war, as his established market in the Medicine Hat area developed further, he also sold his harnesses to the Russian government.[83] Despite his financial troubles, Thomas Hutchinson played a significant role in the coming of specialization to manufacturing in Alberta.

■

Robert J. Welsh: Harness Manufacturer

The early twentieth century also witnessed growth in specialized manufacturing in north central Alberta. A number of individuals, such as Robert J. Welsh of Edmonton, created specialized firms devoted to the production of harnesses.

In 1907, Welsh left Owen Sound, Ontario for Edmonton on a harvest excursion. After working for a farmer and then for a carpenter, in 1908 Welsh used his savings to purchase a harness shop in Edmonton with a partner. A year later, he bought out his partner and began to operate as a single proprietor.[84]

Welsh opened a small New and Second Hand Store, which contained a harness manufacturing shop. It was an important leap into the future in terms of the production of harnesses for homesteaders bound for the area north of Edmonton and especially the Peace River country, to whom Welsh sold harnesses and new and used settlers' goods, including tents, wood stoves, axes, and saws in the period from 1909 to the 1930s.[85]

Welsh's Saddlery in Edmonton in 1969. Robert J. Welsh was among the pioneers of Alberta economic development. (Courtesy of City of Edmonton Archives and Edmonton Journal).

Welsh was constantly on the lookout for new opportunities. During these years, he opened a new market for harnesses for powerful working horses in the northern Alberta logging camps.[86] He also began tapping the market for harnesses at retailers such as the T. Eaton Company.[87] At the same time, Welsh continued to supply farmers in north central Alberta and the Peace River region with harnesses for heavy working horses. All this helped his harness manufacturing business grow modestly.

Robert Welsh's sons also aided him in developing his harness manufacturing business. In 1908, he married Lena Bergey, the daughter of a Mannville area homesteader.[88] Robert and Lena's oldest son Lloyd became an employee in the family business in the late 1930s, and their second son James began working there in the early 1940s.[89] In 1957, Robert incorporated the firm as R. J. Welsh Ltd., and a year later, at the time of his death, Lloyd and James took over the business.[90]

The family firm benefited from James and Lloyd's participation in its management. Like their father, they were always on the lookout for fresh opportunities and, in the early 1960s, began producing dog-team harnesses for the northern dog teams of the Royal Canadian Mounted Police. In the year 1962 alone, Lloyd and James manufactured 100 sets of these harnesses.[91] In that same year they produced about 375 saddles for Albertans devoted to riding in their leisure time.[92] Thus, they successfully followed the family tradition of specialization in manufacturing.

Herbert J. Sissons: Brick Manufacturer

Specialization also appeared in Alberta in the production of building materials. The Redcliff Pressed Brick plant at Redcliff, founded by Herbert J. Sissons and his associates James Hargrave, James Mitchell and A. W. Woodcock in 1912, provides a good illustration. Creating the management structure for the new brick works, Sissons drew from hardware and stove manufacturers. Sissons himself was an experienced hardware and stove salesman before he entered brick making. Born in Montreal in 1881, Sissons became a commercial traveller for the Currie Company of Montreal after completing his education in a high school and a trade school there.[93] In Alberta and elsewhere in Canada, he quickly proved himself an effective salesman for this well-managed company.

In helping to organize the Redcliff Pressed Brick Company, Sissons was involved in developing an administration similar to the one he had worked in at the Currie Company. While James Hargrave, a rancher and a former Hudson's Bay Company factor, became president of the Redcliff Pressed Brick Company and A. W. Woodcock, an experienced brick maker, served as its plant superintendent, Sissons stepped in as general manager and secretary-treasurer to oversee the day-to-day work of the brick-making plant.[94] Management was informal, and Sissons had little difficulty keeping in close contact with Hargrave and Woodcock and the employees. A systematic organizational structure was not needed. In 1916, Sissons married Lisa R. Hargrave, the daughter of James Hargrave, enhancing his social and economic position in Redcliff.

Incorporated for $55,000 in 1912, the Redcliff Pressed Brick Company grew gradually by putting the profits back into the business and using bank credit.[95] By 1939, the company was worth between $50,000 and $75,000 and boasted a high credit rating.[96] Having observed that there was a market for pressed clay brick, Sissons and his associates opened for business in 1913. Over the next three decades the company turned out a variety of brick products, using local clay mined at the gas-fired steam plant. Redcliff Pressed Brick's business was a success from the beginning. The company was able to sell bricks to numerous local customers, such as the St. Theresa Academy in Medicine Hat.[97] Within a few years, many customers across southeastern Alberta had purchased the company's bricks.

Around 1920, the Redcliff Pressed Brick Company adopted the trademark I-XL, a name suggested by Sissons.[98] The trademark came from the words "I excel." Labelled the I-XL brand, the company's bricks became well known for their high quality. The latest brick-making technology was used at the company's plant.

Redcliff Pressed Brick's owners were pleased with their company's performance. In 1929, the company expanded by purchasing the Medicine

Hat Brick and Tile Company, while simultaneously consolidating the administration of both plants at the Medicine Hat plant site.[99] Despite the serious financial problems it faced during the Great Depression, the Redcliff Pressed Brick Company was strong enough to survive those troubles and, in 1944, continued to expand by purchasing the Redcliff Premier Brick Company plant.[100]

In 1949, when Herbert Sissons died, his oldest son Gordon, a University of Alberta trained mining engineer who had served as secretary-treasurer of the Redcliff Pressed Brick Company since 1944, accepted the challenge of becoming general manager of the family firm.[101] Under Gordon's leadership, the company continued to produce high-quality bricks for many years. Redcliff Pressed Brick remained committed to the best possible use of the most advanced technology in the production of bricks.

■

Specialization in Service Businesses

Specialization in service businesses naturally accompanied specialization in commercial and manufacturing activities. Between 1905 and World War II, business enterprises increasingly specialized in banking, insurance, and credit rating services for Alberta's growing economy.

The central Canadian-based chartered banks, besides financing inter-regional and international movements of trade, served local needs in Alberta through their branch systems. Ever since the 1880s these banks, chartered and regulated by the federal government, had operated in Alberta, but they greatly expanded their role in the province after 1905. The chartered banks became increasingly important as sources of short-term commercial and industrial loans. The Bank of Montreal, Imperial Bank of Canada, Molson's Bank, Union Bank of Canada, Canadian Bank of Commerce, Merchants Bank of Canada, Royal Bank of Canada, and Bank of Nova Scotia were among the banks that helped finance many commercial and manufacturing firms across Alberta through branch offices.[102]

The Canadian Bank of Commerce is an especially vivid illustration of this particular type of specialization. Opening its first Alberta branch in Medicine Hat in 1902, this bank grew rapidly and, by the end of 1911, had forty-one branches in the province, including those in Calgary, Edmonton, Innisfail, Ponoka, Red Deer, Nanton, Claresholm, Fort Macleod, Pincher Creek, Lethbridge, Wetaskiwin, Stony Plain, Olds, and Milk River.[103] In this way, the Canadian Bank of Commerce developed into one of the most important banking institutions financing the commercial and industrial segments of the Alberta economy.

In a sense, the history of life insurance companies in Alberta parallels that of chartered banks. Like the chartered banks, the central Canadian-

tion of our cattle; that is, we rounded them up, we brought them home, and we put up feed for them during the winter, with the result that we saved the weak ones, that is, the cows that had calves and the little calves just born, or anything that was liable to die, we kept it at home. Our increase was very much more and our losses were very much diminished.[110]

Cross vigorously defended cattle and land management that would enable him to maximize his profits while simultaneously assuring a steady supply of feed for his cattle by periodically giving some of his pastures a rest so that soil nutrients could be restored.

Alberta entrepreneurs, as they sought personal gain, were confident that they could at the same time accomplish more than that. In this view, individual wealth could help a person work for urban and provincial ends. In 1918, when John A. McDougall told the Edmonton Rotary Club that he had "come West to make my fortune," he also made it clear that he desired to promote the greater good of Edmonton and Alberta.[111]

Some entrepreneurs who did much to develop Alberta's opportunities saw themselves as creative individuals. Louis LaFleche, an Edmonton tailor, once said: "I like to work with my hands, to mould and to form and to create."[112] LaFleche also firmly believed that the suits he made for men could contribute to their success. "Nothing succeeds like success," he emphasized, "and a well-dressed man has a better chance to succeed than his sloppily dressed colleague."[113] Achievement and caring about one's appearance were virtues that businesspeople fostered.

■

Alberta's Changing Business System

Important changes occurred in the business system of Alberta in the forty years following the formation of the province. Newspaper editors drew attention to the striking growth of business activity, the appearance of numerous specialized firms, the expanding market, and transportation and communication technologies that encouraged the rise of larger businesses. New techniques of organization and management fundamentally different from those of earlier times developed with the growth of commerce and the spread of manufacturing in Alberta after World War II.

NOTES TO CHAPTER FOUR

1. *Census of the Northwest Provinces for 1906*, 101; *Census of Canada for 1941*, vol. 10, 2.

2. *Census of Canada for 1941*, vol. 2, 480-487.

3. Ibid.

4. *Census of Canada for 1941*, vol. 1, 46.

5. *Henderson's Edmonton Directory for 1939*, 790-791; *Henderson's Calgary Directory for 1939*, 786-787.

6. *Dun & Bradstreet Reference Book*, July 1939, 41-42, 81-83, 87-89.

7. Ibid., 1-123.

8. City of Edmonton Archives, Ross Bros. clipping file.

9. Alberta Corporate Registry, Ross Bros. Ltd. file.

10. *Dun & Bradstreet Reference Book*, September 1906, 9.

11. Alberta Corporate Registry, Ross Bros. Ltd. file.

12. City of Edmonton Archives, Ross Bros. clipping file.

13. Interview by the author with Art Chesney, 26 September 1975; *Albertan*, 11 November 1957.

14. Chesney interview, 26 September 1975.

15. Ibid.

16. Ibid.

17. Ibid.

18. Interview by the author with Art Chesney, 2 August 1996.

19. *Calgary Herald*, 7, 14, 21 May 1926, 2, 9, 23, March 1934, 6 April 1934, 19 November 1937, 3 December 1937.

20. Chesney interview, 2 August 1996.

21. Ibid.

22. Ibid.

23. Ibid.; *Albertan*, 11 November 1957.

24. *High River Times*, 21 March 1963.

25. Interview by the author with Donald F. Blake, 2 May 1991.

26. Blake interview, 2 May 1991.

27. *High River Times*, 29 July 1954.

28. *Dun & Bradstreet Reference Book*, January 1911, 36.

29. Blake interview, 2 May 1991.

30. *Dun & Bradstreet Reference Book*, September 1921, 33.

31. Blake interview, 2 May 1991.

32. *High River Times*, 21 August 1924, 4 December 1924, 9 April 1925, 5 November 1925, 19 March 1936, 7 May 1936, 18 June 1936, 24 September 1936, 7, 21 January 1937, 13 May 1937, 9 September 1937, 2 December 1937.

33. Blake interview, 2 May 1991; Calgary Court House, Surrogate Division, Estate of Frederick D. Blake file, 21 September 1954.

34. *Henderson's Edmonton Directory for 1939*, 783; *Henderson's Calgary Directory for 1939*, 780.

35. Interview by the author with Stuart W. Dunlap, 20 May 1996.

36. *Stettler Independent*, 6 August 1980.

37. Dunlap interview, 20 May 1996.

38. Alberta Corporate Registry, Dunlap Drug Company Ltd. file.

39. Dunlap interview, 20 May 1996.

40. *Stettler Independent*, 6 August 1980.

41. Ibid.

42. Dunlap interview, 20 May 1996.

43. Ibid.; *Dun and Bradstreet Reference Book*, September 1921, 49.

44. Dunlap interview, 20 May 1996.

45. Ibid.; Alberta Corporate Registry, Dunlap Drug Company Ltd. file.

46. *Henderson's Calgary Directory for 1908*, 309.

47. *Henderson's Calgary Directory for 1910*, 534; *Henderson's Calgary Directory for 1912*, 728; *Henderson's Calgary Directory for 1916*, 727; *Henderson's Calgary Directory for 1917*, 561.

48. Interview by the author with Jack Stokes, 25 May 1991; Alberta Corporate Registry, Kenny & Allin Company Ltd. file.

49. Stokes interview, 25 May 1991.

50. Alberta Corporate Registry, Stokes Drug Company Ltd. file.

51. *Dun & Bradstreet Reference Book*, September 1921, 38.

52. *Lethbridge Herald*, 6, 13 April 1925, 7, 20 May 1925, 7, 14 October 1930, 11, 18 November 1930.

53. Alex Johnston, John E. Stokes, Irma Dogterom, J. A. Sherman, and Carlton R. Stewart, *Lethbridge: Its Medical Doctors, Dentists, and Drug Stores* (Lethbridge: Lethbridge Historical Society, 1991), 73.

54. Stokes interview, 25 May 1991.

55. Ibid.; Alberta Corporate Registry, Stokes Drug Company Ltd. file.

56. Lethbridge Court House, Estate of Ernest B. Stokes file, 21 April 1948.

57. *Henderson's Edmonton Directory for 1939*, 797-798; *Henderson's Calgary Directory for 1939*, 792-793.

58. Red Deer and District Museum and Archives, Clippings file, Shopper, 5 October 1983.

59. Ibid.

60. Interview by the author with Richard Jewell, 16 May 1996.

61. Ibid.

62. *Red Deer Advocate*, 23 January 1920, 12 July 1928, 8 November 1928.

63. Ibid., 2 November 1932.

64. Ibid., 4 May 1938.

65. Jewell interview, 16 May 1996.

66. Interview by the author with Geoffrey Godley, 18 May 1991.

67. *Dun & Bradstreet Reference Book*, September 1906, 7.

68. *Claresholm Advertiser*, 15 April 1914.

69. Ibid., 8 July 1914.

70. Godley interview, 18 May 1991.

71 Fort Macleod Court House, Estate of George M. Godley file, 21 November 1946.

72. Godley interview, 18 May 1991.

73. Estate of George M. Godley file, 21 November 1946.

74. Godley interview, 18 May 1991.

75. Ibid.

76. Interview by the author with James M. Sharp, 21 May 1996.

77. *Medicine Hat News*, 15 February 1913.

78. Ibid.

79. Ibid.

80. Alberta Corporate Registry, the T. Hutchinson Company Ltd. file.

81. Ibid.

82. Ibid.

83. Sharp interview, 21 May 1996.

84. R. J. Welsh Ltd. Archives, Edmonton, "A Brief History of R. J. Welsh Ltd.," one page.

85. *Edmonton Journal*, 28 July 1980.

86. Ibid.

87. Ibid.

88. City of Edmonton Archives, Welsh's Saddlery clipping file.

89. "A Brief History of R. J. Welsh Ltd."

90. Alberta Corporate Registry, R. J. Welsh Ltd. file.

91. *Edmonton Journal*. 16 April 1963.

92. Ibid.

93. Interview by the author with Gordon and Jack Sissons, 22 May 1996.

94. I-XL Industries Archives, Medicine Hat, W. Jack Sissons, "The History of Redcliff Pressed Brick Company Limited," (Medicine Hat: typescript copy, 1995), 1.

95. Sissons interview, 22 May 1996.

96. *Dun & Bradstreet Reference Book*, July 1939, 101.

97. Sissons, "The History of Redcliff Pressed Brick Company Limited," A.

98. Sissons interview, 22 May 1996.

99. Sissons, "The History of Redcliff Pressed Brick Company Limited," 10.

100. Ibid.

101. Sissons, "The History of Redcliff Pressed Brick Company Limited," 11.

102. *Dun & Bradstreet Reference Book*, September 1921, 54-57.

103. Henry C. Klassen, "Canadian Bank of Commerce and Charles Rowley," *Alberta History 39* (Summer, 1991), 9-20.

104. Henry C. Klassen, "The Role of Life Insurance Companies in the Economic Growth of Early Alberta," unpublished paper presented at Project 2005: An Alberta History Workshop, 12-14 May 1988, Red Deer College, Red Deer.

105. Richard E. Bennett, *A House of Quality It Has Ever Been: History of the Great-West Life Assurance Company* (Winnipeg: The Great-West Life Assurance Company, 1992), 44, 103.

106. *Henderson's Calgary Directory for 1910*, 267, 327; *Henderson's Twin City Edmonton and Strathcona Directory for 1910*, 183, 216.

107. Henry C. Klassen, "R. G. Dun & Co.'s Early Years in Alberta, 1880-1900," *Alberta History 44* (Spring 1996), 11-18.

108. Interview by the author with Andrew Carmichael, 9 July 1976.

109. *Calgary Herald*, 13 October 1923; Alberta Corporate Registry, P. Burns & Company Ltd. file.

110. GAIA, M1543, The Calgary Brewing & Malting Company Papers, box 109, file 880, evidence given by A. E. Cross before the Dominions Royal Commission 1917, 51.

111. *Edmonton Bulletin*, 1 February 1918.

112. City of Edmonton Archives, LaFleche Bros. file.

113. Ibid.

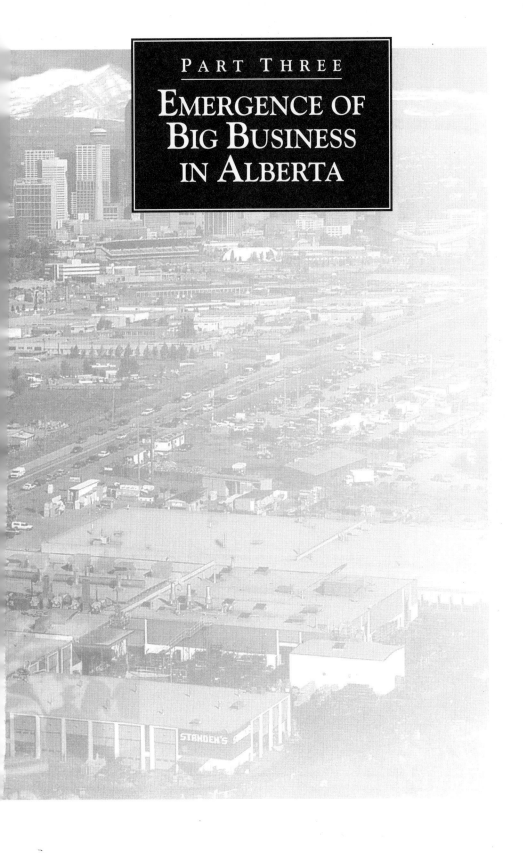

PART THREE

EMERGENCE OF BIG BUSINESS IN ALBERTA

BIG BUSINESS IN ALBERTA

Railways played a significant role in the rise of big business in Alberta, a process that occurred against a background of developments in the central Canadian railway industry. On 27 October 1854, as a result of an operational error, two trains collided on the Great Western Railway in southwestern Upper Canada. Three brakemen and fifty-four passengers were killed; forty-six other passengers were injured. Without question, this accident alarmed the public. The Canadian legislature launched an investigation into the operations of the Great Western.[1] Though they welcomed railways to their settlements, people realized that anyone who travelled by train faced problems of safety.

The Great Western officials responded to the accident by starting to develop a fresh approach to business, an approach that the American business historian Alfred D. Chandler would later see as the managerial revolution.[2] In the mid-and late-nineteenth century, American railways provided models for industrial management. Not surprisingly, Canadian railway managers travelled to the United States to study American management methods during this period. In Canada, as in the United States, it was clear that traditional informal business practices were no longer appropriate. Canadian executives understood the need to control their railways, which gradually helped develop new ways of running businesses. Of greatest importance was the Canadian Pacific Railway, for not only did this venture affect Canada as a whole, but it also had a tremendous impact upon Alberta. The managerial revolution that started in the railway industry after the mid-1850s eventually altered the way Canadians and Albertans did business and contributed to the rise of big business. Clearly, the business scene in Canada was extremely varied, but by the outbreak of World War I, big business had come into its own in Alberta through the presence of the Canadian Pacific.

An event that took place at Leduc, a small town southwest of Edmonton, thirty-three years later symbolized another major theme in the rise of big business in Alberta. On 13 February 1947, Imperial Oil Limited, a subsidiary of Standard Oil of New Jersey and Canada's best-known and largest oil company, discovered the Leduc oil field.[3] This discovery provided the impetus needed to make Imperial Oil huge in Alberta. The presence of this large corporation was a sign that big business had gained a permanent institutional position on the Alberta scene. Beginning to develop important interests in Alberta in 1914, Imperial Oil grew significantly in the province over the next three decades.[4] With the rise of large companies such as Imperial Oil in Alberta during the post-World War I years, personal management so common in earlier times gave way to teams of salaried managers, as big business executives created new corporate organizations necessary to exploit the potential of economies of scale.

The Canadian Pacific and Imperial Oil in Alberta were not self-contained but were related to the availability of natural resources and to Albertan desires for diversification. Besides having an abundance of fertile land, Alberta was a major source of coal. The future of the province, Albertans believed, depended on greater economic diversification and a wider use of its natural resources. Central to the Canadian Pacific's program were land to sustain an agrarian society and thereby create traffic and coal to provide energy for the trains. Alberta was also a major source of oil, in which Imperial Oil came to control much of the production and refining. Early big business operations focused on railway transportation and oil.

The rise of big business brought thoroughgoing changes in the nature of economic decision making in Alberta. Large companies adopted, some more rapidly than others, structures that allowed decisions previously made through market forces to be internalized. The visible hand of business management replaced what Adam Smith called the invisible hand of market forces in monitoring and co-ordinating parts of the Alberta economy.

In the large firms, the first managerial task was to create an internal organizational structure with carefully defined lines of responsibility and authority. Corporate managers began by centralizing authority over geographically dispersed units. The process of centralization involved building effective lines of communication between the central office and the units scattered over wide geographical areas. In an environment changing as rapidly as the Alberta economy was in the early decades of the twentieth century, even the biggest and most powerful centralized companies could not long afford to remain static. Managers had to keep their organizations efficient in order to stay abreast of the times, and there was a need to manage efficiency. The establishment of an efficient business required close control of the finances of the various units.

To meet the needs of and control their growing businesses, entrepreneurs went beyond the general merchant's traditional accounting techniques derived from Italian double-entry bookkeeping. Big businessmen introduced improvements in accounting to help keep track of current and past operations and to plan for the future of their firms. Industrialists developed financial accounting, which involved recording and auditing many financial transactions and synthesizing this information to provide the data needed for compiling their firms' balance sheets and for judging their performance. They developed systematic capital accounting, with its provision for determining depreciation, as a way to plan ahead. Finally, big businessmen developed cost accounting to keep track of and to compare the internal workings of the different parts of their ventures.

Small businesses, however, did not disappear. Instead, Alberta started to develop a dual economy in which big businesses took their places at the centre of the province's economy, with smaller firms at the perimeter.

■

Railways: the First Big Businesses

By the outbreak of World War I, railways had established the foundations of big business management in Canada as well as in Alberta. They were the nation's and Alberta's first big businesses. By this time, entrepreneurs had completed Canada's three transcontinental lines: the Canadian Pacific Railway, the Canadian Northern Railway, and the Grand Trunk Pacific Railway. Each of these lines controlled thousands of miles of track and employed thousands of workers. Constructing these railways was a costly task; the transcontinental lines connecting the East with the West were capitalized at from $100 million to $260 million each.[5] Other pre-World War I business enterprises had not achieved this unprecedented size. Even the largest manufacturing companies in Canada had considerably smaller capitals and workforces than the transcontinental railways.

In Alberta, as in Canada as a whole, railways continued to grow in size after the turn of the century. Between 1909 and 1912, the miles of track in Alberta controlled by the three transcontinental lines increased from 1,365 to 3,055, so that a growing number of urban centres in the province were linked by a transportation network. In 1912, as before that date, the Canadian Pacific Railway was the leader in Alberta with 1,430 miles of track, while the Canadian Northern Railway had 912 and the Grand Trunk Pacific Railway, 638.[6] The building of more than 3,000 miles of track did not finish the system in Alberta, but even by 1912 there was the beginning of an integrated, province-wide railway network available to farmers, ranchers, merchants, manufacturers, and passengers.

Safe railway operations in Alberta and the rest of the nation demanded a meaningful time standard. In the mid-1880s, after Canadian engineer Sandford Fleming had invented standard time in 1879 and American railways had established four time zones and adopted standard time in the United States in 1883, five time zones were created in Canada to allow Canadian railways to use standard time.[7] Railways in Alberta and the rest of Canada therefore adopted standard time as a way of standardizing their schedules; they also adopted a standard-gauge track, which permitted orderly car exchanges and through traffic between different parts of the province and the nation. Despite unpredictable winter snowstorms, the railways made every effort to maintain their schedules.

Safe and orderly operation further demanded the use of improved forms of communications that accompanied the evolution of the railway network in Alberta. There was a close relationship between railways and the telegraph, for the telegraph used railway's rights-of-way for its wires and assisted managers in scheduling trains. To prevent collisions, railways required engineers and conductors to follow thick books of rules so that the meeting places of trains could be indicated exactly in hours and minutes. The use of the telegraph rapidly spread beyond railway managers, as firms across Alberta and Canada employed it to communicate with other businesses. Like the telegraph, the telephone had become an important instrument for long-distance business communication by World War I.

As a result of their swift growth in the early twentieth century, railways in the nation and in Alberta faced new managerial problems. There were far greater capital and workforce requirements than in any other firms of the day. By their very nature, railways were complex and geographically dispersed systems, serving much larger regions. This left them the enormous challenge of operating as unified, co-ordinated organizations. In the railway business, managers had to make decisions quickly and precisely about their services, decisions that affected people over increasingly larger regions, and they had to develop appropriate methods to reach such decisions. Strategic problems, such as dealing with competition and funding growth and development requiring unprecedented amounts of capital, were even more complex.

■

Canadian Pacific Railway: a Pioneer in Big Business

The Canadian Pacific, the first railway to face these managerial problems in Alberta, was a leading pioneer in big business management in the province. Capitalized at $260 million, the Montreal-based Canadian Pacific employed more than 2,000 workers and possessed over 1,400 miles of track in Alberta by 1913.[8] In 1896, Canadian Pacific had 6,500 miles of track and employed about 23,000 workers across the nation.[9] The complexities of the company's strategic and operating problems demanded systematic methods of management. In the late 1880s and early 1890s, American-born William C. Van Horne, the company's president and general manager who had previously gained considerable management experience in the Chicago, Milwaukee and St. Paul Railway, solved these problems by establishing a business bureaucracy. In doing so, Van Horne relied heavily on the Pennsylvania Railroad model.[10]

Between the 1850s and 1870s, J. Edgar Thomson, the Pennsylvania's president, defined relations between the central office of the line and its operating divisions. He separated the responsibilities of head office executives from those of regional division office managers and created the systems needed to allow executives in the central office to co-ordinate the flow of trains and traffic across the railway's various operating units.[11]

Van Horne successfully applied Thomson's methods of management to the Canadian Pacific. To operate the far-flung Canadian Pacific, Van Horne devised a structure by which Montreal head office executives could co-ordinate activities throughout the regional divisions, each of which was headed by a general superintendent.[12] Between 1886 and 1911, William Whyte from his regional office in Winnipeg was responsible for supervising the work of the western division, which included the Canadian Pacific lines in Alberta. In 1899, Thomas G. Shaughnessy replaced Van Horne as the railway's president, and George J. Bury became Whyte's successor in Winnipeg twelve years later. From the Montreal head office, first Van Horne and then Shaughnessy co-ordinated the railway's Alberta operations through its Winnipeg office. Such co-ordination was essential not only for safe operations, but also for the regular, fast, and carefully scheduled movement of goods within Alberta between dozens of points of shipment and into and out of the province.

Van Horne could not create an administrative structure for the Canadian Pacific overnight, but gradually he built a business bureaucracy in which several features stood out. He separated policy making from operations. In Montreal, top management planned for the future of the line and co-ordinated the functions of the railway's different divisions. The general superintendents in charge of the divisions in effect became middle managers. Thus, while top management in the head office focussed on overall strategy, middle managers directed their attention to the day-to-day operations of their divisions. Middle managers like William Whyte received reports from, for example, station agents in Medicine Hat and Calgary, analyzed them, and then sent their own reports to the Montreal head office, establishing a chain that connected the different levels of the Canadian Pacific's bureaucracy. As Van Horne, Whyte, and the Alberta station agents clearly understood, a constant flow of information was needed to keep the big business operating efficiently. Van Horne also developed cost accounting, which involved a systematic recording and analysis of the costs of material and labour and helped him compete with other railways.

As a pioneer in Alberta big business, the Canadian Pacific's success was obvious to Van Horne and to his successor in the president's office, Shaughnessy. In order to operate the expanding railway effectively, Shaughnessy had opened its new locomotive and car shops in Calgary by 1913. He chose to call them the Ogden Shops after Canadian Pacific vice-president I. G. Ogden. Built at a cost of $2,500,000, the Ogden Shops covered six acres of land and employed about 2,000 men.[13] By 1914, the Canadian Pacific had increased its presence in Calgary by opening its posh

In 1914, Canadian Pacific Railway owned enormous production facilities, such as its Ogden locomotive and car shops at Calgary. Ogden Shops in 1998.

(Courtesy of Canadian Pacific Railway).

Palliser Hotel there. The Palliser Hotel's massive size was a reflection of the railway's optimism about the future of Calgary and Alberta.

Making arrangements with the City of Calgary for the building of the Palliser Hotel was part of William Whyte's work as manager of Canadian Pacific's western lines, but the problems of overseeing the new project from Winnipeg had strained his relationship with J. S. Dennis, the Calgary-based Canadian Pacific superintendent of irrigation in Alberta and land commissioner for British Columbia, to its limits. In November 1910, Whyte wrote to Shaughnessy:

> Mr. Dennis has all that he can attend to in connection with irrigation works and the B.C. Land Department without meddling in operating matters and I trust that in the interests of harmony and for the good of the service that you will instruct Mr. Dennis that all matters pertaining to the operation of the line should be referred to me as I am responsible for operating the Western Lines and for the maintenance of harmony between all Departments so as to produce team work which is, I consider, essential to the efficient and economical operation of any large corporation.[14]

Shaughnessy perceptively diagnosed the problem and soon offered the solution. Although he recognized that Whyte had demonstrated his executive capacity, Shaughnessy explained to him that consultation with Dennis as a resident of Calgary was important.[15] Clearly, Shaughnessy had a remarkable understanding of bureaucratic management.

As the Canadian Pacific increased in size in Alberta and as its executives developed new methods of management, the railway became the first business in the province in which the invisible hand of market forces gave way to the visible hand of management. The decisions of the railway's managers played a larger role than market forces in its development. The changes that occurred in the Canadian Pacific's management were important not only for this railway but also for other railways in Alberta. Like the Canadian Pacific, the Canadian Northern Railway and the Grand Trunk Pacific Railway instituted bureaucratic management practices in the province and the nation.

The adoption of bureaucratic methods by the railways was also important for a variety of other businesses and industries in Alberta. As their firms grew in size and complexity in the twentieth century, Alberta's industrialists looked for new management methods to control them. To some degree, they found them in Alberta's railways. The concept of bureaucratic management spread from railways to other industrial firms.

There was another way in which railways were important to the rise of big business in Alberta. In the province, economic growth provided fresh opportunities for business enterprises to expand the scope of their activities, and the development of Alberta's railway network was a critical factor in achieving progress.

■

Spread of Big Business in Alberta

Through population growth and transportation improvements, particularly the railway, Alberta increasingly became a province of interconnected expanding cities, and these changes permitted entrepreneurs to build big business firms. Alberta's population rose from 796,000 in 1941 to 2,510,000 in 1991, and most of this growth took place in cities.[16] In 1941, twenty-seven percent of Albertans lived in cities; in 1991, the proportion had risen to sixty-seven percent. The expansion in population combined with the railway network to create new business opportunities in the province.

Plentiful natural resources continued to play an important role in the development of Alberta's business system, including the rise of big business. Albertans remained the beneficiaries of land capable of supporting agriculture and indirectly along with it industries such as harness making and meat processing, petroleum reserves supplying oil and natural gas, forests providing timber for railway construction and lumber for buildings, and coal not only supplying energy for railway transportation but also generating electricity.

Robert J. Hutchings and Great West Saddlery

The experience of Robert J. Hutchings and the harness and saddlery industry demonstrates the significance of railways and growing cities in the rise of big business. Railways, besides creating Alberta's cities, helped exploit land and open the province to ranching and farming; urban residents and farmers and ranchers provided important markets for Hutchings' harnesses and saddles. Born in Newboro, Ontario in 1866, Hutchings moved to Winnipeg in the early 1880s to become a partner in the E. F. Hutchings Saddlery Company established by his brother Elisha.[17] In this company, Robert Hutchings learned harness- and saddle-making techniques and assimilated managerial skills that helped him become a successful manufacturer, manager, and entrepreneur. In 1889, he came to Calgary to open a branch of the company here. By 1899, the family firm had become the Great West Saddlery Company, with Elisha as its president in the Winnipeg head office and Robert as its vice-president in the Calgary branch office. By 1914, the company had also set up branches in Regina and Saskatoon.

In Calgary, Robert Hutchings as manager, aware of the large and expanding market for harnesses and saddles, developed a substantial factory which by 1914 employed 100 workers.[18] He also opened a branch of the company in Edmonton. By this time, the Great West Saddlery's operations in Alberta had become so big that Hutchings found it difficult to control the family firm. Consequently, he wrote to the Winnipeg head office, asking it to consider "hiring an expert systemizer" to improve his "office, warehouse, and factory system" in Alberta.[19] Whether an expert systemizer was hired is unknown, but Hutchings had an able assistant in the company's auditor, C. D. Edwards, who helped him by outlining ways of gaining better control of the Alberta end of the business. Edwards encouraged Hutchings to install "a proper cost system" and "a perpetual inventory system," among other things.[20]

Hutchings' efforts to control the company proved successful. Under his management, Great West Saddlery in Alberta continued to grow and flourish. By the end of 1914, the company had expanded by acquiring a controlling interest in the T. Hutchinson Company, the harness- and saddle-making firm in Medicine Hat.[21] Comprehensive sales information for Great West Saddlery has not survived, but the available evidence suggests its growing number of Calgary branch customers throughout Alberta as well as in British Columbia: J. H. Ashdown Hardware Company in Calgary; F. E. Algar and Company in Ponoka; Alberta Saddlery Company in Lethbridge; Levi Bradley in High River; Riley & McCormick in Calgary; F. W. Atkins in Cardston; Brewster Trading Company in Banff; Brooks Hardware Company in Brooks; Birkett & Thompson in Coronation; Cranbrook

Trading Company in Cranbrook; and J. H. Anthony in Lytton.[22] By 1921, the Great West Saddlery Company in Alberta was worth more than $1 million, reported the R. G. Dun & Company credit correspondent.[23]

Robert Hutchings helped create the largest harness- and saddle-making business in western Canada and, with financial assistance from banks and individuals such as Harriet Sanford of Hamilton, established Alberta as a leading harness- and saddle-producing province.[24]

•

Big Business in the Alberta Meat Industry

Big business grew in Alberta industry when a number of entrepreneurs took advantage of the new provincial and national markets and advances in technology to integrate mass production with mass distribution. For instance, in the 1940s, John Gainer's son Clifford and his grandson Harold developed a large factory to mass-produce meat in Edmonton and established a network of branches in Alberta and British Columbia to sell it. By this time, completion of the railway and telegraph network across Alberta and Canada had set the stage for the development of the provincial and national mass markets.

Clifford and Harold owed much of their success to what they had learned from John Gainer and from Arthur Gainer, Harold's father and Clifford's brother who was general manager of Gainers from 1911 to 1937. In 1937, after Arthur's death, Clifford became general manager of the family firm, and in 1938, after John's death, Harold became president.[25] A major opportunity came with the outbreak of World War II in 1939, which directly affected Gainers. Production of meat at the firm grew at a tremendous pace, as the demand for meat products greatly increased. Sensitive to Canada's rising needs, Harold and Clifford Gainer expanded production by purchasing a meat packing plant in Vancouver in 1945.[26]

In the 1950s, Gainers faced the problem of fierce competition, but Clifford and Harold could take justifiable pride in establishing the firm as a major producer of meat for people in Alberta and British Columbia. Initially incorporated for $150,000, the company had raised its authorized capital to $600,000 by 1951.[27] In celebrating its seventieth anniversary ten years later, the company's then general manager Alexander M. MacDonald wrote a short biography of the firm, in which he emphasized that it was an all-Alberta company.[28] To meet the growing demand for pre-cut and packaged meats and the need for more meat-cooling facilities, Gainers expanded its Edmonton plant in 1962.[29] Funding was available, largely from Gainers' careful retention of profits but also from loans provided by the Imperial Bank of Canada.[30] By 1966, Gainers had opened branches in Calgary, Victoria, and Vancouver, building a marketing network across Alberta and British Columbia.[31]

Central in importance for Gainers' future were close family ties and bonds of friendship in the firm. Controlled by some fifteen shareholders, most of whom were descendants or relatives of John Gainer, the firm continued to grow and prosper in the early and mid-1960s. While Harold Gainer remained president, John A. Young, an engineer who had married John Gainer's granddaughter Lois, had become general manager and treasurer of the firm by 1963.[32] By 1969, Young had succeeded Harold Gainer as president.

Important as well for Gainers' future was its willingness to explore and make use of the latest technology in the meat packing process. The development of curing bacon and hams provides an excellent example. Before World War II, Gainers' capabilities allowed the firm to cure bacon in fourteen to twenty days and hams in forty to sixty days. Gainers made progress, however and by the early 1960s, the firm was able to cure bacon in three days and hams in seven days.[33] This high-speed production helped Gainers grow and keep pace with the rising demand for meat. By 1972, the firm employed about 500 workers.[34]

Further growth occurred at Gainers soon after November 1972, when the Gainer family sold the business to Saskatoon-based Agra Industries.[35] Retaining its old name, Gainers began enlarging its Edmonton plant in 1973.[36] By 1979, one year after Peter Pocklington had become the new owner of Gainers, the firm's work force had grown to 650 while its annual sales had reached $85 million.[37] By 1982, the Edmonton plant had the capacity to process 10,000 hogs and 2,500 head of cattle per week.[38]

■

Mass Distribution

The unification of Alberta and national markets through the completion of the railway network during the first half of the twentieth century permitted manufacturers to set up their factories in one or two cities and sell throughout Alberta and other parts of Canada. The creation of provincial and national markets through such transportation improvements revolutionized the marketing and distribution of goods in Alberta. Before World War I, the traditional mercantile firm, operating as a general merchant, marketed and distributed most of Alberta's goods. By the 1930s, a number of general merchants had been replaced by mass retailers — the department store and the chain store.

These mass marketing firms in Alberta saved money by bypassing wholesalers and purchasing directly from manufacturers. All of them possessed similar buying and selling systems by using the railways and the telegraph to co-ordinate the flow of goods from manufacturers to consumers. Mass marketers organized centralized distribution facilities, where workers handled a growing volume of goods, making it possible to lower costs and expand markets. In the increasingly urbanized Alberta economy, what dominated distribution were volume and speed of sales. General merchants, from territorial times to World War I, had stressed making large profits on a relatively small quantity of goods. By contrast, mass marketing firms flourished by selling many goods at low margins. The strategy of profit through volume represented a new way of doing business in Alberta.

By selling mostly branded, packaged goods, mass retailers enhanced their potential for growth. The earlier general merchants had dealt mainly in undifferentiated commodities. As a result, consumers often needed time to find out what was desirable about a product before buying it. In contrast, name-brand goods such as Blue Ribbon Coffee in small packages instantly conveyed important information to consumers and speeded the marketing and distribution process. By advertising such branded, packaged goods in big-city newspapers, mass marketers reached a growing number of potential consumers. And by making shopping a pleasurable activity, they fostered a consumer culture in Alberta.

Of the new mass marketers in Alberta, the department store was the oldest. The department store appeared initially in Calgary in the 1880s when I. G. Baker & Company opened a small one there.[39] A little later, in 1891, the Winnipeg-based Hudson's Bay Company set up a small department store in Calgary and, by 1905, had also established small department stores in Edmonton, Fort Macleod, Lethbridge, and Pincher Creek.[40] The name of one of these pioneers, the Hudson's Bay Company, has remained a household word in Calgary and Edmonton to the present. Another department store, the Toronto-based T. Eaton Company, opened for business in Calgary in 1929 and, by the outbreak of World War II, also had stores in Edmonton, Red Deer, Medicine Hat, and Lethbridge. Eaton's remains one of the leading department stores in Alberta more than half a century later.

Alberta entrepreneurs also created department stores and by 1939, there were a number of such mass retailers, including Reach & Company in Fort Macleod, J. Lawrence & Company in Camrose and Stettler, and Johnstone Walker in Edmonton.

■

Johnstone Walker: a Department Store

The evolution of Johnstone Walker presents a good case study in the development of a department store in an expanding city. Its founder, W. Johnstone Walker, helped transform the Alberta retail industry by using mass-distribution methods.

A native of Scotland, Walker engaged in farming in South Africa before he came to Edmonton in 1885. Aided by John A. McDougall, Walker opened a small general store on Ninety-eighth Street in 1886.[41] Realizing that the store was crowded, Walker looked elsewhere for growth

Mass retailing developed first in Alberta's large cities, the biggest markets in the province. Large–city department stores, such as Johnstone Walker's in Edmonton (1915), introduced new ways of selling, including the creation of attractive public places filled with handsome displays of inviting merchandise.

(Courtesy of City of Edmonton Archives and the Edmonton Journal).

possibilities. In 1892, he found larger premises in the Power-Loney Building on Jasper Avenue. In the expanded business, there was no mass distribution, and Walker was simply one of a number of general merchants.

Walker moved ahead of other general merchants in 1900 by constructing a two-storey, brick building on Jasper Avenue for his newly organized department store.[42] Walker's business survived for many years after 1902, when he retired because of poor health, and Cecil S. Sutherland became the store's manager. Like Walker, Sutherland, who was born in Trackadie, Nova Scotia and had been with the store since 1896, was a man of imagination and vision. Sutherland was responsible for the pioneer store's growth over the next ten years and beyond. In 1912, when Walker died, his son Grahame incorporated the business as Johnstone Walker, became its president, and appointed Sutherland managing director.[43] Three years later, in 1915, while Grahame Walker was serving overseas with the Glasgow Highlanders Light Infantry in World War I, Sutherland moved the store into a larger building at the corner of Jasper Avenue and 102nd Street.[44]

Capitalized at $250,000, Johnstone Walker Limited received backing not only from Grahame Walker and Sutherland, but also from the Imperial Bank of Canada and the Mutual Life Assurance Company of Canada.[45]

The store had $232,200 in paid-in capital when it opened for business in the larger premises. Between 1915 and 1916, the firm's net worth increased from $105,984 to $111,965. Owned primarily by the Walker and Sutherland families, Johnstone Walker was a family business.

By 1918, Johnstone Walker had emerged as an impressive department store occupying 30,000 square feet on three floors, employing 86 regular workers and 125 in rush seasons, and handling many lines, including ladies' wear, silks, furs, ready-to-wear, millinery and fancy goods, men's and boys' clothing and furnishings, boots and shoes, toilet goods, groceries, house furnishings, and toys.[46] Among the most popular items were Dorothy Dodd shoes for women and Wear-Better suits for boys.

A mass retailer, Johnstone Walker's policy was aimed at expansion of sales volume through low prices, low margins, and high turnover in the rapidly growing Edmonton market. Volume, not markup, was to create profits. From the beginning, Johnstone Walker as a department store advertised itself as "the store that sells for lowest prices."[47] For a firm with about 100 salespeople making thousands of sales, it was also logical to adhere to a one-price policy. Prices on goods were fixed and the same for all customers, not a matter for negotiation. Records of stock-turn have not survived, but the available evidence suggests that Johnstone Walker's extensive local advertising, which announced both the availability of products and their prices, helped maintain a fairly high level of stock-turn. A fundamental characteristic of Johnstone Walker was its success in providing a bright and friendly environment in the store, which contributed to the flow of customers into the establishment by the hundreds. Award-winning window displays, created by senior staff member W. Oliver Johnson, added to the exciting and attractive atmosphere.[48]

To cope with the increasing volume of business, Johnstone Walker took over the Heimick Building next to it in 1920. By 1931, after making two more additions to the original structure, Johnstone Walker utilized 40,000 square feet of floor space and employed 120 full-time workers.[49]

Johnstone Walker also maintained a relatively high stock-turn by developing a well-defined management structure. While the firm's president, Grahame Walker, lived in Glasgow, Scotland, managing director Sutherland had become vice-president and general manager by 1918.[50] P. E. Engel served as secretary treasurer. By 1936, Fred V. Hollands, who joined the firm in 1911, had become advertising and sales manager. Experienced buyers for the various departments had emerged, for example, E. E. Davies, who had been with the firm for thirty-three years, had become the buyer for the all-piece goods, staples and bedding department. Maud McGregor had become the buyer for the lingerie department, while Mrs. M. Hawson and Edith Maloy had become the buyers for the infants and children's wear department and the knitting wools and art needlework department respectively. McGregor, Hawson, and Maloy had all been with Johnstone Walker for at least twenty-one years. In addition, John Hampton, with twenty-two years of store work under Sutherland behind him, served as shipper.[51] By 1918, Johnstone Walker provided an automobile delivery service for its customers in all parts of Edmonton.[52]

Johnstone Walker's early success was also based on its mail-order distribution. By 1910, Sutherland had created an efficient mail-order department to reach the store's small town and rural customers in Alberta and other sections of western Canada. As an advertisement in the *Edmonton Capital* promised, "mail orders promptly executed."[53] Aided by its illustrated price catalogue which went out to many householders, Johnstone Walker sold a wide variety of goods by mail.[54] In the mid-1930s, Sutherland learned from research that customers in the region surrounding Edmonton were likely to place mail orders if they read Johnstone Walker's Daily Store News in the *Edmonton Journal*, and he vigorously pursued this business: "Realizing the disadvantage of out-of-town readers who have no alternative to shopping by mail, Johnstone Walker's always gives every possible consideration to meeting their needs. And in instances where lines are sold out, we often go to the length of substituting a better article if possible."[55]

Despite the drop in Johnstone Walker's sales during the depth of the Great Depression in the 1930s, the firm survived these difficult years. Like the city of Edmonton, the firm shared in World War II prosperity. Post-war Johnstone Walker was led by a new president, Cecil Sutherland, who took over the position on Grahame Walker's retirement in 1951.[56]

Described by the *Edmonton Journal* as "dean of Edmonton department store managers," Sutherland still had vision.[57] In 1959, he expanded Johnstone Walker's operations by opening a new department store with floor space of 28,000 square feet in Edmonton's Bonnie Doon Shopping Centre.[58] Further expansion occurred five years later, in 1964, when Sutherland opened a new department store with more than 32,000 square feet of floor space in the city's Westmount Shopping Centre at a cost of $500,000.[59]

Upon Cecil Sutherland's death, sometime between 1964 and 1967, his son Sydney became president of Johnstone Walker. A University of Alberta commerce graduate who had started in the business as a stockboy before World War II and worked his way up through the ranks, Sydney Sutherland owned a substantial block of Johnstone Walker stock.[60] Like his father, Sydney had a deep interest in his work and sought to expand the business. In 1970, the newly erected department store in the Southgate Shopping Centre became the firm's fourth outlet in Edmonton.[61] It had a similar outlet in Calgary. By this time, Johnstone Walker employed more than 200 workers. To administer his extensive investment in mass retailing, Sydney Sutherland worked closely with the managers of his outlets.

Among other early mass retailers that emerged in Alberta were chain stores. The growth of chains encompassed food, drugs, and apparel. Chain stores of significant size appeared first in the grocery business.

■

Jenkins' Groceteria: a Chain Store

The first chain store to make a long-term impact on the distribution of food in Alberta was Jenkins' Groceteria. Founded in 1909 in Calgary at 1229 Ninth Avenue Southeast by Henry Marshall Jenkins and John Cornfoot, the firm sold mainly groceries and had two clerks. The following year, Jenkins, a man of extraordinary ability, energy, and initiative, bought out his partner Cornfoot and became sole owner of the small grocery store.[62]

Born on a farm at Mount Albion, Prince Edward Island in 1881, Henry Jenkins relied heavily on family and friends back home in building up his grocery business in Calgary. He expanded this trade, using funds from his older brother Robert Harold. In 1911, Henry married Josephine Peebles, who also came from Prince Edward Island. Initially, Henry and Josephine, who did her best to be supportive, lived above the store.[63] By 1913, Jenkins employed eight men and had two delivery wagons to handle his growing grocery trade.[64]

Six months after the outbreak of World War I, Jenkins saw half his staff leave to join the Canadian armed forces.[65] Around the same time, as a result of the closure of a competitor's five stores when he enlisted, more business went to the Jenkins store. To handle the increasing volume of distribution, Jenkins hired two young women to sell groceries. The sales staff, however, could not keep up with their work.

Jenkins recognized that a new sales approach was needed and, in 1917, he travelled to Seattle to study the marketing and distribution methods used at Walter Monson's chain store, the Seattle Groceteria.[66] Under the guidance of Monson, Jenkins learned how to use the grocery chain store as an instrument for mass retailing.

In March 1918, Jenkins quickly transformed his firm in Calgary into a self-service grocery establishment — the first in Canada. Under federal law, he incorporated it as Groceteria Stores Company, capitalized at $45,000. Henry Jenkins became president of the new company, and he, his wife Josephine, and their baker, Arthur R. Watt, served as directors.[67] Jenkins was operating one self-service grocery store in Calgary at the end of 1918 and, by 1924, had opened an additional seven such stores in the city. In his stores, Jenkins looked at groceries from the customers' perspective; customers wanted groceries at a lower price.

Jenkins was lowering prices and mass marketing high-quality goods. As his son Ronald later explained,

The interior of Jenkins' Groceteria store in Calgary in 1959. The emergence of Jenkins' Groceteria, with its chain of stores across Alberta and commitment to self-service and low prices, reflected the grocery retailing revolution in the province during the early twentieth century. (Courtesy of Canadian Grocer).

> *There was a greater turnover and such volume that he was able to reduce prices drastically. The idea just caught fire. The big attraction was just the fact that they [self-service stores] were cheaper in their prices. In fact, very drastically cheaper prices, probably ten to fifteen percent cheaper because the wages were lower and the volume that each clerk could produce was very much greater, double probably.*[68]

Jenkins' decision to stop granting credit to customers and rely completely on cash sales further increased his capacity to cut costs and lower prices.[69] In order to keep customers, however, he gradually returned to offering them credit. This service was now more limited than it had been earlier.

To reach other parts of Alberta, Jenkins expanded his distribution network for groceries by setting up small-town stores in centres such as Drumheller, Banff, Hanna, Olds, Didsbury, Lacombe, Stettler, High River, Nanton, and Fort Macleod. Growth quickened and, by 1929, the Jenkins chain was operating thirty stores — seventeen in Calgary and thirteen outside the city.[70] Jenkins had opened self-service stores at an unprecedented rate in Alberta retailing.

At first, Jenkins purchased his groceries from wholesalers, especially Louis Petrie Limited in Calgary. Soon, however, Jenkins started to assume the warehousing function himself. In 1928, he integrated backward into wholesaling, acquiring control of Louis Petrie Limited, and changed the name of his company from the Groceteria Stores Company to Jenkins' Groceteria Limited.[71] In the process, Jenkins brought new investors into the picture, including Louis Petrie and John E. Prince, a lumber manufacturer. Pat Burns was among those who saw the potential of self-service grocery stores. He guaranteed the dividend on the Jenkins' Groceteria shares for ten years. In return, during this period, Jenkins sold only Burns meats in his chain of stores.[72]

During the Great Depression in the 1930s, Jenkins faced serious financial problems for the first time in his business career. "Many times," he said, "I thought we were out of the woods, only to find we had reached merely a clearing."[73] There were danger signals at Jenkins' Groceteria. For instance, the controlling interest in the firm slipped from Jenkins' grasp. In these years, he made impressive contributions in money management. He demonstrated his own confidence by expanding his grocery business and, by 1939, was operating thirty-six stores in Alberta, including those in Red Deer and Brooks. Jenkins remained the dominant influence and single largest shareholder in the firm.

World War II brought changes to Jenkins' Groceteria. To begin with, there was growth in volume of sales, as well as a gradual, though not steady, increase in net profits.[74] Henry Jenkins died in March 1945. There was provision in Henry's will for his son Ronald to succeed him. Ronald received his education at the Commercial High School, Western Canada High School, and Mount Royal College in Calgary. He began at Jenkins' Groceteria as an employee in 1934, working first as an inventory clerk and then as a commercial traveller.[75] After serving overseas with the Royal Canadian Air Force between 1941 and the summer of 1945, Ronald became head of Jenkins' Groceteria.

Jenkins' Groceteria came out of World War II with profitable operations, but a company in need of transformation.[76] Aided by the Bank of Nova Scotia, Ronald Jenkins started by purchasing control of the company.[77] He then reorganized the firm's administration, recruiting new managers. Headed by Jenkins as president and general manager, the company soon had an effective team of managers: H. C. Hilton, director, treasurer, and store engineering manager; T. H. Royds, merchandise manager and wholesale operations manager; R. P. Pearpoint, credit manager and personnel and staff training manager; I. D. Howden, store operations manager and country supervision manager; and P. J. Harrison, advertising and public relations manager.[78]

Ronald Jenkins' work as creator of this management team demonstrated his remarkable skill, breadth, and understanding as a general executive. By purchasing a large factory in Calgary and transforming it into a modern office and warehouse complex, he revealed his ability to meet the challenge of developing and enhancing his distribution system.[79] Jenkins' contributions to cutting costs and reducing the sale price of groceries by gradually discontinuing charge accounts was additional proof of his talent as top manager. He understood the techniques of chain store management.

Under Ronald Jenkins' administration, Jenkins' Groceteria growth, in terms of number of stores, number of employees, and sales, was impressive. By 1954, the company owned and operated forty-seven stores: twenty-one in Calgary, two in Red Deer, and one in centres such as Claresholm, Lethbridge, Milk River, Olds, Taber, Bow Island, Vulcan, Trochu, Eckville, Hanna, Drumheller, High River, and Sylvan Lake. From 1945 to 1959, the firm's workforce grew from 210 to 425. In the same period, sales increased more than four times, from $3 million to more than $13 million.[80]

Some other grocery chains also came on the scene in Alberta during the first half of the twentieth century. One of these was Canada Safeway, a subsidiary of the Delaware-headquartered Safeway that had 2,660 stores in the United States in 1929 when it started new retail outlets over the border in Alberta.[81]

The entry of foreign firms broke down long-standing relationships in Alberta's business system. The grocery industry was a case in point. With the growth of international trade and the expansion of the grocery markets, foreign firms such as Safeway were sometimes more successful than Alberta companies. During his career at Jenkins' Groceteria, Ronald Jenkins saw his company experience difficulty in engaging profitably in the grocery business in Alberta, while Safeway, a grocery chain based in the United States, was not only succeeding in its home base but also penetrating Alberta's distribution system and markets. The penetration of Alberta industries by foreign firms brought about fundamental changes in the Alberta business system. One change was the restructuring achieved by Alberta companies through the refocussing of investments. For instance, the sale of Jenkins' Groceteria to Western Grocers, a Winnipeg-based firm, in 1959 reshaped ownership patterns in the Alberta grocery industry.[82] Meanwhile, foreign investments in Alberta reshaped the Alberta business landscape with new names. The grocery industry was one area where this development was obvious to Albertans.

■

Canada Safeway and Mass Retailing in Alberta

The continuing growth of the Alberta market provided new business opportunities, as the history of Canada Safeway reveals. In January 1929, the firm was incorporated as Safeway Stores in Manitoba. As Canada Safeway began operations, American-born and -trained Walter J. Kraft served as Alberta manager.[83] By the end of 1929, this grocery chain was operating sixteen self-service stores in Alberta.[84] Considerable growth occurred over the next decade, and by 1939 Safeway was running thirty-

The growth of chain stores, such as Canada Safeway, was dramatic in Alberta towns and cities in the half century after World War II. Canada Safeway continued to develop, in order to tap the ever-growing urban market. A showplace of the Canada Safeway chain in the Manning district in Edmonton in 1997.

(Courtesy of Canada Safeway).

five stores in Alberta: twelve in Edmonton, eleven in Calgary, and one in each of the following centres: Wetaskiwin, Camrose, Lethbridge, Red Deer, Vegreville, Medicine Hat, Stettler, Leduc, Vermilion, Lacombe, Wainwright, and Ponoka.[85]

Kraft, and those who later assumed top-management responsibilities at Safeway in Alberta, offered high-quality goods at low prices but not credit.[86] The keystone of Safeway's strategy was to sell many goods at low margins instead of a few goods at high margins. By making groceries available in large quantities to thousands of customers all over Alberta, the firm became a mass retailer in the province.[87]

Safeway in Alberta understood the advantages of vertical integration. Over the years, the firm integrated backward into mass manufacturing. It concentrated especially on producing highly perishable goods. Safeway discovered that, rather than relying on independent suppliers, it could deliver a number of products to customers more cheaply through its own plants — its Lucerne milk-producing plants in Edmonton, Empress bread-making plant and Lucerne meat-packing plant in Calgary, and Empress vegetable-processing plant in Taber, among others.[88] By the last third of the twentieth century, Safeway had created a great, vertically integrated organization, with major departments for marketing, purchasing, and processing, tightly controlled from its head office in Calgary.

Besides pursuing economy operation vigorously, Canada Safeway in Alberta branched rapidly. By 1982 Canada Safeway owned and operated a chain of ninety-seven stores in the province, a chain that stretched from Lethbridge in the South to Fort McMurray in the North. By the mid-1990s,

Safeway employed more than 9,000 workers in Alberta.[89] Covering 20,000 square feet in the 1930s, each store had about 55,000 square feet by the mid-1990s. As the years passed, Safeway's store design gained not only in size, but also in efficiency. By developing cost-saving techniques in mass distribution and mass production, Safeway as a big chain store helped change business operations in the Alberta grocery trade.

■

Mass Production

Mass demand in the marketplace called not only for mass distribution but also for mass production, and the Alberta economy responded well. Significantly, mass production developed almost concurrently with mass distribution in the province. Mass production promised economies of scale, a reduction in unit costs over a wide variety of manufactured goods. The rapidly expanding market encouraged manufacturers to increase their production, and new technologies made greater output possible.

The development of new technologies allowed Alberta manufacturers to speed up the process of production, achieve more output, and decrease the number of workers needed to produce a specific amount of output. Indeed, they helped manufacturers mass produce grains, meat, sugar, milk, and other foods. They also made feasible mass production in the oil industry. To achieve production in high volume required massive capital investment in plants and equipment.

The early twentieth century left its mark on the Alberta oil industry. As the nation's prime storehouse for oil, Alberta occupied a significant place in the development of Canada's oil products. Albertans enthusiastically greeted the new importance of their extractive industries such as oil, particularly after the depression of 1913. Of course, they hoped for immediate short-range profits, but beyond these gains they viewed the development of the oil industry as an opportunity to advance their long-range goal of diversifying Alberta's economy and speeding industrial growth.

The penetration of the Alberta oil industry by foreign firms helped to reshape Alberta business. In 1914, Calgary Petroleum Products dominated the market.[90] Six years later Calgary Petroleum Products saw its market share shrink substantially while it competed with a company based in the United States — Imperial Oil — for production leadership. Capital availability became uncertain for Alberta companies. Imperial Oil began operations in the Turner Valley oil field, and Calgary Petroleum Products responded by establishing a partnership with them. Imperial Oil was the dominant partner, however. The American penetration reshaped the Alberta oil industry in the 1920s. By 1923, Imperial Oil was the largest oil company in Alberta. Many Albertans welcomed the expansion of Imperial Oil in their province as a unique chance to diversify Alberta's economy.

Imperial Oil and Mass Production

The evolution of Imperial Oil provides a striking example of mass production in Alberta. Founded in 1880 by entrepreneur Frederick Fitzgerald of London, Ontario, its first president, and fifteen other local businessmen, the company was capitalized at $500,000. In 1898, after opening refineries at Petrolia and Sarnia, Imperial Oil brought a new investor into the picture — the Standard Oil Company of New Jersey, a big American firm which, at that time, acquired a majority interest in Imperial Oil.[91] Thus, Imperial Oil became a subsidiary of Standard Oil. Under the leadership of president Walter Teagle, Imperial Oil had, by 1917, become a large, integrated industrial corporation with its Canadian head office in Sarnia and its central sales office in Toronto.[92]

In 1923, nine years after the discovery of oil at Turner Valley, Imperial Oil opened a refinery in Calgary with a daily rated capacity of 4,000 barrels.[93] C. M. Moore, Imperial Oil's superintendent at Calgary, had incorporated improved refining processes into the refinery.[94] The use of enlarged, low pressure stills and catalytic cracking units permitted high-volume, large-batch or continuous-process production.[95] By spring of 1924, Imperial Oil's operation at its Calgary plant was refining about 3,000 barrels of gasoline and oil a day.[96]

Over the years, output grew. Significant increases in the production of gasoline and oil at the Imperial Oil's Calgary plant interlocked with the booming automobile industry in Alberta. The company set up its own marketing facilities and, by 1931, it had a network of 299 service stations in the province.[97]

As in numerous other industries, in oil, the processors rather than the producers of raw materials created the big industrial business.[98] Imperial Oil in Alberta had a considerably greater potential for economies of scale in refining oil than in producing crude oil.

Imperial Oil remained a symbol of Alberta big business. In 1948, the firm expanded its facilities in Alberta by opening a continuous-process refinery with the most advanced technology in Edmonton.[99] By 1949, two years after its discovery of oil at Leduc and one year after its discovery of oil at Redwater, Imperial Oil's operations at Edmonton and Calgary were refining well over 21,000 barrels a day. Five years later, in 1954, this figure had risen to about 28,000.[100] The scale of these operations resulted in important cost advantages.

Simultaneously, Imperial Oil was expanding the production of crude oil in Alberta. Between 1947 and 1950, the company's crude oil production in the province increased from 457,000 to 13,000,000 barrels. By 1950, Imperial Oil was producing forty-eight percent of Alberta's crude.[101]

The Imperial Pipe Line Company, a wholly-owned subsidiary of

The important crude-oil discovery near Leduc on 13 February 1947 opened the way for rapid growth of Imperial Oil in Alberta. This strike led to oil booms throughout Alberta, as well as in Saskatchewan, Manitoba, and British Columbia, during the following decades. (Courtesy of Imperial Oil).

Imperial Oil, gathered all the crude oil produced in the Leduc-Woodbend field as well as a major part of the Redwater-Simmons production. It delivered this crude to the Interprovincial Pipe Line and to Imperial Oil's Edmonton refinery by pipeline and by tank car to refineries with no pipeline connection. During 1950, Imperial Oil expanded its Leduc-Woodbend gathering system from forty miles to a total of 103 miles and its Redwater-Simmons gathering system from twenty-seven miles to a total of sixty-nine miles.[102]

Developing its marketing and distribution facilities across Canada and abroad, Imperial Oil contributed to a technological innovation: long-distance pipelines. The company participated in building not only the Interprovincial Pipe Line, a crude oil trunk line system that ran from Redwater to its refinery at Sarnia, but also the Trans Mountain Pipe Line, a crude oil trunk line system that ran from Edmonton to Vancouver and Anacortes, Washington.[103] The Interprovincial Pipe Line was completed to Sarnia by 1953, and the Trans Mountain Pipe Line was completed to Vancouver by 1953 and to Anacortes by 1955.[104] These pipelines, over which Imperial Oil had partial control, helped increase the importance of its presence in Alberta.

By the 1950s, besides being a big crude oil producer and a big refiner, the company had extensive transportation and distribution facilities in Alberta and Canada. Also, in the 1950s, large managerial hierarchy was co-ordinating, monitoring, and planning for this big industrial corporation from its chief executive office at 56 Church Street in Toronto.[105]

As its marketing network grew, Imperial Oil expanded and diversified its output in Alberta. In 1969, the company opened a $50 million fertilizer complex near Redwater.[106] Six years later, in 1975, Imperial Oil replaced its refineries in Edmonton, Calgary, Regina, and Winnipeg with the large Strathcona refinery on Edmonton's outskirts.[107] To manage all its natural resource activities, in 1978 Imperial Oil created Esso Resources Canada Limited, a Calgary-based wholly-owned subsidiary.[108] In 1985, the company began to extract bitumen from the oil sands at Cold Lake.[109] Besides piping part of the bitumen to its refineries for conversion into crude oil, Imperial Oil sold some of it for uses such as producing asphalt for roads and shingles. By 1995, Cold Lake bitumen production — the firm's largest single source of non-conventional oil production — had reached 90,000 barrels a day.[110] Bitumen production at another oil-sand operation, Syncrude Canada at Fort McMurray, in which Imperial Oil had a twenty-five percent interest, had increased to 202,000 barrels a day.[111] Imperial Oil had its head office in Toronto. Seventy percent owned by the United States oil company Exxon Corporation, Imperial Oil nonetheless had an all-Canadian board of directors and more than 19,000 Canadian shareholders.[112]

Big business developed in Alberta industry when entrepreneurs took advantage of new opportunities. At Imperial Oil, there were many such entrepreneurs. For instance, in 1986 Saskatchewan-born Arden Haynes, chairman and chief executive officer of the company, could say confidently, "I am not thinking in terms of survival but in terms of opportunity. Our human resources and our financial resources will carry us to new opportunities."[113] Haynes's policies proved successful. He recruited a managerial team to co-ordinate the flow from the oil fields through Imperial Oil's refining facilities and its distribution network to retailers. In the process, Haynes helped maintain Imperial Oil as the largest oil company in Alberta and Canada and did much to consolidate Alberta's position as the leading oil-producing province.

■

Frederick C. Mannix and the Rise of Big Business

The story of Frederick C. Mannix and the railway and pipeline construction industries illustrates the importance of railways and oil to the rise of big business in Alberta. Possessing the knowledge and experience required to meet the needs of specific customers in the areas of railway expansion and pipeline development, Mannix could offer valuable construction services. Born in 1913 in Edmonton, Mannix moved with his family to Calgary four years later. Educated at Brentwood College, a boys'

In the late 1950s, Frederick C. Mannix's urban construction, coal mining, and pipeline construction businesses became known as LORAM enterprises. Running the operations with skill, Mannix played a major role in the economic growth of Alberta. (Courtesy of LORAM Corporation).

private boarding school north of Victoria on Vancouver Island, Mannix owed much of his success to what he learned in the construction business.[114] In Alberta, Mannix held several low-paying jobs, including that of hauling oil, gas, oats, and hay by truck at a project to construct the grade for the Canadian Pacific branch line between Drumheller and Rosemary, before becoming the superintendent at a dam his father, Frederick S. Mannix, was building for a sugar refining plant near Picture Butte in the mid-1930s.[115]

Introduced to the world of high finance by his father and Harry Morrison of M K Construction, Boise, Idaho, Frederick C. Mannix became an investor in numerous business enterprises: an urban construction business, a coal mine, and a pipeline construction company, among others.[116] With the success of these enterprises, Mannix became a prosperous businessman. Operating from his head office in Calgary, he continued to make money, but wealth alone did not satisfy him. He wanted to create something of lasting importance, and it was this desire that led him to diversify into the oil industry.

When Mannix entered the oil industry in the early 1950s, he brought with him some important lessons from his construction experience. For instance, he knew about the large and expanding market for construction services that oil was creating with its requirements for plants and pipelines. In 1954, he established the Pembina Pipe Line to build and operate the pipeline gathering and transmission system for the big Pembina oil field southwest of Edmonton.[117] In managing his pipeline company Mannix took to heart the passion of oil executives for low-cost operations. Like oil production, pipeline construction and ownership was a capital-intensive business, and Mannix always sought to lower costs and increase the efficiency of his pipeline. Keeping down costs, he believed, would help to develop a profitable business. Mannix's enterprises were able to grow as they did in part because of his willingness to adopt a long-range view, something that led him in 1957 to adopt the name LORAM (Lo standing for long, ra for range, and M for Mannix).[118]

Mannix's policies proved successful. He continued to diversify, creating Alberta Coal, the largest coal-mining company in Canada, designed especially to generate electricity, and, with bankers, helped maintain Alberta as the leading coal-producing province. Markets beyond Alberta also attracted attention from Mannix. The expansion of his operations saw him become involved in mining iron ore on Vancouver Island, manufacturing railway equipment and constructing railways in the United States, engineering pipelines in Iran, and building railways in Australia.[119]

To carry out his far-flung ventures, Mannix relied heavily on family and friends. He married Margaret Ruth Boughton of Hull, Quebec in 1939. The couple had children: Frederick Philip, born in 1942; Maureen Gail, in 1944; and Ronald Neil, in 1948.[120] Frederick C. Mannix's wife, Margaret, played an important role in the development of the family businesses. "I owe everything to her," Frederick C. Mannix observed many years later. "She gave F. C. the support that he needed. He was a very dynamic individual, but we are not islands, and she complemented everything he did," noted Dorothy Larson, a long-time employee.[121]

To assist him in running his big enterprises, Mannix created and maintained a strong management team. For many years, Eric Connelly, a chartered accountant, served as chief financial officer; Karl Collett was head of construction operations; Brock Montgomery served as chief engineer; and Si Fraser was head of business development for Mannix's coal-mining operations. "Everyone in the company was working together and operating as a family. We went all out to make the company really go. There were no politics. It was most rewarding just to be there," observed Eric Connelly.[122]

Frederick C. Mannix lived to see his enterprises in mass production and mass distribution benefit from a number of years of accelerating growth before his death in 1995.[123] He had in several decades built up one of Alberta's leading businesses, an integrated concern known throughout the West for the scope and quality of its products. Long before that, however, his capacity to take the long range view included planning succession. Experienced people guided the expansion of the Mannix enterprises from the late 1970s onward, as the business continued to be led by a closely held group of owner-managers. Family ties remained of great importance to the concern's management. Frederick C. had groomed his two sons, Frederick P. and Ronald N. Mannix, for leadership. Frederick P. Mannix, who had graduated with a commerce degree from the University of Alberta, and

Ronald N. Mannix, who was also a University of Alberta commerce graduate, rose to become the heads of the Mannix enterprises.[124] By 1995, the Mannix enterprises stood as an important business complex employing thousands of men and women.[125]

■

Restructuring the Business Firm in Alberta

As firms started to integrate mass production with mass distribution, they became much different from earlier Alberta business enterprises. The new companies were considerably larger, Alberta's first big industrial businesses. Besides growing in size and complexity, these companies differed from their forerunners in other ways.

Many of them emerged as corporations, as corporate enterprise became more and more widespread in Alberta after World War I, especially among manufacturing firms. Manufacturing companies had to raise large amounts of capital to construct new factories and improve machinery and other equipment in existing plants. The corporate form of organization, offering the advantage of limited liability to investors, appealed particularly to manufacturers. The corporation also proved attractive to manufacturers because, unlike a partnership, it did not have to be dissolved and reorganized when an investor withdrew from the business or died.

As they expanded, new big businesses in Alberta developed internal structures different from those of most earlier firms. In creating these structures, the big firms were responding to opportunities in the growing market as well as to the ever-increasing complexity of manufacturing and manufactured goods. The expanding market presented great opportunities to Alberta businesspeople, at the same time, forcing them to face new problems. The province-wide and nation-wide railway network undermined local monopolistic operations, intensifying competition across Alberta and requiring changes in business methods.

■

Vertical Integration

In an effort to decrease competition and stabilize their positions in the market, Alberta business managers restructured their firms. Vertical integration provided one mechanism by which this could be done. Indeed, vertically integrated companies became a distinguishing feature of big business in Alberta. In vertical integration, a firm that at first engaged in only one step in the making and selling of a product might integrate backward to supply its own materials and might also integrate forward into the marketing and distribution of its goods. By means of vertical integration, big businesses in Alberta brought together mass production and mass distribution and grew larger in the process.

The Burns Meats' Calgary Plant, around 1920, was a model of efficiency. Pat Burns' strategy of backward vertical integration into raw material sources and forward into distribution facilities, including many retail stores, enabled him to develop better meat products at lower prices and reduce business risks. This strategy helped his meat-packing business grow. (Courtesy of Nuburn Capital Corporation).

Pat Burns' desire to control production costs while also seizing the opportunities offered by the growing market for meat moved him to create a vertically integrated business firm. Initially, P. Burns & Company relied on other businesses for most of its raw materials: cattle, hogs, and sheep. This situation worried Burns, because he felt he was paying too much for raw materials and, even more importantly, because during times of peak production he could not always get enough of them. To lower costs and ensure a steady supply of livestock for his mass-production plant in Calgary, Burns sought to control his sources of raw materials. In 1892, he acquired a ranch at Olds, where he was soon fattening as many as 1,000 head of cattle.[126] Seven years later, in 1899, Burns purchased the McIntosh Sheep Ranch on Rosebud Creek northeast of Calgary along with its herd of 7,000 sheep.[127] In 1902, Burns bought William Roper Hull's large cattle ranch on Fish Creek. Burns took steps to control the sale of his meat products, purchasing a number of Hull meat shops in Alberta and British Columbia.[128] In addition, Burns set up other sales offices in Alberta and British Columbia cities and towns. Burns's integrated firm was one of the most influential institutions in the Alberta economy.

The development of vertical integration at the Burns meat-packing business and other meat companies reflected a basic change in the way the meat industry was organized in Alberta. The pre-1890s meat industry was largely unintegrated: different firms handled different stages of the production and distribution processes and relied on independent merchants to move their products from one stage to the next. As entrepreneurs such as Burns altered the structure of the meat industry, however, small merchants became less significant, and big firms emerged that integrated all the steps in production and marketing. Similarly, Alberta business executives in other industries, such as oil, used vertical integration to control the costs of production and take advantage of opportunities in the growing market.

■

Horizontal Integration

Horizontal integration was a second common response to the problems and opportunities of Alberta's expanding market. In horizontal integration, several firms, using similar processes to make similar products for similar markets, joined together. The reasons for horizontal integration, just as for vertical integration, were to lessen competition and carve out secure economic positions for firms. Such horizontal integration could enhance organizational capabilities, especially when the firms that combined were administratively centralized.

P. Burns & Company was a good example of horizontal integration, as Burns sought to control the rapidly growing meat industry in Alberta. In 1902, P. Burns & Company acquired William Roper Hull's meat-processing plant in Calgary.[129] Burns quickly established centralized administrative control over the Hull plant. Besides giving P. Burns & Company substantial cost advantages, this helped increase its organizational capabilities.

■

Alberta's Early Merger Movements

Business integration in Alberta, vertical as well as horizontal, occurred through mergers of previously independent firms. The holding company played a relatively small role in the mergers that took place in the province in the late nineteenth and early twentieth centuries. Some firms that grew by merger followed the path of consolidation, bringing together two or more enterprises into a holding company in which the formerly independent firms retained their firm names as the operating parts of the new corporation. For example, in 1923 United Dairies of Calgary became a holding company, consolidating Union Milk, Crystal Dairy, Central Creameries (Calgary), Central Creameries (British Columbia), and Red Deer Dairy Products.[130]

In contrast, acquisition figured prominently in the mergers that occurred in Alberta. A firm already in existence acquired control of small companies, which disappeared into the merger and saw their individual names vanish. Acquisition, as distinguished from consolidation, played the principal part in the merger movements that rolled over Alberta business in the late nineteenth and early twentieth centuries. Such acquisitions clustered in two time periods.

The first period came between the 1880s and 1914. During these years, acquisitions took place in nearly every type of business in Alberta. For instance, in 1899 Great West Saddlery Company acquired Edmonton Saddlery Company.[131] When J. H. Ashdown Hardware Company was formed in 1902, it absorbed Calgary Hardware Company.[132] In 1907, Thompson, Codville Company became a part of Georgeson and Company, a Calgary wholesale grocery establishment.[133] In 1909, James A. Powell & Company, an Edmonton farm implement firm, acquired Great West Implement Company.[134] Alberta Pacific Grain Company absorbed Alberta Grain Company of Edmonton in 1914.[135] Several of these firms soon started the move toward administrative centralization.

The second period of mergers by way of acquisition in Alberta began in the 1920s. Again, acquisitions occurred in almost every kind of business. For instance, in 1923, the Canadian Farm Implement Company acquired Alberta Foundry & Machine Company of Medicine Hat.[136] Redcliff Pressed Brick Company absorbed the Medicine Hat Brick and Tile Company in 1929.[137] In 1934, British American Oil Company acquired Bell Refining Company in Calgary.[138] The Edmonton hardware firm W. W. Arcade Limited absorbed W. W. Sales, a local hardware store, in 1947.[139] In 1954, Pioneer Grain Company acquired the Calgary-based Cummings Grain Company.[140] Five years later, in 1959, Western Grocers absorbed Jenkins' Groceteria.[141] These examples of mergers illustrate the growth in size of many firms.

There were numerous business motives for mergers in Alberta. The main one being to gain market power by uniting two or more firms in a single corporate enterprise, and another to control prices. Undeniably, many firms that grew big through mergers sought to lessen price competition. Mergers also occurred in order to exploit economies of scale.

A number of mergers did not succeed, however, some lasting only a few years. Among failed mergers was Canadian Farm Implement Company.[142] Sustained success in the market was often determined by a large corporation's ability to operate more efficiently than smaller firms that remained independent. Mergers that successfully exploited economies of scale frequently lasted.

■

Big Business as a Social Institution

During the decades after World War II, big business firms grew in significance beyond their economic role in Alberta society. Many of these companies offered security and good pay for rising numbers of managers as well as for workers. Albertans enjoyed a high standard of living in the 1950s and 1960s. Compared to the Great Depression of the 1930s, recessions were short-lived. After some contentious strikes during the war, labour relations were much calmer than they had been in the 1930s, partly because the executives of corporations learned that an improvement in personnel policies could lead to fewer disruptions to the workflow within a firm.

Like managers, workers during the prosperous postwar decades were relatively confident of the security of their jobs. In return for their security, workers and managers gave their loyalty to their companies in this period of economic growth. Large firms, in turn, were loyal to management. With the evolution of personnel policies, a typical big Alberta company provided security from the time of a person's initial employment to retirement and into the retirement years. Firms had set up a variety of benefit programs for employees before the end of World War II that were extended during the postwar prosperity. For example, in 1950, Jenkins' Groceteria launched a pension plan for its employees. In the process, the company committed itself to making an important contribution to the plan for past and future service. During the same year, the company established a hospitalization and surgical benefits program for its employees and their dependents, in addition to broadening its long-standing group life insurance policy for its employees.[143] Jenkins' Groceteria titled its employees magazine *Gold N Drule* and offered its employees security in exchange for good work, as well as recreation, including participation in the company's bowling league.

Similarly, in 1950, Imperial Oil provided additional security for its employees by improving its group life insurance plan for them. As well, in that year the company enhanced its training program for its senior managers through the expansion of supervisors' conferences. Five years later, in 1955, Imperial Oil renewed its emphasis on the benefits it offered to the surviving members of the families of deceased employees. The company paid particular attention to meeting the needs of widows, children, and even grandchildren.[144]

Many corporate Albertans enjoyed company-owned recreational facilities, attended festive parties and picnics, and participated in singing groups. For instance, employees, family, and friends always joined Frederick C. Mannix and his wife Margaret at the Mannix enterprises' annual Christmas party. Frenchie Hamilton, a supervisor in the company's railway construction division, observed:

The Christmas party was the highlight of the year for most of us. You were treated like a king. You got a beautiful hotel room, nice meals, dancing, and then the big get-together, where you'd meet people you'd known for years. Fred and Margie and the family, all of them would be there, and they just treated you like you were part of the family, coming home for Christmas dinner.[145]

Most leaders in big firms in Alberta during the 1950s and 1960s came from middle- or upper-income families. Rags to riches careers were exceptions, rather than the rule, in Alberta business. Many of Alberta's leading business executives benefited from an upbringing in comfortable circumstances and from a superior education. A fairly large number had attended college or university. Coming from backgrounds of some privilege, nearly all executives running big businesses were men. They sought acceptance as members of the larger society in Alberta. The 1950s were the years of the business executive in the gray flannel suit, men who tried to blend into the downtown crowds.

In the 1950s and 1960s, the prosperity of the Alberta economy and the handsome profits earned by many big businesses allowed executives to carry forward traditions of philanthropy and social responsibility. Corporation executives played active roles in the development of community philanthropic organizations, providing financial support as well as leadership, and participated in the formation of local business groups intended to foster urban renewal and growth. The Canadian National Railways and other large corporations, for instance, helped finance the rebuilding of downtown Edmonton in the 1960s.

■

Persistence of Small Businesses in Alberta

Despite its importance, the rise of big business did not permeate the entire Alberta economy. Small firms persisted as a significant part of Alberta's business system. In manufacturing, commerce, farming, and service industries, small enterprises remained viable concerns. In 1939, at least half of Alberta's industrial workers had jobs in firms of 100 or fewer employees. Hundreds of small businesses with five to twenty workers continued in manufacturing and commerce on the eve of World War II.

Small manufacturing businesses in Alberta survived and flourished by using important strategies. They succeeded by specializing in a particular product: in this way, they found niche markets that big firms could not easily exploit with scale advantages. Sometimes these were local and regional markets and sometimes markets for products that required specialized processes involving custom work. The small manufacturers did not mass-produce large quantities of standardized goods for Alberta and Canadian consumers. Instead of attempting a large-scale approach, they turned out relatively small quantities of precision products with limited total demand. Small manufacturers also succeeded by providing special services to customers and developing a reputation for dependability. Indeed, service was one of the most important products sold by small industrialists. The route to survival for small manufacturing businesses lay in their ability to combine service with the discovery of markets of a specialized nature that could be satisfied by small production runs of specialty goods. Small manufacturers in Alberta continued to respond in these ways throughout the twentieth century.

The experiences of Edmonton textile makers illustrate continuing opportunities for small businesses in manufacturing in the age of big business. Their owners sought out new market niches, niches provided by changing fashions and seasons. The growth of the tailoring firm La Fleche Brothers of Edmonton suggests the continuing importance of small businesses in manufacturing across Alberta. Formed in 1906 by brothers Joseph and Tripoli La Fleche, La Fleche Brothers developed a specialty product for a niche market, custom-tailored men's suits.[146] Over the years, orders for suits grew, and La Fleche Brothers emerged as a highly successful business, an important family firm in Alberta lasting to the present time.[147]

■

Alberta's New Business System

The rise of big businesses, coupled with the persistence of small businesses, changed Alberta's business system during the twentieth century. A dual system appeared, with big businesses at the centre and small businesses at the periphery of the province's new business system. Central businesses, such as P. Burns & Company and Imperial Oil, were capital-intensive firms. Most central firms, besides enjoying significant economies of scale, were vertically integrated. They used mass-production and mass-distribution methods. In addition, they engaged in research and development and were managed by executives who supervised activities related to the production and distribution of goods. In contrast, small businesses or peripheral firms were usually labour-intensive instead of capital-intensive and seldom used mass-production techniques.

With the rise of big business, there was also a change in the nature of government-business relations in Alberta. At the federal, provincial, and municipal levels, governments continued their developmental policy of assisting Alberta business enterprises in order to build up the local, provincial, and national economies. By World War I, however, a new element had made its appearance in government-business relations, the regulation of business by the government, especially the federal government. Beginning with railways in the 1880s, the federal government went on to exercise its regulatory powers over other businesses as well in the early twentieth century.

NOTES TO CHAPTER FIVE

1. *Journals of the Legislative Assembly of the Province of Canada*, vol. 13, 1854-55, Appendix (Y.Y.), Reports of the Commissioners appointed to inquire into a series of Accidents and Detentions on the Great Western Railway, Canada West, 7 February 1855; *Lambton Observer and Western Advertiser*, 2 November 1854.

2. Alfred D. Chandler, Jr., *The Visible Hand: The Managerial Revolution in American Business* (Cambridge, Mass.: Harvard University Press, 1977).

3. *Edmonton Journal*, 14 February 1947.

4. Imperial Oil Archives, Toronto, *The Story of Imperial Oil* (Toronto: Imperial Oil Limited, 1991), 10.

5. Harold A. Innis, *A History of the Canadian Pacific Railway* (Toronto: University of Toronto Press, 1971), 284; T.D. Regehr, *The Canadian Northern Railway: Pioneer Road of the Northern Prairies, 1895-1918* (Toronto: MacMillan of Canada, 1976), 479.

6. *Albertan*, 28 February 1913.

7. Pierre Berton, *The National Dream: The Great Railway, 1871-1881* (Toronto: McClelland & Stewart, 1970), 18.

8. *Albertan*, 28 February 1913.

9. John A. Eagle, *The Canadian Pacific Railway and the Development of Western Canada* (Montreal: McGill-Queen's University Press, 1989), 3-4.

10. Ibid., 22.

11. Mansel G. Blackford and K. Austin Kerr, *Business Enterprise in American History*, Third Edition (Boston, Mass.: Houghton Mifflin Company, 1994), 130-131.

12. Eagle, *The Canadian Pacific Railway*, 22.

13. *Albertan*, 28 February 1913.

14. Canadian Pacific Railway Corporate Archives, Montreal, Canadian Pacific Railway Letterbook, Winnipeg, 18 November 1910, William Whyte to Thomas G. Shaughnessy.

15. Ibid., Montreal, 19 November 1910, Thomas G. Shaughnessy to William Whyte.

16. Alberta Municipal Affairs Archives, Edmonton, *Alberta Census for 1991*.

17. *Albertan*, 13 February 1937.

18. *Henderson's Calgary Directory for 1914*, 601.

19. GAIA, M1470, Great West Saddlery Company Papers, box 1, file 3, Calgary, 27 March 1914, C. D. Edwards to R. J. Hutchings.

20. Ibid.

21. Alberta Corporate Registry, T. Hutchinson Company Ltd. file.

22. Great West Saddlery Company Papers, ledgers, 1900-1912.

23. *Dun & Bradstreet Reference Book*, September 1921, 12.

24. Calgary Land Titles Office, mortgage records, 1890-1905.

25. Alberta Corporate Registry, Gainers Ltd. file.

26. *Edmonton Journal*, 29 January 1966.

27. Alberta Corporate Registry, Gainers Ltd. file.

28. City of Edmonton Archives, Gainers clipping file, A. M. MacDonald, "An All-Alberta Company, 1891-1961," pamphlet (Edmonton, 1961).

29. *Edmonton Free Press*, 24 January 1962.

30. Alberta Corporate Registry, Gainers Ltd. file.

31. *Edmonton Journal*, 29 January 1966.

32. Alberta Corporate Registry, Gainers Ltd. file; *Edmonton Journal*, 3 February 1979.

33. *Edmonton Free Press*, 24 January 1962.

34. *Edmonton Journal*, 25 November 1972.

35. Ibid.

36. *Edmonton Journal*, 22 June 1973.

37. *Edmonton Journal*, 28 April 1979; *Globe and Mail*, 12 August 1991.

38. *Edmonton Journal*, 3 August 1982.

39. Henry C. Klassen, "The Hudson's Bay Company in Southwestern Alberta, 1874-1905," in Jennifer S. H. Brown, W. J. Eccles and Donald P. Heldman, eds., *The Fur Trade Revisited: Selected Papers of the Sixth North American Fur Trade Conference, Mackinac Island, Michigan, 1991* (East Lansing: Michigan State University Press, 1994), 400.

40. Ibid., 401-408.

41. *Edmonton Journal*, 1 November 1946.

42. Ibid., 9 September 1964.

43. Alberta Corporate Registry, Johnstone Walker Ltd. file.

44. *Edmonton Bulletin*, 1 July 1918.

45. Alberta Corporate Registry, Johnstone Walker Ltd. file.

46. *Edmonton Bulletin*, 1 July 1918.

47. Ibid., 11 July 1907.

48. *Edmonton Journal*, 29 October 1936.

49. City of Edmonton Archives, Johnstone Walker clipping file.

50. *Edmonton Bulletin*, 1 July 1918.

51. *Edmonton Journal*, 29 October 1936.

52. *Edmonton Bulletin*, 1 July 1918.

53. *Edmonton Capital*, 3 January 1910.

54. City of Edmonton Archives, Johnstone Walker Ltd. clipping file.

55. *Edmonton Journal*, 2 May 1935.

56. Alberta Corporate Registry, Johnstone Walker Ltd. file.

57. *Edmonton Journal*, 11 November 1963.

58. *Edmonton Journal*, 19 August 1959.

59. *Edmonton Journal*, 9 September 1964.

60. Alberta Corporate Registry, Johnstone Walker Ltd. file.

61. *Real Estate Weekly* (Edmonton), 9-15 November 1989.

62. Interview by the author with Ronald H. Jenkins, 8 November 1973.

63. Ibid.

64. *Calgary, Alberta* (1911), 180.

65. Jenkins interview, 8 November 1973.

66. GAIA, M6494, Jenkins' Groceteria Ltd. Papers, "35 Years of Progress, 1909-1944."

67. Alberta Corporate Registry, Groceteria Stores Company Ltd. file.

68. Jenkins interview, 8 November 1973.

69. *Calgary Herald*, 13 October 1923.

70. *Calgary Herald*, 9 December 1929.

71. Jenkins interview, 8 November 1973; Alberta Corporate Registry, Louie Petrie Ltd. file.

72. Jenkins interview, 8 November 1973.

73. Jenkins' Groceteria Ltd. Papers, "35 Years of Progress 1909-1944."

74. Jenkins' Groceteria Ltd. Papers, "Historical Sketch of Jenkins' Groceteria Limited," 3.

75. GAIA, Interview by Charles Ursenbach with Ronald Henry Jenkins, September 1975.

76. Ibid.

77. Henry C. Klassen, "Family Businesses in Calgary to 1939." In Max Foran and Sheilagh Jameson, eds., *Citymakers: Calgarians after the Frontier* (Calgary: The Historical Society of Alberta, Chinook Country Chapter, 1987), 317.

78. *Canadian Grocer*, 20 June 1959, 20.

79. "Historical Sketch of Jenkins' Groceteria Limited," 1-3.

80. *Canadian Grocer*, 20 June 1959, 18-20.

81. Blackford and Kerr, *Business Enterprise in American History*, 229; Mira Wilkins, *The Maturing of Multinational Enterprise: American Business Abroad from 1914 to 1970* (Cambridge, Mass.: Harvard University Press, 1974), 135.

82. Klassen, "Family Businesses in Calgary to 1939," 317.

83. *Edmonton Journal*, 6 September 1989; *Calgary Herald*, 6 September 1989.

84. Max Foran and Heather MacEwan Foran, *Calgary Canada's Frontier Metropolis* (Toronto: Windsor Publications, 1982), 296.

85. *Dun & Bradstreet Reference Book*, July 1939, 1-123; *Henderson's Edmonton Directory for 1939*, 660; *Henderson's Calgary Directory for 1939*, 657.

86. *Edmonton Journal*, 6 September 1989.

87. *Alberta Report*, 27 March 1989, insert, "Canada Safeway Turns Sixty," 1-104.

88. *Edmonton Journal*, 6 September 1989; James Careless, "Happy Birthday, Safeway," *Canadian Grocer* 103 (October 1989), 22-26.

89. Canada Safeway Archives, Calgary, Safeway records.

90. David H. Breen, *Alberta's Petroleum Industry and the Conservation Board* (Edmonton: University of Alberta Press, 1993), 15.

91. Imperial Oil Archives, Calgary, *The Imperial Oil Story* (Toronto: Imperial Oil Limited, 1991), 7.

92. Graham D. Taylor, "From Branch Operation to Integrated Subsidiary: The Reorganisation of Imperial Oil under Walter Teagle, 1911-1917," *Business History 34* (July 1992), 49-68.

93. *Calgary Herald*, 13 October 1923.

94. *The Imperial Oil Story*, 11; Calgary Herald, 13 October 1923.

95. *The Maple Leaf*, April 1924, 54.

96. Ibid.

97. Alberta Corporate Registry, Imperial Oil Ltd. file.

98. Alfred D. Chandler, Jr., *Scale and Scope: The Dynamics of Industrial Capitalism* (Cambridge, Mass.: Harvard University Press, 1990), 92.

99. *Edmonton Journal*, 17 July 1948.

100. Alberta Corporate Registry, Imperial Oil Ltd. file.

101. Ibid.

102. Ibid.

103. Ibid.

104. David H. Breen, *Alberta's Petroleum Industry*, 659-660.

105. Imperial Oil Archives, Toronto, Organization Chart of Imperial Oil Limited, 1962; Alberta Corporate Registry, Imperial Oil Ltd. file.

106. City of Edmonton Archives, Imperial Oil Ltd. clipping file.

107. *The Imperial Oil Story*, 1.

108. Ibid.

109. *The Imperial Oil Story*, 24; Russell Felton, "Thick Black Gold," *Imperial Oil Review*, Winter 1987, 12-16; Peter McKenzie-Brown, Gordon Jaremko, and David Finch, *The Great Oil Age: The Petroleum Industry in Canada* (Calgary: Detselig Enterprise, 1993), 80-81.

110. Imperial Oil Archives, Calgary, Imperial Oil Ltd., Annual Report for 1995, 11.

111. Ibid.

112. *The Imperial Oil Story*, 47.

113. Quoted in Kenneth Bagnell, "The Shape of Change," *Imperial Oil Review, Vol. 70*, Winter 1986, 5.

114. *Calgary Herald*, 8 June 1983.

115. *Financial Post*, 26 November 1977; *Frederick Charles Mannix, 1913-1995* (Calgary: Loram Group, 1995).

116. *Calgary Herald*, 6 June 1998.

117. *Frederick Charles Mannix, 1913-1995*.

118. Ibid.

119. *The Mannix Story, 70th Anniversary Issue* (April 1968).

120. *Frederick Charles Mannix, 1913-1995.*

121. Ibid.

122. Ibid.

123. *Calgary Herald*, 6 June 1998.

124. *Frederick Charles Mannix, 1913-1995.*

125. Calgary Herald, 3 August 1995.

126. Grant MacEwan, *Pat Burns: Cattle King* (Saskatoon: Western Producer Prairie Books, 1979), 131-134.

127. Ibid., 102.

128. Ibid., 139-141.

129. Ibid., 139-140.

130. Klassen, "Family Businesses in Calgary to 1939," 311.

131. Alberta Corporate Registry, Great West Saddlery Company Ltd. file; City of Edmonton Archives, Tax Revisions file; *Dun & Bradstreet Reference Book*, September 1899, 363.

132. Alberta Corporate Registry, J.H. Ashdown Hardware Company Ltd. file; *Dun & Bradstreet Reference Book*, September 1900, 364; *Dun & Bradstreet Reference Book*, September 1906, 6.

133. *Calgary Herald*, 13 October 1923; Alberta Corporate Registry, Georgeson and Company Ltd. file.

134. City of Edmonton Archives, newspaper clipping file, James A. Powell & Company; Alberta Corporate Registry, Great West Implement Company Ltd. file.

135. Alberta Corporate Registry, Alberta Grain Company Ltd. file.

136. Alberta Corporate Registry, Alberta Foundry & Machine Company Ltd. file.

137. I-XL Industries Limited Archives, Medicine Hat, W. Jack Sissons, "The History of Redcliff Pressed Brick Company Limited," Medicine Hat, typescript copy, 1995, 13.

138. Gulf Canada Archives, Calgary, *Gulf Oil Canada ... Proud Past, Exciting Future* (1969), 23.

139. City of Edmonton Archives, newspaper clipping file, W. W. Arcade Ltd.

140. Klassen, "Family Businesses in Calgary to 1939," 315.

141. Ibid., 317.

142. Alberta Corporate Registry, Alberta Foundry & Machine Company Ltd. file.

143. Historical Sketch of Jenkins' Groceteria Limited, 3.

144. Alberta Corporate Registry, Imperial Oil Ltd. file.

145. *Frederick Charles Mannix, 1913-1995.*

146. City of Edmonton Archives, newspaper clippings files, La Fleche Brothers file.

147. *Edmonton Sun*, 7 July 1995.

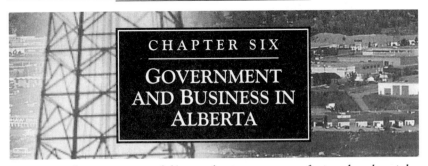

CHAPTER SIX

GOVERNMENT AND BUSINESS IN ALBERTA

The emergence of the new business system of central and peripheral firms led to a debate over the character of the Alberta political economy. Although a number of Albertans admired big businessmen, others looked upon them with suspicion. Some argued that if the economic power of large corporations continued, it would threaten fundamental democratic values. In general, the Alberta response to the coming of big business was to attempt to control it through regulation by the government, particularly the federal government.

Despite the diversity of interests and attitudes, there was widespread agreement in Alberta that economic development should be promoted. Whether moved by a desire to get ahead or by the profit motive, Albertans favoured a world of economic growth. In the striving society that existed in the province, individuals pushed themselves to take advantage of the opportunities appearing in their developing economy. An intense work ethic embraced adventurous young men and women in Alberta. They exalted the ancient virtue of industry, not only because they felt that it could help lead to personal success in business, but also because they believed it could contribute to economic growth in the province. Then, too, if business success was a primary goal of Albertans, the development of the province's natural resources was a widely accepted objective of public policy. In possession of an abundant supply of productive land, favourable climate, rich coal fields, and huge oil and natural gas reserves, Alberta attached importance to speedier growth aided by federal government encouragement.

Both large and small business leaders in Alberta interested themselves in town and city politics to serve the interests of their firms, as well as to serve their community and gain personal status. Local politics were often aimed at preventing higher assessments, increases in taxes, and other financial burdens, as well as securing cash bonuses and property tax exemptions. Businessmen, who dominated the early city and town councils in Alberta, found it helpful to build the reputation of their communities for reliable goods and reasonable prices through regulations.

As the business world in Alberta grew in size and complexity, many entrepreneurs in a variety of businesses devoted themselves to provincial politics. Attendance at the Alberta legislature in Edmonton became important to establish a regulatory structure. Provincial regulatory activity often occurred in response to the needs of sound business. For instance, the legislature set weights and measures, established rules regarding corporations, mortgages, sale of personal property, and probate, and enacted laws of contract and agency. Businessmen-politicians, however, sometimes supported only those provincial expenditures that would directly assist their communities. Battles in the Alberta legislature tended to revolve around the issue of which area would benefit from what provincial action.

The rise of large-scale business enterprise in Alberta brought political protest and especially federal legislation during the late nineteenth and early twentieth centuries. A major political theme was control and regulation of railways, department stores, and large industrial firms. Farmers, merchants, and small manufacturers led the protest against big business in Alberta. Despite political campaigns and legislative action at the federal level, large corporations continued to expand.

Small and big business leaders, however, shared a set of beliefs about the nature of the Alberta economy and the role of the federal government. Both agreed that there should be a measure of government-business co-operation in economic planning. Traditionally, both big and small businesses appreciated federal government policies aimed at promoting economic development. Both wanted the government's developmental policies to continue in the late nineteenth and early twentieth centuries. Although small businesses desired legislation to check large corporations' power, they sought laws designed to promote economic growth in Alberta.

Big businesses, which also supported federal government intervention to boost Alberta's economic fortunes, criticized government, urging the development of a laissez-faire policy. Like Adam Smith in the eighteenth century, they took the position that too much government action would inevitably stifle private initiative. For corporate leaders in Alberta, laissez faire was wrapped up in the whole issue of economic freedom. In reaction to calls for government regulation of their business practices, they advocated the development of a political economy that permitted entrepreneurs to participate freely in Alberta's economic growth.

Entrepreneurs organizing new railways and factories in Alberta, though they had a reputation for great political influence, often found it difficult to trust politicians. Such entrepreneurs wanted predictability in their relationship with federal officials. Most Albertans, unwilling to forgo the benefits of big businesses, turned to politics to regulate but not to drive them out of the province. The major issues of the political economy that dominated Alberta's agenda concerned railways, the tariff, labour, combinations, banking, farming, and the oil and natural gas industry. The policies that the federal government adopted in its effort to resolve these issues significantly affected the development of business in Alberta.

Government Promotion and Regulation of Railways

The evolution of early railway promotion in Alberta by the federal government, and then regulation as well, can best be understood by a look at the development of the Canadian Pacific Railway. Still underdeveloped, Alberta in the late nineteenth and early twentieth centuries needed a better transportation system to marshal its resources for growth. To make progress in that direction, the province depended to an amazing extent on active, interventionist government.

From the beginning, the railway business in Alberta was a heavily subsidized service. The federal government helped create the market, long before railway technology could sustain province-wide and nation-wide freight and passenger service. During the 1880s, the federal government funded the construction of the Canadian Pacific Railway with a land subsidy of 25,000,000 acres in the prairie West and a cash subsidy of $25,000,000.[1] There was some income for the railway from land sales out of its land grant, but this income decreased as settlement in the prairies slowed in the mid-1880s. The railway also used the land grant as collateral for loans, including one of $22,500,000 in 1884 and another of $5,000,000 in 1885 from the federal government, to provide a portion of the capital needed.[2]

Federal political leaders took their first reluctant steps to consider the regulation of Canada's railways only after the Canadian Pacific Railway was completed in 1885. Responding to pressure from Ontario Conservative member of parliament D'Alton McCarthy to create an independent commission to investigate the affairs of railways, Prime Minister John A. Macdonald appointed a royal commission in 1886 to study the question. A commission of four members, led by Alexander Galt, former finance minister, recommended not the creation of an independent railway commission, but rather that the old Railway Committee of the Privy Council be given stronger powers to enforce legislation pertaining to railway affairs, including charges for moving freight and passengers.[3] Macdonald's response was to extend such powers to the Railway Committee through the revised railway law enacted by parliament in 1888.

The Railway Committee was assisted by a three-member Railway Rates Commission of civil servants appointed by the Conservative government of John Thompson in November 1894 to hold public hearings on railway rates in the prairie West. All three commissioners — chairman P. S. Archibald, William Pearce of Calgary, and W. H. Allison — were officials in the federal Department of the Interior. Although the Railway Rates Commission left unresolved the important question of the need to apply independent public expertise to the affairs of railways in the prairies, it did provide a forum for the discussion of prairie rates.

Small shippers in Alberta and other parts of the prairies lacked the leverage of big shippers to negotiate with the railways for favourable rates and turned to the Railway Rates Commission. At public hearings in Edmonton and Calgary in February 1895, small merchants and other business owners, supported politically by small farmers in the surrounding areas who had organized as the Patrons of Industry, pressed for stronger federal regulation of Canadian Pacific Railway rates than was possible under existing laws.[4] They demanded a reduction in the railway's rates. Operating in an industry burdened with high fixed costs during the difficult years in the mid-1880s, the Canadian Pacific had strong economic reasons to maintain a rate structure designed to maximize income. At the hearing in Calgary, small wholesale merchant James Bannerman complained: "I am speaking now from the standpoint of a Calgary merchant doing a jobbing trade north and south on the branch lines. High rates retard trade and travel."[5] The Railway Rates Commission, however, concluded that the Canadian Pacific's rate structure was acceptable.[6]

A new stage in the history of railway regulation began when the Liberal government under Wilfrid Laurier secured the passage of the Railway Act of 1903 to create the Board of Railway Commissioners as the nation's first federal independent regulatory railway commission, one that was separate from the executive, legislative, and judicial branches of government.[7] The law gave this three-member Board, led by Andrew G. Blair, former railways minister in Laurier's government, the power to regulate what railways charged large favoured shippers as well as small shippers. The law required the Board to ensure that freight rates were reasonable and just.[8]

The growth of the Alberta economy in the early twentieth century complicated railway politics. Rapid economic development meant that railways faced increasing demands for service, and these demands made it necessary to improve their tracks and equipment in the province. The capital needed for improvements was not easy to raise, however, because of the railways' rising costs. The opposition railways faced from shippers made it difficult to increase freight rates and plough the resulting savings back into their businesses. The Board of Railway Commissioners often found itself adjusting railway rates after careful investigation.

The Railway Commissioners had considerable impact upon Alberta's business system. For instance, in July 1909, in *Cardston Board of Trade v. Alberta Railway & Irrigation Company*, the Railway Commissioners ruled in favour of the Cardston Board of Trade. The small merchants in the Cardston Board of Trade had close ties with small farmers and ranchers in the surrounding region. Generally sympathetic to the needs of merchants, ranchers, and farmers, all of whom relied on railway service, the Railway Commissioners ordered the Alberta Railway & Irrigation Company, which was controlled by the Canadian Pacific Railway, to reduce its passenger charges from four to three cents per mile on its line south of Lethbridge, making them the same as the Canadian Pacific's rates north of Lethbridge.[9]

In some other rate disputes in Alberta, the Board of Railway Commissioners ruled in favour of the railways, including the Canadian Northern, the Grand Trunk Pacific, and the Canadian Pacific.[10] The Board did not always respond positively to the complaints of small merchants and farmers, but required railways to demonstrate the necessity of higher charges, for freight and passengers, and adhere to published rates. In addition to the crucial rate issue, there were concerns about railway service. One of the chief functions of Board regulation was to settle a variety of disputes about service important to business owners. For the Board, these disputes revolved around issues such as the placement of a grade crossing in Edmonton, the extension of a spur line in Okotoks, and the provision of moveable partitions in cars to enable Clover Bar farmers to maintain the identity of their small shipments of cattle or hogs.

While railway regulation remained an important matter of concern, the federal government's policies still tended toward development. For example, in 1897, the Laurier government subsidized the Canadian Pacific's branch line, the Crow's Nest Pass Railway linking Lethbridge to Nelson, British Columbia, with a cash subsidy of $11,000 per mile. This was a large subsidy, aimed at meeting forty-five percent of the estimated cost of building the Crow's Nest Pass Railway.[11] In return, the Canadian Pacific agreed to reduce rates on certain classes of merchandise shipped from Fort William to all points on the company's railway in the prairie West including Alberta: a thirty-three and one third percent reduction on all green and fresh fruits; a twenty percent reduction on coal oil; and a ten percent reduction on agricultural implements, binder twine, livestock, cordage, iron, wire, window glass, building paper, roofing felt, paints, household furniture, and wooden ware.[12] The Canadian Pacific also agreed to a reduction of three cents per 100 lbs on grain and flour shipped from all points in the prairie West to Fort William. These rates, soon known as the Crow rates and later also largely adopted by the other railways, pleased many farmers and merchants in Alberta.

World War I brought changes to the situation, however. Farmers and merchants in Alberta, favoured by the Crow rates, saw their advantage disappear in July 1918 with the Robert Borden government's decision to suspend the Crow's Nest Pass Agreement of 1897 by order-in-council under the War Measures Act to help railways meet wartime inflation. Then, in 1919, an amendment to the Railway Act placed the Crow rates under the jurisdiction of the Board of Railway Commissioners.[13] The Board had to deal with a bitter dispute, in which the railways opposed the restoration of the Crow rates and the farmers in Alberta, Saskatchewan, and Manitoba sought to bring them into force once again.

Railways faced an especially significant development in the years immediately after World War I: the rise of a farmers' movement in the prairie West that created the Progressive Party, the second largest party in the House of Commons after the federal election of 1921. In the same year, the Liberal Party took power under Prime Minister Mackenzie King, who defended the right of the federal government to enact regulatory legislation. In 1922, in response to pressure from the Progressives, he restored by statute some of the Crow rates — grain and flour moving from Alberta, Saskatchewan, and Manitoba to Fort William.[14] Yet, the legislation did not require the railways to lower their rates on westbound commodities. Thus, King used the power of the state to promote simultaneously the growth of the farmers' and the railways' business.

Despite King's action, the old regulatory machinery — the Board of Railway Commissioners — remained and continued to have jurisdiction over the Crow rates and other railway rates. Many Albertans knew that regulation, with or without the Board, would often be a political activity. Generally speaking, regulation of railways in Alberta was a political settlement, made in an attempt to protect the different interests of all the businesses affected.

■

Tariff and Federal Regulation

In the history of federal regulation in Alberta during the early twentieth century, the tariff was also important. A subject of substantial controversy, the tariff became an issue that divided party platforms. In spite of complaints from prairie farmers and the efforts, particularly of the Liberals led by Wilfrid Laurier, to have Parliament lower customs duties, the general trend of Canadian tariff policy was protectionist, similar to the policy championed by John A. Macdonald. Central Canadian manufacturers could look forward to new opportunities. In 1911, the Conservative Party under Robert Borden gained power, partly because he forged a significant measure of agreement that a protective tariff would help the federal government foster economic growth and increase the nation's prosperity.

In the years that followed, partisan debates over the tariff continued to reflect conflicting business interests. During the early 1920s, Alberta farmers who purchased manufactured goods felt that a low tariff would be to their advantage. George G. Coote, a Nanton area farmer, former local manager of the Bank of Hamilton, and Progressive Member of Parliament for Macleod, was a low tariff advocate.[15] Lowering customs duties on American farm implements, he believed, would help the Alberta agricultural industry. On the other hand, there were central Canadian farm machinery manufacturers, such as the Massey-Harris Company of Toronto that depended on tariff protection for their growth and development.

George G. Coote (1880-1959), a Nanton area farmer who first became a Progressive and then a United Farmers of Alberta member of the House of Commons, helped focus Canadian attention on the solution of farmers' economic problems at parliamentary sessions in the 1920s and 1930s. Eventually, Coote became a director of the Bank of Canada, as well as a director of its subsidiary, the Industrial Development Bank.

(Courtesy of Donald H. Coote and Blank & Stoller).

Emotions surrounding the tariff issue flared, coming to a climax in 1924, as prairie Progressives led by Robert Forke stepped up their demand for lower tariff duties on farm implements.

The popularity of the Progressive rhetoric worried Prime Minister Mackenzie King, whose political fortunes were tied to the Progressives. It meant that he must favour lower customs duties to stay in power. Accordingly, he made a skillful effort to win the backing of the Progressives. He had no trouble defining his own position. "I had Mr. Forke, Leader of the Progressives, to lunch," King noted in his diary on 27 February 1924, "and talked with him of the line I was intending to take. To go in for taking the duties off of Agric. Implements, etc. if the Progressives would be half decent in their support."[16] Shortly thereafter, James Robb, minister of finance, maneuvered the budget through Parliament that made significant reductions in the duties on agricultural implements. The reductions pleased most farmers in Alberta and the other prairie provinces, but aroused the resentment of central Canadian manufacturers. The negative reaction of the manufacturers was hardly surprising to King. After all, he knew that the conflicting business interests in the tariff issue made it impossible for him to arrange a compromise that was fully satisfactory.

What to do with the tariff in the long run remained a puzzle. In his quest for a solution to the problem, King turned to the idea of a tariff board. "I advocated today again," he wrote in his diary on 5 April 1924, "a board to advise Gov't on tariff matters, not to shape the tariff, but secure information. The idea carried" cabinet.[17] King was not convinced that a tariff commission as suggested by Montreal manufacturers was appropriate.[18] Cabinet "discussed question of a board to advise the Minister of Finance on Tariff matters," King noted. "We have become unanimous on agreeing to it, as necessary for purposes of information — permanent informed trained officials — not a tariff commission to take the tariff out of politics."[19] From King's viewpoint, political pressures would continue to shape the tariff. Also, the federal government needed to retain control of the tariff as a way to secure revenues.[20]

Gradually, manufacturers and farmers came to support the board idea. On 7 April 1926, King created the Advisory Board on Tariff and Taxation. This new Board was not a federal regulatory body. Rather, it was to serve as an instrument of information for the Department of Finance, and submit reports to King. The Tariff Advisory Board, however, got off to a rough start. King attempted to make a careful search for helpful appointees, but for a variety of reasons not one of the three original members remained in office for longer than several months. King soon appointed W. H. Moore, a former lawyer, as chairman and H. H. Racine, a wholesaler in Montreal, and F. S. Jacobs, a farmer in Alberta, as the other two members.[21]

The Tariff Advisory Board and King did not, however, fulfill the expectations of many farmers, manufacturers, and other business owners. Between April 1926 and February 1927, King received fifty-one applications for changes in the tariff. Robb instructed the Board to investigate and report to him on these applications for tariff changes. By mid-February 1927, the Board had completed a thorough investigation of most of the applications by holding numerous public hearings and had submitted its reports to Robb.[22] A negative response greeted these reports. King, with the support of Robb and the other members of the government, decided not to include any changes in the tariff in the 1927 budget. Though faithfully carrying out its tasks, the Board was making little impact.

Meanwhile, King had proceeded to make changes in the tariff on automobiles and motor trucks without referring this particular issue to the Tariff Advisory Board.[23] His action came in response to dissatisfaction with automobile and motor truck prices in many provinces, including Alberta. Alberta farmer George Coote, like many other Canadians, was disturbed at the high prices of automobiles and motor trucks. "The only reason that I can see why we have only one car to fourteen of our population, and the United States one to every six is that cars are too expensive in this country and the people cannot afford to buy them," said Coote on 29 March 1926 in the Commons. He added:

> in one town in my constituency this fall there were fifty-seven men delivering wheat to the elevator with motor trucks. Some of them were hauling the wheat a distance of twenty-eight miles. There are many others still hauling wheat with horses. I wish hon. Members in this House could realize what a boon it would be to these farmers if they could afford to own motor trucks and deliver their wheat with them.

The automobile *"industry,"* Coote emphasized, *"does not need a thirty-five percent protection in order to carry on. If the tariff were reduced they would have to reduce prices; more cars would be sold, and they would have an increase of employment rather than a decrease. I do not think that statement can be successfully challenged."*[24]

King did not challenge the statement; he persuaded Robb to accept Coote's argument.

Shortly afterward, on April 15, Robb presented his budget. "There is a pronounced sentiment throughout Canada," he stated, "that the automobile industry enjoys more protection than is needed to maintain it on a reasonably profitable basis, and in deference to that sentiment we propose a downward readjustment."[25] The duty was reduced on automobiles valued at not more than $1,200 and on motor trucks and motor cycles from thirty-five to twenty percent. In an effort to encourage domestic production, the government provided a drawback, by which Canadian manufacturers received a twenty-five percent rebate on any duty paid on parts for their vehicles if the Canadian content in the finished product was at least fifty percent.[26] The automobile industry mounted a strong critique of the reductions in the tariff. Despite the tariff changes, however, manufacturers such as Ford-Canada continued to do well over the next few years.[27] Farmers and other business owners in Alberta who purchased cars and trucks now naturally felt elated. The new tariff regulations proved to be of considerable help in improving their situation.

Although King had decided to lower the tariff on cars and trucks without seeking information from the Tariff Advisory Board, he allowed it to continue to investigate and report to Robb on applications for tariff changes. King believed that the federal government should establish the tariff policy.[28] The final authority over the tariff remained in the hands of elected officials.

■

Labour and Business Regulation

Besides this important tariff issue, there were concerns about federal government policy on relations between employers and workers in Alberta. Bitter conflict between workers and management often resulted in strikes.

For instance, on the morning of 9 March 1906, most of the 524 miners who worked in the Alberta Railway and Irrigation Company coal mine at Lethbridge walked off the job.[29] Mine cars being loaded at that time were abandoned on the spot. Like the disturbances that had marked the strike at the mine in 1894, violence accompanied this strike.[30] Lasting nearly nine months, the 1906 miners' strike caused an acute shortage of fuel in Alberta and especially in Saskatchewan. The human problem of unemployment and distress among the workers was serious. Interruption of regular income made for a poorer diet and deterioration in health in the labour force at the Lethbridge coal mine. For unemployed workers, there was no such thing as adequate public relief and assistance, and private charity was usually insufficient. The reaction of Mackenzie King, then deputy minister of labour in Laurier's government, revealed that the federal method of regulation did not provide a perfect solution to labour-management disputes.

The strike occurred against a background of important developments in Alberta's coal industry in the previous year. Increased competition and falling coal prices had squeezed the coal companies' profits, forcing them to economize. Like most companies, the Alberta Railway and Irrigation Company held down its employees' wages. This refusal to increase wages, more than anything else, precipitated the strike by the United Mine Workers of America. Under the leadership of Frank Sherman, the Alberta Railway and Irrigation Company employees demanded higher wages, an eight-hour day for underground workers, a ten-hour day for surface workers, and union recognition.[31] When they failed in their attempt to enter into negotiations with the company, they walked out.

The Conciliation Act of 1900 empowered the federal government to appoint conciliation officers, at the request of either employers or workers involved in a dispute. As it happened, neither the Alberta Railway and Irrigation Company nor its employees requested government intervention. The dismay of prairie people faced with coal shortages and extremely cold weather in mid-November 1906, after the strike had dragged on for more than eight months, was felt more keenly in Saskatchewan than anywhere else in the prairie West. Premier Walter Scott of Saskatchewan impressed upon Laurier the seriousness of the situation. Pressures from Scott and others forced the federal government into a searching examination of the strike. On 17 November, Laurier sent King to Lethbridge to intervene.[32]

King arrived in Lethbridge five days later. In keeping with his usual method, he first undertook to ascertain the facts of the case. He interviewed the representative of the Alberta Railway and Irrigation Company and the representative of its employees, offering to serve as a conciliator. Soon both the company and the workers accepted King's offer. Using his talent for finding the peaceful ground, along with reference to Saskatchewan people who were freezing because of lack of coal, King worked out a harmonious compromise between the interests of the workers and those of the Alberta Railway and Irrigation Company.[33] On 2 December, the strike at last ended.[34] The settlement included a ten percent increase in wages for the workers and a process by which they could work with management to settle their grievances. The company, however, did not recognize the union. A more complete solution would require the federal regulatory system to acknowledge and accept the principle of collective bargaining.

For the Alberta Railway and Irrigation Company, the settlement meant that it resumed its normal operations and supplied coal dealers in Alberta, Saskatchewan, and elsewhere with much-needed coal. Because of the company's critical role in the prairie economy, the production and distribution of coal clearly promoted general economic growth in Alberta and the rest of the prairie West. Prairie society so depended on coal for present prosperity and future development that no regulatory effort was too much to keep coal companies in operation.

Acutely conscious of this situation, King undertook to show how the federal government could more effectively do the job of regulation. The best solution to the coal problem, he thought, was to find some means of coping with the whole question of labour-management disputes. In order to perform this function, the government must create an expert body — a regulatory board.

Pursuing this line of thinking, King prepared the Industrial Disputes Investigation Act which Parliament passed in March 1907.[35] Through the passage of this law, Parliament asserted its authority, albeit with little impact, over labour and business. The law provided that it was illegal to declare a strike or lockout in mines, transportation and communication firms, and public utilities before a three-man conciliation board representing the employer, the workers, and the public had investigated the dispute. Although the parties to the dispute were not required to accept the board's recommendation, always in the background, as the workers and the employer well knew, lay the pressure of public opinion. Behind most of the difficulties with this law was the fact that it neither embodied a major goal that the workers had in mind — collective bargaining — nor outlawed dismissal of employees and hiring of strike-breakers by the employer.

Although the Industrial Disputes Investigation Act compelled the federal government to intervene in an industrial dispute on the application of either party, there remained a substantial measure of uncertainty. The law, in the years immediately after its passage as well as in later decades, could not prevent strikes and lockouts. For example, in May 1907, miners at the H. W. McNeill Company in Canmore went on strike while an effort was being made to establish a board of conciliation.[36] In 1920, the Grand Trunk Pacific Railway in Edmonton suspended some of its machinists.[37] For the most part, business firms had the upper hand in labour-management conflict handled by a federal board of conciliation. This was also the case when a provincial board of conciliation was charged, under the Alberta Settlement of Labour Disputes Act of 1926, with the task of dealing with a labour-management dispute.[38]

The Industrial Disputes Investigation Act foreshadowed augmented federal authority over business and labour in Alberta. Many business owners in the province understood that success depended on co-operative relations with employees. Although labour-management conflict remained a province-wide concern, the first half of the twentieth century saw a reconciliation of interests between managers and workers at many business firms in Alberta. Overall, the conclusion is inescapable that important attempts at federal government regulation of labour and business began in the early years of this period, and these experiences provided a foundation on which a later generation of Canadians and Albertans built a stronger governmental system to regulate relations between employers and workers.

■

Regulation and the Anticombines Movement

Regulation of business combinations was also becoming a significant matter of concern in Alberta. During the late nineteenth and early twentieth centuries, this concern came from small merchants, farmers, and manufacturers, all of whom wanted an agency with wide investigatory powers that could put a stop to monopolistic practices by large corporations and combinations of firms. Alliances among firms robbed individual entrepreneurs of business opportunities. Small businesses desired a marketplace governed by the interactions of hundreds of small independent firms.

Initially, Parliament did not make a serious attempt to meet these wishes.[39] Rather, it passed the Prevention and Suppression of Combinations formed in restraint of Trade Act in 1889.[40] This statute declared business combinations illegal but created no new regulatory board or other machinery. Parliament left it to attorneys-general of the provinces to decide whether or not to prosecute businesses for combining with competitors in mergers or associations. But the Alberta attorney-general, like those in the other provinces, did not prosecute aggressively.

In 1908, in *Rex v. Clarke*, the Supreme Court of Alberta ruled against William Harold Clarke, an Edmonton lumber dealer, and other lumber merchants, formally known as the Alberta Retail Dealers' Association.[41] This association dominated its industry in Alberta and was reaching out to combine with its remaining competitors. The Court saw violation of the law and ruled that the Alberta Retail Dealers' Association was clearly preventing competition. Further, the Court noted that it was easy to demonstrate the association's price-fixing practices. Certainly, the decision informed the lumber dealers that they could not collaborate to fix prices. The Anticombines Act of 1889 thus remained a potentially important weapon against business combinations.

Small independent firms in Alberta and elsewhere in the nation felt that the law was not powerful enough. Parliament responded to this sentiment by passing the Combines Investigation Act in 1910.[42] This act, drafted by Mackenzie King, then minister of labour in Laurier's cabinet, empowered the federal government to set up temporary boards with broad investigatory powers to protect small firms from business combinations. The law required the government to appoint such federal boards after complaints against combinations had been aired in provincial courts. Once a provincial court had made a decision in regard to a particular business combination and a federal board had investigated the case, it was up to the government to decide whether or not to impose penalties on the combination. The law, however, established no permanent regulatory body.

No rash of penalties followed the enactment of the Combines Investigation Act of 1910. King was generally sympathetic to the needs of business firms to gain control over the competitive jungle of the marketplace. He accepted most business combinations as legitimate, even though he was opposed to monopolies that were harmful to small firms. For Albertans who sought a vigorous application of the Combines Investigation Act, there was great disappointment. For instance, in 1917, in *Stewart v. Thorpe*, the Supreme Court of Alberta ruled in favour of the Canadian Anthracite Coal Company and the Canmore Coal Company.[43] These two companies had combined to purchase the Georgetown Collieries. The Court found no violation of the law and upheld the purchase on the grounds that the Georgetown Collieries was still free to acquire other properties and in this way to continue to compete with the Canadian Anthracite Coal Company and the Canmore Coal Company. In effect, the Court ruled that in these circumstances the federal government had no power to interfere. Thus, the Combines Investigation Act of 1910 had little impact on business firms in Alberta.

Thirteen years later, Parliament passed a new anticombines law, the Combines Investigation Act of 1923, an act prepared by Mackenzie King, and created a new permanent regulatory agency, the registrar of the act.[44] Like other forms of federal regulation, this event involved a compromise and was a product of widespread agitation by small businesspeople.

By 1923, public sentiment in Canada had crystallized: it was necessary to do something about combinations, trusts, and mergers. Small businesspeople — small merchants, farmers, manufacturers — wanted an agency that would be more attentive to violations of legal prohibitions against the fixing of prices and the limiting of competition. They disliked a powerful monopoly because it interfered with the independence of small business firms that were absorbed into a trade combination. Big business owners, on the other hand, desired freedom in the management of their firms. To be a viable big business, they thought, a firm must be at liberty to achieve growth through the acquisition of formerly competing enterprises.

Although the Combines Investigation Act of 1923 gave more structure to the anticombines law, because of conflicting business interests, Parliament was unable to offer more than a compromise. While the act provided effective machinery to identify combines operating in ways that were harmful to the public, the new regulatory body fell short of an investigatory agency that would always aid small businesses threatened by the monopolistic practices of big firms. Many monopolies remained in existence. The act provided for a permanent registrar and permanent or special commissioners.[45] The core of the registrar's or commissioner's authority lay in the provision that he/she must conduct an investigation, on receipt of a complaint regarding a combination operating against the interest of the public. The registrar or commissioner in effect had the power to determine which combinations were harmful.

For Albertans who wanted a more energetic application of the new law, some of the commissioner's decisions were encouraging. For example, in 1938, Commissioner F. A. McGregor investigated the Northern Alberta Tobacco Jobbers' Association and discovered a combine that was carrying on business to the detriment of the public.[46] This investigation involved an association which operated as an unincorporated group of wholesale distributors of tobacco products, made up mainly of firms engaged in business in Edmonton. The selling policies of the Northern Alberta Tobacco Jobbers' Association did indeed cause injury to the small tobacco dealers in Edmonton and the surrounding region. The highly publicized decision told tobacco wholesalers that they could not combine to fix prices. The Combines Investigation Act of 1923 could and sometimes did serve as a powerful weapon against business combinations in Alberta.

Mass retailers in Alberta also came under increased regulation during this period. By the 1930s, the growing importance of mass retailers in the province made it possible for a larger percentage of the population to buy a greater variety of goods and services than even the most visionary consumers in earlier decades would have dreamed. Alberta's business system had placed an unprecedented array of products into the hands of the average citizen by the 1930s. In household appliances, as well as in food and clothing, Alberta had become a province of consumers. An interest in purchasing consumer products came to be a significant characteristic shared by many people. In a sense, the purchase of a standardized, branded item created a bond among buyers. One result of increased advertising was a sharp decline in sales of products in bulk as Albertans in ever greater numbers turned to packaged goods with brand names. In the retail world, Alberta was well along the road toward democratizing consumption.

One of the major pieces of Prime Minister R. B. Bennett's New Deal legislation reflected the growing role of the federal government in supervising the retail industry. The Dominion Trade and Industry Commission Act of 1935 was central to Bennett's attempt to meet the recommendations of the Royal Commission on Price Spreads. In 1934, the Price Spreads Commission, which grew out of Trade and Commerce Minister Harry H. Stevens' investigation of price spreads in distribution, particularly in regard to the affairs of Simpson and Eaton's department stores, recommended the creation of a federal trade and industry commission to regulate competition through the rigorous enforcement of the Combines Investigation Act.[47]

Donald M. Kennedy, a member of the Price Spreads Commission who was a farmer and rancher at Fairview, Alberta and United Farmers of Alberta Member of Parliament for Peace River, found good reason to cooperate with the government. Kennedy explained:

I think it was very well established in the evidence that some organizations in this country were able to buy commodities from manufacturers and others at prices that would put the manufacturers out of business unless they got higher prices from someone else. Whether it is done deliberately or not, the result is a differential between the price at which the mass buyer gets his commodities and the price at which his competitor obtains his. And so the question arises whether or not the spread is fair. I think it is quite evident, and it was generally agreed by the commission, that the spread was unfair.[48]

The Dominion Trade and Industry Commission Act of 1935 empowered the federal Tariff Board to prohibit unfair competitive practices in the retail industry. As a regulatory agency, the Tariff Board might have imposed harsh federal discipline on mass retailers in Alberta and elsewhere in Canada involved in unfair methods of competition. Instead, the Board tried to shape business policy without smothering private entrepreneurship.

∎

Banking Regulation

The appearance of chartered commercial banks in Alberta in the mid-1880s presented new opportunities to Albertans and produced new issues in the political economy. With the emergence of branches of these banks, along with the arrival of the Canadian Pacific Railway at this time, the localism of the Alberta political economy during the 1870s and early 1880s began to recede after 1886, to be gradually replaced by the federal government's national policies. Federal government policies regarding chartered banks had the overall effect of promoting these institutions as well as regulating them.

The enactment of the Bank Act of 1871, besides reflecting these policies, was deeply rooted in many Canadians' conceptions of the political economy. This act was an expression of a generalized belief that the chartered banks were essential to economic development in the nation. Through the act, the federal government placed requirements on the banks aimed at ensuring their growth and soundness. To encourage them to grow, the government permitted the banks to open branch offices in all parts of Canada, including Alberta. After running for concurrent ten-year periods, the act and all the bank charters were to be reviewed to meet changing needs.[49] The law provided for the creation of new chartered banks by individual acts of Parliament. By setting capital requirements, the government tried to provide a minimum level of security for those who held a bank's liabilities. Each new bank had to have a minimum capital of $500,000, and twenty percent of this amount had to be paid in before it could begin operations. The privilege of the bank note issue was intended to attract banks into the chartered banking system. But the law limited the note issue to the value of a bank's paid-in capital. While a bank could issue notes in denominations of $4 and $5 and multiples of $5, the federal government issued Dominion notes in denominations of $1 and $2 in addition to coins.

The law did not fully define the cash reserve that was required, but a bank had to secure its circulation by keeping one-third of its cash reserves in Dominion notes. The banks made profits from lending money at interest but, until they established a reserve fund, were limited to paying eight percent in dividends. A bank was allowed to grant short-term loans, usually of ninety days or less, but it could not make these loans by taking real estate as collateral. This legal limitation, necessary in the eyes of the government to avoid a volatile real estate market, imposed a constraint on banks' lending. Banks could, however, accept merchandise, cattle, and horses as security. No federal examination of banks occurred. By requiring banks to submit detailed monthly reports on their operations to the government, the law sought to regulate and foster the development of an important service industry.

In general, this system pleased chartered banks, but it did not always serve business in Alberta well. The bank law contributed to a concentration of financial power in Toronto and Montreal, where most of the head offices of the chartered banks were located. In the late nineteenth and early twentieth centuries, many small farmers, merchants and manufacturers in Alberta believed that the banking system provided unfair advantages to the large banks and other big businesses that formed a central Canadian establishment.

During this period, Alberta was still largely an agricultural society, and many Albertans believed that the banking system was not geared to the needs of such a society. From their position in an agricultural community, they felt insecure in the face of the financial forces that dominated their province. Far from controlling events, farmers — like other Albertans — were frequently bewildered by them, especially during times of economic depression. They were concerned about some of the restrictions the federal government placed upon chartered banks. For example, a large amount of capital was required to obtain a banking charter, making it hard to found banks in small Alberta towns. The law prohibited banks from making loans secured by land, the principal asset in agricultural communities. These circumstances prompted dissatisfaction over the credit question in the minds of many Albertans, including small farmers, merchants, and politicians. After the severe economic depression in 1907, there was growing pressure for reform in the Canadian banking system.

Parliament responded to this situation by amending the Bank Act in 1908.[50] W. S. Fielding, Minister of Finance in the government of Wilfrid Laurier, took the initiative in pushing this important amendment through the House of Commons. To assist farmers in moving their crops to market in the fall of the year, the amendment permitted the chartered banks to increase their note circulation during this season to 115 percent of their paid-up capital. By thus regulating the banks, the federal government helped make more funds available to farmers in Alberta, particularly in the very months of the year when their credit needs surged.

Chartered banking came under increased federal regulation a few years later. For more than a decade, bank merger policy disputes had affected the Canadian political system. Albertans, like other Canadians, witnessed a partial resolution of these disputes with the revision of the Bank Act of 1913. Politicians and bankers reached agreement on what they considered an appropriate relationship between the federal government and banking and the merger question.

The Bank Act revision of 1913 came only after years of disagreement between banks and other businesses over bank mergers and control of the banking system. In Alberta, the controversy over mergers arose because chartered banks were becoming larger through consolidations, although the availability of bank credit for small businesses was sometimes shrinking. The change brought about by the Bank Act of 1900 had provided that a special act of Parliament was no longer required for bank mergers. Banks could merge with the federal cabinet's approval based on the Treasury Board's recommendation. But now that more mergers were occurring, including the Royal Bank of Canada's acquisition of the Traders Bank of Canada in 1912, farmers and other small businesspeople in Alberta and elsewhere in the country were pressing for reform in the banking system. Once persuaded that action was needed, Prime Minister Robert Borden and Finance Minister Thomas White saw to it that certain provisions were included in the revision of the Bank Act in 1913. One provision was that banks could not finalize an agreement to merge through their shareholders before seeking the federal government's approval.[51] They had to demonstrate that their proposed merger would serve the public interest. Another provision was that banks could lend money to farmers on the security of their threshed grain.[52]

Not even with the federal law on their side were farmers able to gain everything they wanted. In June 1922, in the Commons, George Coote complained about the Mackenzie King government's approval in that year of the Bank of Montreal's acquisition of the Merchants Bank of Canada, many of whose branches were in Alberta. Coote found it unacceptable that the Bank of Montreal "now controls approximately one-quarter of the savings bank deposits in Canada" because this made it too powerful, especially in Alberta, where farmers still had insufficient access to bank credit.[53]

During the 1920s, one of Coote's main concerns as a farmer and former bank manager centred on a critical area: easier access for Alberta farmers to credit at chartered banks in the province. At the provincial level, most efforts to provide adequate farm credit had accomplished little. Nor did the Royal Commission on Banking and Credit with Respect to the Industry of Agriculture in the Province of Alberta, which the Herbert Greenfield United Farmers of Alberta government appointed in 1922, bring sufficient bank credit to Alberta farmers, despite Commissioner D. A. MacGibbon's recommendation that the aim of the next "revision of the Bank Act should be to revise the Act so as to enable the banks to become as convenient and flexible agencies for the dispensing of credit to the farming as to the mercantile and industrial side of our economic life."[54] There was no provision for such reform in the revision of the Bank Act in 1923. Coote never had a great deal of confidence that the federal government's attempt to regulate banking in that year would include an effort to provide benefits for Alberta farmers. The policy he advocated was the creation of a nationally owned and controlled central bank, and he believed that this policy would be more beneficial to farmers than the help afforded them in possible Bank Act revisions.

With the onset of the Great Depression of the 1930s, as a United Farmers of Alberta member of the Commons, Coote went on to suggest to the Conservative government led by R. B. Bennett ways to improve the nation's banking and currency system. Voluntarily co-operating with Bennett in an effort to end hard times, Coote tried to provide members of the government with the practical knowledge of banking they lacked. His ideas about a central bank as a regulatory body evolved from at least 1931 to 1934. In 1931, he introduced a motion in the Commons to establish a nationally owned central bank. One of the goals of regulation, Coote felt, should be to democratize the control of credit.[55] Bennett responded to this call for reform by appointing the Royal Commission on Banking in 1933. Lord MacMillan, a well-known British banker, was named commission chairman, and Premier J. E Brownlee of Alberta became one of its members. The result of the commission's recommendation was the Bank of Canada Act of 1934. This law, which chartered banks except the Royal Bank did not favour, gave the newly created private Bank of Canada authority to regulate interest rates and the nation's supply of money.

Further legislation in 1936 and 1938, authored by Prime Minister Mackenzie King, nationalized the Bank of Canada. This increased Coote's faith in the bank, as it did that of Brownlee, the only member of the commission who, like Coote, wanted a nationally owned and controlled central bank. Government officials initiated these banking reforms between 1934 and 1938, and Alberta farmers such as Coote and other small businessmen helped shape the laws. Bennett appointed Graham Towers, previously a successful general manager of the Royal Bank, as the first governor of the Bank of Canada. Despite the grumbling that came from some bankers who now had to face new regulations issued by new federal bureaucrats, Towers generally succeeded in getting the banks to act in accordance with the new regulatory standards.[56] He apparently enjoyed good relations with George Coote, one of the Bank of Canada's directors.

In trying to solve the problems of the Great Depression, the Social Credit government in Alberta led by William Aberhart interfered with federal control of banking. The Credit of Alberta Regulation Act and the Bank Employees Civil Rights Act, both passed by the Alberta legislature in 1937, gave the Alberta government responsibility for the regulation of chartered banks in the province. The federal government under Mackenzie King immediately responded by disallowing this new legislation. When the Alberta legislature enacted the Bank Taxation Act in 1938, in another attempt to control chartered banks in Alberta, the Supreme Court of Canada ruled that the act was *ultra vires* of the province.[57] All this meant, among other things, that the Bank of Canada continued to regulate banking practices and the money supply in Alberta. Some critics believed that this power to regulate might inhibit economic recovery in Alberta in the 1930s. But because its economic principles were sound, the Bank of Canada Act made a positive impact. Indeed, it promoted recovery and financial rehabilitation. By and large, Alberta farmers and other business owners, chartered banks, and government officials in the Bank of Canada co-operated in an effort to bring about economic stabilization and recovery.

■

Farmers and the Canadian Wheat Board

Government-business co-operation reached fresh heights in 1935; prairie farmers and government officials worked together through federal government agencies, the most important of which was the Canadian Wheat Board. One of Bennett's solutions to the problems of the Great Depression was a New Deal law passed by Parliament in July of that year, the Canadian Wheat Board Act, to regulate the wheat industry. Under this law, the Canadian Wheat Board was required to market the wheat produced in Alberta, Saskatchewan, Manitoba, and British Columbia.[58]

This significant piece of legislation came only after years of disagreement between farmers and other business leaders over the control of wheat marketing. The controversy over marketing arose because the price farmers received for their wheat had dropped drastically, and the Winnipeg Grain Exchange continued to regulate the prairie West's wheat trade to the advantage of speculators. The system established in 1917, during World War I, had provided for a new federal Board of Grain Supervisors to purchase the annual wheat crop at a fixed price and serve as a selling agent for the entire crop, thereby controlling the rapidly rising wheat price in the interests of Canada's war effort and the Canadian consumer.[59] After the return to peace at the end of 1918, the temporary resumption of the free market and the Winnipeg Grain Exchange's operations became controversial.[60] The debate revolved around the special interests of two business groups. Prairie farmers, by now deep in debt and facing the post-war depression, favoured the continuation of a fixed price for their wheat through sale by the federal government. The Winnipeg Grain Exchange, on the other hand, wanted the free market to continue. The response of the federal government was to create the Canadian Wheat Board to sell the 1919 wheat crop. In marketing their wheat, the Board guaranteed the farmers a minimum price. However, the price of wheat began to fall sharply at the end of August 1920, when the government terminated the Board and permitted the Winnipeg Grain Exchange to re-open.[61]

The marketing controversy continued as discontented prairie farmers demanded a return to the federal guarantee of a minimum price for their wheat. In June 1922, George Coote, one of many Alberta farmers who had been affected by the declining wheat price, rose in his place in the Commons to say that "the farmers of western Canada, as hon. members know, or should know, are asking for a wheat board to distribute their wheat."[62] Albertans in part solved their marketing problem in 1923 by organizing the farmer-owned Alberta Wheat Pool and co-operating with the Saskatchewan and Manitoba wheat pools during the following year in setting up the Central Selling Agency to market their wheat, but, by the early 1930s, the three pools were greatly overextended and struggling to carry on with the help of bank loans guaranteed by the federal government. In June 1935, Coote supported Bennett's resolution in the Commons to establish a wheat board. "I am very pleased the Prime Minister has introduced a resolution looking to the setting up of a wheat board," said Coote.[63] Despite strong opposition from the Winnipeg Grain Exchange, Parliament asserted its authority over the wheat industry by passing the Canadian Wheat Board Act a month later.

A great flurry of prairie wheat sales by the Canadian Wheat Board followed the enactment of the Canadian Wheat Board law.[64] For instance, the new Board sold twenty-two million bushels of wheat to Argentina. By the end of October 1935, the Board had undertaken to market, among other wheat deliveries, the wheat Coote had delivered to the Alberta Wheat Pool elevator in Cayley that month.[65] Although the law was a compromise between the farmer and Winnipeg Grain Exchange interests that made the Canadian Wheat Board a voluntary marketing agency and allowed the Winnipeg Grain Exchange to continue, the Board had considerable power. Also, in 1943, the sale of wheat through the Board became compulsory.

In the 1930s and 1940s, then, federal policymakers generally believed that market forces left to themselves would create widespread injustice. They therefore held the conviction that an active federal government in the regulation of the wheat industry in Alberta and the other western provinces was essential to the well-being of the Canadian people.

■

Government Promotion and Regulation of Oil and Natural Gas Businesses

The oil and natural gas industry in Alberta was also a recipient of this kind of federal government regulation in the early twentieth century. Federal policymakers became convinced that a government active in the regulation of oil and gas businesses in the province would serve the public interest.

Regulation of oil and gas firms functioned as a promotional or developmental device. As we have seen, this was also the case with railways. The federal government provided significant help for railways before World War I. Government aid was particularly significant in providing railway transportation for Alberta in the late nineteenth and early twentieth centuries. During the early twentieth century, federal government assistance was also important in helping oil and gas businesses.

This assistance occurred against a background of developments in federal government policy. Initially, two orders-in-council shaped the regulation of the oil industry in Alberta. In 1890, the Conservative government under John A. Macdonald issued an order-in-council that provided for the leasing of Dominion land in southern Alberta to individuals who wanted to prospect for petroleum on it, as well as for the sale of the property to them after five years if they had produced at least one paying oil well. The Department of the Interior was given authority to regulate the development of petroleum on such land. In 1898, the federal government led by Wilfrid Laurier passed an order-in-council that created the opportunity for prospectors to purchase up to 640 acres within six months of their entry if they had succeeded in discovering oil and making their business a paying proposition.[66] The issue of new orders-in-council continued into the next decade, with provisions permitting the sale of Dominion oil as well as natural gas lands in all of Alberta.

This remained the situation until 1910, when a further order-in-council removed the opportunity for Albertans to obtain private ownership rights to Dominion oil and natural gas lands and expressly provided that occupation was to be subject to leasing rules. In so doing, the federal government retained title to the oil and gas lands without stifling private entrepreneurship. The government continued to aid oil and gas businesses. By following the new federal rules, Albertans obtained leasing rights to up to 1,920 acres for twenty-one years at twenty-five cents per acre for the first year and fifty cents per acre after that. Under the leasing system, which allowed them to renew their lease for another twenty-one years, they were not required to pay royalties on oil until 1930, even though they had to make royalty payments on natural gas.[67] Further federal assistance came in the form of the government's acceptance of development expenditures as credits against the rent paid for leases.

Even as the federal government continued to assist the development of oil and gas businesses in Alberta, new issues regarding the control of these businesses started to appear. The new issues grew from the emergence of big firms in the oil and gas industry. The large firms tried to guard their interests, and injustices in the eyes of the small firms began to surface.

For instance, in 1919, William S. Herron, a small independent oil and gas producer in the Turner Valley field, complained that the great financial resources of the big American oil firms in Turner Valley gave them an unfair advantage. As Herron explained to L. B. Beale, a British visitor:

> The latest news in oil circles which I think you heard when you were here, is that the Union Oil Company of California has filed on 100,000 acres south along the anticline from the Imperial Company's holdings. I know that a Geologist or scout of the Union Oil Co. looked the field over during the past summer. I met him and talked with him a number of times. A clerk in the land office told me he was quite sure that the filing was done for the Imperial Oil Co. Whether his supposition is correct or not I cannot say, but the filing has been done by some big American interests. There is no question about that. They come in and pick the plums right under the Canadians' nose.[68]

At the same time, Herron himself found it extremely difficult to meet the rent on his leases in the Turner Valley field. Because his rent payments were in arrears, the Department of the Interior cancelled two of his most valuable oil and natural gas leases. Herron's lawyer, H. P. O. Savary, protested the Department of the Interior's action:

> if there is one man in the Province of Alberta who is deserving of fair treatment and special consideration at the hands of the Department in matters pertaining to petroleum and natural gas leases, that person is William Stewart Herron. Mr. Herron took out the first petroleum and natural gas lease in the territory west of Okotoks. Until the outbreak of the War, Mr. Herron was endeavouring in every way possible to procure the development of his holdings and his faith in the future of this territory was such that he had invested every dollar which he could raise in this work. Today, as the result of his faith in the Field

A small independent oil and gas producer in the Turner Valley field, William S. Herron, pictured here around 1930, joined other small producers in trying to enlarge opportunities for business in the period from 1911 to the 1930s.

(Courtesy of Glenbow Archives, NA-4607-1).

and the free investment of his monies in the development thereof, he finds himself very seriously embarrassed financially.[69]

The Department of the Interior responded by leaving Herron in possession of his leases and giving him more time to pay his rent.

Small and big oil and gas firms alike pressed for an increase in the credits they received from the federal government against annual rent on their leases. The costs of development were high, and by the early 1920s, all firms concluded that it was time to request federal regulation that would transform a larger portion of their expenditures into credits. Imperial Oil was especially instrumental in persuading the government to increase the credits by the end of 1921.[70]

The efforts of big and small oil and gas firms to take advantage of new business opportunities and the attendant problems that arose in Alberta in the early twentieth century led to a search by the federal government for common interests between small and big businesses. By the late 1920s, on the eve of the transfer of the control of natural resources in the province from the federal to the Alberta government, this search produced a policy aimed at creating more friendly federal regulations for oil and gas firms, both large and small.

■

A Changing Political Economy

By the 1930s, the Alberta political economy had undergone significant changes from the late nineteenth century. Changes occurred as Parliament established a regulatory system and tried to assert its authority over big business. The creation of important federal regulatory agencies — the Board of Railway Commissioners, Tariff Advisory Board, and Canadian Wheat Board — had served to augment federal authority. Also, the federal government had assumed major new responsibilities under the Industrial Disputes Investigation Act of 1910, Combines Investigation Act of 1923, and Bank of Canada Act of 1934. Further, the Department of the Interior was charged, under an order-in-council of 1910, with regulation of the important oil and gas industry in Alberta.

Federal regulation and control of a maturing Alberta economy had become significant matters of concern. From time to time, this concern came from small businesses distressed by the practices of big corporations, such as railways and chartered banks. Corporate leaders in Alberta also felt the need for federal regulation. Because the market was always the main factor in management decisions, the federal government's most important role was in shaping markets for the goods and services of large and small businesses in the province.

Business leaders' experience during the Great Depression of the 1930s had a significant impact on the conduct of business in Alberta, particularly in big central firms. The depression disrupted business and the Alberta economy, but World War II in the next decade created fresh opportunities. When the war was over, industrial firms emerged at the forefront of the business system. Alberta executives organized diversified, decentralized big businesses in an attempt to assure the long-term health of their firms.

NOTES TO CHAPTER SIX

1. Peter James George, *Government Subsidies and the Construction of the Canadian Pacific Railway* (New York: Arno Press, 1981), 91-93.

2. Harold A. Innis, *A History of the Canadian Pacific Railway* (Toronto: University of Toronto Press, 1971), 120-126.

3. Ken Cruikshank, *Close Ties: Railways, Government, and the Board of Railway Commissioners, 1851-1933* (Montreal: McGill-Queen's University Press, 1991), 51-57; Peter B. Waite, *Canada 1874-1896: Arduous Destiny* (Toronto: McClelland & Stewart, 1971), 181-183.

4. *Calgary Herald*, 11 February 1895; W. L. Morton, *The Progressive Party in Canada* (Toronto: University of Toronto Press, 1950), 10-11.

5. *Calgary Herald*, 11 February 1895.

6. Canada, *Sessional Papers*, 1895, no. 30, *Report of the Railway Rates Commission*, 7 May 1895.

7. Innis, *A History of the Canadian Pacific Railway*, 186.

8. Cruikshank, *Close Ties*, 81.

9. *Fifth Report of the Board of Railway Commissioners for Canada for 1910*, 236-240.

10. *Fourth Report of the Board of Railway Commissioners for Canada for 1909*, 116-124.

11. John A. Eagle, *The Canadian Pacific Railway and the Development of Western Canada, 1896-1914* (Montreal: McGill-Queen's University Press, 1989), 44-45.

12. Innis, *A History of the Canadian Pacific Railway*, 184-185.

13. Morton, *The Progressive Party in Canada*, 156.

14. Ibid., 157.

15. Canada, House of Commons, *Debates*, 9 June 1922, 2725.

16. University of Calgary Library, Mackenzie King Diaries, Transcript 50, 27 February 1924, G3982.

17. Mackenzie King Diaries, Transcript 50, 5 April 1924, G3982.

18. Tom Traves, *The State and Enterprise: Canadian Manufacturers and the Federal Government, 1917-1931* (Toronto: University of Toronto Press, 1979), 99.

19. Mackenzie King Diaries, Transcript 50, 8 April 1924, G3983.

20. H. Blair Neatby, *William Lyon Mackenzie King Volume II, 1924-1932: The Lonely Heights* (Toronto: University of Toronto Press, 1963), 98-99.

21. Traves, *The State and Enterprise*, 99.

22. Canada, House of Commons, *Debates*, 17 February 1927, 391.

23. Neatby, *William Lyon Mackenzie King*, 125.

24. Canada, House of Commons, *Debates*, 29 March 1926, 1997-2003.

25. Ibid., 15 April 1926, 2450.

26. Ibid.

27. Mira Wilkins and Frank Ernest Hill, *American Business Abroad: Ford on Six*

Continents (Detroit: Wayne State University Press, 1964), 131-133; Traves, *The State and Enterprise*, 113.

28. Mackenzie King Diaries, Transcript 52, 16 March 1925, G4185-4186.

29. A. A. den Otter, *Civilizing the West: The Galts and the Development of Western Canada* (Edmonton: University of Alberta Press, 1982), 285-286; *Albertan*, 10 March 1906.

30. *Lethbridge Herald*, 5 April 1906.

31. den Otter, *Civilizing the West*, 285-286.

32. Ottawa, 8 December 1906, Report of Mackenzie King to Rodolphe Lemieux, in *Labour Gazette*, December 1906, 649.

33. Ibid., 650-659.

34. *Lethbridge Herald*, 6 December 1906.

35. Mackenzie King Diaries, Transcript 21, 5 January 1907, G2001; Robert Craig Brown and Ramsay Cook, *Canada, 1896-1921: A Nation Transformed* (Toronto: McClelland & Stewart, 1974), 119-123; Stuart Jamieson, *Times of Trouble: Labour Unrest and Industrial Conflict in Canada: 1900-66* (Ottawa: Information Canada, 1968), 126-132; Paul Craven, *An Impartial Umpire: Industrial Relations and the Canadian State, 1900-1911* (Toronto: University of Toronto Press, 1980), 264-270; R. MacGregor Dawson, *William Lyon Mackenzie King: A Political Biography, 1874-1923*, Volume One (Toronto: University of Toronto Press, 1958), 132-144.

36. Canada, *Sessional Papers*, 1920, vol. 20, no. 36a, *Report of the Registrar of Boards of Conciliation and Investigation for the year ending 31 March 1916*, Proceedings, 1907-08, 16.

37. Canada, Sessional Papers, 1920, vol. 10, no. 37, Report of the Deputy Minister of Labour for the year 1919, 37.

38. *Labour Gazette*, May 1947, 641.

39. Michael Bliss, "Another Anti-Trust Tradition: Canadian Anti-Combines Policy, 1889-1910," *Business History Review 47* (Summer 1973), 177-188.

40. Canada, *Statutes*, 1889, 52 Victoria, chap. 41.

41. *Alberta Law Reports*, 1908, vol. 1, *Rex v. Clarke*, 358-383; *Journal of the House of Commons, 1906-07*, Appendix no. 6, Proceedings of the Select Committee Appointed for the Purpose of Inquiring into the Prices Charged for Lumber in the Provinces of Manitoba, Alberta, and Saskatchewan; Lloyd G. Reynolds, *The Control of Competition in Canada*, (Cambridge, Mass.: Harvard University Press, 1940), 136.

42. Canada, *Statutes*, 9-10 Edward VII, chap. 9; Dawson, *William Lyon Mackenzie King*, 204-206.

43. *Dominion Law Reports*, 1917, vol. 36, *Stewart V. Thorpe*, 752-760.

44. Canada, *Statutes*, 13-14 George V, chap. 9.

45. Ibid.

46. Canada, Department of Labour, *Report of Commissioner on investigation under the Combines Investigation Act into an alleged combine in the distribution of Tobacco Products in the Province of Alberta and elsewhere in Canada*, 31 August 1938.

47. *Report of the Royal Commission on Price Spreads* (Ottawa: King's Printer, 1935), 274-275; Larry A. Glassford, *Reaction & Reform: The Politics of the Conservative Party under R. B. Bennett, 1927-1938* (Toronto: University of Toronto Press, 1992), 157-159.

48. Canada, House of Commons, *Debates*, 11 June 1935, 3535-3536.

49. Michael Bliss, *Northern Enterprise: Five Centuries of Canadian Business* (Toronto: McClelland & Stewart, 1990), 262; Duncan McDowall, *Quick to the Frontier: Canada's Royal Bank* (Toronto: McClelland & Stewart, 1993), 30; Robert MacIntosh, *Different Drummers: Banking and Politics in Canada* (Toronto: MacMillan Canada, 1991), 68-69.

50. McDowall, *Quick to the Frontier*, 129-130.

51. Ibid., 140.

52. Ibid., 209; Robert Craig Brown, *Robert Laird Borden, A Biography, Volume I:1854-1914* (MacMillan of Canada, 1975), 217-218.

53. Canada, House of Commons, *Debates*, 9 June 1922, 2727-2728

54. Provincial Archives of Alberta, accession no. 70.414/556, *Report of the Commissioner on Banking and Credit with Respect to the Industry of Agriculture in the Province of Alberta 1922*, 102-103.

55. Canada, House of Commons, *Debates*, 22 February 1934, 831-833.

56. Douglas H. Fullerton, *Graham Towers and his Times: A Biography* (Toronto: McClelland & Stewart, 1986), 64-65; Franklin L. Foster, *John E. Brownlee: A Biography* (Lloydminster: Foster Learning, 1996), 216-224.

57. J. R. Mallory, *Social Credit and the Federal Power in Canada* (Toronto: University of Toronto Press, 1954), 67-90; Lewis H. Thomas, *William Aberhart and Social Credit in Alberta* (Toronto: Copp Clark Publishing, 1977), 86-91.

58. Canada, *Statutes*, 25-26 George V, chap. 53.

59. Morton, *The Progressive Party in Canada*, 108-109.

60. Allan Levine, *The Exchange: 100 Years of Trading Grain in Winnipeg* (Winnipeg: Peguis Publishers, 1987), 100-103.

61. William Kirby Rolph, *Henry Wise Wood of Alberta* (Toronto: University of Toronto Press, 1950), 125-126.

62. Canada, House of Commons, *Debates*, 9 June 1922, 2728.

63. Ibid., 10 June 1935, 3459.

64. William E. Morris, *Chosen Instrument A History of the Canadian Wheat Board: The McIvor Years* (Winnipeg: The Canadian Wheat Board, 1987), 86-97.

65. GAIA, George G. Coote Papers, box 2, file 19, Alberta Wheat Pool, Elevator Department, statement, 22 October 1935.

66. David H. Breen, *Alberta's Petroleum Industry and the Conservation Board* (Edmonton: University of Alberta Press, 1993), 5-6.

67. Ibid., 7.

68. Calgary, 15 November 1919, W. S. Herron to L. B. Beale, in David H. Breen, ed., *William Stewart Herron: Father of the Petroleum Industry in Alberta* (Calgary: Alberta Records Publication Board, Historical Society of Alberta,

1984), 75.

69. Calgary, 15 October 1918, H. P. O. Savary to the minister of the interior, in Breen, ed., *William Stewart Herron*, 139.

70. Breen, *Alberta Petroleum Industry and the Conservation Board*, 36-37.

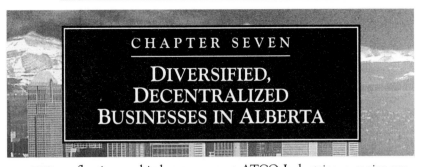

CHAPTER SEVEN

DIVERSIFIED, DECENTRALIZED BUSINESSES IN ALBERTA

R eflecting on his long career at ATCO Industries, a major producer of mobile housing, Ronald D. Southern — who as president and chief executive officer reshaped the company's management structure in the 1980s — commented on an important change he had made in the firm: "You will not see a return to monolithic, centralized management of the company. I think that's gone forever."[1] Led by ATCO Industries and other firms during the 1980s, some Alberta businesses made the transition from centralized to decentralized management structures, particularly as they tried to direct their strategies toward new markets. Establishing decentralized management systems, Southern and his counterparts in other companies were beginning a process of restructuring big businesses that was to continue after this period. Such firms grew especially by moving into new geographical markets and diversifying their product lines. This growth increased the size of management structures and made decision making at the top more complex.

In developing new management systems, individual firms contributed to the evolving business system in Alberta. Corporate executives gradually learned that a change in strategy was likely to succeed only if a change in organizational structure occurred at the same time. In particular, they found that a decentralized structure was a crucial complement to a firm's diversification strategy. Companies that successfully implemented the diversification strategy had the opportunity to reap significant profits. It was in the United States that the decentralized structure first appeared, at the chemical firm Dupont and General Motors, shortly after World War I, and this structure was the forerunner of the decentralized management system that ATCO Industries began to fashion in the 1980s.[2]

■

Changes in the Alberta Business System

There were dramatic changes in business opportunities after World War II, as Alberta developed from a producer-oriented to a consumer-dominated society. Ups and downs in the general economic climate of Alberta also led to variations in opportunities.

Economic and social changes in Alberta following World War II challenged business executives more than in earlier times. In big firms, management sought to achieve greater control over resources. Besides trying to cope with the increasing complexity of the economic system, it had to adjust to the expansion of governmental authority. The Alberta economy, which declined sharply during the Great Depression, grew rapidly from 1939 on. Shortly after the declaration of war, there were new business opportunities in Alberta. With the armed forces seeking much-needed supplies, entrepreneurs attempted to place themselves in a favourable position in the new market. The federal government worked closely with business in awarding contracts for war supplies. Alberta business leaders and federal officials made effective arrangements for reorganizing industry and directing the flow of industrial products and foodstuffs to the Canadian war effort. With the return of peace, many business executives in Alberta tried to preserve the wartime changes that permitted business and government to become involved in co-operative planning in dealing with economic uncertainties.

In addition to seeing the need to consider the effects of their policies on relations with government, chief executives in Alberta believed that good community relations would contribute to the survival and well-being of their big companies. Company public relations plans often reflected this conviction. Plant managers were made responsible for community relations within their areas. The ambitious manager tried to become a good citizen of his community, using company money to support civic causes and generally co-operating with movements for local improvements. In the process, public relations expenditures frequently helped enhance the public image of the company and its products.

In creating markets for their products, business executives started to think increasingly in terms of diverse product lines. Within the development of diversification, two important trends stood out: a new conception of marketing and a new conception of advertising. After World War II, a new view of marketing began to appear that affected business strategy and contributed to changes in the structure of Alberta businesses. Marketing involved conceiving of a firm as selling products compared to merely making them. The new marketing meant developing the firm's strategy in accordance with the needs of customers, focussing on planning for the whole firm, and co-ordinating production, distribution, sales, and service. It required a greater degree of administrative specialization, concentrating on individual products, product lines, or markets.

Structure followed strategy in Alberta business. As a company became more diversified in terms of products and markets, it was logical to set up management that was decentralized. In this kind of structure, operating divisions were established for each product, product line, or geographic region and charged with a number of functions: production, purchasing, sales, research and development, and transportation. Each of these divisions enjoyed a fairly large measure of autonomy, which made it possible for them to satisfy the demands created by their line of products. During the post-World War II years, pioneers in this marketing approach to management in Alberta discovered the importance of differentiating their goods from those of their rivals and offering a range of goods to consumers.

As this marketing orientation became dominant, firms started to spend more heavily on advertising to influence the behaviour of consumers. Alberta businesses fostered the growth of consumerism through advertising, encouraging the purchasing of consumer goods. Aimed at selling particular goods or services, advertising emerged as a major industry in the province after World War II. Advertising was as old as Alberta business, but after the war it became a significant part of the province's business culture. The tremendous growth in advertising expenditures, besides reflecting the rise of the consumer society, was important to increase demand.

The manufacturing industry in Alberta responded to the growing demand for consumer goods by expanding the volume of investment. Compared with central Canada's economy, capital for investment in production in Alberta was scarce. Bountiful natural resources environment in the province helped compensate for shortages of private stocks of capital. Alberta's natural resources were an important part of the province's endowment. Searching them out and putting them to use gave employment to capital and labour. The economy of the province was still based on a variety of resources: land, timber, petroleum, coal, and water power sites. These, along with agricultural produce, were the foundations of Alberta industry.

Electricity, available in all Alberta cities by World War II, enabled plants to operate their machines fairly efficiently. Relatively cheap small-scale transportation of products by truck helped many manufacturers survive and grow. Despite the spread of large firms with decentralized management, small businesses continued to be important in distribution and in manufacturing areas where they developed specialty products for niche markets. With the passage of time, some small industrial concerns like ATCO Industries became big, diversified, decentralized firms. When demand for one of their products fell off, they could move some of their resources to a more promising segment of the market.

■

ATCO Industries

ATCO Industries, one of Alberta's most important firms in the post-World War II period, was among the industrial concerns that created a plan to decentralize management. Founded in 1946 in Calgary as a small trailer company, ATCO eventually became a producer of mobile housing. Donald Southern, a native of Plymouth, England who served as fire chief with the

Royal Canadian Air Force during World War II, was the founder of ATCO Industries. A member of the fire department in Calgary, Southern first became interested in trailers in 1946, when he organized the Alberta Trailer Hire Company to rent two-wheeled trailers in the city.[3] The original capital of $4,000 to start the company came from Donald Southern and his son Ronald, with each supplying half. The growth of the oil and gas workforce following the discovery of oil at Leduc in 1947 significantly increased the demand for mobile housing. In 1949, Donald Southern worked to broaden the firm's offerings by beginning to sell mobile homes and, two years later, incorporated the business as the Alberta Trailer Company.

Growing up to serve the oil and gas market in Alberta, the Alberta Trailer Company expanded to a factory in Edmonton in 1953 to begin manufacturing mobile industrial housing. By the following year, according to a Dun & Bradstreet credit reporter, the company was worth between $50,000 and $75,000.[4] The destruction of the Edmonton factory by fire in 1955 led Southern to relocate his manufacturing business to Airdrie. Knowing that he had a product that customers appreciated, he remained a producer of mobile homes, completing an existing order for sixty-eight units on schedule.[5]

Donald Southern's son Ronald, who had completed his B.Sc. at the University of Alberta, began to run the company in 1956. Together Ronald and Donald built the Alberta Trailer Company into a large international company, with Ronald serving as president and chief executive officer and Donald acting as chairman. They were pioneers in the mobile housing industry. "Prior to ATCO coming along," Ronald Southern recalled many years later, "if you wanted to house people in temporary areas, you either put them in tents or you built a town: We decided to build something portable, strong and warm. And in doing so, we created a whole new industry for the world."[6]

Ronald and Donald Southern clearly emerged as effective leaders and soon took the firm into a period of growth and diversification. The Alberta Trailer Company expanded steadily as a producer of industrial mobile housing until 1959, when growth soared. In 1962, the company was incorporated as ATCO Industries with its head office in Calgary. Between 1959 and 1968, the company opened new plants in Adelaide, South Australia; Nampa, Idaho; southwest Calgary; and Montreal. In the same period, the firm completed a number of major export orders, supplying mobile homes for a project in Alaska, the Mangla Dam project in Pakistan, and the Boeing Company Minuteman ICBM project in Montana, North Dakota, South Dakota, Missouri, and Wyoming. By 1967, ATCO Industries' assets totalled $21 million and, between 1963 and 1967, its net profits increased from $410 thousand to $1.6 million. ATCO began diversifying production as the Southerns sought investment outlets for the substantial profits. Industrial mobile homes remained the company's most important product but, by 1968, ATCO had entered new fields, moving beyond industrial housing into residential homes, schools, hospitals, office complexes, and recreation centres.[7] In 1968, ATCO became a public corporation, with Ronald and Donald Southern owning a majority of shares in it.

As owner-managers of the company, the Southerns continued to diversify. They diversified their product lines by setting up a large research and development department to bring out new products and improve existing ones.[8] Their major contribution to diversification came through their role in investing in oil and gas exploration and production in Alberta in the early 1970s, acquiring Thomson Industries, an oil and gas well-drilling and well-servicing contractor in Canada and the United States, in 1978, and purchasing Canadian Utilities of Edmonton, a distributor of natural gas and electricity, in 1980.[9] Diversification was a large and satisfying part of Ronald Southern's work as president of ATCO. He firmly stated in 1981:

Manufacturing started it all for us and it holds a special significance for me, but we have reached the point where we can use much more selective marketing techniques. Diversification gives us strength and we do not have to keep reaching in a single direction with the attendant, sometimes, crazy risks.[10]

Diversification, however, demonstrated the limitations of ATCO's management structure, even though this very structure, with its functional departments overseen by the Calgary head office including the president, chairman, and vice-presidents, had successfully carried the company through the great challenges of the 1950s, 1960s, and 1970s. In 1981, ATCO was still centralized. Originally ATCO, like most of Alberta's newly integrated industrial firms, had been organized around functional departments. In the three decades prior to 1981, under the leadership of Donald and Ronald Southern, the company had created departments for each of its major operations, including production, sales, purchasing, finance, and research and development.[11] Dividing the company into functional departments served it well only as long as its focus on a single product provided a matching unifying power. Fresh lines such as utilities, oil, and gas did not fit easily into an organization established for mobile homes, because they brought ATCO into several businesses and undermined its coherent whole. The business cycle further complicated things when the recession of 1981 drove down ATCO's profits.

Undeniably, a reorganization of ATCO's management structure was necessary to accommodate the new diversification strategy. Otherwise, the fresh lines might disrupt what had emerged as a clearly profitable mobile housing firm. ATCO's response was to shift to a new course.

The Southerns reorganized in the mid-1980s by adopting a decentralized management structure. In this new structure, they treated each group

A leading corporation in Alberta, ATCO could offer a promising future for a new generation of executives, employees, and customers in the 1990s. Ronald Southern, ATCO's chairman and chief executive officer, and his daughter, Nancy Southern, deputy chairman and deputy chief executive officer, 1998.

(Courtesy of ATCO Group).

of products as a separate business enterprise. Ronald and Donald Southern reorganized ATCO around three operating companies: Canadian Utilities, ATCOR, and ATCO Enterprises. Canadian Utilities, with its head office in Edmonton and 4,100 employees, distributed natural gas and electricity. With headquarters in Calgary and employing 1,100 workers, ATCOR engaged in the exploration, production, and marketing of oil and gas. ATCO Enterprises, with its head office in Calgary and 1,100 employees, produced and sold industrial housing and other structures and provided oilfield services.[12]

In adopting formal and complete restructuring, ATCO, an enterprise worth $3 billion, committed itself to three product divisions, each headed by a chief executive officer with full responsibility and authority for all the functions of his business. Each chief executive officer answered to the Calgary head office including Ronald and Donald Southern and the vice-presidents. Head office staff, in turn, provided advice and concerned themselves with the broader economic strategies for the operating companies.[13] Rebuilding ATCO, the Southerns were greatly assisted by the chief executive officers of the operating companies, all of whom had already proven themselves with the enterprise: Norman Robertson, head of ATCO Enterprises; John Wood, president of Canadian Utilities; and Bill Elser, head of ATCOR. ATCO's president, Ronald Southern, had full confidence in them. "If they," he stated, "want to do something different from what I'm saying and they can get the approval of their board, it's guaranteed they're going to do it."[14]

The decentralized management structure established at ATCO Industries by Ronald and Donald Southern generally worked quite well. During the three months ending 30 June 1987, ATCO's profits amounted to $10.1 million and then increased to $12.9 million during the same period in 1988.[15] The company's profits continued to rise, reaching $78 million for the year 1995.[16] The decentralized management system, with divisions organized around product lines, allowed the company's executives to handle the growing size and complexity of ATCO's operations. By 1996, ATCO had more than 5,500 employees.[17] Donald Southern died in 1990 at the age of eighty.[18] Ronald Southern continued to lead the company as chairman and chief executive officer of ATCO.[19]

■

Foremost Industries and Decentralized Management

ATCO Industries shifted to a decentralized system of management when its operations became complex and diverse, but it was not the only firm in Alberta to do so. The more diversified and complex their products and markets grew, the more reason companies had to use decentralized management structures similar to that of ATCO. This was certainly the case with Foremost Industries in Calgary, a producer of massive, all-terrain tracked and wheeled off-road vehicles that had adopted decentralized management by the mid-1970s.

Foremost Industries' lineage can be traced back to the company Bruce Nodwell founded in Calgary to manufacture large all-terrain vehicles in 1952. This business was known as Bruce Nodwell. As would be true of many others involved with Foremost Industries in later years, Bruce Nodwell had close personal and business ties with the Calgary business community. Born in Asquith, Saskatchewan in 1914, Nodwell was the son of a homesteader.[20] He left public school after Grade 8 and worked for a number of firms, including a creamery, a trucking concern, and an electrical contracting business. Striking out on his own during the Great Depression of the 1930s, Nodwell purchased a second-hand truck, moving from one prairie town to another to paint buildings, erect signs, and construct service stations.[21] Along with his three brothers, he settled in Calgary in 1942, and by the following year, the four of them had formed Nodwell Bros., a contracting company organized around a machine shop.[22] Over the next eight years, the company turned out a variety of metal products, especially for the local market.

Bruce Nodwell's well-known technical ability eventually brought him an order from Imperial Oil for an all-terrain vehicle for its exploration work in northern Alberta, where it faced deep snow, muskeg, and swamps. In

Better all-terrain vehicles — such as the all-terrain truck made at Foremost Industries — remained significant in linking the different regions of Alberta as the twentieth century entered its last years. Chairman and chief executive officer, Jack Nodwell, in Calgary in 1993.

(Courtesy of Calgary Herald).

1952, he produced a crude machine that did not work well.[23] Nodwell nevertheless continued his efforts to design and manufacture a usable all-terrain vehicle and, in the same year, left the family contracting firm to organize his own company, Bruce Nodwell. In 1956, at his small plant in northeast Calgary, Nodwell created an efficient, powerful all-terrain vehicle for Imperial Oil that could carry geophysical equipment across muskeg in northern Alberta.[24] The success of this machine soon brought orders for more from Imperial Oil. After these initial steps, Nodwell also built an all-terrain vehicle for Shell Oil.[25]

With the security of major clients and confidence in the future of the oil and gas industry in Alberta, Nodwell built up his manufacturing capacity. The numerous improvements he made in his all-terrain vehicles allowed him to find a ready market for them. Then, in 1965, he turned to reorganizing his business to meet future needs. To secure the capital essential to continue operations, Nodwell looked to personal friends in Alberta, such as Percy Smith, Elmer McDougall, Lawrence Harrington, Bruce McLean, John McMillan, and Vern Easterbrook, a Peace River caterpillar contractor.[26] In return for a significant investment, Nodwell's son Jack, a University of Alberta mechanical engineering graduate who had earlier opened his own landbreaking business in the Peace River country, became the owner of a substantial interest in Nodwell's reorganized company, Canadian Foremost.[27] Canadian Foremost was incorporated in 1966.[28]

Jack Nodwell served as president, while his father Bruce became vice-president.[29]

Jack and Bruce Nodwell brought growth to Canadian Foremost through the production of high-quality all-terrain vehicles. They were owner-managers who understood and were interested in their firm's technology. In 1965, with seven employees, their plant turned out only two machines. By 1967, the Foremost workforce had grown to thirty, and its output had increased to thirty vehicles; the company's total sales came to $1,500,000.[30] With Foremost's growth came public recognition of the firm's rising importance as part of Calgary's industrial base and the Alberta manufacturing scene.

Highly motivated entrepreneurs, the Nodwells sought additional expansion opportunities. The first important prospect for growth beyond Canada came in 1966. During that year, Foremost's executives met Soviet Union officials at Rainbow Lake in northwestern Alberta. Impressed by the company's all-terrain vehicles at the Rainbow Lake drilling site, the Soviets proposed to buy a number of them for their oil and gas industry in Siberia. Jack Nodwell spent a great deal of his time arranging the sale and, in 1968, shipped thirty-two vehicles to the Soviet Union.[31] Thereafter, an ever-increasing share of Foremost's efforts went into the production of all-terrain vehicles for the Soviet market.

Foremost remained a manufacturer of all-terrain vehicles, but, in an attempt to continue to grow, the company diversified into a new product. In 1976, Foremost's executives moved in a new direction, beginning production of heavy hydraulic oil pumps for use in drilling operations in oilfields. As the years passed, Jack and Bruce Nodwell worked to refine the design of these pumps. They appreciated the need for technological progress. "We came out with too many valves and whistles," said Jack in 1982. The pumps "were too exotic. Over the past few years we have simplified them. We have three models that will cover the majority of the market spread in terms of size and capacity."[32] By this time, Foremost had sold about 200 hydraulic oil pumps.

Foremost's oil pumps were a technical success, yet there were economic problems. The depression in 1981 and its aftermath hit the company hard. Significantly, this depression seriously retarded business development in Alberta. A partial solution to these problems soon appeared, however. In the spring of 1982, the Nodwells moved their oil pump manufacturing division from Calgary to Lloydminster in an effort to be in a better position to increase their business once the oil and gas industry recovered.[33]

As Foremost's operations became more diverse and complex during the period from the mid-1970s to the early 1980s, the Nodwells succeeded in providing a rational management system for their business. In these years, they introduced a decentralized management structure at Foremost by carefully identifying the responsibilities of the Calgary head office executives and the divisions and establishing effective communications among the different components of the firm.[34] The Nodwells' objective was to combine semi-autonomous divisions with supervision by a strong central office.

The Nodwells started with important changes in their firm's management at the level of the operating divisions. Each division — wheeled and tracked vehicles, oil pumps, and others — was organized around a distinct product line.[35] Adopting the product-line organization, Jack and Bruce Nodwell also created a strong head office for Foremost. Central office executives, among whom they themselves remained the most important, supervised the work of the product divisions, set policies for the whole company, and planned for its future.

With their decentralized management system going well, the Nodwells turned, once again, to new markets. By 1977, they had diversified into the airport firefighting field.[36] At its Calgary plant, Foremost had already produced and sold four specialized firefighting units for use at airports in Canada and the United States. Conventional fire trucks were not always suitable for putting out airplane fires. Some airport authorities were beginning to favour Foremost vehicles with firefighting equipment. To handle fire and rescue work in difficult terrain conditions found in heavily forested areas and swamps, Foremost had also manufactured and sold specialized vehicles with fire and rescue equipment. Foremost had also moved into the production of tracked cane haulers for use in Hawaiian sugar cane fields.[37] By employing these vehicles to carry cane from their fields to road transport, sugar cane growers could avoid field damage.

Besides pursuing diversification within its plant, Foremost diversified further by acquiring an interest in other companies. In 1980, Foremost purchased a forty percent interest in Volk Precision Industries, a local firm that provided precision machining and fabrication services.[38] The same year, Foremost acquired a five percent interest in a joint venture oil-drilling program in Kansas. By 1983, Foremost had a forty-nine percent interest in the Calgary firm of Macedon Resources, a junior oil and gas exploration company.[39] Foremost, a family enterprise owned and run by Jack and Bruce Nodwell, financed its diversification efforts mainly through retained profits. As early as 1978, remaining largely in the hands of the Nodwells, the company had gone public to attract additional capital.[40]

Diversification gradually helped increase Foremost's sales, and sales were essential for the company's growth and development. Total sales, including all-terrain vehicles and oil pumps, rose from $9 million in 1974 to $20 million in 1980.[41] In 1981, sales increased to about $28 million. As a result of the economic depression, sales plunged to $14 million in 1982.[42] "It was a turbulent year," said Jack Nodwell, "but we are used to fluctuating markets and our production systems are designed to allow a quick reaction to changing conditions."[43]

Foremost's strategy at its plant was to make extensive use of outside suppliers for parts. While the company manufactured some of the parts it needed for its products, it was able to draw on the large number of external parts suppliers that sprang up. The company relied heavily on outside suppliers for many components. This provided Foremost with considerable flexibility and permitted it to respond quickly to changing markets. As Bill Pusch, vice-president manufacturing at Foremost in 1977, explained:

> We do three things here. We design the equipment, we do the final assembly and we market it. We don't manufacture many of the components since we believe that the more we can sub-contract out, the better. We use suppliers from all over North America but Canadian content in our vehicles is better than 80 percent.[44]

To help get its products to the market fast, Foremost combined internal manufacturing with heavy dependence on external sourcing. For example, in the 1970s, Volk Precision Industries provided Foremost with precision machining and fabrication services.[45] Foremost relied on Standen's in Calgary for springs and axles.[46]

To improve product lines and meet customer needs, the Nodwells invested in research and development. From the beginning, a research, engineering and development team at Foremost concentrated on improving the company's product lines.[47] The knowledge needed for research and development came from Jack and Bruce Nodwell, as well as from a number of skilled technicians at the company's plant. The Nodwells and their technicians understood the importance of research and development in keeping Foremost viable as a business over the long term. They focussed on continually evaluating the operating divisions' performance. To provide a steady flow of information to enable the top executives to monitor performance, each division carried on research and developed new products. Such product development required testing at the plant and in the field. Expenditures for research were substantial. For instance, in 1980, the company spent $1.5 million on research and development.[48] As the need arose to respond to changing markets, research and development became an important stimulus to diversification at Foremost.

Foremost's operations became increasingly diversified. In March 1988, the company moved into the manufacture of drilling rigs by purchasing Drill Systems International, a producer of drilling rigs for oil and gas exploration.[49] By making this acquisition and selling hydraulic pumps to Amoco Canada, Foremost increased its income. In the nine months ending 30 September 1988, the company's net profits reached $344,000, as compared to a loss of $398,000 during the same period in 1987.[50] Foremost's move into drilling rigs was important, but its core business still lay in the manufacture of all-terrain vehicles for carrying heavy oil and gas equipment to remote regions.

Seldom do a firm's diversification efforts proceed as smoothly as its executives hope. Nowhere was this more evident at Foremost than in the company's attempt to produce all-terrain vehicles for the Canadian military. In July 1988, Foremost secured a major contract from the Conservative government led by Brian Mulroney to supply the Canadian Armed Forces with 820 large all-terrain vehicles for use in the defence of Canada and to maintain the nation's commitment to the North Atlantic Treaty Organization.[51] Production of these vehicles was to begin in 1992. The Nodwells thought this new phase of diversification would help reduce Foremost's dependence on the highly cyclical oil and gas industry. In April 1989, however, they saw the contract get chopped to half the original $420 million deal as Finance Minister Michael Wilson presented his budget. Disappointed as he was, Jack Nodwell believed Foremost could survive the cut. "It does make it difficult," he said, "but it's the nature of this business to be able to handle the swings."[52] Later, in May 1991, when the federal government cancelled the entire contract on the grounds that dismantling the Berlin Wall and the gradual withdrawal of the Soviet military from central Europe had brought the Cold War to an end, Foremost was once again able to handle the change even though the company had already undertaken initial studies for the vehicles.[53] "This cancellation will have no impact on Foremost's ongoing business," stated Nodwell.[54]

In the first three months of 1991, after reporting large losses for several years, Foremost showed a profit $221,000.[55] In part, this improvement in the company's performance came from its continuing diversification drive. Foremost created new products for new markets, including trucks for the oil sands development work of Syncrude Canada.[56] Foremost also diversified through acquisitions. For instance, at the end of 1991, the firm acquired the Bronco Tank and Testing Company, a Red Deer oilfield services concern, to provide specialized services, including equipment for vapour-tight recovery of oil and gas effluents during well testing.[57]

Around 1991, Canadian Foremost's managerial system underwent change as Bruce Nodwell withdrew from active management of the company. Jack Nodwell, Foremost's chairman and chief executive officer, continued to take responsibility for the overall direction and management of the firm.[58] Vehicle sales abroad, especially in Russia and China, became increasingly important as time progressed. In recognition of this alteration in the firm's sales picture, Jack Nodwell changed the name of the company to Foremost Industries in 1994.[59] In that year, the company's total sales reached $64 million.[60] The skilled workforce at Foremost's Calgary plant had increased to 150. Further growth resulted from another diversification effort. Between 1988 and 1993, Foremost continued to diversify its operations through the acquisition of three Calgary drilling companies: Drill Systems, Canterra Drills, and the drilling equipment division of Barber Industries.[61] These companies focussed on operations such as water-well and environmental drilling.

Foremost Industries had become a highly diversified business. The company had gone into not only off-road, all-terrain tracked and wheeled vehicles, but also drill rigs, hydraulic pumps, and other services. By 1995, these services included Foremost's energy systems, with offices in Calgary, Red Deer, and Grande Prairie, providing oil and gas well testing services for western Canada's petroleum industry.[62] "Foremost has always been thought of as an off-road vehicle manufacturer, but that area now makes up less than half of our business," said Jack Nodwell in the spring of 1995. "Our off-road business did very well last year as well — but with the product mix we now have, we are no longer dependent on those sales."[63] By the end of 1996, Foremost had become even more diversified, as drilling rigs with their many applications had emerged as Foremost's main product line.[64]

■

Standen's and Diversification

Standen's, a producer of springs and axles, moved almost as quickly as Foremost Industries and ATCO to adopt decentralized management. The change came in an evolutionary manner, as Standen's responded to opportunities to diversify its products. Structure followed strategy in most large twentieth-century Alberta businesses, such as ATCO and Foremost Industries, and this was also true in the development of Standen's. Standen's strategy of growth through diversification had a profound impact on its management structure. When its operations became diverse and complex, Standen's switched to a decentralized system of management.

Standen's was founded in Calgary in 1924 by Cyril Standen, a twenty-year-old blacksmith, and his father William, a harness and saddle maker. Born in Oxfordshire, England in 1904, Cyril Standen moved with his family to Calgary eight years later, where he took drafting and electrical courses at James Walker School.[65] He got his first job as a blacksmith at George Edwards' blacksmith shop.[66] In 1924, Cyril Standen and his father, who had worked as a harness and saddle maker first at Riley & McCormick and then at the Great West Saddlery, established a small springs and trunk shop in southeast Calgary. Their partnership, in which each had an equal share, was set up to allow Cyril to manufacture springs and William to produce trunks. For help in making these products, they relied on two employees. From the beginning, Standen's was short of capital. Cyril and his father each had less than $1,000 when they began business.[67]

Cyril and William were soon borrowing a variety of tools from friends to stay afloat. In the trunk department, William produced goods for the

Standen's rose to the challenge of producing and offering new and improved springs and axles for oil and gas trucks, all-terrain vehicles, buses, automobiles, and trailers providing vital supplies to freight and passenger transportation, Calgary, 1998. (Courtesy of Standen's).

local market, including steamer trunks, wardrobe trunks, and automobile trunks, as well as sample cases for commercial travellers, leather hand luggage, and leather riding boots and gloves. He managed his department carefully. Similarly, Cyril was careful in the management of the springs department, where he manufactured parts for trunks.[68] He devoted most of his time to repairing springs on cars and trucks. Often working late into the night on repair jobs, he also began to manufacture steel springs for trucks and cars.[69] Cyril Standen's interests centred on technology and crafting quality products, which remained his passion throughout his business career. He sold his products to customers in Calgary and the surrounding area and serviced their cars and trucks as well. Among his major customers were the Crystal Dairy, the Alberta Ice Company, the Hudson's Bay Company, Eaton's, all the local taxi companies, the City of Calgary, farmers, ranchers, and Turner Valley oil and gas firms.[70]

The Great Depression of the 1930s was difficult for Standen's. As customers curtailed their orders, the firm cut back production and struggled to survive. Cyril and William Standen, however, continued to manage their firm carefully, which helped them weather the Great Depression and enhanced Standen's position in the long run. Cyril's three younger brothers, Sid, Reg, and Alex had also joined the firm by this time, contributing to its success.[71] By the end of the 1930s, production for cars and trucks dominated the firm's activities.

With sales improving in the late 1930s, the Standens decided to expand their facilities. In 1938, they spent $35,000 for a new brick factory building.[72] Brightened by fluorescent lighting, the building was steamheated throughout and well ventilated by exhaust fans. The Standens also developed new products in the springs department, which, remaining primarily a manufacturer of springs for automobiles and trucks, diversified into the production of springs for hair-triggered guns, pipe organ pedals, and other things.[73] Every year the firm used sixty tons of steel, much of which was imported from Sheffield, England, to produce springs. "If we haven't got what you want in stock, we'll make it for you," Cyril and William Standen confidently told their customers.[74] The Standens looked on their employees as essential partners in production. By 1938, their workforce had increased to eleven.[75]

World War II brought important changes to Standen's physical plant, organization, and day-to-day operations. Working with business leaders, federal government officials co-ordinated wartime planning and encouraged the expansion of industrial plants. Standen's responded in 1940 by enlarging its factory to provide more space to service trucks and cars.[76] This work included vehicles of the Canadian Army and the Royal Canadian Air Force maintenance units in Alberta. In addition, Standen's overhauled hundreds of heavy truck springs for military vehicles involved in the building of the Alaska Highway. The firm continued to service cars and trucks for civilians.

In early 1941, William and Cyril Standen felt that the time had come to incorporate their firm and, within a few months, had transformed the partnership into an Alberta-chartered corporation, Standen's. Initially capitalized at $20,000, Standen's received backing from the Bank of Montreal.[77] The company was still financed largely through retained profits.[78] William Standen acted as president, while Cyril Standen was vice-president. By the end of the war, the firm's service department was handling more than 3,000 vehicles per year for customers in western Canada. To provide fast and efficient service, Standen's adopted the policy of carrying over 10,000 complete springs of all sizes in stock at all times. In 1943, the firm installed a large, new furnace to improve the heat-treating process in the manufacture of springs.[79] Good management-labour relations was an important factor in the company's success up to this time as well as in later years. "This is a well-oiled machine," Cyril Standen noted later as he talked about the history of management-labour relations at the company.[80]

Standen's emerged from the war with a substantially enlarged and improved plant. In the late 1940s, the firm developed along lines established earlier, remaining committed primarily to production of springs for cars and trucks and servicing these vehicles. With the death of William Standen and the sale of the trunk business in 1949, Cyril Standen soon became principal owner of the company, serving as its president and general manager.[81] Even more than before, the company's operations now focussed on the manufacture of springs for trucks and cars and on service work.

During the 1950s and early 1960s, Cyril Standen once again pushed the firm into a period of growth and diversification. In 1953, he enlarged the plant, providing the company with 18,000 square feet of space for operations and storage. By 1959, Standen employed thirty workers.[82] The workforce increased to forty-seven by 1964. Besides building up the spring manufacturing department and the spring service department for all types of vehicles including oil and gas trucks, buses, cars, and trailers, Standen added an alignment and frame department, which provided mechanical service for suspension and steering systems, wheel balancing, and frame and axle straightening.[83] Standen spent a significant proportion of the company's profits on research and development and used the newest machines and equipment. "Some people in the past thought that we spent too much money on machinery and equipment," said Standen. "This is nonsense. Machines may cost money, but they save a lot of time, and time is something you just can't buy."[84] By the late 1960s, the company's total sales had reached $1 million.[85]

As the company grew, Standen created a workable management system for it. He found that the centralized management structure he developed could still handle his needs. The company had four major functional departments: spring manufacturing, spring service, alignment and frame service, and parts and accessories.[86] Standen placed a manager in charge of each department, with direct responsibility for all its operations. Standen and his senior office staff oversaw and co-ordinated the work of the departments, providing advice and making policy decisions based on the flow of financial information from the department managers.

Developing the company, Cyril Standen was greatly assisted by his son-in-law, Walter Kilbourn, who had married Cyril's daughter Margaret. Previously the body shop manager at General Motors in Calgary, Kilbourn came to Standen's in 1959 to open and manage the alignment and frame department.[87] In 1970, Kilbourn acquired a majority interest in Standen's and became the company's vice-president of operations, while Cyril Standen became chairman of the board of directors and a salaried consultant to the company.[88] Joe Iozzi, who had been with the firm since 1944 and worked his way up through the ranks, served as vice-president of manufacturing. Kilbourn and Iozzi, acting on Cyril Standen's advice, brought the company into yet another period of expansion and diversification.[89] In 1970, when the plant burned down, the company's officers rebuilt and enlarged it.[90] Four years later, in 1974, the company moved into larger quarters in a new location. In that year, the firm's officers invested $3 million in building a new 90,000 sq. ft. plant on a seven-and-a-half-acre site on the corner of Fifty-eighth Avenue and Eleventh Street Southeast.[91] By 1976, the plant employed more than 160 workers.

During the early and mid-1970s, under Kilbourn and Iozzi's leadership, Standen's diversified by expanding into the manufacture of axles for trailers and other vehicles.[92] The company also started producing farm implement parts such as cultivator shanks.[93] Further, Standen's moved in a new direction by manufacturing steel grouser bars — a driving component of tracked vehicles — for firms like Canadian Foremost.[94] "We can also rebuild, repair, manufacture and balance any driveshaft for any vehicle in use today," noted Kilbourn.[95] Standen's was able to develop and manufacture these new items because of its research efforts and the improvements in its plant. The company upgraded the heat-treating facilities required in the production of steel needed in springs, axles, grouser bars, and farm machinery parts. Besides expanding its market share in Canada, Standen's was selling its products abroad, particularly in the United States.

Standen's thus became an increasingly diversified business in the 1970s. As Kilbourn and Iozzi succeeded in leading Standen's into new paths of development, they recognized the need to build up an organization required to manage the company's complex operations. Standen's officers developed a decentralized system of management to satisfy the firm's changing needs.[96] This decentralized structure evolved over the years. During the period from the 1970s to the 1980s, the spring-manufacturing operations became the spring division and the axle-manufacturing operations became the axle division. Finally, the farm machinery parts manufacturing operations emerged as a new division in the mid-1980s.

Standen's central office, composed of Kilbourn, Iozzi, and their senior staff, established policies for the firm and planned its overall growth and development.[97] Central office decided company matters such as environmental protection, labour relations, and so on. Kilbourn and Iozzi also supervised the operations of the product divisions. The division heads ran the day-to-day operations of the company, and as a rule enjoyed considerable autonomy. Accurate information on finance, production, and sales flowed from the division heads to the central office. In the early 1980s, Standen's began to expand its market share abroad, especially in the United States. In addition to establishing warehouses in Toronto and Vancouver, the company opened a warehouse in Seattle.[98]

Apart from minor changes, the decentralized management system developed in the 1970s and 1980s remained the basic administrative structure of Standen's through the mid-1990s. Under the leadership of Mel Svendsen, who became president in 1990, and secretary-treasurer Gerald Lockey, Standen's continued to strike a good balance between the responsibilities of its central office and those of the operating divisions. Svendsen grew up with Standen's, serving as head of manufacturing operations from 1971 to 1985 and as general manager from 1985 to 1990. His long service with the firm clearly made him familiar with all its operations. He knew the company had the products people wanted to buy. Svendsen sought to link employee education and training more closely to the firm's needs. "The ongoing education and training of our workforce," he noted, "has allowed us to implement various high technology processes to what is basically a primary industry."[99] Svendson remained committed to his company's tradition of research, as seen in his purchase of a production robot in 1988. Like top managers before him, he looked to research and development as one way to keep the company profitable in the future.

The fire that ripped through the plant in July 1991 was a temporary setback, not seriously affecting production. Svendsen was prepared, and his good relations with the workforce soon led to a cleanup of the mess and the reopening of the plant for business. "We have excellent contingency plans in the event of something like this," said Svendsen. "We have a responsibility to the community and our customers to get our products out."[100] As head of Standen's, Svendsen held the diversified company together for further growth and development. He placed renewed emphasis on quality products and service. By the end of 1996, Standen's workforce had grown to 420 and its total sales had reached $50 million.[101]

■

Canbra Foods: a Diversified Company

Another Alberta company that undertook diversification was Canbra Foods. Canbra Foods — by 1995 a diversified corporation with annual sales of $175 million — had inauspicious beginnings.[102] Canbra Foods evolved out of Western Canadian Seed Producers, established in Lethbridge in 1957.[103] Until 1964, like most new businesses then as now, this forerunner was unprofitable. The company did survive and grow, however.

Western Canadian Seed Producers began as a public company, producing vegetable oil shortening at its plant in Lethbridge for the local market. Robert L. Greer served as president, and Hugh H. Michael, district agriculturist at Claresholm, was vice-president. Greer and Michael's desire to control production costs and take advantage of the opportunities offered by the regional and national markets led them to build a vertically integrated business. At first, the company cleaned seed grain, such as wheat.[104] To lower costs and ensure adequate supplies, Greer and Michael integrated backwards into purchasing networks. They gained control of their sources of raw materials by entering into contracts with local farmers to provide them with sunflower and canola seeds.[105]

Alberta's significant industrial growth included the rise of Canbra Foods, manufacturer of products such as West Premium Blend Margarine, West Sunflower Oil, Heartlight Canola Cooking and Salad Oil, and high protein meal. Head office of Canbra Foods in Lethbridge, 1995. (Courtesy of Canbra Foods).

By 1960, Western Canadian Seed was developing new or improved branded, packaged products. The company manufactured vegetable oil shortening products using sunflower and canola seed oil as raw materials. After struggling for several years, the company posted a gain of $52,000 in 1965. As the market for vegetable oil shortening grew, so did Western Canadian Seed's profits, which reached $412,000 in 1966.[106] In 1973, the company began making Tasty-Fry, a liquid shortening. Growing by diversifying into new products, by 1970 Western Canadian Seed had begun production of hard and soft margarines.[107] The company's diversification efforts continued in 1972, when it purchased Stafford Foods of Toronto, a manufacturer and national distributor of a wide variety of food products.[108]

The company's stockholders, in recognition of its altered nature, changed its name to Canbra Foods in 1974.[109] Company officers adopted a national and even international point of view for Canbra Foods. They integrated forward into mass marketing and distribution. Their overall goal was to expand their share of the margarine and shortening market. They made arrangements for the sale of the company's products across Canada, as well as in other countries such as the United States and Great Britain. Between 1966 and 1984, total annual sales at Canbra Foods increased rapidly, jumping from $6 million to $137 million.[110] Like most small businesses, Canbra Foods had to finance its early expansion internally through retained profits. But, while retained profits continued to be the mainstay in the company's financing, it received backing from the Bank of Montreal.[111]

By the mid-1960s, the main raw material used in the manufacture of the company's products was canola seed.[112] Growth by adding a canola seed cleaning plant in Prince Albert, Saskatchewan led to a more adequate supply of canola for the Lethbridge factory.[113] Of the brand-name products Canbra Foods manufactured, advertised, and sold by the early 1980s, few were more successful than West Soft Margarine, West Premium Blend Margarine, West Canola Oil, and West Sunflower Oil.[114] The company also produced high-protein canola meal for use as livestock feed. In 1990, the proteins division of Canbra Foods sold more than 100,000 tonnes of canola meal in Alberta, British Columbia, and the northwestern United States.[115]

At Canbra Foods, top executives continued to rely on diversification for further growth. Believing that this strategy of growth was the answer to Canbra Foods' future, they made extensive investments in improving the Lethbridge plant and in fundamental research essential to develop new products for new markets.[116] In 1990, they moved in a new direction by beginning to produce and sell a new line of products — Heartlight canola products — including Heartlight margarine and Heartlight canola cooking and salad oil.[117] They broadened the base for growth in 1994 by starting to manufacture and sell environmentally-friendly lubricants, a line of vegetable oil products.[118]

Diversification into new products brought new management methods at Canbra Foods. The company's senior executives realized that their functionally departmentalized central management system was no longer adequate to handle the increasing size of their firm and the growing complexity of their work. By 1995, they had partially adopted a decentralized management structure consisting of divisional offices to administer the two major product lines — vegetable oils and high-protein meal — and a central office to manage the company as a whole.[119] Total annual sales at Canbra Foods had reached $175 million.[120] Spurred by energetic management, the company continued to grow; by the end of 1996, Canbra Foods employed 250 workers.[121]

Growing Importance of Alberta Multinationals

Some Alberta companies undertook another form of diversification: multinational operations. Central to the continuing development of these businesses was the strategy that led to adding production and distribution facilities in other countries. Diversified firms were the types of companies that most frequently ventured abroad to do business. Multinational companies, usually defined as corporations with production facilities in more than one nation, were an important response by Alberta businessmen to growing business opportunities abroad. Before expanding abroad, these Alberta companies built up their plants and distribution networks at home. As they extended their marketing organizations to other countries, they built factories there, making direct investments in plants and other physical properties to improve access to raw materials and to enable them to operate behind tariff barriers erected abroad, as well as to avoid high transportation costs. Through direct investments, Alberta multinational corporations hoped to increase their market share beyond national borders and to lower the costs of producing and selling their products in foreign lands. When demand fell off at home, Alberta multinationals could move some of their investments to one or more countries abroad.

During the post-World War II era, Alberta corporations had significant opportunities to expand abroad, and a number of businesses took advantage of these conditions. For the Alberta firm, this was an important transition. In the previous half-century, Alberta businesses had been largely occupied with local, regional, and national markets. Alberta possessed rich natural resources and a growing population that offered all the opportunities required by most provincial companies. In general, foreign populations and resources had been left to the attention of entrepreneurs from elsewhere, particularly the British, Dutch, German, and American businessmen.

After the war, however, the European nations' economies were so disrupted that they could not easily regain the markets they had been forced to give up overseas. During the decades following 1945, Alberta businesses saw these opportunities and, with their decentralized management structures, they were in a good position to move into markets abroad. In this favourable environment, Alberta corporations became multinational in the postwar years. Before long, doing business in foreign countries was normal for them.

Alberta multinationals had considerable direct foreign investments in manufacturing and oil by the 1970s. The role of Alberta affiliates in industry abroad grew in size and importance as the years progressed. Initially, the United States was the largest host for Alberta direct foreign investment in industry, but later other countries also became significant host economies.

Ronald and Donald Southern's mobile housing firm, ATCO Industries, was a classic example of a multinational corporation, as the Southerns sought to continue to diversify their company. The growth of the mobile housing industry in Alberta, like that of the oil and gas industry, was explosive. The Southerns became steadily stronger in the industrial housing market. After making major investments in the production and distribution of industrial housing in Alberta, they created a marketing organization in Alaska. As they expanded production at Airdrie and increased sales in Alaska, they recognized the need for constructing production facilities in the United States. America's similar culture and language and its proximity to Alberta helped reduce the information costs faced by the Southerns as investors. In 1959, the Southerns incorporated the Northlands Camp Company in Alaska as the first non-Canadian ATCO company and opened the company's plant on a twelve-acre site at Nampa, Idaho six years later.[122]

The Southerns believed that markets could be developed in the American Northwest beyond Alaska. Soon the Northlands Camp plant at Nampa was manufacturing mobile housing units and selling them not only in Alaska, but also in the states of Idaho, California, and Washington. The plant supplied living quarters for off-shore drilling platforms and for military purposes, as well as schools for Alaska.[123] The Northlands Camp Company expanded its business in the United States through superior production and marketing. In addition to the company's sales branches established in Nampa, Los Angeles, San Francisco, and Seattle, others were formed in New York City, Washington, DC, and Houston.[124] Recognizing the scope of possible American operations, the company was ready to tackle them vigorously.

Oceans away, Adelaide, South Australia saw the opening of another ATCO plant as early as 1962, as Ronald and Donald Southern incorporated the Worldwide Camps Pty. Company in Australia for the purpose of manufacturing mobile housing in this city.[125] The Southerns picked Australia, as they did the United States, in the early stages of their expansion abroad in part because Australia represented a culturally similar investment location. By 1968, the Adelaide plant had the capacity to produce fifteen industrial housing units per day. The Southerns astutely adapted their housing units to the tastes of their customers and the tropical conditions in Australia. Pushing ahead to develop their business, they set up sales offices in Adelaide, Perth, Sydney, Melbourne, and Brisbane.[126] All the offices sold mobile housing, and together they penetrated the vast land of Australia. By 1971, the Southerns' Adelaide plant was also supplying the Australian market with classrooms and nurses' quarters.

A vital place for additional overseas activity was Saudi Arabia. By 1977, Ronald and Donald Southern had opened plants in Jedda and Medina, Saudi Arabia to produce mobile housing.[127] In addition to providing Saudi

Arabia with many housing units, these plants supplied furniture for Saudi Arabian schools. To manage and co-ordinate these operations, the Southerns formed the ATCO Saudi Arabia Company. In the process, they learned to adjust to the social and political environments within this host country.

Generally profitable operations in Alberta and abroad, along with a willingness to accommodate to political and social environments within host countries, allowed ATCO to expand around the world.[128] By 1995, the highly diversified company was operating in sixty-seven countries, including Kirghizstan.[129] Around this time, ATCO opened a plant in Hungary to manufacture mobile industrial housing.[130] The multinational corporation needed all Ronald Southern's abilities as it faced numerous problems across the world, such as the company's poor performance in foreign countries where there were economic downturns. Southern noted:

There's real difficulty in operating in many foreign markets. Many companies enticed to foreign markets by the fads of success are ill-equipped to judge the risks and may not have the financial power to sustain the risks. It's one thing to have grand announcements when you go to market. It's quite another to sustain earnings.[131]

Yet, ATCO had its own strengths which provided the financial, organizational, and technological advantages required to support the company's position as Alberta's leading direct investor abroad.

The ATCO story was repeated by an increasing number of large Alberta companies in the years after 1945. Among the many new Alberta direct investments abroad in the second half of the twentieth century was Foremost Industries. Like ATCO, Foremost innovated in a variety of products which were then sold in foreign markets as these products became mature. By 1980, Jack and Bruce Nodwell's Foremost Company was exporting tracked and wheeled all-terrain vehicles and oil pumps to the United States, the Soviet Union, Brazil, West Germany, and Australia, among other foreign places. The growing frequency of transactions required the establishment of sales offices or marketing subsidiaries in some countries. For instance, by 1980, the Nodwells had opened a Foremost sales office in Enid, Oklahoma and invested in service facilities in this office.[132]

In 1988, the Nodwells incorporated Foremost Progress in the Soviet Union as a marketing subsidiary. With headquarters in Moscow, Foremost Progress was a joint venture, owned by Canadian Foremost and VPO Soyuztransprogress, a Soviet Ministry of Oil and Gas Construction Industries manufacturing concern.[133] After doing business with the Soviets for over two decades, during which time they sold them more than 500 tracked and wheeled all-terrain vehicles representing total sales of $125 million, the Nodwells created an enterprise to manufacture and market the Yamal, an all-terrain vehicle that was larger than any previous Foremost product. In this joint venture, the Nodwells agreed to build part of the vehicle — the cab, power train, main frame, and undercarriage — at their Calgary plant, and the Soviets agreed to provide the tracks, wheel-drive sprockets, and walking beams from their factory in Kropotkin.[134]

Foremost Progress, of which the Nodwells at first owned fifty percent, handled trade in an immense area. It was Jack Nodwell who had planned the formation of this joint venture, worked on the styling of the new Yamal all-terrain vehicles, and increasingly took a larger role in the subsidiary. He had early set himself the goal of producing vehicles that the Soviets would purchase. Using excellent skilled workers and high-quality materials, he had achieved this goal. Another secret of his success in the Soviet Union, he emphasized, was that:

> you've got to be prepared to do business in their environment, by their method of negotiations. If a person's not patient enough to adjust and learn, exporting will be difficult. For example, in 1970, I negotiated with the Soviets for eleven weeks straight on our third contract. I was relatively accustomed to the Soviet negotiating process from the previous two negotiations, but I didn't expect it to go so long – eleven weeks of grinding face-to-face negotiation for an hour and a half to three hours a day.[135]

Jack Nodwell's sustained success in the Soviet market was also determined by his willingness to adopt the joint venture strategy. It was important, he stressed:

> ...to be prepared to enter into some sort of joint enterprise. Foreigners now have the ability to work inside the country through forming associations with Soviet organizations to produce and pursue markets together, inside and outside the country. That will give the Soviet participants an opportunity to reduce their foreign net currency expenditures, because they'll be building part of a product for domestic consumption and part for export, as well as servicing it themselves. They'll also benefit by acquiring some new technology and learning marketing methods.[136]

The joint venture worked fairly well, leading to the sale of numerous Foremost Yamal all-terrain vehicles to the Soviets over the years, and by 1992 the Nodwells held a seventy percent interest in Foremost Progress.[137]

Jack Nodwell, however, faced problems as the market for his other vehicles in the Soviet Union declined between 1988 and 1991 owing to the Soviet Union's economic restructuring.[138] He had a way of coping with the situation. However, in his Calgary plant, he continued to produce tracked and wheeled all-terrain vehicles that Soviets wanted to buy. For example, in December 1991, he delivered four large tracked vehicles valued at $2.5 million to the Oilfield Production Association in Siberia, to be used especially for servicing pipeline breakages that occurred in areas filled with swamps.[139] Sales grew as the years passed, and, during the first six months of 1996, Foremost's total vehicle sales to Russian customers amounted to $11.7 million.[140]

By 1989, Foremost had made its first move into production in the United States, opening a pipe manufacturing plant in Reno, Nevada.[141] This plant manufactured drill pipe and provided parts and accessories for the mineral and environmental drilling industry. The production of drill pipe designed specifically for the western United States market was followed by an improvement in the company's customer service. By 1990, Foremost's Reno plant was engaged in fundamental research work.[142] It diversified by beginning to manufacture drill rods and tools and specialized tools for the environmental drilling business two years later.[143]

In 1994, Jack Nodwell expanded his manufacturing business in the United States by purchasing a seventy-nine percent interest in the Mobile Drilling Company in Indianapolis, Indiana.[144] In doing so, he acquired one of the largest United States manufacturers of drilling rigs and associated tooling.[145] In 1995, besides changing the name of the company to the Foremost Mobile Company, Nodwell diversified by moving into the production of a new line of drill rigs at the Indianapolis plant.[146] Nodwell was the right man to supervise Foremost's complex multinational business. In addition to his familiarity with the field, he had imagination and was able to preside over Foremost's business abroad and develop its great possibilities.

The history of Alberta multinationals also includes Canbra Foods. During the 1980s, the company formed part of a general surge in Alberta direct investment in the United States. The officers of Canbra Foods took their first major step in the direction of multinational operations by opening a packaging plant at Butte, Montana in 1989.[147] At the beginning of 1990, after manufacturing its new Heartlight canola products at its Lethbridge plant, Canbra Foods started to send a substantial portion of them to its Butte plant to be packaged for distribution in the United States market. By the end of that year, the company was selling Heartlight 100 percent pure canola oil and Heartlight soft margarine in California, Montana, Arizona, Colorado, Utah, and Idaho.[148] To handle the continuing multinational business, Canbra Foods' officers obtained a $12.5 million loan from the John Hancock Mutual Life Insurance Company of Boston.[149]

The Heartlight canola product line of Canbra Foods was a commercial success in the United States in 1990. Because the U.S. Food and Drug Administration blocked further use of the Heartlight brand by Canbra Foods in 1991 on the grounds that this brand name might mislead consumers about the effects of the products on cholesterol, Canbra Foods experienced more trouble than some other Alberta multinationals doing business in the United States.[150] A partial solution to this problem appeared before long; Canbra Foods replaced the old brand name with a new one — Canola Harvest.[151]

Economic problems remained. Canbra Foods had difficulty improving its position in the United States market. The company hoped to change this situation through its plan to add a factory to its packaging plant at Butte. The growing importance of canola crops in Montana provided incentive to manufacture canola products within the state. Unable to find enough Montana farmers to contract to grow canola seed, however, Canbra Foods shelved its plan for building a factory in Butte in the autumn of 1992.[152]

Volume shipments of canola products, nonetheless, continued to come from the company's Lethbridge manufacturing plant to the Butte packaging plant over the next three years.[153] As 1995 came to an end, prospects for the Canbra Foods business in the United States had never looked better. The most successful year to date in the company's history, 1995, witnessed the Lethbridge plant making an ever-increasing volume of canola products. The company was purchasing more than 270,000 tonnes of canola seed from contract growers for use at its Lethbridge plant each year. Canbra Foods' total sales in 1995 reached $175 million, over half of which were made in the United States.[154] Like some other large diversified Alberta firms, Canbra Foods was successful not only at home, but also abroad as a multinational corporation.

Alberta multinationals understood that they had to adapt to and respect the laws and customs of foreign countries in which they did business. Where host country regulations impeded the activities of Alberta companies abroad, their managers often modified procedures and made adjustments in operations. They realized that a compromise with nationalism was essential for doing successful business abroad. Generally speaking, Alberta multinationals did not respond by curtailing investment in foreign lands or withdrawing from international business completely. Many persisted. Their managers knew that flexibility was essential to their success.

∎

Large Diversified Alberta Firms in Politics

At home, the success of large diversified Alberta firms depended in part upon their ability to maintain good relations with government officials and agencies. The management of these firms sometimes took an active part in politics in Edmonton and Ottawa. As competition grew within their own industries, firm officers frequently intensified their political efforts as one way of attempting to cope with the numerous problems they faced.

During the years after World War II, business leaders still turned to the federal government, as well as to the provincial government, to guide economic prosperity in Alberta. The premier's office in Edmonton became increasingly involved in promoting the well-being of Alberta capitalism. Government, at both the federal and provincial levels, expanded significantly during the 1950s and thereafter. Unquestionably, the growing public sector was a reflection of increased work undertaken by government agencies. Government expansion also signalled growth of government involvement in Alberta's economy. More than ever before, the provincial government shouldered responsibility for the long-term health of the economy in an effort to ensure that the postwar period would not see a return of the Great Depression to Alberta.

The Social Credit government led by Ernest C. Manning played a major role in assisting diversified firms that undergirded the power of the Alberta oil and gas industry in the years after World War II. Almost universally respected for his firm grasp of the inner workings of the Alberta economy, Manning was able to exert much influence on the province's oil and gas industry in the postwar years. The Oil and Gas Resources Conservation Act of 1950 embodied Manning's desire to prevent the recurrence of the Great Depression in Alberta and stimulate the provincial economy. The Alberta legislature had originally, in 1938, passed a bill which created a new provincial regulatory agency, the Petroleum and Gas Conservation Board. Renaming it the Energy Resources Conservation Board later, Manning gave the Board more authority through the Oil and Gas Act of 1950 to regulate the exploration and production of oil and gas in Alberta.[155] The three-member board, headed at this time by I. N. McKinnon, provided the technical expertise that Manning needed in promoting private business initiatives for the development of oil and gas and greater general prosperity and growth.

Manning's role, together with that of the Energy Resources Conservation Board, began to have a significant impact on the conditions in which oil and gas executives made decisions in their industry. The success of the premier's policy had the effect of stimulating the growth of oil and gas businesses. Among diversified firms that benefited indirectly from Manning's work was ATCO Industries, a major producer of mobile industrial housing for the oil and gas industry in Alberta. As the oil and gas business grew, so did ATCO's mobile industrial housing business. Similarly, Foremost Industries, as a large manufacturer of all-terrain vehicles for the oil and gas industry, benefited indirectly from Manning's oil and gas policy. So, too, the premier's work helped provide opportunities for Standen's, an important producer of springs for all-terrain vehicles as well as for oil and gas trucks. Manning was instrumental in improving the position of these diversified firms.

Under Prime Minister Pierre Trudeau's leadership, the federal government could also take some of the credit for helping to improve the position of diversified firms in Alberta. For example, in 1970, ATCO approached the customs and excise division of the Department of National Revenue, seeking a modification of the federal sales tax on mobile residential and industrial housing units. High taxes restricted the mobile housing market.

The response of the Department of National Revenue was to adjust taxes downward, as well as to simplify the process by which they were collected.[156]

In October 1980 came the unwelcome news from Ottawa that the Liberal government led by Trudeau had launched the National Energy Program. The National Energy Program came into being against a background of developments in the Middle East. In 1979, in response to war in the Middle East, the international oil cartel, the Organization of Petroleum Exporting Countries (OPEC), greatly increased the price of crude oil to other nations. Canada's growing dependence on supplies of crude oil from the OPEC nations complicated the situation Trudeau faced. He tried to deal with the energy problem created by the OPEC nations through the National Energy Program, a program which significantly reduced Alberta's share of production revenues through new taxes, provided federal exploration grants to companies with a high level of Canadian ownership, and increased federal power in the energy field.[157]

The oil shocks generated by the OPEC nations and the coming of the National Energy Program stunned the Alberta business world. Besides stimulating inflation, the oil shocks augmented business uncertainties in Alberta. In spite of the severe recession that began in 1981, inflationary pressures mounted in the province. ATCO Industries and Canadian Foremost found it difficult to adjust to these changes. "Uncertainties over the price of oil, coupled with the National Energy Program in Canada, reduced rig utilization significantly" in Alberta, Ronald Southern told ATCO shareholders in his 1983 annual report.[158] At the same time, he brought good news for those who hoped that Premier Peter Lougheed, head of the Conservative government, would continue not only to be the strong leader Alberta needed in the eighties but also to be supportive of ATCO. "In October of 1982, ATCO was awarded the Alberta Provincial Government sponsored International Marketing Award for continuous and outstanding achievement in export performance," Southern reported to the shareholders.[159]

The oil shocks and the National Energy Program also hurt Canadian Foremost. In his 1980 message to the shareholders in Canadian Foremost, Jack Nodwell said:

> the recent federal National Energy Program will, unfortunately, have a serious adverse effect on Canadian sales [in the all-terrain vehicle and oil pump] divisions during 1981. Foremost's domestic activities are closely tied to the oil industry. We cannot help but suffer as industry activity declines, due to a reassessment of exploration and production levels stemming from the federal program.[160]

For Albertans, the National Energy Program and the oil shocks brought wrenching and painful changes in business activity. International and

Canadian political currents outside direct Albertan control were dramatically affecting relationships between the federal government and Alberta's economy.[161]

New political arrangements, however, shaped new business opportunities in Alberta. The North American Free Trade Agreement (NAFTA) started to take form in 1989, when Prime Minister Brian Mulroney and President Ronald Reagan signed the Canada-United States Free Trade Agreement and started lowering trade barriers, a process to be completed over the next decade. Three years later, in 1992, both nations enlarged their 1989 trade agreement to bring in Mexico.

From the very beginning in 1989, benefits from the agreement flowed to large diversified Alberta firms such as Standen's and Canbra Foods. As Alberta's leading manufacturer of steel springs and axles, Standen's did well. Free trade allowed Standen's to increase significantly its share of the springs and axles market in the United States. Sales south of the border rose to heights well above those of the years prior to the advent of free trade.[162] The story was the same at Canbra Foods. "Free trade and health consciousness are rapidly improving the marketability of canola oil in Canada and the United States. The opportunity exists to make significant inroads into the U.S. market," Robert E. Burpee, president and chief executive officer of Canbra Foods, told the company's shareholders in 1990.[163] Reflecting growing confidence in free trade in 1995, Larry P. McNamara, Canbra's president and chief executive officer, spoke of the company's impressive achievements:

> The North American Free Trade Agreement (NAFTA), General Agreement on Tariffs and Trade (GATT), and health consciousness are rapidly improving the market for canola in Canada, the United States, Mexico and other international markets. The Company has positioned itself as a major supplier in meeting the growing demand for canola products in the North American food industry.[164]

By actively participating in the NAFTA and GATT agreements, Alberta and Canadian political and business leaders were taking steps aimed at increasing the prosperity of Alberta and Canada.

As large diversified Alberta firms expanded in the global market and in Canada's domestic market, small business persisted in Alberta during the years after World War II. The persistence of small businesses reflected continuity in the province's business system. Although this period saw fluctuations in the fortunes of small businesses, they continued to play important roles in Alberta's economic evolution and often became sources of economic revitalization.

NOTES TO CHAPTER SEVEN

1. *Calgary Herald*, 17 September 1988.

2. Alfred D. Chandler, Jr., *Strategy and Structure: Chapters in the History of the American Industrial Enterprise* (Cambridge, Mass.: MIT Press, 1962), 96-142.

3. Alberta Corporate Registry, Edmonton, ATCO Industries Ltd. file; *Alberta Report*, 9 April 1990; *Calgary Herald*, 26 March 1990.

4. *Dun & Bradstreet Reference Book*, January 1954, 8.

5. Alberta Corporate Registry, ATCO Industries Ltd. file.

6. *Alberta Report*, 9 January 1995.

7. Alberta Corporate Registry, ATCO Industries Ltd. file.

8. Ibid.

9. *Calgary Herald*, 17 September 1988; Alberta Corporate Registry, ATCO Industries Ltd. file.

10. *Globe and Mail*, 12 October 1981.

11. Alberta Corporate Registry, ATCO Industries Ltd. file.

12. *Calgary Herald*, 17 September 1988.

13. Ibid.

14. Ibid.

15. Ibid.

16. *Calgary Sun*, 29 June 1996.

17. Ibid.

18. *Globe and Mail*, 27 March 1990.

19. *Calgary Herald*, 16 November 1996; *Calgary Sun*, 29 June 1996.

20. GAIA, M908, Reminiscences of Bruce Nodwell, Calgary, 1971; Max Foran, "Calgary, Calgarians and the Northern Movement of the Oil Frontier, 1950-1970," in A. W. Rasporich, ed., *The Making of the Modern West: Western Canada Since 1945* (Calgary: University of Calgary Press, 1984), 124.

21. *Calgary Herald*, 23 May 1993.

22. Ibid.

23. Ibid.

24. *Financial Post*, 3 April 1982.

25. Foran, "Calgary, Calgarians and the Northern Movement of the Oil Frontier," 124.

26. Ibid., 125, 131.

27. *Calgary Herald*, 23 May 1993.

28. Foremost Industries Archives, Calgary, Canadian Foremost Ltd., *Annual Report for 1991*, 2.

29. Interview by the author with Jack Nodwell, 8 December 1996.

30. *Calgary Herald*, 23 May 1993.

31. Nattalia Lea, "Calgary's Russian Connection," *Alberta Business*, March 1990, 1.

32. *Financial Post*, 3 April 1982.

33. Ibid.

34. Nodwell interview, 8 December 1996.

35. Alberta Corporate Registry, Canadian Foremost Ltd. file.

36. Carl Radimer, "Canadian Foremost Ltd., Calgary," *Trade and Commerce*, October 1977, 13.

37. Ibid.

38. Alberta Corporate Registry, Canadian Foremost Ltd. file.

39. *Globe and Mail*, 11 June 1983.

40. *Calgary Herald*, 23 May 1993.

41. Alberta Corporate Registry, Canadian Foremost Ltd. file.

42. *Globe and Mail*, 11 June 1983.

43. Ibid.

44. Radimer, "Canadian Foremost Ltd.," 14.

45. Alberta Corporate Registry, Canadian Foremost Ltd. file.

46. Interview by the author with Cyril Standen, 11 November 1991.

47. GAIA, M909, Bruce Nodwell Papers, a Foremost pamphlet, n.d.

48. *Financial Post*, 3 April 1982.

49. *Globe and Mail*, 11 March 1988.

50. *Financial Post*, 29 November 1988.

51. *Calgary Herald*, 30 May 1989.

52. Ibid.

53. *Calgary Herald*, 18 May 1991.

54. *Globe and Mail*, 19 June 1991.

55. Ibid.

56. Ibid.

57. Foremost Industries Archives, Canadian Foremost Ltd., *Annual Report for 1991*, 3; *Globe and Mail*, 3 December 1991.

58. *Financial Post*, 25 March 1992.

59. *Financial Post*, 29 June 1994.

60. Foremost Industries Archives, Foremost Industries, *Annual Report for 1994*, 1.

61. *Calgary Herald*, 24 March 1995.

62. Foremost Industries Archives, Foremost Industries, *Annual Report for 1995*, 3.

63. *Calgary Herald*, 24 March 1995.

64. Nodwell interview, 8 December 1996.

65. Interview by the author with Cyril Standen, 11 November 1991.

66. GAIA, Charles Ursenbach, "Captain of Local Industry," interview with Cyril Standen, 15 March 1979.

67. Standen Interview, 11 November 1991.

68. Ibid.

69. Ibid.

70. Ibid.

71. *Trade and Commerce*, April 1976, 3.

72. *Albertan*, 29 July 1938.

73. Ibid.

74. Ibid.

75. Ibid.

76. *Western Business & Industry*, May 1945, 66.

77. Alberta Corporate Registry, Standen's Ltd. file.

78. Standen interview, 11 November 1991.

79. *Western Business & Industry*, May 1945, 68.

80. Standen interview, 11 November 1991.

81. Ibid.

82. *Alberta Automotive Retailing News*, February 1959, 14.

83. GAIA, Cyril Standen Papers, "The Standen's Story."

84. "The Standen's Story."

85. Interviews by the author with Mel Svendsen, 9, 17 December 1996.

86. "The Standen's Story."

87. Standen interview, 11 November 1991.

88. Ibid.

89. Ibid.

90. Ibid.

91. *Trade and Commerce*, April 1976, 2.

92. Ibid., 4.

93. Standen interview, 11 November 1991.

94. *Trade and Commerce*, April 1976, 3.

95. Ibid., 3

96. Mel Svendsen Interviews, 9,17 December 1996.

97. Ibid.

98. Cyril Standen Interview, 11 November 1991.

99. *Canadian Machinery and Metalworking*, June 1988, 19-20.

100. *Calgary Herald*, 14 July 1991.

101. Svendsen interviews, 9,17 December 1996.

102. Canbra Foods Archives, Canbra Foods, Lethbridge, *Annual Report for 1995*, 10; Alberta Economic Development and Tourism Library, Edmonton,

Western Industrial Selectory, 1995.

103. Canbra Foods Archives, *Canbra Foods Ltd., 25th Anniversary, Sept. 13,1982*, pamphlet, 3.

104. Ibid., 5.

105. Ibid., 7-9.

106. Ibid., 10.

107. Ibid., 6.

108. Ibid., 14.

109. Ibid., 15.

110. *Lethbridge Herald*, 31 December 1966; Canbra Foods Archives, Canbra Foods Ltd., *Annual Report for 1985*, 2.

111. Canbra Foods Archives, Canbra Foods Ltd., *Annual Report for 1985*, 8.

112. *Lethbridge Herald*, 31 December 1966.

113. Canbra Foods Archives, Canbra Foods Ltd., *Annual Report for 1985*, inside front cover.

114. Canbra Foods Archives, *Canbra Foods Ltd., 25th Anniversary, Sept. 13, 1982*, advertising on back cover.

115. Canbra Foods Archives, Canbra Foods Ltd., *Annual Report for 1990*, 6.

116. *Food in Canada*, October 1988, 9.

117. Canbra Foods Archives, Canbra Foods Ltd., *Annual Report for 1990*, 4.

118. Canbra Foods Archives, Canbra Foods Ltd., *Annual Report for 1995*, 6.

119. Ibid., 16.

120. Ibid., 15.

121. Interview by the author with Jason Elliott, 24 December 1996.

122. Alberta Corporate Registry, ATCO Industries Ltd. file.

123. Ibid.

124. Ibid.

125. Ibid.

126. Ibid.

127. Ibid.

128. *Globe and Mail*, 19 August 1982.

129. *Alberta Report*, 9 January 1995.

130. Ibid.

131. Ibid.

132. Alberta Corporate Registry, Canadian Foremost Ltd. file.

133. Jack Nodwell, as told to Dave Greber, "Doing Business Soviet-Style," *Report on Business Magazine*, November 1988, 141; Nattalia Lea, "Calgary's Russian Connection," *Alberta Business*, March 1990, 1.

134. *Calgary Herald*, 20 August 1988.

135. Nodwell, "Doing Business Soviet-Style," 144.

136. Ibid.

137. Foremost Industries Archives, Canadian Foremost Ltd., *Annual Report for 1992*, 6.

138. Foremost Industries Archives, Canadian Foremost Ltd., *Annual Report for 1991*, 5.

139. Ibid.

140. Foremost Industries Archives, Foremost Industries, Corporate Fact Sheet, 16 September 1996.

141. Foremost Industries Archives, Canadian Foremost Ltd., *Annual Report for 1989*, 1.

142. Foremost Industries Archives, Canadian Foremost Ltd., *Annual Report for 1990*, 7.

143. Foremost Industries Archives, Canadian Foremost Ltd., *Annual Report for 1992*, 5.

144. *Calgary Herald*, 12 May 1994.

145. *Financial Post*, 12 May 1994.

146. Foremost Industries Archives, Foremost Industries Inc., *Annual Report for 1995*, 9.

147. Canbra Foods Archives, Canbra Foods Ltd., Annual Report for 1990, 7.

148. Ibid., 4,7.

149. Ibid., 2.

150. *Calgary Herald*, 18 September 1992.

151. Ibid.

152. Ibid.

153. *Financial Times of Canada*, 10 April 1993.

154. Canbra Foods Archives, Canbra Foods Ltd., *Annual Report for 1995*, 14-15.

155. David H. Breen, *Alberta's Petroleum Industry and the Conservation Board* (Edmonton: University of Alberta Press, 1993), 307-308.

156. Alberta Corporate Registry, ATCO Industries Ltd. file.

157. Michael Bliss, *Northern Enterprise: Five Centuries of Canadian Business* (Toronto: McClelland & Stewart, 1990), 541-545; Graham D. Taylor and Peter A. Baskerville, *A Concise History of Business in Canada* (Toronto: Oxford University Press, 1994), 456-459; Larry Pratt, "The Political Economy of Province-Building: Alberta's Development Strategy, 1971-1981," in David Leadbeater, ed., *Essays on the Political Economy of Alberta* (Toronto: New Hogtown Press, 1984), 194-222; David G. Wood, *The Lougheed Legacy* (Toronto: Key Porter Books, 1985), 157-183.

158. Alberta Corporate Registry, ATCO Industries Ltd. file.

159. Ibid.

160. Alberta Corporate Registry, Canadian Foremost Ltd. file.

161. Michael Bliss, *Right Honourable Men: The Descent of Canadian Politics from Macdonald to Mulroney* (Toronto: Harper Collins Publishers, 1994), 269-271.

162. Standen Interview, 11 November 1991.

163. Canbra Foods Archives, Canbra Foods Ltd., *Annual Report for 1990*, inside front cover.

164. Canbra Foods Archives, Canbra Foods Ltd., *Annual Report for 1995*, inside front cover.

PART FOUR
RECENT TRENDS IN ALBERTA BUSINESS

CHAPTER EIGHT

SMALL BUSINESS IN THE MATURING ALBERTA ECONOMY

Once, when asked how his small business competed with larger companies from the 1940s to the 1990s, Steve Kovacs, the owner of a Red Deer shoe concern specializing in the production and distribution of big shoes, succinctly articulated how many small firms succeeded. "You can't compete with them. You can't buy like them. I don't carry anything they carry. I stay away from it 100 percent," he observed. "I got a name," he continued, "for having the biggest stock of wide shoes."[1] Small firms came under more and more pressure from larger enterprises in Alberta in the decades after World War II. In one field after another, business became increasingly consolidated, and small firms faced growing competition, suffering from great risks and uncertainties.

During the postwar years, the pace of growth in Alberta business was uneven, and on the downturn of the economy small firms were often forced to cut the prices of their goods and services. As profits dropped, they also cut costs. Yet, costs were not as flexible as prices. When demand and prices were declining, most small firms had very few resources to fall back on. If they could not solve their problems, bankruptcy could be the result, particularly during an extended downswing such as that beginning in the last third of 1980. Failures were common among small businesses, even in good times. A number of them, however, survived and prospered. Like the Steve Kovacs firm, many small businesses in Alberta specialized in particular products and services to develop market niches that large enterprises could not easily exploit.

Small businesses remained significant especially in manufacturing, sales and services, and agriculture from the 1940s to the 1990s, a period when the completion of Alberta's home market led to the maturing of the province's economy. In these years, Alberta's bountiful natural resources — forests, land, petroleum — continued to be powerful magnets that pulled entrepreneurs, investment capital, and workers into new small businesses. Willing to take risks, the entrepreneurs of this era put their own money and credit on the line to create new firms and develop them. The question of exactly what constitutes a small business must be approached with caution, but in the early 1990s, the Canadian Federation of Independent Business (CFIB) defined any firm with fewer than fifty employees as small. A complete breakdown of the size categories in use by the CFIB at that time was as follows: under 50 employees, small; 50-499, medium-sized; and over 500, large.[2]

The CFIB definitions are helpful, however, the functional approach in viewing small businesses is taken in this study wherever possible. The emphasis on functional characteristics, instead of on absolute measures of size, is useful, for most small firms in Alberta during the last half of the twentieth century shared several qualities. Often their management arrangements were fairly simple and uncomplicated. The top manager, who was usually also the owner, ran the company personally. The owner's hands-on style of management characterized small firms. He or she knew firsthand what was happening at all levels of the business. In small firms, hierarchies of top, middle, and lower salaried managers did not exist. Most small businesses were single-unit enterprises and operated in only one geographic area. Usually, besides recruiting their workers from their communities, small firms took part in the activities of local organizations.

Yet, although the CFIB's quantitative definitions of small business do not tell the whole story, they do help us in approximately measuring the position of small firms in the Alberta economy. Complete information on the operations of small businesses in the province is difficult to obtain. The available data frequently point consistently in directions that make it possible to provide a general picture of the economic position of small firms.

Measured as firms with under fifty employees, small business in 1982 accounted for 94.5 percent of the total number of business enterprises in Alberta. This figure increased slightly to 95.2 percent ten years later.[3] During the 1980s, the private sector in Alberta created some 214,000 net new jobs. Over four-fifths of them were created by independent small businesses with under fifty employees.[4] Job creation by small firms in Alberta continued despite the recession in the early 1980s and at a faster pace during the recovery of the provincial economy.

■

Small Business in Manufacturing

In 1992, companies employing under fifty workers accounted for twenty-four percent of Alberta's manufacturing employment.[5] Big manufacturers with over 500 employees accounted for a much larger share of Alberta's manufacturing employment: forty-six percent. Despite its relatively small share of employment, small business played a significant role as a components supplier and subcontractor to big manufacturers. Small companies were also a vital force in flexible manufacturing requiring craft skills. Other manufacturing sectors in Alberta where small firms had an important part were furniture, furs, apparel and textiles, and forestry machinery.

Some small craft-oriented manufacturers in Alberta during the twentieth century found themselves unable to compete with large manufacturing businesses and went out of existence. Others succeeded in making the transition to industrial production without abandoning their skills as craftspersons. Individual manufacturing firms in particular fields of endeavour, such as Risley Manufacturing in forestry machinery manufacturing, were typical of small companies that remained in business in the last quarter of the twentieth century.

Risley Manufacturing's lineage can be traced back to the firm Fluidic Power, which was formed in Grande Prairie by Reg Isley in June 1978. Born in Beaverlodge, Isley was educated at Elmworth High School. At Fluidic Power, a small hydraulic repair shop in Grande Prairie, he provided services to other businesses, repairing their hydraulic equipment.[6] The small building he rented gave him the space needed to begin work. The late 1970s were prosperous years for Fluidic Power. Within its first two years, the firm increased the size of its workforce from three to twenty.[7] In the fall of 1978, Fluidic Power finished construction of its own new building and moved in machinery to repair hydraulic equipment.

A severe depression that began in the fall of 1980 shattered hopes for further expansion. Reg Isley was an optimistic man, however, not easily dispirited by what he viewed as a temporary setback. Intrigued by what he noticed in the logging industry, Isley spent the next few years trying to develop a saw that would leave the butt surface of a tree smooth and level.[8] Isley's wife Emily, who was born in Fairview and educated at Grande Prairie High School, encouraged him in his efforts and played an important role in the development of the family enterprise in Grande Prairie. Isley's attempts to design a usable saw set the stage for his entrance into the forestry machinery manufacturing business.

In 1984, Isley discovered how to make the kind of saw he needed: a rotosaw. With this discovery, the manufacturing of forestry machinery took off. In that same year, Isley formed the Risley Equipment Company, a corporation set up to manufacture rotosaws and other forestry machinery. As it grew, Risley Equipment's plant manufactured a diversified range of high-quality products, but always dominated by specialized products for niche markets. With a population of 28,000 by 1991, Grande Prairie had an expanding industrial workforce ready for employment in the company's growing plant. Several specialty goods were paramount in the company's product line by the early 1990s: rotosaws, lim-mit delimbers, slingshot wood harvesters, and sets of grapples.[9]

Risley Equipment's sales were in Grande Prairie and the surrounding region, the rest of Canada, the United States, western Europe, Australia, New Zealand, and Japan. In response to Hurricane Hugo, which swept through the eastern United States in 1989, Risley Equipment manufactured and sold the Hugo rotosaw, a special, small version of the standard rotosaw, to eastern Americans to enable them to harvest the tangled trees hit by the hurricane.[10] Scientific research, an element that lay behind the Hugo rotosaw, was always important to Risley Equipment. Personally involved in the company's research efforts, Reg Isley had great success in using research to bring new products to the market.

Risley Equipment's strategy — several specialized products for niche markets, a strong emphasis on high-quality goods, and personal service — led to the growth of the concern. Sustained success in the market, as Reg Isley put it in 1990, was determined by three factors:

First in this business you have to be innovative. You've got to have a better idea than the next fellow and you've got to stay one jump ahead all the time. Second, you've got to design machines for high availability. We always try for that magic ninety-six per cent and most of the time we come pretty close. If the guys out in the bush are going to make a buck, the machines have got to work. Loggers can't afford to be broken down, waiting for parts and repairs. That leads to a third point, which is backup, parts and service. These services are equally important as the first two points. None of my points is any more important than the other – they are equally important. We always try to keep a good supply of parts on hand and if a machine needs attention, we get there as fast as we can.[11]

By 1989, the enterprise had two incorporated companies: Risley Manufacturing, headed by Reg Isley, and Risley Equipment, with Emily Risley as president. A willingness to try new things, deal with problems, and push on characterized Reg and Emily's work. Their son, Dean, who had incorporated computer technology into the manufacturing process, served as vice-president of both companies. By 1996, the family venture employed more than 200 men and women and earned $30 million in annual sales.[12]

The history of the LaFleche Bros. Company also illustrates how small manufacturing firms could prosper in Alberta in the twentieth century. Founded in 1906 in Edmonton by Quebec-born brothers Joseph A. and Tripoli J. LaFleche, the company experienced remarkable success as a personal, family business producing clothing for niche markets.[13] By the mid-1990s, the fourth generation of the LaFleche family in Alberta was running the company.

After serving an apprenticeship as tailors at the American Fashion Company in New York City, Joseph and Tripoli LaFleche had begun manufacturing men's clothing in that city.[14] When their business found itself squeezed by the growth of competition, they went to Brattleboro, Vermont to start again. Failing to make any progress in the tailoring business there, they moved to Edmonton in 1906 to begin once more.

Organized as a partnership in that year, LaFleche Bros. was family-owned and -operated. Using $600 borrowed from several individuals, Joseph and Tripoli LaFleche entered the clothing industry in Edmonton with the production of men's custom-tailored suits. During World War I,

LaFleche Brothers' tailoring workshop in 1955. Owners of the firm were proud of their products — uniforms and custom-made men's suits.

(Courtesy of City of Edmonton Archives and Edmonton Journal).

LaFleche Bros. successfully broke into established markets with their product. By 1921, the R. G. Dun & Company credit correspondent estimated that the firm was worth between $10,000 and $20,000.[15] In 1925, by which time the business had been incorporated, the LaFleche brothers set up the Westcraft System to produce custom-made suits. "We call it modernized tailoring, the system whereby high-class custom tailoring is turned out at moderate prices," explained Joseph LaFleche.[16] In addition to being innovative in design, the custom-made suits were backed by reliable, quick service. LaFleche Bros.' early success was attributable not only to a specialty product, innovation, and service, but also to the existence of a favourable external environment, for spending on the production of uniforms for City of Edmonton mayors, policemen, bus drivers, and fire fighters, provincial forest rangers, Greyhound bus drivers, and officers of the Princess Patricia Light Infantry Regiment increased LaFleche Bros.' sales.[17]

Relations between management and labour were good. As owners and managers, the LaFleche brothers' actions were paternalistic. The company was hard hit by the Great Depression in the 1930s, but Joseph and Tripoli LaFleche survived the difficult times and did not lay off their employees. They sent them home temporarily when orders for custom-made suits and uniforms dried up from time to time.[18]

LaFleche Bros.' emergence as a custom-tailored suit maker of national repute during World War II marked the beginning of two decades of rapid growth. By 1963, the company's thirty-five workers were producing 100 suits and uniforms a week.[19] A combination of inter-related elements helped bring about this success. Louis LaFleche, son of Joseph LaFleche, ran the firm from 1933 until the early 1970s and, like the founders, he was innovative. Trained in custom suit making himself at the American Fashion

Company's Cutting and Design School in New York City, he spent a good deal of time at the machines on the Edmonton plant floor creating new patterns and new suits. "We have always demanded the highest possible quality in workmanship and materials, and in this way there is a constant demand for our product," noted Louis LaFleche.[20] He worked closely with his three sons, Gordon, LeRoi, and Arthur, who by 1963 had joined the firm, as well as with employees, developing new ways of producing suits.

After the death of Louis LaFleche in 1975, his three sons became the key individuals running the company.[21] Besides formulating policy and providing general supervision of the company's operations, Gordon and LeRoi concentrated on designing and production, while Arthur managed the sales end of the business.[22] By 1992, LeRoi had become the company's president and head designer and his two sons Bryan and LeRoi Jr. had become junior managers. LaFleche Bros., still a family-owned concern, continued to depend on its reputation for high-quality products and personal service. In 1992, LaFleche Bros.' total sales rose to $1.5 million and the company employed thirty-five full-time and three part-time persons. Fifty-five percent of these sales came from uniforms and forty-five percent from custom-tailored men's suits.[23]

Under the leadership of LeRoi LaFleche and his two sons, the company successfully adjusted to the computer age in 1992 and 1993, adding computer design and laser cutters to its operations to speed production. LaFleche Bros. continued to do well in part through constant innovation in the company's specialty products: uniforms and custom-made men's suits. The owners, father and sons, continued to get their hands dirty on the plant floor, with no managerial hierarchies dividing them from their workforce. These developments left LaFleche Bros. well prepared to meet the growing competition in the mid-1990s.[24]

Furs by Sam was similar to LaFleche Bros. in some respects. Founded in Medicine Hat in 1950 by Sam Stone, Furs by Sam produced fur coats especially for women and found a profitable market niche in the late 1950s and 1960s.[25] Furs by Sam never tried to challenge any of the larger fur producers in areas where their economies of scale gave them an edge. Like LaFleche Bros., Furs by Sam was a small family enterprise that relied on a reputation for high-quality products and personal service.

Sam Stone was born in Winnipeg in 1919. He was educated there and served with the Royal Canadian Air Force during World War II. Stone had gained previous experience in specialty fur operations, working during the late 1930s first as an apprentice and then as a journeyman for W. Cohen Furs on Portage Avenue in Winnipeg in the production of furs for sale in the local market.[26] In 1947, Stone struck out on his own, leaving his salaried job and establishing his own firm, Stone Furs, in Winnipeg. But in 1950, he sold this fur business and moved to Medicine Hat to open a small

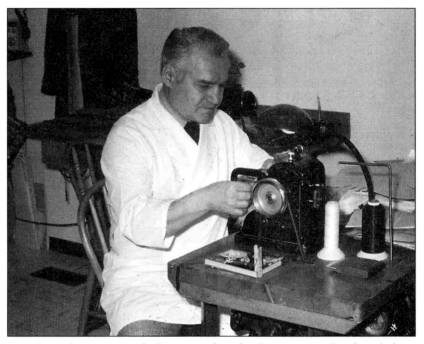

Sam Stone fur coats, mostly for women but also for men, were hand-crafted products. Sam Stone at work in his shop on 2nd Street Southeast in Medicine Hat in 1952. (Courtesy of Sam and Sheri Stone).

fur shop and take advantage of new opportunities.

Using one of his old personal Winnipeg contacts, Henry Chevrier, a travelling fur salesman for Eaton's, Stone began in Medicine Hat serving in his own shop, Furs by Sam, as a fitter for Eaton's local store.[27] Then, Stone went on to manufacture new fur coats, mostly for women but also for men. He also took in old fur coats to make any necessary repairs. To develop his business, Stone adopted the most advanced production technologies of the day. By 1959, Furs by Sam was worth between $10,000 and $20,000, reported the Dun & Bradstreet credit correspondent.[28] Stone employed five persons, most of them women.[29] The relations between Stone and his employees were cordial and mutually beneficial, complete with opportunities for some of them to stay with the firm as long as twenty-five years. In his shop, work was divided into different tasks by the late 1950s and 1960s. Stone's establishment had two main departments, one devoted to manufacturing fur coats and the second concerned with doing repair jobs. The shop also served as a retail outlet for fur coats Stone himself produced as well as for those he sold as an agent for Winnipeg, Toronto, and Montreal fur companies.

Furs by Sam survived and prospered by specializing in women's fur coats. Rather than competing directly with big fur companies, Furs by Sam co-existed with larger enterprises in Alberta turning out products for a niche market. Stone's wife Sheri, whom he had married in Winnipeg in 1942, played an important role in the growth of the family business in Medicine Hat from the beginning.[30] A graduate of Success College in Winnipeg, Sheri assisted Sam in keeping the books and selling fur coats. She helped create a friendly environment in the shop for their many customers in Medicine Hat and the surrounding region. By 1974, total annual sales had reached $150,000.[31]

The efforts of Sam and Sheri formed the basis for a strong and continuing firm in Medicine Hat in the late 1980s and 1990s. Important for the development of their fur business in this period as well was their son Perry, who began to run the enterprise in the mid-1980s. Sam's technical creativity remained one of the keys to the firm's success. Another factor that contributed to the growth of Furs by Sam was Sam's close involvement in community affairs and deep interest in his community. In addition to belonging to the local Rotary Club from 1955 onward, he served as city alderman and played an active role in the development of the hospital in Medicine Hat at different times.[32] Furs by Sam continued in the mid-1990s as a significant element in the fur industry, servicing a fairly highly specialized market niche.

Like Furs by Sam, the furniture manufacturing firm John Tynan & Co. succeeded by differentiating its products from those of its larger counterparts in Alberta. Founded as a partnership in Calgary in 1929, John Tynan & Co. was incorporated a few years later but continued to be run as a family business into the 1980s. John Tynan & Co. became a successful firm by developing technological innovations in the manufacturing of specialty products — especially upholstered furniture — and by maintaining close personal connections between owner-managers and retailers buying its goods.

John Tynan, who was born on a farm in County Donegal, Northern Ireland in 1892, began as a salesman in the furniture department of Eaton's department store at Toronto in 1912. Tynan quickly proved to be a good furniture salesman, but, in 1914 at the outbreak of World War I, he left for County Donegal to run the family farm when his older brothers joined the British armed forces.[33] Moving to Vancouver in 1927, he was employed by his brother Allan as a furniture maker. He performed well as a furniture maker because he thoroughly understood the manufacturing techniques that had been developed. In 1929, he went to Calgary where, in partnership with his brother, he opened a plant to produce upholstered furniture. While his brother remained in Vancouver to continue running his plant there, John Tynan soon purchased his brother's share of the Calgary business.[34] In 1932, he reorganized the venture as John Tynan & Company.

Incorporated for $30,000, the company was backed by the Canadian Bank of Commerce from the beginning.[35]

Headed by John Tynan as president and general manager, the company brought a new investor into the picture, James Orr, who became vice-president and secretary-treasurer.[36] Employing eighteen workers, the company turned out upholstered furniture, especially chesterfields and chairs, mostly for the local market. The times, however, did not favour new businesses. Alberta was suffering from the Great Depression in the early and mid-1930s, which hurt the province's furniture industry. John Tynan & Company led a shaky existence. The business posted losses in 1932, 1933, 1935, and 1936.[37] "We could close up, and perhaps we should," said Tynan to Orr, "but there'd be no point to it. We can't go back any further than we are already."[38] Several times during these years, Tynan talked the Calgary sheriff out of closing the company down.[39]

Short of money from the outset, John Tynan & Company had only $20,000 in paid-in capital when it started business, and in 1936 the firm's stockholders were still $10,000 short of paying in their full subscriptions.[40] Despite the shortage of funds, the company survived and grew; how it did so illustrates some of the ways small enterprises were able to co-exist with their larger counterparts in Alberta. In the early 1940s, John Tynan & Company developed a specialty product for a niche market, Kant-Sag upholstered furniture. Made of top-quality wood and hand-tied steel coil in an adjustable web to permit tightening, this highly sophisticated upholstered furniture gave John Tynan & Company an edge over its competitors and allowed the firm to break into the regional market.[41]

Entering a regional market, John Tynan relied heavily on his personal ties with other businesspeople. In business in Calgary, he had come to know the executives at Eaton's, Hudson's Bay Company, Woodward's, Sears, and other retailers. These retailers began purchasing John Tynan & Company's Kant-Sag upholstered furniture and liked it so much that they continued as customers.[42]

John Tynan's son William played an important role in helping to expand the company's marketing organization. Born in County Donegal, Northern Ireland in 1925, William attended Central High School in Calgary and served overseas with the Canadian Navy during World War II from 1943 to 1945. From 1939 to 1942, he worked in his father's factory, learning to make upholstered furniture. His skill in furniture manufacturing rapidly won the admiration of his father. In 1946, after returning from overseas, William joined his father's company as a travelling salesman in Alberta, Saskatchewan, and British Columbia.[43]

Rapid growth in demand for Kant-Sag upholstered furniture and the concomitant expansion of the company's marketing organization led to increased investment in manufacturing facilities. In 1951, retained profits, always an important source of funding, helped pay for an addition to John Tynan & Company's plant. The value of the plant's output reached $750,000 in 1954, and the company employed fifty-five workers.[44] Furniture construction required a broad range of skills, and the workers clearly possessed the skills that were needed. Relations between management and labour were amicable. William, who had obtained a diploma in business administration from Mount Royal College in 1947, had become sales manager with a staff of three travelling salesmen who secured orders especially in the prairie West. "Our market is limited to the prairie, but that's all the market we will need for a long time. The prairie is growing, and we plan to grow with it," said John Tynan.[45]

The mid-1950s were prosperous years for John Tynan & Company. Total sales rose to $1 million in 1957.[46] In that year, John Tynan retired from active management of the company and turned over the reins to his son William. John provided advice by remaining a director until his death in 1967. Under William Tynan's leadership, the family enterprise continued to flourish. The start of another expansion drive at John Tynan & Company came in 1958, as the firm increased its authorized capitalization to $130,000.[47] Considerable money was spent on improvements over the next several years. As its modern plant continued to manufacture high-quality Kant-Sag upholstered furniture in the late 1950s and 1960s, John Tynan & Company became an increasingly important element in the upholstered furniture industry.

In his approach to business, William Tynan, like his father before him, adopted the most advanced techniques. He experimented with new construction methods, organized the furniture plant in an efficient way, and employed effective inventory controls.[48] He also maintained control over transportation costs by using his own trucks for furniture deliveries. As in the past, John Tynan & Company relied heavily on skilled workers, a number of whom stayed with the firm for many years.[49] The company continued to benefit from good management-labour relations.

The business philosophy at John Tynan & Company also remained unchanged. A commitment to high-quality Kant-Sag upholstered furniture characterized William Tynan's efforts. Certainly, the company was still at the high-quality end of the market in the 1970s. John Tynan & Company still aimed at a distinct niche in the market and grew significantly. In 1981, total sales climbed to $2.5 million.[50]

In that year, William Tynan sold the family furniture plant to his daughter Maureen.[51] The dedication to high-quality Kant-Sag upholstered furniture remained unshaken, as Maureen began to run the business. She reorganized the company as Tynan Furniture.[52] Trained earlier at the plant as a furniture maker under her father's supervision and educated in interior design at Mount Royal College, Maureen settled in to servicing a small

Denoon's Meat Market, founded by William A. Denoon and still operated by his son Gordon, Nanton, 1997. (Courtesy of Gordon Denoon).

upholstered furniture market niche. This meant that her company was able to co-exist with its larger counterparts in Alberta in the late twentieth century. She made the most of new opportunities in the 1980s and 1990s. For instance, she supplied the Palliser Hotel with Kant-Sag upholstered furniture for Queen Elizabeth's visit in June 1990.[53] Retaining its reputation for high-quality production, Tynan Furniture continued to prosper in sales.

Denoons' of Nanton, a small meat producer, also succeeded by differentiating its products from those of its larger Alberta counterparts. Rather than compete with big companies in the large-scale production of meat, Denoons' of Nanton co-existed side by side with them by producing specialized meat products for niche markets in the last third of the twentieth century. Pursuing this strategy, the firm's approach to business closely resembled the approach taken by Tynan Furniture in its competition with the larger furniture companies in Alberta.

The origins of Denoons' of Nanton can be traced back to the firm Denoons' Meat Market established in Nanton in 1917. This business was owned and managed by William A. Denoon. Born into a family of Scottish descent in Peterborough, Ontario in 1887, Denoon attended a local school and began serving an apprenticeship as a machinist in the Peterborough branch of General Electric.[54] After breaking his contract with this company in 1906 to go to High River, where in the following year his brother George found a job for him with a local horse breeder and dealer, William Denoon became acquainted with the livestock industry in Alberta. Denoon returned to Peterborough in 1908 to complete his apprenticeship with General Electric, but instead of pursuing a career as a machinist, he opened a butcher shop in Didsbury in 1909.[55] Eight years later, after selling his Didsbury shop, working at a variety of jobs, and failing in the meat business in Calgary, the restless Denoon moved to Nanton to begin again as a butcher.[56]

By 1921, the R. G. Dun & Company credit correspondent estimated that Denoons' Meat Market in Nanton was worth between $5,000 and $10,000.[57] Over the next nine years, William Denoon purchased cattle and hogs from local ranchers and farmers and produced fresh and cured meats for local markets.[58] The Great Depression in the 1930s severely retarded the development of his business. During these years, he found the going tough as he had $50,000 in bad debts on his books.[59] In 1939, Denoons' Meat Market was worth only between $3,000 and $5,000, reported the R. G. Dun & Company credit correspondent.[60]

Central in importance for the future of Denoons' Meat Market was the frozen food locker plant William Denoon built in 1941.[61] He hired Archie Taylor, an experienced meat packer. The 184 individual lockers in which Denoon stored high-quality frozen meat products for his customers allowed him to provide a specialized service. He was able to service a specialized market niche that helped insulate his products from competition.

Denoon's son Gordon also played an important part in building up the small firm. Born in Nanton in 1924, Gordon attended the local high school, joined the air cadets at age sixteen, and served overseas with the Royal Canadian Air Force Medical Corps during World War II from 1943 to 1945.[62] Entering Denoons' Meat Market as an employee in 1945, Gordon learned how to slaughter livestock and cure and cut meat from his father and Archie Taylor. In 1952, Gordon became a partner and the family firm changed its name to W. A. Denoon & Son. During the next sixteen years, the firm produced a variety of meat goods and found a ready market for them.[63] Reaching beyond Nanton, the business also sold its meat products to customers in the surrounding region. William and Gordon's personal connections were of great importance in securing these sales. Total annual sales in this period reached $50,000.[64]

In 1968, Gordon took the firm into the second generation of control, as William retired from active management.[65] By this time, Gordon had the kind of all-round knowledge of the meat business that was essential to run the family concern. The founder, William, died in 1976, but the family component endured as Gordon later hired his nephew Donald Kitchen.[66] There were hints, however, that the old order was beginning to change. Under Gordon's leadership, the small firm eventually came to be called Denoons' of Nanton.

During the late 1960s and 1970s, Gordon Denoon began innovating in high-quality meat products, preventing competitors from usurping his trade. For example, he experimented with garlic sausage, pepper sausage, and spiced beef and found a specialized market niche in which he could survive and prosper.[67] Denoon's growing trade remained closely linked to home demand in Nanton and the surrounding area, but his increase in business also came from substantial sales in Calgary, Vancouver, Hong Kong, Hawaii, and Germany.[68] As orders from outside markets grew, Denoon's involvement with meat production intensified. By 1978, total annual sales had increased to $100,000. This figure rose to $150,000 ten years later.[69]

Denoon made steady progress. He had three employees in the 1980s.[70] Relations between Denoon and his workers were friendly and mutually supportive. Significantly, he carried his concern for his employees into a similar interest in the economic and social development of Nanton as a community. Besides being a founder of the Nanton Chamber of Commerce, Denoon helped start the local tennis club, directed the town's United Church Choir, and played a leading role in organizing the Foothills Regional Choir.[71] Denoon was thinking of retirement and willing to sell his meat business. Unable to sell, however, in 1989 he closed his shop.[72] He continued to make his well-known products, especially sausages, for a number of his customers. Those who knew Denoon well were aware that he remained committed to high-quality meat products.

As the examples of Risley Manufacturing, LaFleche Bros., Furs by Sam, John Tynan & Company, and Denoons' of Nanton illustrate, manufacturing presented many opportunities to aspiring small businesspeople in Alberta after World War II.

■

Small Business in Sales and Services

Sales and services offered even more hope during this period. The province's retailers had been a traditional stronghold of Alberta small business. In 1992, fifty-one percent of retail employment in Alberta was accounted for by firms with under fifty employees.[73] The importance of small business was also apparent in services at this time. For instance, small firms with under fifty employees accounted for fifty-seven percent of business service employment.[74]

For many years, the small Alberta retailer had been losing ground to big chains. In 1992, retailers with over 500 employees accounted for thirty percent of all retail employment in Alberta.[75] Most large retailer growth came through the addition of store units in the province. The rise of chain stores after World War I undermined the significance of independent retailers in numerous trades. In variety goods, stores such as the F. W. Woolworth Company, an American chain, came to small as well as large cities in Alberta. As we have seen, the Alberta chain, Jenkins' Groceteria, opened stores in both small towns and cities.

Some small firms, however, continued to prosper, frequently through specialization in the lines of merchandise they offered. Others thrived by

banding together in associations to gain benefits obtained by big businesses, such as discounts secured through high-volume purchases.

Reach & Co., a small department store in Fort Macleod, typifies how
some independent retailers managed to hold their own. Founded in 1886,
Reach & Co. originally sold lime, tents, wagon covers, groceries, and many
other products.[76] As Fort Macleod grew, the store built a profitable business
by providing reliable goods and service. The store's founder and owner,
Charles J. Reach, was a man who could make the firm grow. Reach's personal and business connections in the community were an important factor in his store's growth.

Born in Ipswich, England in 1852 and educated in a boys school there,
Reach served an apprenticeship in Eaton's department store in Toronto.[77]
By the end of World War I, Reach & Co. had emerged as a small department store. Total sales amounted to $132,000 in 1919.[78] Reach & Co. was
incorporated in November 1922, several months after Reach's seventieth
birthday.[79] Authorized capitalization was $100,000. Of the 1,000 shares of
stock at a par value of $100 per share, Reach, the president, took 998.
Harry C. Winter, the manager, took one share, and one share went to the
grocery manager, Wesley Shield. Total paid-in capital amounted to
$100,000 by 1924.[80]

After Charles's death in 1928, Reach & Co. continued to grow as a
family-owned and -operated department store, with Charles's son Charles
Sydney, who was educated at St. Joseph's College in Edmonton and
Garbutt's Business College in Calgary, going into the family business as a
small shareholder and clerk.[81] Offering three main lines of products — groceries, dry goods, and men's wear — Reach & Co. placed an increasing
emphasis on grocery sales. This specialization served the company well.

Reach & Co. faced growing competition from large department stores
in Alberta. A partial solution to this problem appeared in 1929, when
Charles S. Reach became a founder and member of Associated Grocers
Ltd., an organization of independent Alberta retailers with its head office
and warehouse in Calgary.[82] Among other founding members of Associated
Grocers were Craig & Co. of Olds, Joseph M. Thomson of Milo, and F. M.
Thomson & Co. of Blairmore.[83] Through the scale of operations of
Associated Grocers, Reach & Co. was able to reduce its costs of doing business and offer lower prices to customers. Associated Grocers cut out middlemen in distribution, instead making purchases directly from growers and
manufacturers of goods. As a shareholder in Associated Grocers, Reach &
Co. also received dividends. Despite the onset of the Great Depression in
1929, Reach & Co.'s profits from its department store business came to
$4,572 in 1930.[84] Most of the company's profits were ploughed back into
the firm to meet its development needs.

This happy state of affairs, however, soon came to a halt as the

By the early twentieth century, Reach & Co.'s small department store in Fort Macleod was a marketplace where town and country people mingled. Around 1998, one of the main lines of products in the store was groceries. The photographs above the groceries show scenes from the early years of the century, including the front of Reach & Co.'s store on the right. (Courtesy of Charles G. Reach).

depression deepened. Reach & Co. was led by a new president; Charles S. Reach had taken over this position by 1931. Charles was an able executive, but the depression hurt the store. Reach & Co. posted losses in 1931, 1932, and 1934.[85] Fortunately for the company, it was able to obtain loans from the Canadian Bank of Commerce to keep going. Soon afterward, business picked up, and in 1935 the company reported a profit of $252.[86] Reach & Co.'s connection with Associated Grocers also contributed to its survival during these years.

The Second World War helped revive Reach & Co.'s financial fortunes. As markets expanded, the company's total sales increased to $159,719 in 1941.[87] The company shared in wartime prosperity and, in 1946, made net profits of $18,143 on total sales of $196,696.[88] In the period from the mid-1940s to the 1950s, Reach & Co. developed along lines established in earlier times. Grocery sales, more than $105,000 in 1946, continued to dominate the company's activities.[89] Reach & Co.'s heavy reliance on groceries was fortunate, for in these years grocery customers were a growing market for the products of the company. Dry goods sales and men's wear sales remained important.

Charles George Reach assumed the presidency at Reach & Co. at the death of his father Charles S. in 1954.[90] Born in Fort Macleod in 1931, Charles G. had worked his way up through the ranks at Reach & Co.[91] He, too, understood that specialization in groceries and a continuing link with Associated Grocers was good for his family firm. In 1963, Reach & Co.'s total sales rose to $372,000, with grocery sales amounting to $268,625.[92] Like his father and grandfather before him, Charles G. never abandoned other principal lines of stock, dry goods and men's wear, in the department store. Like them, he also enjoyed a great deal of help from women in the Reach family.

The store offered women in the Reach family opportunities for owner-ship and management from the beginning.[93] Pearl Reach, wife of Charles J. and part owner, helped run the business until shortly before her death in 1902.[94] Although Jennifer, Charles J.'s second wife, did not become involved in management, she participated in the ownership of the store as did her daughters Winnifred and Catherine.[95] Catherine and Winnifred also assisted in managing the family business, especially the grocery and ladies' wear departments. Marion Reach, wife of Charles S. and part owner, played an important role in running the store, particularly after her hus-band's death.[96] Similarly, Betty Reach, Charles G.'s wife and part owner, was significantly involved in managing the store.[97]

As president, Charles G. Reach spent much of his time planning the development of the company. Tremendous growth resulted from his effort. Reach & Co. supplied a growing number of families in Fort Macleod and the surrounding region with groceries, dry goods, men's wear, and ladies' wear. There was almost a threefold increase in Reach & Co.'s sales between 1963 and the early 1990s. In 1990, the company's total sales reached $1 million.[98] Service and personal connections continued to be of consider-able importance in making sales. Taking a long-term approach to business, Charles G. Reach retained a good deal of the company's earnings for devel-opment purposes. Reach & Co.'s ongoing relationship with Associated Grocers remained a significant factor in the company's ability to co-exist with large enterprises.

Small retailers also banded together in other fields to secure some of the benefits obtained by large firms. One such field was the hardware industry in Alberta. In 1955, the High River Hardware Company joined other small Alberta hardware retailers to form the Link Hardware Company, a corporation organized to meet competition from big chains, such as Marshall Wells.[99] The five founders of the Link Hardware Company were Donald Blake of the High River Hardware Company and four Calgary hardware merchants: Art Chesney, George Webber, William Hislop, and Kenneth Burlock.[100] They opened their head office in the Lancaster Building in Calgary.[101] To secure merchandise at lower prices,

Blake and Webber journeyed to Toronto to purchase 100 ironing boards directly from a manufacturer.[102] Each of the five founders took twenty iron-ing boards. Through this direct purchasing, they realized a saving of more than twenty-five percent. Initially, The Link Hardware Company used an old shed behind Webber's hardware store as a warehouse. Gradually, the company gained direct access to many other manufacturers' products, such as batteries and paint.[103]

As the last half of the twentieth century progressed, the Link Hardware Company grew, spreading across Alberta as well as into British Columbia, Saskatchewan, Manitoba, the Yukon, and the Northwest Territories.[104] The good news of lower costs travelled quickly by word of mouth from one small hardware dealer to another.[105] By the late 1960s, there were more than 400 western Canadian hardware stores on the company's list of share-holders. In Alberta, such stores were especially numerous: Wilfred W. Lilges in Grande Prairie, D. Brookhart's in Hinton, Burrell Gibson's in Wainwright, Raymond Renaud's in Westlock, H. W. Soley's in Lacombe, A. L. Phillips' in Trochu, Carl Leeson's in Didsbury, and John M. Wolfe's in Vulcan, among others.[106] The company had warehouse facilities not only in Calgary, but also in Edmonton, Winnipeg, and Victoria.

Donald Blake's association with the Link Hardware Company contin-ued to play a major role in the growth of his small hardware firm in High River. The High River Hardware Company co-existed side by side with larger hardware enterprises by cutting its costs of doing business through its connection with the Link Hardware Company. At High River Hardware, Blake sold a wide range of goods, including paint, batteries, ironing boards, dinnerware sets, table lamps, radios, linoleum, duo therm oil heaters, tube skates, sleighs, plastic wading pools, camp cook sets, lawn mowers, and chain saws, and provided dependable service.[107] Between the late 1940s and the 1970s, total annual sales at High River Hardware increased from $75,000 to $200,000.[108]

A management change spurred diversification at High River Hardware. In 1977, Donald Blake's son John began in the company as a clerk. Two years later, John Blake took over the firm.[109] With a BA from the University of Calgary, he was prepared to lead the family business in a new direction. Around 1979, John Blake diversified by adding building products to the goods he sold at his hardware store.[110] As time passed, building products came to account for a growing share of the store's sales.

High River Hardware's move into building products occurred around the same time the company gained direct access to goods through a new organization. In 1980, the Link Hardware Company and the Home Hardware Stores Company, a large central Canadian group of independent hardware dealers, united to become the Home Hardware Stores Company.[111] Like Link before it, Home offered substantial savings in the cost of goods for John Blake's High River Hardware. His reliable service helped bring an increasing number of customers into his store. With the store's business going well, its total annual sales soon reached $1.5 million.[112]

Blake faced the problem of the recession in 1981, trying to keep his small hardware company economically viable.[113] When the construction industry declined in the early 1980s, High River Hardware had difficulties with building products, which slowed the company's diversification drive. Blake had succeeded in leading High River Hardware into a new path of development, a considerable accomplishment in the small business world, but unstable and falling sales to building contractors made it difficult for him to turn the store around. In 1990, Home took over Blake's hardware store.[114] Vanishing as an independent firm, the High River Hardware shared the experience of numerous small Alberta retailers in the late twentieth century.

Other small retailers in Alberta, however, did not suffer the same fate. In fact, many survived the perils of the 1980s and grew. The growth of the Alberta Machinery Company of Camrose indicates the continuing importance of small businesses in sales across Alberta. By the outbreak of World War I, settlers were pouring into the province, eager to make a living on its fertile soil. The Alberta Machinery Company had its start in these settlement years.

The story of the Alberta Machinery Company is rooted in the firm Francoeur Bros., which was formed in Camrose in 1914.[115] This business was a partnership of two brothers, David R. (D. R.) and Fernand Francoeur. Like those involved with the Alberta Machinery Company in later years, the partners in Francoeur Bros. had close personal and business connections with the Camrose business community. These ties were especially strong in the case of D. R. Francoeur. Born in St. Roche des Aulnaies, Quebec, he was educated in a local classical college. He moved from Quebec to Camrose in 1911 and, by the following year, had become an agent for the Quebec farm machinery manufacturer, the C.A.R. Desjardins Company of St. Andre. At first, Francoeur sold threshing machines, small engines, and a few other products.[116] He had an early opportunity to expand his business in 1914, when his brother Fernand joined him to organize Francoeur Bros. and open a small farm implements shop in Camrose.

Their venture reflected the hope that a farm machinery enterprise represented. The new retail firm was to make implements available to farmers and help bring hinterland trade to Camrose. In doing so, Francoeur Bros. would contribute to the town's growth. Even as the firm stimulated the development of the town, its efforts fostered mechanization in the farming community. As more and more farmers moved into the Camrose region, Francoeur Bros. built a substantial business selling Moody and Desjardins

Serving the Alberta farm economy with merchandise, including small threshing outfits, became a significant area of enterprise in the 1920s for many retail businesses like Francoeur Bros.' Alberta Machinery Company. The first office and showrooms of Alberta Machinery Company on the corner of Bakken Street and Alberta Avenue at Camrose around 1920. (Courtesy of J. Maurice Francoeur).

threshing outfits, as well as engines, fanning mills, pumps, windmills, and many other items that farmers needed. The machines the firm provided, often through credit sales, were backed by reliable, fast service. Financing the retail farm machinery business required the retention of profits, but the firm also depended on credit from suppliers and banks to grow. The entrepreneurial drive of the Francoeur brothers was evident in their opening of branches in Edmonton and Saskatoon during World War I, but the postwar depression forced them to close these branches in 1919 and confine their trade to Camrose and the surrounding area.[117]

In recognition of the altered geographical area in which the firm traded, the Francoeur brothers changed its name to the Alberta Machinery Company in 1920. During the next two decades, however, troubles hampered the company's operations. After recovering from the postwar depression in the mid-1920s, the Alberta Machinery Company was handicapped by the withdrawal of D. R. Francoeur in 1927, who was suffering from tuberculosis. He left a gap that was difficult to fill. Although the company benefited from the entry of Victor Forster as a partner in 1932, it had a hard time coping with the economic problems caused by the Great Depression. The situation was further complicated by the death of Forster in the late 1930s and Fernand Francoeur's death in 1942.[118]

With an improvement in his health, D. R. Francoeur took over the family firm in 1942; his sons Louis and Paul became his partners in 1942 and 1944 respectively.[119] Born in 1918 and a graduate of Camrose High School, Louis served with the Royal Canadian Air Force during World War II until he was injured in 1942.[120] Louis had already made a name for himself at the Alberta Machinery Company in the mid- and late 1930s by, among other things, successfully delivering the horses that the firm had taken in trade for machinery to Quebec customers.[121] Desjardins was no longer supplying the company with farm implements. Alberta Machinery Company obtained farm machinery from Oliver, Minneapolis Moline, Monitor, and especially Allis-Chalmers.[122] Allis-Chalmers machines had lasting popularity and advanced the company's trade for many years. After joining the Alberta Machinery Company in 1942, Louis played a vital role in helping his father manage the business.

Led by a new management and sharing in the wartime prosperity, the Alberta Machinery Company entered an era of growth during the early and mid-1940s. A land purchase enlarged the company's Camrose property in the downtown area. In 1942, the Alberta Machinery Company bought the property formerly occupied by another farm implements dealer.[123] The mid- and late 1940s and the 1950s were prosperous years for the company. While the Alberta Machinery Company centred its attention on selling Allis-Chalmers tractors and combines, it also supplied farmers with other products. The Francoeurs used some of the profits to improve their retail facilities and provide better service. In 1960, the year D. R. Francoeur retired, the Alberta Machinery Company was incorporated.[124] Further growth came in the 1960s and the 1970s, as the company bought several downtown lots and an abandoned curling rink.

The entrepreneurial drive, so evident in the company's management in earlier decades, continued to be characteristic of its leadership from the 1970s to the 1990s. In 1971, Louis Francoeur's sons Maurice and Robert purchased Paul's interest in the Alberta Machinery Company.[125] The father and two sons managed their company well. Spurred by the growing demand for farm implements, they began thinking of further expansion. In 1979, they constructed and moved into a considerably enlarged farm machinery shop in Camrose's industrial park. At the same time, Louis retired and sold his interest in the business to his two sons.[126] In 1986, Maurice bought Robert's share in the firm and took over the Alberta Machinery Company.

Born in Camrose in 1943, Maurice Francoeur received his B. Ed. from the University of Alberta and taught school in Alberta for five years.[127] After joining the Alberta Machinery Company in 1971, he played an important part in its success. By the time he took over the small family business fifteen years later, its total annual sales had reached $5 million.[128] As Camrose grew through its continuing involvement with the surrounding agricultural region, so did the Alberta Machinery Company. By 1991, Camrose had become a city of nearly 13,000 people.[129] To maintain his competitive edge, Francoeur installed a computer system in the farm machinery shop in the mid-1980s and continued to provide dependable, rapid service. Francoeur's reliance on Allis products as well as on other items, such as Monitor reciprocating water systems, was fortunate, for the Alberta Machinery Company continued to flourish as a small retailer in the late 1980s and 1990s.

With the development of an urbanized and industrialized society in Alberta, services remained the home of small business firms even more than retailing did in the last half of the twentieth century. Service industries, a rapidly growing segment of the Alberta economy, were clearly a stronghold of small businesses. Small local businesses played an important role in engineering, computer, architectural, accounting, legal, and other types of service industries. Only with the development of engineering firms, such as Associated Engineering Services of Edmonton, could local and regional oil and gas companies grow to become large enterprises in the 1970s and 1980s.[130] Fast growth characterized the computer industry, so that by 1990 there were about 400 small computer businesses in Alberta offering services in areas like software development and systems analysis, computer leasing, and data entry and processing.[131]

The architectural industry was dominated by small businesses. Small architectural firms could become prosperous in the years after World War II — as shown by the experience of Stevenson Raines Barrett Hutton Seton & Partners, a firm whose lineage can be traced back to the partnership of Leo Dowler and James M. Stevenson formed in Calgary in 1911.[132] Between 1911 and 1915, the architectural firm Dowler & Stevenson grew and stayed close to its customers by offering personal services. Over the next three decades, Stevenson, a native of Airdrie, Scotland who attended Glasgow School of Arts, demonstrated his capacity for growth in other roles as well: overseas as a private with the First Pioneer Battalion, Canadian Expeditionary Force, during World War I, as a federal architect with the Dominion Department of Public Works in Alberta for nine years after the war, and as an architectural partner of George Fordyce in Calgary from 1928 to the early 1940s.[133] Through sound planning, good management, hard work, and close ties with the Calgary business community, the Fordyce & Stevenson architectural firm grew to become an important force in the local architectural industry.

Even for individuals as diligent as Stevenson and Fordyce, however, the Great Depression years were an unpropitious time to do business.[134] Through personal connections, they continued to find work. Stevenson's son John, who received his B.Sc. Arch. from the University of Alberta and served overseas with the Royal Canadian Engineers during World War II, joined the firm as a partner in 1945, when it became J. M. Stevenson & Son.[135] Over the next eleven years, the firm's growth took place as part of the expansion of Calgary's architectural industry. Personal and business ties remained important in carving out a market for J. M. Stevenson & Son's high-quality services. After his father's retirement in 1956, John took new partners, and in 1967 the firm was reorganized as Stevenson Raines Barrett Hutton Seton & Partners. As the years passed after 1945, the Calgary International Airport, the University of Calgary, Mount Royal College, the Calgary Exhibition and Stampede, and schools and hospitals in Red Deer, Drumheller, and Medicine Hat became some of the firm's most important customers.

Just as much as the architectural industry, accounting was a home for small businesses in Alberta. In Edmonton, for instance, the certified management accountants firm McDonald & Co. was established in 1972. Over the next twenty-four years, the firm grew by specializing in owner-managed businesses and providing personal, professional accounting, tax, and computer services.[136] By the mid-1990s, many other small accounting firms had made their appearance in Edmonton, including Small Business Accounting Services, which provided a full range of services to small owner-managed enterprises, especially services involving corporate and personal income tax returns, financial statements, bookkeeping, payroll, and management and tax planning.[137]

Small firms thrived in the legal industry as well, as illustrated by the experience of Skene, Gorman & Stewart, a firm founded in Calgary in 1914, when George W. Skene entered the practice of law with his brother Stanley D. Skene and Mark B. Peacock.[138] Within two years, however, Stanley D. Skene left the firm. Born in Ontario, George W. Skene received his BA from Queen's University. In 1914, Calgary was a small dot on the map of Alberta. As the city steadily grew, Skene's commitment to high-quality personal service helped him do significant work for a variety of local businesses.[139] There was a complex inter-relationship between Calgary's emergence as a larger city and Peacock & Skene's growth into a substantial small law firm. As Peacock & Skene evolved to meet the legal needs of a commercial and industrializing city, other important lawyers achieved positions as name partners. The firm took on a new name partner in 1945 with the addition of John C. Gorman, and another in 1971, G. C. Stewart. Thus, by the early 1970s the firm had taken the name Skene, Gorman & Stewart. Like Skene, his partners Gorman and Stewart contributed to the development of the firm, providing dependable service.

■

Small Business in Farming and Ranching

Although Alberta was rapidly becoming an urban industrial province in the last half of the twentieth century, agriculture remained a significant part of the Alberta economy. In 1990, Alberta farms and ranches produced about twenty percent of the agricultural output in Canada.[140] Farming in Alberta saw a decline in small businesses after World War II. Long-term economic developments combined with short-term difficulties to favour larger farm holdings over small family farms in the province. A number of family farms, however, continued to prosper, many of them, like other kinds of small business enterprises, by specializing in their operations.

In Alberta, the depression in the early 1920s and the Great Depression in the 1930s hurt small family farms more than the larger units. During World War I, many Alberta farmers expanded their activities as the demand for foodstuffs soared, frequently using loans secured by mortgages on their farm holdings. With the collapse of wheat prices in the early 1920s, numerous farmers could not pay back these loans and had to kiss their farms goodbye. Wheat prices dropped even lower during the Great Depression, with the result that there was more farm distress across Alberta.

As the demand for foodstuffs skyrocketed again during World War II, the substantial advance in mechanization in response to this demand made farming much more capital-intensive. The postwar years witnessed a continuation of this trend. Many farmers found it difficult to raise the funds needed to acquire larger tractors and mechanized equipment. The minimum profitable size of farms in Alberta grew larger as big power machinery came into ever-increasing use in agriculture. Between 1966 and 1986, the average farm size in the province rose from 706 to 883 acres.[141] Of the new forms of agriculture, the large vertically integrated agribusinesses were the most important, their operations the most complex. They were companies that raised, processed, and marketed agricultural commodities, with processing and marketing earning the bulk of the profits.

A number of family farms were able to prosper, however. Among the success stories was the Rouse family, owners of a farm near Stettler. Oscar Rouse, a homesteader who founded the farm in 1904, had gained previous experience in farming in his native community — Liberal, Missouri.[142] In 1930, Rouse's son Jacob, after working in a successful partnership with his father for many years, took over the family farm. Like many Alberta farmers, Jacob Rouse suffered from the Great Depression. Producing cream, eggs, and especially pigs for sale in the local and regional markets and growing wheat for the larger national market, Rouse managed to recover and expand during World War II.[143] To acquire more land and make it productive, he borrowed $44,000 from a local bank in 1944 and, by 1950, had paid back the entire loan.[144]

Jacob Rouse's achievements also depended on other family members, particularly his wife Nellie, who greatly assisted him in running the farm, and his sons James and Ronald.[145] As schoolboys, James and Ronald helped build up the farm in a variety of ways, such as milking cows, feeding and watering livestock, cleaning pig pens, and picking roots on freshly broken land. In 1965, after the death of his father, James took over the family farming business.[146]

Despite the rise of large corporate farmers, the family farm still lay at the centre of Alberta agriculture in the last half of the twentieth century. Family farm of James A. and Jeanette Rouse at Stettler in 1960. (Courtesy of James A. and Jeanette Rouse).

Born in Stettler in 1927, James Rouse graduated from the local high school.[147] In 1953, as his father's partner, James began to specialize in raising hogs. He also owned a small Holstein dairy herd. Planning to exploit the growing demand for fluid milk, in 1958, James dropped hogs and started to specialize in dairying. Using the most advanced production methods, he expanded his dairy operations, specializing in the delivery of high-quality milk to the Alpha Milk Plant in Stettler.[148] After succeeding as a milk producer for twenty-one years, James Rouse sold his dairy herd in 1979 and switched his attention to the more profitable business of raising wheat and canola.[149]

Specializing in growing wheat and canola was rewarding in the 1980s and 1990s for Rouse and his wife Jeannette, who helped him run the farm. Rouse trained their sons, Darren and Stephen, by giving them an opportunity to become involved in the practical work of the farming business. Both sons made rapid progress, Darren eventually becoming his father's partner and Stephen becoming a freelance writer, but at the same time remaining tied to the family farm.[150]

Like the Rouse family, John (Jack) A. McBride, another Alberta farmer, adopted the strategy of specialization. Born in Calgary, McBride took up the task of developing a farm along the Medicine River near Benalto in 1923 at the age of seventeen.[151] In 1927, he married Lillian Krause. On what they called Riverbend Farms, Jack and Lillian and their growing family made a living for the next forty years. A graduate of Garbutt's Business College in Calgary, Lillian did all the paperwork on the farm.[152] After surviving the Great Depression of the 1930s, Jack McBride prospered as a specialized farmer, raising high-quality, registered Aberdeen Angus cattle, and participating in the commercial market for them in Canada and the United States.

Agriculture based on cattle in particular boosted the growth of a number of Alberta family farms, such as Jack and Lillian McBride's Riverbend Farms at Benalto, in the decades before and after World War II. Jack McBride beside a sign featuring purebred Angus on Riverbend Farms in 1965.

(Courtesy of Canadian Cattlemen).

Like many Alberta farmers, McBride acquired his farm on credit, gradually paying off his debt.[153] He made most of his profits raising and purchasing Angus cattle, fattening them on grass, and then selling them throughout North America. During the late 1940s and early 1950s, growing seed grain on Riverbend Farms was also an important source of income. A progressive farmer, McBride practised rotational grazing, moving his cattle from one pasture to the next every two weeks, always took an interest in new farming techniques, and improved the Angus herd.[154]

In the early 1960s, McBride expanded by purchasing a large herd of Angus cattle for $100,000.[155] By 1965, he was grazing 1,000 head of purebred cattle on Riverbend Farms.[156] Riverbend Farms continued to grow as a family-owned and -operated farm, with McBride's son Bud taking over the business in 1967. Like his father, Bud prospered over the next thirty years, employing the most advanced methods in raising Angus cattle.

Numerous Alberta ranchers were no less progressive than the McBrides; for many ranchers, advanced techniques were essential to the successful conduct of agricultural affairs. The career of Hugh Lynch-Staunton illustrates this aspect of ranch life. Raised in a southwestern Alberta ranch family, Lynch-Staunton became part owner of the small

In the last quarter of the twentieth century, Alberta family ranches such as Hugh and Betty Lynch-Staunton's Antelope Butte Ranch at Lundbreck remained important, producing cattle for local consumption and long-distance trade. 1998, Longhorns in the foreground and a Beefbooster calf behind the fence. (Courtesy of Hugh and Betty Lynch-Staunton).

family ranch at Lundbreck in 1967. Born in 1943, he received his B. Comm. from the University of Alberta, and then worked for Esso Resources for a while.[157] He married Betty Galeski in 1965 and, two years later, became a partner of his father, Frank Lynch-Staunton, the owner of a ranch established by his father in the late nineteenth century. In 1967, Hugh and Frank incorporated the family business as the Antelope Butte Ranch. The partnership was capitalized at $20,000. Frank was president, while Hugh served as secretary.[158]

Hugh and Frank Lynch-Staunton prospered as ranchers, specializing in raising high-quality Hereford cattle. This situation was not new at the small Antelope Butte Ranch, for Frank had successfully raised Hereford cattle previously.[159] Together Hugh and Frank were able to increase the size of the herd of cattle from 400 to nearly 500 between 1967 and 1969.[160] Hugh Lynch-Staunton took over the Antelope Butte Ranch in 1979, when his father became lieutenant-governor of Alberta.[161] Like his father, Hugh took a keen interest in new ranching methods and improved the Hereford cattle, relying on retained earnings and bank credit to expand the business. By 1991, there were 1,400 cattle grazing on the Antelope Butte Ranch.[162] It was clearly a tightly knit family affair, with Hugh and his wife Betty and their children all playing a part in the ranch's growth and development.

Women in Small Business Management

Small business ownership and management also offered more and more opportunities for women in Alberta after World War II. During the 1980s, women established new businesses, almost all of which were small, at a rate more than twice as fast as that of men in the province. Of all the self-employed persons in Alberta in 1993, women comprised thirty-three percent.[163]

Alberta businesses owned and managed by women clustered in services and sales. At the same time, the industry distribution of businesses owned by women in the province was becoming more diverse, as women moved into industries such as transportation. Some prospered in both production and distribution.

Few Alberta women were as successful in small-scale production and distribution as Jean Páre of Vermilion, the owner and manager of a commercial kitchen and a publishing company. Raised in a general store family in Irma, Páre graduated from the local high school. An important aspect of her life at home was the kitchen, where she quickly learned how to cook from her mother. It was soon evident that Páre was a gifted cook. In 1963, she became a caterer in Vermilion.[164] She began by providing food and service for 1,000 people attending the fiftieth anniversary of the Vermilion School of Agriculture. Aided by her husband Larry, who was an electrical contractor, Páre went on to prepare and serve hot meals on other occasions, sometimes to as many as 1,500 people.[165]

Many people were soon exchanging recipes with Páre. Then someone asked her to write a cookbook. Central in importance for the future of Páre's catering business was her willingness to accept the suggestion of her son Grant that she focus on one type of food in her proposed cookbook. Páre decided to specialize in squares for a niche market. Forming Company's Coming Publishing in the fall of 1980, she published her first cookbook, *150 Delicious Squares*, in April of the following year.[166] The first printing of 15,000 copies sold out in three months. Before long, the second edition appeared, with even healthier sales of 25,000.[167]

Encouraged by her success, Páre made plans to expand operations. She was well on the way to raising adequate financing for Company's Coming Publishing. Headed by Páre as president and with its head office in Edmonton, the company was incorporated for $1 million.[168] Her son Grant became vice-president and played an important part in running the company. By 1990, still working out of what had become her Vermilion Test Kitchen, Páre had written and published fourteen cookbooks.[169] She continued to prosper by specializing in one particular kind of food in each volume.

By the late 1980s, Páre had helped establish a sister company, Comac

After World War II, women started a number of businesses in Alberta. Jean Paré, in her Vermilion Test Kitchen in 1997, developed an important business in the fields of catering and publishing. Eventually Paré became president of Company's Coming Publishing. (Courtesy of Jean Pare).

Food Group organized around snack bars, to market her food products.[170] By 1990, Comac had twenty-five snack bars across Canada, the three in Edmonton in the West Edmonton Mall, ManuLife Place II, and Kingsway Garden Mall.[171] Under the leadership of Páre and her associates, Comac diversified in 1990 by purchasing Grabbajabba, a gourmet coffee chain with two stores in Calgary and one in Edmonton.[172]

To grow in these ways, Company's Coming Publishing invested some of its profits in Comac.[173] Still the heart of the family business, Company's Coming expanded its kitchen facilities. Continuing to work out of her Vermilion Test Kitchen with its two stoves, three fridges, and two freezers, Páre had by 1996 published twenty-six Company's Coming cookbooks as well as five cookbooks in another series — *Pint Size*.[174] She had sold over eleven million copies of her books at home and abroad, all the volumes in the English language and a number of them in French as well.[175]

Although Alberta women were underrepresented in senior management of large businesses, they made considerable progress in management of small businesses. Among women managers of small Alberta firms was Mabel Macdonald. In 1963, she became assistant manager of Imperial

Women's Wear, a small specialized business founded by Ernie Wilson in Lethbridge in 1935.[176] Wilson's son Donald, who had graduated from Garbutt's Business College before he served overseas with the Canadian Army during World War II, became the manager of Imperial Women's Wear in 1963, when his father died. Donald Wilson and Mabel Macdonald were partners and, in that year, they transformed their partnership into a corporation, the Imperial Women's Wear Company capitalized at $50,000. Since 1945 Donald Wilson had been helping to run another branch of his father's business in Lethbridge: "Junior's," a children's wear concern.[177] While Wilson remained in charge of Junior's as well as Imperial Women's Wear after 1963, Mabel Macdonald assisted him in running Imperial Women's Wear until she retired around 1981.

In 1981, two years after Donald Wilson had sold Junior's, his wife Shirley, who had graduated from Lethbridge Collegiate Institute, began to manage Imperial Women's Wear with him.[178] The business was owned by both Shirley and Donald. By the late 1980s, the firm was specializing in clothing for middle-class women. At Shirley Wilson's suggestion, the name of the firm was changed to Imperial Fashions. The business prospered by staying close to its clients through the provision of personal, reliable service. By 1990, the stock at Imperial Fashions was turned over five times a year and total annual sales had reached $700,000.[179]

The years after World War II brought expanded business ownership opportunities for women elsewhere in Alberta as well. The developing boomtown of Fort McMurray attracted the attention of Bernard and Frances Jean who, with their five children, moved there in 1967. Bernard, who had served with the Canadian Army after graduating from the H. B. Beale Technical School in London, Ontario, began to work for Catalytic at the Great Canadian Oil Sands Plant which was exploiting the Athabasca oil sands near Fort McMurray. Frances had graduated from George Pringle High School in Westbank, British Columbia. Bernard and Frances were optimistic enough about their future to form a new business — Jean's Gifts & Stationery, a small Alberta corporation — in Fort McMurray in 1968.[180] The cost of the Main Street lot on which they erected their own office building came to $9,000. Frances and Bernard sold office supplies, books, gifts, and a variety of toys to local people, many of whom had young families. From the beginning, Jean's Gifts & Stationery provided the personal, dependable service that was essential in securing business in Fort McMurray.

The management of the family firm Jean's Gifts & Stationery was standard. On a daily basis, control of the company rested with Bernard and Frances. Frances was in charge of personnel and ordering and selling goods, while Bernard was responsible for planning and maintenance.[181] The Jean family owned all of the company's stock. At Jean's Gifts and Stationery, the owners managed their business.

Fort McMurray was growing quickly in the late 1960s, and with its development came fresh opportunities for its residents.[182] Before long, the Jeans were thinking of diversifying and, in 1970, they started a weekly newspaper, the *McMurray Courier*.[183] With a broad knowledge of business and civic affairs in Fort McMurray as well as of developments in the outside world, they ran a good paper. Using an electronic Gestetner at first and then an offset press, the Jeans published a paper every Wednesday morning. Frances wrote the news, their son Mark made the negatives and plates, and Bernard was especially involved in the final stages of production.

By 1971, Fort McMurray was emerging as an industrial town of nearly 7,000, and thereby had the people and businesses to support a weekly newspaper. Soon after its inception, the *McMurray Courier* had a circulation of 1,600. With the growth of the town's population resulting from the organization of the Syncrude Canada project in 1973, the Jeans were able to increase the scope of their newspaper operations. By 1974, when they sold their paper for $100,000 but kept their new Heidelberg presses and printing equipment, the circulation had reached 6,500.[184]

The funds from the sale of their newspaper allowed them to expand the operations of Jean's Gifts & Stationery. Much of the growth in the late 1970s and 1980s occurred as an extension of the developments begun earlier. Stationery, toys, gifts, books, and the printing shop remained important in the evolution of the business. Fort McMurray became large enough to support the Jeans' gift and book trade increasingly geared to a middle-class market. In the gift department, items such as Waterford crystal were popular. Frances and Bernard Jean diversified again by moving into selling Chestnut canoes and bedding plants.[185] Their personal experience in gardening helped them participate in Fort McMurray's growing market for bedding plants, trees, and shrubs, which they brought in from Edmonton.

As Bernard reached retirement age around 1987, the business he and Frances had run together for nearly two decades was healthy. Merchandise industry profits were encouraging, even in the face of mounting competition. Although Jean's Gifts & Stationery had slipped so much in its traditional toy market that it had discontinued this product line, the other parts of the business remained successful.[186] Management succession was no problem, and in 1987 Jean's Gifts & Stationery smoothly entered a new stage in its development under Frances's leadership.

Jean's Gifts & Stationery continued to enjoy a favourable position in the Fort McMurray business community while Frances Jean remained in charge over the next ten years. The development of the oil sands industry brought continuing population growth to Fort McMurray. By 1991, about 34,000 people lived in the city.[187] In this setting, Frances Jean was able to assemble a talented group of young family members, son Brian, a lawyer, and daughter Evelyn, around her.[188] She had a personal and trusting

By the 1990s, Fort McMurray had
became a bustling city. Frances Jean
next to a display of flowers in Jean's
Gifts & Stationery store at Fort
McMurray in 1997. (Courtesy of
Calgary Herald).

business relationship with both Evelyn and Brian. Like Frances, Brian and
Evelyn were entrepreneurial in spirit, enthusiastic about the prospects of
Jean's Gifts & Stationery, and they supported Frances in her projects.

The late 1980s and early 1990s were risky times for Alberta business, a
period of ups and downs in the business cycle. A severe depression hurt
many businesses in the early 1990s. "We've had some tough times here in
the past few years," recalled Frances Jean later.[189] But with her persistent
entrepreneurship, Jean's Gifts & Stationery survived the difficulties and
even expanded. Frances Jean sought an increasing volume of book sales, a
strategy that proved successful in the late 1980s when she secured a long-
term contract with Syncrude Canada to supply that corporation with
books, videos, and training materials. Evelyn, who took charge of the contract, was an excellent salesperson for the business. Frances and Brian
directed their attention to fostering improvements in the printing shop to
develop new markets. In 1994, Jean's Gifts & Stationery became an agent
for Xerox Canada and installed an Instant Copy Centre complete with a
reprographic machine and colour copier, which had a positive impact on
the offset printing business.[190] Brian's willingness to oversee marketing
and the computer system at Jean's Gifts & Stationery helped the firm
immensely.

The economic and social environments within which Jean's Gifts &
Stationery operated also aided the enterprise. Frances Jean's acceptance by
the Fort McMurray business leaders was particularly important. They had

quickly accepted Frances Jean as one of their own. Jean served as secretary-treasurer of Fort McMurray's Chamber of Commerce for three years. The Chamber of Commerce awarded Jean's Gifts & Stationery the Retail Business of the Year and the Small Business Award in 1983. By 1997, when total annual sales at Jean's Gifts & Stationery had reached $1.5 million and the firm employed fifteen full- and part-time staff, Frances Jean was chairperson of Fort McMurray's Downtown Business Revitalization Zone.[191]

■

Government Policies for Small Business

During World War II, the federal government, besides becoming deeply involved in trying to ensure the economic well-being of the nation, engaged in activities designed to shape the business environment for both men and women in small business. One aspect of these activities was planning to meet the interests of the business community at the end of the war during the anticipated conversion from a wartime to a peacetime economy.

In the early stages of the war, the Liberal government led by Mackenzie King set up the Economic Advisory Committee to participate in planning for the postwar period.[192] During 1943, King asked this committee to study the financial problems that might face small and medium-sized industrial firms as they made the transition from wartime to peacetime production. He accepted the committee's main recommendation that the federal government create an industrial credit bank through legislation to meet the financial needs of small and medium-sized industrial concerns. Parliament took action with the passage of the Industrial Development Bank Act of 1944, which sought to increase small business participation in the development of the economy by setting up the Industrial Development Bank as a subsidiary of the Bank of Canada. The Industrial Development Bank was charged with ensuring adequate credit for small businesses across the nation, including those in Alberta.[193]

Aided by good leadership, the Industrial Development Bank was often successful in achieving its goal. Numerous loans flowed to small Alberta businesses. Alberta experienced accelerating economic growth during the decades following World War II. Some political and business leaders feared a postwar recession, which never materialized, as Albertans rushed to invest their savings in the oil and gas industry. Many who went into business on their own did so by borrowing money. Max Ward, for instance, had to supplement income saved during the war years with loans from the Industrial Development Bank to pursue a career in the airline business.[194]

Born in Edmonton, Ward graduated from Victoria High School, married Marjorie Skelton, worked as a bush pilot, and served as a flying instructor with the Royal Canadian Air Force during World War II. Using his war savings and money borrowed from his father-in-law, William Skelton, as well as from a family friend and the finance company Industrial Acceptance Corporation, Ward established a small charter airline in Yellowknife, Northwest Territories in 1946.[195] Over the next few years, Ward constantly faced financial problems, and then abandoned his airline business, only to begin again in 1953 after he had secured financing from the Industrial Development Bank.

"In Toronto," Ward wrote many years later, "I met an IDB officer, Ritchie Clark, who was to be my banker for years to come. I told him what I wanted to do: buy an Otter, start my own airline, pay off the Otter, buy another airplane, and keep on going." Responding positively, Ritchie asked for a financial pro forma to show him how it would all work.

That was going to be a facer. I really didn't know, in detail, how it could be done. Still, I sat down with a pen and paper and began to work on it. From my own experience, I was able to put together a pro forma that looked very practical and promising. The main elements were not that hard to calculate: the charge for a mile of flying airfreight, the costs of fuel, capital, insurance, and administration, all things I had been dealing with for years. When I divided all the costs against the projected revenue, I came up with a net gain. Now if I could only make it work out in practice. I presented my handiwork to Ritchie, who looked it over for a long time.[196]

On Ritchie's recommendation, the Industrial Development Bank lent Ward $75,000, taking the aircraft as security. This loan helped make possible the birth of Wardair, which in 1961, after receiving further assistance from the Industrial Development Bank, moved its head office to Edmonton to launch its international charter service.[197]

The Industrial Development Bank sought to encourage the development of the Alberta economy through aid to Wardair and tried to assist other small Alberta businesses as well. Between 1944 and 1975, the Industrial Development Bank lent a total of $286 million to 5,142 Alberta borrowers.[198]

Most Canadian politicians favoured the growth of small business, which they felt was a vital part of the national economy. Just before he became prime minister at the head of the Conservative government in 1957, John Diefenbaker promised "to take necessary effective action to assist small business, the backbone of our national business."[199] To promote small business, Diefenbaker set up a Small Business Section in the Department of Trade and Commerce in 1958. Important small business legislation followed: the Small Business Loans Act of 1960 authorized the federal government to guarantee chartered bank loans limited to $25,000 per borrower to small businesses in the manufacturing, wholesale, retail, and service industries.[200]

The maximum loan size under the Small Business Loans Act had increased considerably by 1994.[201] By this time, these chartered bank loans across the nation totaled $2 billion.[202] Like their counterparts in the other provinces, small businesses in Alberta benefited greatly from access to this type of bank credit.

Alberta government policies also strengthened small businesses. During World War II, business and provincial government leaders had worked together in a variety of industries, including food production, producing goods and materials needed for fighting overseas. Many big and small business leaders wanted co-operation with the government to continue after the war. To co-ordinate the reconstruction of the Alberta economy in the postwar years, Premier William Aberhart established the Postwar Reconstruction Committee early in 1943. Among prominent members of this committee was Ernest C. Manning, who collaborated with business leaders in planning for the future. The co-operation between government and business begun in the Aberhart years continued into the Manning years. When Manning took office on 31 May 1943, eight days after Aberhart's death, he wanted government and business to work together to bolster the economic strength of Alberta. To this end, Manning set up the department of economic affairs in March 1945.[203] This department fostered business opportunities, for both large and small firms. Large businesses generally benefited more than small businesses from the department's activities, but small firms grew as they participated in transforming Alberta's wartime economy into a peacetime one.

Manning also sought to bring about economic growth by having the government continue to make loans to businesses through the Treasury Branches, and here small businesses generally benefited more than large ones.[204] Established in 1938 under Premier Aberhart, the Treasury Branches, a provincial agency, were empowered to make loans to agricultural, commercial, and industrial businesses.[205] By 1944, the Treasury Branches had made 386 loans, totalling $1.6 million. They had made 10,286 loans, amounting to $63.1 million, twenty years later.[206] Much of the money went to small businesses.

Like chartered banks, the Treasury Branches channelled funds in their communities into profitable investment opportunities. Treasury Branch managers served their local areas, making loans to merchants, farmers, ranchers, and manufacturers they knew personally. Living in their communities, managers kept in close contact with the business needs of their city neighbourhoods, towns, and surrounding regions. By 1944, there were thirty-three Treasury Branches in Alberta; by 1968, 70; and by 1997, 147.[207] They continued to loan the bulk of their resources to small business enterprises.

Coming to power in 1971, Premier Peter Lougheed realized that there was a need to help small businesses in other ways as well. In 1977, he established a Small Business Development Program within the department of business development and tourism to provide management counselling for small businesses.[208] By 1979, this program had published several small business guides, including *Starting a Business in Alberta, Financing a Business in Alberta, Marketing for the Small Manufacturer in Alberta, Operating a Small Retail Business in Alberta, Operating a Small Manufacturing Business in Alberta,* and *Operating a Small Service Business in Alberta,* and distributed thousands of copies of these guides throughout the province.[209]

The various federal and Alberta government policies designed to further the development of small businesses accomplished a great deal. Effective action on behalf of small business mirrored public attitudes. Most Albertans wanted the federal and Alberta governments to take steps to preserve small business enterprises. As it turned out, these actions helped maintain the place of small firms in Alberta's business system.

NOTES TO CHAPTER EIGHT

1. *Red Deer Advocate*, 28 October 1995.

2. Pat Thompson, "Small Business and Job Creation in Alberta 1991," *Research* (Toronto: Canadian Federation of Independent Business, May 1994), 1.

3. Industry Canada, Ottawa, Entrepreneurship & Small Business Office, "Small Business in Canada: A Statistical Overview," December 1993, 19.

4. Thompson, "Small Business and Job Creation in Alberta, 1991," 3.

5. Industry Canada, Entrepreneurship & Small Business Office, "Regional Extension of the Reference Handbook on Small Business Statistics for 1992."

6. Interview by the author with Emily Isley, 3 March 1997.

7. L. Ward Johnson, "Reg Isley Spent Years Searching for the Kindest Cut," *Logging & Sawmilling Journal*, June 1990, 8.

8. Ibid., 9.

9. Isley interview, 3 March 1997; Johnson, "Reg Isley Spent Years Searching for the Kindest Cut," 9-11; Jim Stirling, "Risley on a Roll," *Logging & Sawmilling Journal*, April 1993, 8-10; Alberta Municipal Affairs Archives, Edmonton, *Alberta Census for 1991*.

10. Johnson, "Reg Isley Spent Years Searching for the Kindest Cut," 10.

11. Ibid., 11.

12. Isley interview, 3 March 1997; Alberta Economic Development and Tourism Library, Dun & Bradstreet data.

13. *Edmonton Bulletin*, 23 August 1926.

14. *Business Press*, March 1982, 5.

15. University of Calgary Library, *Dun & Bradstreet Reference Book*, September 1921, 25.

16. *Edmonton Bulletin*, 23 August 1926.

17. City of Edmonton Archives, LaFleche Bros. file.

18. *Edmonton Sun*, 7 July 1995.

19. City of Edmonton Archives, LaFleche Bros. file.

20. *Edmonton Journal*, 9 December 1968.

21. *Business Press*, March 1982, 18.

22. *Alberta Report*, 6 February 1981.

23. *Edmonton Sun*, 27 September 1993.

24. *Edmonton Sun*, 7 July 1995.

25. Interview by the author with Sam Stone, 22 May 1996.

26. Ibid.

27. Ibid.

28. *Dun & Bradstreet Reference Book,* July 1959, 75.

29. Stone interview, 22 May 1996.

30. Ibid.

31. Ibid.

32. Ibid.

33. Interview by the author with William J. Tynan, 18 November 1991.

34. Ibid.

35. Alberta Corporate Registry, John Tynan & Company Ltd. file.

36. Ibid.

37. Ibid.

38. *Western Business & Industry*, December 1954, 26.

39. Tynan interview, 18 November 1991.

40. Alberta Corporate Registry, John Tynan & Company Ltd. file.

41. *Calgary Commerce*, July/August 1978, 36.

42. Tynan interview, 18 November 1991.

43. Ibid.

44. *Western Business & Industry*, December 1954, 27.

45. Ibid.

46. Tynan interview, 18 November 1991.

47. Alberta Corporate Registry, John Tynan & Company Ltd. file.

48. Tynan interview, 18 November 1991.

49. Ibid.

50. Ibid.

51. Ibid.

52. Alberta Corporate Registry, Tynan Furniture Ltd. file.

53. Tynan interview, 18 November 1991.

54. Interviews by the author with Gordon W. Denoon, 9 March, 12 December 1991.

55. Ibid.

56. Nanton and District Historical Society, *Mosquito Creek Roundup* (Nanton: Nanton and District Historical Society, 1975), 382-383.

57. *Dun & Bradstreet Reference Book*, September 1921, 42.

58. *Nanton News*, 7 October 1926, 19 January 1928, 6 December 1928, 13 June 1929.

59. Denoon interviews, 9 May, 12 December 1991.

60. *Dun & Bradstreet Reference Book*, July 1939, 93.

61. Denoon interviews, 9 May, 12 December 1991.

62. Ibid.

63. *Nanton News*, 26 January 1956, 28 March 1957, 27 September 1962.

64. Denoon interviews, 9 May, 12 December 1991.

65. Ibid.

66. *Nanton News*, 26 February 1976; Denoon interviews, 9 May, 12 December 1991.

67. Denoon interviews, 9 May, 12 December 1991.

68. Ibid.

69. Ibid.

70. Ibid.

71. Ibid.

72. Ibid.

73. Industry Canada, Entrepreneurship and Small Business Office, Regional Extension of the Reference Handbook on Small Business Statistics for 1992, n.p.

74. Ibid.

75. Ibid.

76. *Macleod Gazette*, 20 July 1886, 5 April 1887, 9 August 1887, 22 April 1898, 3 July 1903; Fort Macleod History Book Committee, *Fort Macleod — Our Colourful Past: A History of the Town of Fort Macleod, from 1874 to 1924* (Fort Macleod: Fort Macleod History Book Committee, 1977), 424.

77. Interview by the author with Charles G. Reach, 22 May 1991.

78. Ibid.

79. Alberta Corporate Registry, Reach & Co. Ltd. file.

80. Ibid.

81. Ibid.

82. Reach interview, 22 May 1991.

83. Ibid.

84. Alberta Corporate Registry, Reach & Co. Ltd. file.

85. Ibid.

86. Ibid.

87. Reach interview, 22 May 1991.

88. Alberta Corporate Registry, Reach & Co. Ltd. file.

89. Ibid.

90. Ibid.

91. Reach interview, 22 May 1991.

92. Alberta Corporate Registry, Reach & Co. Ltd. file.

93. Reach interview, 22 May 1991.

94. Macleod Court House, Estate of Pearl Reach file, 4 March 1903; *Macleod Gazette*, 14 November 1902.

95. Reach interview, 22 May 1991.

96. bid.

97. Ibid.

98. Ibid.

99. Interview by the author with Donald F. Blake, 2 May 1991.

100. Ibid.

101. Alberta Corporate Registry, Link Hardware Company Ltd. file.

102. Blake interview, 2 May 1991.

103. Ibid.

104. Alberta Corporate Registry, Link Hardware Company Ltd. file.

105. Blake interview, 2 May 1991.

106. Alberta Corporate Registry, Link Hardware Company Ltd. file.

107. *High River Times*, 4 October 1956, 8 November 1956, 10 January 1957, 18 July 1957, 10 January 1963, 7 March 1963, 3 February 1972, 19 April 1979.

108. Blake interview, 2 May 1991.

109. Ibid.

110. Ibid.

111. Alberta Corporate Registry, Home Hardware Stores Ltd. file.

112. Blake interview, 2 May 1991.

113. Ibid.

114. Ibid.

115. Interview by the author with Maurice Francoeur, 18 May 1996.

116. Ibid.

117. Alberta Machinery Company Archives, Camrose, Louis Francoeur, "Looking back on Alberta Machinery Co.," *The Alberta Machinery Report*, January 1989, 1,3.

118. Ibid.

119. Ibid.

120. Francoeur interview, 18 May 1996.

121. Ibid.

122. Francoeur, "Looking back on Alberta Machinery Co.," 3.

123. Ibid.

124. Ibid.

125. Ibid.

126. Ibid.

127. Francoeur interview, 18 May 1996.

128. Ibid.

129. Alberta Municipal Affairs Archives, Edmonton, *Alberta Census for 1991*.

130. *Edmonton Journal*, 29 September 1975.

131. Alberta Economic Development and Tourism Library, Alberta Industry and Resources 1990, 88.

132. *Calgary Herald*, 1 December 1956.

133. Interview by the author with John Stevenson, 23 May 1974.

134. Ibid.

135. *Calgary Herald*, 1 December 1956.

136. *Edmonton Directory for 1996*, 48.

137. Ibid.

138. Interview by the author with George W. Skene, 28 September 1974.

139. Ibid; See also Henry C. Klassen, "Lawyers, Finance, and Economic Development In Southwestern Alberta, 1884-1920," in Carol Wilton, ed., *Beyond the Law: Lawyers and Business in Canada, 1830-1930.* (Toronto: The Osgoode Society, 1990), 299-319; Henry C. Klassen, "The George F. Downes Firm in the Development of Edmonton and its Region, 1903-1930," in Carol Wilton, ed., *Inside the Law: Canadian Law Firms in Historical Perspective.* (Toronto: University of Toronto Press, 1996), 248-279.

140. Alberta Economic Development and Tourism Library, Alberta Industry and Resources 1990, 45.

141. Ibid.

142. Interview by the author with James Rouse, 17 May 1996.

143. Ibid.

144. *The United Farmer*, August/September 1982, 4-5.

145. Ibid., 3-4.

146. Rouse interview, 17 May 1996.

147. Ibid.

148. *The United Farmer*, August/September 1982, 5.

149. Rouse interview, 17 May 1996.

150. Ibid.

151. Interview by the author with John A. McBride, 28 June 1994.

152. Ibid.

153. Ibid.

154. *Canadian Cattlemen*, October 1965, 14.

155. McBride interview, 28 June 1994.

156. *Canadian Cattlemen*, October 1965, 12.

157. Interview by the author with Hugh Lynch-Staunton, 24 May 1991.

158. Ibid; Alberta Corporate Registry, Antelope Butte Ranch Ltd. file.

159. GAIA, Frank Lynch-Staunton Papers, financial statements, 1948-1956; Elva Fletcher, "Open-hearted Hospitality," *Country Guide*, May 1964, 46-47.

160. Lynch-Staunton interview, 24 May 1991.

161. Ibid.

162. Ibid.

163. Industry Canada, Entrepreneurship and Small Business Office, August 1994, "Reference Handbook on Small Business Statistics," 18.

164. Interview by the author with Jean Páre, 4 July 1996.

165. Ibid.

166. Ibid.

167. Ibid.

168. Alberta Corporate Registry, Company's Coming Publishing Ltd. file.

169. *Calgary Herald*, 22 October 1990.

170. Páre interview, 4 July 1996.

171. *Edmonton Sun*, 15 October 1990.

172. Ibid.

173. *Edmonton Sun*, 23 June 1995.

174. Páre interview, 4 July 1996.

175. Ibid.

176. Interview by the author with Donald G. Wilson, 25 May 1991; Alberta Corporate Registry, Imperial Women's Wear Ltd. file.

177. Wilson interview, 25 May 1991.

178. Ibid.

179. Ibid.

180. Interviews by the author with Frances Jean, 2, 13 February 1997.

181. Ibid.

182. Howard Palmer with Tamara Palmer, *Alberta: A New History* (Edmonton: Hurtig Publishers, 1990), 330.

183. Jean interviews, 2, 13 February 1997.

184. Ibid.

185. Ibid.

186. Ibid.

187. Alberta Municipal Affairs Archives, *Alberta Census for 1991*.

188. Jean interviews, 2, 13 February 1997.

189. *Calgary Herald*, 1 February 1997.

190. Jean interviews, 2, 13 February 1997.

191. Ibid.

192. E. Ritchie Clark, *The IDB: A History of Canada's Industrial Development Bank* (Toronto, University of Toronto Press, 1985), 14-15.

193. Ibid., 18-32.

194. Max Ward, *The Max Ward Story: A Bush Pilot in the Bureaucratic Jungle* (Toronto: McClelland & Stewart, 1991), 39.

195. Ibid., 48-51.

196. Ibid., 103-104.

197. *Edmonton Journal*, 29 May 1974.

198. Clark, *The IDB*, 394.

199. Quoted in Clark, *The IDB*, 120.

200. Clark, *The IDB*, 121-123.

201. Ted Mallett, "Small Business: Banking on Job Creation, Results of 1994 CFIB Survey on Banking Issues," (Toronto: Canadian Federation of Independent Business, 1994), 23.

202. Industry Canada, Entrepreneurship and Small Business Office, "Quarterly Report on Small- and Medium-Sized Enterprises June 1994," 4.

203. Ernest Watkins, *The Golden Province: A Political History of Alberta* (Calgary: Sandstone Publishing, 1980), 154-155.

204. Ernest C. Manning, "A White Paper on Human Resources Development," March 1967, 62-63.

205. Lewis H. Thomas, ed., *William Aberhart and Social Credit in Alberta* (Toronto: Copp Clark Publishing, 1977), 119-120; Alvin Finkel, *The Social Credit Phenomenon in Alberta* (Toronto: University of Toronto Press, 1989), 46.

206. Alberta Treasury Branches, Head Office Library, Edmonton, *Annual Report for 1968-1969.*

207. Alberta Treasury Branches, Head Office Library, financial statements for the years 1944-1997.

208. Alberta, Department of Business Development and Tourism, *Annual Report 1976-77*, 29.

209. Alberta, Department of Business Development and Tourism, *Annual Report 1979*, 25

CHAPTER NINE

CHALLENGES TO ALBERTA BUSINESS AT HOME AND ABROAD

On Tuesday morning, 24 July 1973, Pierre Trudeau, Prime Minister of Canada, took a seat at a U-shaped table in Mount Royal College in Calgary.[1] Trudeau was leading the Western Economic Opportunities Conference aimed at clarifying his new administration's commitment to assist western Canada.[2] Trudeau had won the prime ministership even though he had lost his majority in the House of Commons in a federal election nine months before, observers agreed, because a substantial minority of Canadian voters were concerned about the course of the economy. There was growing unemployment, inflation rates were high, the cost of living was rising, and many citizens felt ill-prepared to face the challenges of competition.[3] Trudeau had promised the voters that if he became Prime Minister he would focus on, among other things, the economic growth of the country.

The Western Economic Opportunities Conference, unprecedented in Canada's history, was one result of Trudeau's pledge. Besides the four western premiers — Peter Lougheed of Alberta, Dave Barrett of British Columbia, Allan Blakeney of Saskatchewan, and Ed Shreyer of Manitoba — other government officials such as federal Finance Minister John Turner and Alberta Industry and Commerce Minister Fred Peacock came to Calgary. Some prominent business leaders, such as executives of the Canadian Petroleum Association, also participated in the deliberations.[4]

Like Trudeau, Lougheed and the other western premiers, and oil and gas executives were active participants in a debate that arose at the conference about federal government-business relations and economic policy. Reflecting the views of the oil and gas leaders, Lougheed told reporters that he was cautiously optimistic about the new Trudeau administration's willingness to aid business development in Alberta.[5] Details of the Prime Minister's program included federal commitments to provide information on the costs that went into railway freight rates, to seek a reduction in U.S. tariffs on Canadian petrochemicals, and to develop policy initiatives helpful to small business.[6] Trudeau generally respected the tradition begun in 1867 of federal support for developmental economic policies.

Alberta Business in the New World Order

Many Albertans worried that they and their children were ill-equipped to face the challenges of competition at home and abroad. Some Alberta firms began to suffer in the competitive environment, as global economic conditions changed in the 1970s and 1980s. In addition to the confusion stemming from economic factors, pressures came from the dramatic changes that occurred in the world's political arrangements. Inflation and oil shocks hurt Alberta firms in their competition with foreign businesses. First in 1973 and then again in 1979, through the OPEC cartel, oil-producing countries increased the price of crude oil to other nations. In response to the Arab-Israeli War, they raised prices fourfold in 1973. In 1979, similar action took place. The oil shocks stimulated inflation in Alberta, enlarging uncertainties in the business community. By the early 1980s, in spite of a recession, inflation had soared in Alberta. Alberta business leaders experienced great difficulty in their efforts to come to grips with inflation.

The Cold War, which had made its appearance in the aftermath of World War II, influenced economic decisions in Alberta for four decades. With the reunification of Germany in 1989 and the collapse of the Soviet Union in 1991, the Cold War suddenly ended. The political map of Europe had to be redrawn after the end of the Cold War, with new nations appearing in what had formerly been the Soviet Union. These political changes brought greater risks to the international economy as western countries, including Canada, tried to do business in what had once been Soviet economies. For Albertans, the end of the Cold War brought important changes in business activity. Multinational firms based in Alberta were now looking more closely at Russia as a new investment opportunity. For example, Foremost Industries executives hoped their Russian venture would lead to further multinational growth.

■

Regulation: Canadian Politics and Economic Uncertainty in Alberta

As the business environment in the international sphere transformed from 1973 onward, the federal government responded by establishing new regulatory machinery. Trudeau's response contributed to the uncertain conditions characterizing Alberta business during this period. In the autumn of 1973, he limited domestic oil prices by using direct controls and imposed heavy taxes on oil exports.[7] Trudeau's approach specified an increasingly important role for the federal government in energy, and in 1980 this led to his National Energy Program (NEP). During the mid- and late 1970s, world oil prices had risen dramatically, but the NEP did not allow Alberta oil producers to take full advantage of them. Under the NEP Albertans saw the prices for their new oil involving expensive production rise to world levels, but they had to accept prices at no more than seventy-five percent of world levels for their old oil derived from sources developed prior to 1973.[8] In addition, they faced higher oil production taxes created by the NEP.

For many Albertans, the new federal regulations ultimately meant a foreclosure of their business opportunities. Any argument in favour of the NEP as a way to promote national interests, therefore, raised difficult questions about its ability to foster business enterprise in Alberta. The oil industry had come to play a critical role in the Alberta economy.[9] In Albertans' view, the regulatory program was a drag on the growth of this industry. Premier Peter Lougheed naturally felt that the NEP had brought nothing but grief for many businesses in the province. His argument had great appeal, and the negative effects of the NEP became a theme that was struck again and again by critics of this federal regulatory system.

■

Deregulating the Oil and Gas Industry

Prime Minister Brian Mulroney, who served from 1984 to 1993, and his advisors started thinking of new ways for the federal government to aid business firms that were faltering in the competitive business environment. Shortly after achieving power in 1984, Mulroney turned to deregulation as a policy to improve the climate for business. The oil and gas industry was the first to experience the full force of deregulation. Mulroney began by dismantling the NEP.[10] In the process, he removed tax increases on oil. The NEP did not disappear without adding new uncertainty in the Alberta economy, but under deregulation many Alberta oil and gas firms increased their business.

Federal government action spurred diversification in the Alberta economy. To promote economic diversification in Alberta and the rest of the West, Mulroney set up a Western Economic Diversification Office in 1987.[11] With headquarters in Edmonton and regional offices in Alberta, Saskatchewan, Manitoba, and British Columbia, the Western Economic Diversification Office initially had a budget of $312 million to aid diversification efforts within the western Canadian economy.[12] In Alberta, progress was significant, as Premier Don Getty co-operated with Mulroney in his diversification drive.[13]

■

Growth through Free Trade

Getty also supported Mulroney's free trade efforts. Mulroney helped work out an arrangement for free trade between Canada and the United States in 1989 in the hopes of stimulating economic activity. In 1992, he played an important role in expanding this trade agreement to include Mexico.[14] The creation of free trade did not occur without bringing new uncertainties to the Alberta economy, but many Alberta businesses, including Standen's and Canbra Foods, benefited from free trade arrangements.

The volume of Alberta-U.S. trade, already large, grew larger. The Canada-U.S. Free Trade Agreement "is providing brand new, exciting opportunities for entrepreneurs in our stronger businesses," observed Ted Newall, chief executive officer of Nova Corporation, a large Alberta oil and gas firm, in October 1993. "The facts are in; the evidence is compelling."[15] Alberta enjoyed a favourable balance of trade in United States commerce. During the period from 1992 to 1996, the value of Alberta's exports to the United States rose from about $14 billion to about $25 billion.[16] Petroleum oils, natural gas, petroleum gases, live cattle, polyethylene, and propane were the most important products in the southbound Alberta-U.S. trade. Between 1992 and 1996, the value of Alberta's imports from the United States increased from about $3 billion to about $6 billion.[17] Automobiles and trucks were the most significant articles in the northbound U.S.-Alberta trade.

The period between 1992 and 1996 was also one of growth for Alberta-Mexico trade. Alberta enjoyed a favourable balance of trade with Mexico. In the two years before the enforcement of NAFTA in 1994, the value of Alberta's exports to Mexico increased from about $72 million to about $84 million.[18] The value of Alberta's exports to Mexico rose to about $140 million in 1994 and to about $192 million two years later. Rapeseed, wheat, milk powder, sulphur, bituminous coal, chemical wood pulp, and canola oil were the most important articles in the southbound Alberta-Mexico trade. In the two years before 1994, the value of Alberta's imports from Mexico climbed from about $35 million to about $42 million. The value of Alberta's imports from Mexico increased to about $60 million in 1994 and to about $98 million by 1996.[19] Bananas, melons, television receivers, tomatoes, peppers, and telephone sets were the most significant products in the northbound Mexico-Alberta trade.

■

Big Business and New Opportunities

As part of the development of Alberta's business system, big businesses experienced significant growth in the 1970s, 1980s, and 1990s. Alberta remained a hospitable environment for the conduct of business. Geography and abundant natural resources, such as oil, natural gas, and waterpower and coal for the production of electricity, continued to play important roles in the development of the business system. Corporations benefited from urban growth and the exploitation of natural resources in this period. Alberta cities, large and small, continued to grow as commercial and industrial cities exploiting natural resources in the surrounding areas at their command. Industrial and service firms evolved to serve the growing populations of the urban centres and their hinterlands. In many cases, firms reached beyond local and regional markets to national and even international markets.

In the decades after 1970, business provided new economic opportunities for Albertans and, at the same time, became more competitive. Market opportunities and investments were changing rapidly in Alberta and across the world. Some Alberta firms, like Gulf Canada Resources, a subsidiary of the U.S. firm Gulf Oil Corporation, were generally successful in adapting to these changes. With assets of $4.9 billion in 1983, Gulf Canada was truly a big business.[20] In the late 1980s, Gulf Canada executives in corporate headquarters in Calgary decided policy for the entire company, co-ordinated the work of the firm's various divisions, and employed sophisticated financial techniques to monitor their business in Alberta and across the globe. Other Alberta businesses fell by the wayside, as expanding competition swept over them.

Gulf Canada Resources survived and grew. Founded in 1906 as the British American Oil Company in Toronto by Albert L. Ellsworth, who had gained experience in the oil business in the United States, Gulf Canada began with eight shareholders who invested $135,000 in the venture.[21] By 1909, the British American Oil Company was operating a refinery on Toronto's eastern waterfront. Its works were the third largest in Canada. After making investments in oil wells in the United States, especially in Oklahoma, and in Alberta's Turner Valley field, the company built a refinery at Calgary in 1936 with a daily capacity of 4,500 barrels.[22]

The opening of a new field at Leduc in 1947 created new opportunities for British American Oil.[23] By the mid-1950s, however, the company had not developed the crude oil production capabilities in Alberta to build a substantial marketing and distribution organization in the province.[24] It turned to Gulf Oil Corporation. By then, Gulf Oil was a large crude oil producer in Alberta. British American Oil soon came under the financial control of Gulf Oil[25] and British American Oil gained control of huge oil and gas reserves in Alberta.

British American Oil changed its name to Gulf Oil Canada in 1969. Around this time, Gulf Oil Canada invested in a refinery of optimal size at Edmonton using crude from Alberta fields, and so was able to take full advantage of economies of scale.[26] The company also set up an extensive marketing and distribution network in Alberta. Significantly, the company was fully integrated, from production of crude oil to marketing in retail outlets. It took the name Gulf Canada in 1978 and Gulf Canada Resources in 1987.

As its marketing network expanded, Gulf Canada Resources enlarged its research laboratories and its output in Alberta.[27] For some years, Gulf Canada executives had wanted to sell the refining and marketing operations and, in the mid-1980s, they achieved this goal.[28] They had already moved ahead in another direction. Aggressive expansion in oil exploration and drilling in the Beaufort Sea during the early 1980s, as well as off the coast of Australia and in the Gulf of Suez in later years, reinforced the company's position.[29] With the company's investments in physical facilities came the recruitment of the necessary managerial and operating personnel. In this way Gulf Canada built up organizational capabilities that assured its position in the Alberta and international oil industry.

The extent of Gulf Canada's investment in Alberta was indicated by the move of its head office from Toronto to Calgary in 1987. In January 1995, increasing difficulties running the company and lack of funds essential to build a strong organization led management to bring J. P. Bryan to Calgary to serve as the new president and chief executive officer. Born in Houston, Texas, Bryan was an entrepreneurially-minded executive with long experience in the oil industry.[30] Bryan's first step was to restructure Gulf Canada by downsizing its management, reducing its Canadian workforce from 1200 to 700, and reorganizing its finances.[31] Under his leadership, the company then sold its interest in Komi Arctic Oil, withdrew from northern Russia, purchased the Alberta government's interest in the Syncrude Canada oilsands project, and acquired Mannville Oil & Gas in Alberta.[32] Gulf Canada also expanded its operations in Indonesia by investing in field and gas plant facilities for the Corridor Block gas project. The company acquired important assets in the United States. By the end of 1995, Gulf Canada held 185,000 acres in three northern states, permitting it to begin exploring and developing oil pools in North Dakota's Lodgepole Trend, Montana's Sheep Mountain Basin, and Wyoming's Minnelusa Trend.[33]

Bryan provided a good example of a highly successful builder of big business in Alberta. Members of Gulf Canada's management team in Calgary were amazed at Bryan's accomplishments. Andrew Wiswell, Gulf Canada's senior vice-president finance and chief financial officer wrote:

> I wouldn't have thought it possible to pass so many financial milestones in one year, attracting new equity, repaying and refinancing debt, addressing preferred share dividends, gaining a credit rating upgrade, increasing cash flow and posting positive earnings for the last nine months. Our journey delivered results for all Gulf stakeholders in 1995.[34]

The continuing growth of the Alberta economy provided new opportunities, as the history of the Canadian Western Natural Gas Company reveals. The Canadian Western Natural Gas Company's seventy-fifth anniversary in 1987 marked an important milestone in its development. The company was a significant natural gas utility concern in Alberta serving 288,000

An enormous capital investment was required to hold a significant position in the natural gas industry in Alberta. One aspect of Canadian Western Natural Gas operations in the summer of 1998: work on the fourth phase of the five-phase Banff Loop Pipeline project, which twinned the existing pipeline from Jumping Pound to Banff. (Courtesy of Canadian Western Natural Gas and Trudie Lee Photography Inc.).

customers from Red Deer to the U.S. border and earning about $309 million in annual sales. Through the board of directors and executive officers, stockholders controlled about $433 million in total assets.[35] Canadian Western was truly a big business, an economic institution that occupied an important position in the natural gas industry. With facilities at sites across southern Alberta, it sold its product and services to homes and other businesses in 114 communities.[36] As the *Lethbridge Herald* put it, these communities had come to "depend on the Canadian Western Natural Gas Company to heat their homes, cook their food, warm their water, dry their clothes and fuel their barbecues."[37]

The firm celebrating its seventy-fifth anniversary was a complex human organization. Top officers focused on the company's strategic decisions, while middle-level executives co-ordinated the work of the departments. Lower-level managers looked after operations. As opportunities grew for the investment of capital and expansion of the workforce, business executives at Canadian Western struggled to develop long-term advantages for their company.

The Canadian Western Natural Gas Company of 1987 was a far cry from the fledgling corporation, Canadian Western Natural Gas, Light, Heat and Power Company, which organized in Calgary in 1911 and began providing service in southern Alberta in 1912. The founding entrepreneur, Eugene Coste, a mining engineer and geologist earlier employed by the Geological Survey of Canada, could not have foreseen how the firm would develop over the next seventy-five years. Born in Ontario and educated in Grenoble and Paris, Coste had come to Alberta seeking his fortune after gaining experience in the Ontario natural gas industry.[38] An employee of the Canadian Pacific Railway, he spent much of the period from 1906 to 1909 searching for oil in southeastern Alberta.[39] Coste's discovery of natural gas at Bow Island, southwest of Medicine Hat, in 1909 led to the formation of the Canadian Western Natural Gas, Light, Heat and Power Company in Calgary two years later. Coste derived much of the financial support for the founding of the company from several individuals: capitalist N. Scott Russell of London, England; Clifford Sifton, former minister of the interior; William Mackenzie, president of the Canadian Northern Railway; and Pat Burns of Calgary.[40] In 1912, the company laid a 170-mile pipeline from the Bow Island field to Calgary via Lethbridge and began to distribute natural gas in these cities in July of that year. Before long, branch pipelines brought natural gas to other communities, such as Fort Macleod, Granum, Claresholm, Nanton, and Okotoks.[41]

Coste's was a relatively small business, founded in a city that was in the early stages of its industrial development. In 1913, the Canadian Western Natural Gas, Light, Heat and Power Company employed a handful of people, sold its product in a small region, and had only 6,790 customers.[42] Responsible for the company's daily management, Eugene Coste, the first president and a major stockholder, personally oversaw the drilling of the early natural gas wells at Bow Island.[43] "He would pay an inspection visit to a drill crew," recalled Tiny Phillips, one of his drillers in those years, "and if an overnight stay was required and no cots were available, he would roll up in a blanket on the floor of the tent."[44]

With the growing demand for natural gas by homes as well as by commercial and industrial customers in urban southern Alberta, Coste, who remained president until 1921, and other executives at Canadian Western had to focus attention on the problems of increasing production and expanding the marketing network. As the Bow Island natural gas reserves depleted rapidly between 1917 and 1920, the company sought fresh sources of supply. By 1930, it was obtaining natural gas from several new sources, including especially the Turner Valley and Foremost fields.[45] Even before 1930, Canadian Western was cash-poor, a situation that led the company to turn in the late 1920s to International Utilities of Maryland for capital. International Utilities rescued the company. In securing this funding, however, executives at Canadian Western soon yielded control of their company to International Utilities.[46] The company now had sufficient capital to carry on its business. By 1960, the firm had changed its name to Canadian Western Natural Gas Company, and the Jumping Pound field supplied forty-eight percent of its total natural gas needs.[47] Opening new fields was accompanied by the laying of new branch pipelines, as well as the recruitment of the managerial and sales personnel necessary to compete seriously in the production and distribution of natural gas.

The voracious demand for natural gas in southern Alberta in the 1960s and 1970s permitted Canadian Western to grow. Concentrating on this vast and rapidly expanding market, the company moved quickly and systematically to gain access to new sources of supply. By 1970, the Jumping Pound, Jumping Pound West, and Sarcee fields supplied fifty-six per cent of Canadian Western's natural gas requirements. A significant amount — twenty-four percent — of the company's natural gas supply came from the Turner Valley, Redland, Strathmore, and Okotoks fields.[48] Several smaller fields, such as the one at Stirling, supplied the remainder of Canadian Western's natural gas needs. By 1980, the company was drawing a large volume of natural gas from the Carbon field.[49] During the 1960s and 1970s, Canadian Western grew, not only by serving an increasing number of industrial and commercial customers and homes in urban centres, but also by beginning to bring natural gas to farms, ranches, and irrigation systems in southern Alberta through plastic pipe.[50]

By 1980, Canadian Western had become a big business. The company employed nearly 1,200 men and women and achieved about $257 million in annual sales. Stockholders, through their board of directors and executive officers, controlled about $228 million in total assets.[51] Emerging as a big business, Canadian Western reflected the fashion of the 1970s and 1980s, a time of rapid institutional growth among Alberta companies in several industries such as utilities. It was also a period when many large firms restructured and rearranged their businesses to lower production and distribution costs and increase profits.

As executives at Canadian Western faced increasing financial pressures, a fundamental restructuring of their company occurred in 1972. In that year, none of the changes Canadian Western underwent was more dramatic than the takeover of the company by Canadian Utilities. Then, in 1980, Canadian Utilities was taken over by ATCO Industries.[52] In the process, Canadian Western became an ATCO company.

Only firms willing and able to invest substantial sums of capital in new, modern facilities did well in the big business world in Alberta during the 1980s and 1990s. Another key to success was low-cost, efficient production. In this context, the growth of Canadian Western was noteworthy. By 1995, the company achieved about $343 million in annual sales. Through their board and executive officers, the stockholders of the company controlled about $750 million in total assets. In southern Alberta, Canadian Western provided natural gas service to 348,143 customers in 115 communities.[53]

Transalta Utilities Company's seventy-fifth anniversary in 1986, one year before Canadian Western's, marked a significant milestone in its evolution. Transalta Utilities Company was an important electric utility enterprise in Alberta employing 2,500 men and women and achieving about $909 million in annual sales. Stockholders of the company, through the board of directors and executive officers, controlled about $3.7 billion in total assets. Like Canadian Western, Transalta Utilities was a big business, an economic institution that commanded an important position in the electric utility industry. Transalta Utilities' facilities were at sites across central and southern Alberta, and it sold its product and services to homes and other businesses in 600 communities.[54]

Transalta Utilities was a sophisticated human organization in 1986. Top officers decided policies for the whole company, while lower-level managers were responsible for operations. A third, or middle, level of officers co-ordinated the different departments' activities. As opportunities for the production and distribution of electricity broadened, business executives at Transalta faced the future with a desire for continued growth.

The Transalta Utilities Company of 1986 developed from the new corporation, Calgary Power Company, which was formed in Montreal in 1909 and delivered its first electric power to Calgary on 21 May 1911.[55] The founding entrepreneurs, Max Aitken (later Lord Beaverbrook), and R. B. Bennett, could not have anticipated how the firm would evolve over the next seventy-five years. Aitken, a Montreal financier, and Bennett, a Calgary corporate lawyer, were the initial guiding forces in the company. Along with entrepreneur Herbert S. Holt of Montreal, they provided a substantial part of its capital. After Aitken and then Holt each briefly served as president, Bennett assumed the presidency on 3 August 1911, two and a half months after the company brought power to Calgary.[56] Bennett remained president until 1920.

Bennett's was a relatively small enterprise, doing business in an area of Alberta that was beginning to industrialize. In 1911, the Calgary Power Company employed fifteen men, was located in the central business district of a small city, and produced electricity for the local market.[57] Active in the firm's management, Bennett, a major stockholder, personally looked after its financial and legal affairs.

Transalta Utilities, originally called Calgary Power Company, was the first large electrical power corporation in Alberta. Head office of Transalta Utilities at Transalta Place, 110-12 Avenue Southwest, Calgary in 1998.

(Courtesy of Transalta Utilities).

Particularly important to Bennett, the Calgary Power Company had major hydro plants at Horseshoe Falls and Kananaskis Falls, upstream from Calgary on the Bow River. These plants, however, presented problems for years, because they lacked sufficient water after freeze-up to operate at full capacity.[58] By 1913, high-voltage transmission lines carried electricity from the plants not only to Calgary, but also to Exshaw and Cochrane.[59] Growing demand for power ensured that electricity found customers, especially in Calgary. Between 1913 and 1920, the company's net profits increased from $88,000 to $236,000.[60]

The early 1920s was a risky period for Alberta business. A severe depression shut down many businesses in the years immediately after World War I. Calgary Power, however, survived the depression and expanded in southern Alberta during the mid-1920s. Through the extension of the company's high-voltage transmission system, a number of urban centres, including High River, Blackie, Vulcan, Stavely, Claresholm, Nobleford, Lethbridge, and Taber, received electricity.[61] "Calgary Power Company reaches out through the richest agricultural districts of the South with transmission lines. Dozens of communities and hundreds of farms [are] supplied with power from the Bow River plants. Hydro [has been] put to increasing uses," such as street lighting, domestic appliances, store light, farm machinery, and oilfield equipment, noted the *Calgary Herald* on 7 December 1927.[62]

Calgary Power, however, suffered in the Great Depression. With the deepening of the depression in the early 1930s, one response of the company was to ask its employees to take a ten percent wage cut. They agreed to this request. The reduction in wages enabled all the employees to retain their jobs.[63]

Alberta recovered from the Great Depression slowly. There was economic growth by the late 1930s, with full recovery occurring during World War II. Calgary Power participated in Alberta's economic upswing. During the early and mid-1940s, the company's sales increased significantly. Calgary Power continued to grow and, in 1947, with the appearance of new opportunities to sell electricity following the discovery of oil at Leduc, the company moved its head office from Montreal to Calgary and changed its name to Calgary Power Ltd.[64] With division offices in Edmonton, Camrose, Wetaskiwin, and Lethbridge and twenty-four district offices, Calgary Power employed 400 men and women. By 1950, the company's sales had reached $6.2 million.[65]

Growth at Calgary Power in the late 1940s and 1950s, besides stemming from the company's response to increasing industrial demand for electricity, came from its growing involvement in rural electrification and the opening of new hydro plants in Alberta, including the Spray, Three Sisters, Rundle, and Cascade plants. By 1955, 25,000 farms received electricity from Calgary Power.[66] The company was supplying power to 2,554 oil well pumps in Alberta by 1956.[67] Further expansion at Calgary Power during the 1960s and 1970s was made possible by opening its coal-fired Wabamun and Sundance electric plants west of Edmonton.[68] After the late 1940s, investment in research and development increased. Moving into new geographical markets in Alberta became the accepted strategy of growth. This growth enlarged the size of management and significantly increased the complexity of the decision-making process at the top.

In recognition of the broad scope of the company's operations in Alberta, its name was changed to Transalta Utilities Corporation in 1981. The scrawny little firm that had started in 1911 was a big business seven decades later. An important electrical utility concern, Transalta Utilities employed 2,500 men and women and enjoyed about $403 million in annual sales. Through its board of directors and executive officers, the company controlled $483 million in total assets.[69]

As a result of Transalta Utilities' growth in size and complexity, the company adopted a departmental structure in 1981, formalizing a direction in which the firm had been moving for a number of years.[70] Under Marshall M. Williams, president and chief executive officer, and Albert W. Howard, chairman of the board of directors, a middle level of management was created: seven men became vice-presidents, serving as heads of the departments of planning, plant engineering and construction, engineering, human resources, finance, power system operations, and customer service operations. Another management group, composed of lower-level directors and managers, was established to assist the vice-presidents.

By the 1980s, Transalta Utilities had emerged as one of the most successful electrical utilities in Alberta. Marshall Williams and the other executives were innovative and persistent entrepreneurs. Aiming at providing high-quality service, they were willing to take risks and never looked back, even in the hard times of the early 1980s when their company faced major difficulties and a takeover attempt by ATCO Industries.[71] Among Marshall Williams's contributions to the firm was his optimism. In spite of the problems he encountered in the electrical utilities industry in Alberta in the 1980s, he continued to work closely with other executives in top management to make Transalta Utilities a success.

The early and mid-1990s were years of growth for Transalta. By 1995, the company supplied work to about 2,200 people, and its total sales reached $1.4 billion.[72] With assets of $4.6 billion, Transalta was the largest electric utility in Alberta.[73] Transalta generally proved successful in its foreign as well as in its Alberta and Canadian operations during the early and mid-1990s. By 1995, the company had opened two hydro plants in Ontario, one in Ottawa and another in Mississauga. In its overseas activities, Transalta had turned to Australia to construct the Parkeston Power Station there. A joint venture with the Gold Mines of Kalgoorlie, this natural gas-fired power plant was scheduled for completion in August 1996. By 1995, New Zealand, Argentina, Brazil, and Chile had become home to Transalta investments in the production and distribution of electricity.[74]

Transalta executives doubtless hoped that expansion overseas and in Ontario would offset the problem of competition in Alberta during the 1990s. They sought to make profits quickly in their Ontario and overseas power ventures. To some extent, these hopes were realized. There were difficulties in setting up foreign and Ontario power enterprises. Nonetheless, by 1995 some of Transalta's Ontario and overseas operations were profitable.[75] The company meanwhile remained strong in the Alberta power market despite competition.

■

Restructuring Alberta Business

During the 1980s and 1990s, the Alberta political economy underwent important development. Although a great deal that was traditional in federal policy toward business remained, some long-standing views of regulation changed. The federal government did not greatly affect the permanence of big Alberta businesses as institutions dominating the creation of industrial wealth. Even though big business remained a major feature of the Alberta economic system, new complexities appeared in the politics of business as the federal government enacted new regulations. Regulations sometimes combined with the growth of competition and strategic emphasis on financial affairs to influence business-government relations and to spark a restructuring of Alberta business in areas such as the airline industry.

Prime Minister Brian Mulroney echoed the complaints of Alberta business that federal regulation of the airline industry brought high costs and consequently imposed excessive burdens on consumers. In an effort to slow inflation, Mulroney turned to deregulation as a policy for lowering business costs. Deregulation of the airline industry through the National Transportation Act of 1987 significantly affected Wardair. From a small company formed in Edmonton after World War II, in 1953, Wardair had become a big business by 1987.

In the decades after 1953, Wardair was one of the fastest growing airlines in aviation history. Max Ward, president of Wardair, had a profound economic and social vision, a vision he tried to bring to fulfillment. He provided an environment in which his airline could expand. Wardair's planes were kept in the air a significant number of hours a day, the pilots flew many hours a month, and the flight attendants were attentive and friendly. By the late 1970s, Wardair's planes carried over a million passengers a year. Max Ward's efforts met with phenomenal success. Building up a large fleet of planes, he pleased the flying public by providing high-quality service in international charter markets.

Wardair had many of the ingredients for success, but the road to success was not smooth. Especially important, under federal government airline regulation Edmonton-based Wardair was neither permitted to become a scheduled carrier in the international arena nor allowed to operate scheduled domestic flights between Edmonton, Vancouver, Calgary, and the large central Canadian cities of Toronto and Montreal. These restrictions prevented Wardair's entry into several major markets. Since the late 1970s, Ward had sought deregulation. After Congress deregulated the airlines in the United States by enacting the Airline Deregulation Act of 1978, Ward began his quest for similar legislation in Canada. "In August 1978," said Ward, "I wrote, rather desperately, to Prime Minister Pierre Trudeau. I begged him to direct the Canadian Transport Commission to loosen the rules that were binding us, and I asked, not for the first time, that Wardair be designated Canada's third international scheduled carrier." [76] Unlike Air Canada and CP Air, however, Wardair was not permitted to provide international scheduled service.

Once deregulation came with the passage of the National Transportation Act of 1987, all-out competition provided Ward with new opportunities in the scheduled service market but, at the same time, caused real structural problems at his airline. There was external pressure on Ward to restructure his Edmonton-based company. The early and mid-1980s

Max Ward's Edmonton-based company, Wardair, became one of the most important airlines in Canadian aviation history. Shown here is Wardair's CF-FUN, 100 series, the "Romeo Vachon" named for a famous French-Canadian bush pilot. It was Wardair's second 747, purchased in 1974.

(Courtesy of Maxwell W. Ward).

were years of increased merger activity in Alberta, with acquisitions often in the province's business news. Because its stock price was low, Wardair was a ripe takeover target for other companies on the hunt. Internal pressures also led to restructuring at Wardair. Having operated at a loss in the late 1970s and still suffering from the depression of the early 1980s and its aftermath, Wardair was a company in deep trouble by 1987.[77] Ward responded to the growing problems by undertaking a review of the company's activities and prospects. Restructuring was the result of this review. In an attempt to deal with the firm's huge debt load, Ward cut costs and made new financial arrangements with creditors. As well, he sold old planes and purchased new ones.[78] Wardair had become an international scheduled carrier and had also initiated scheduled service on the high-density route between Edmonton, Vancouver, Calgary, and Toronto.

Ward's airline faced increasing competition from Air Canada and Calgary-based Canadian Airlines International at home and abroad; by the fall of 1988, its long-term debt — $300 million — had become unmanageable.[79] In January 1989, he sold to Canadian Airlines International. Max Ward had changed the face of Canadian aviation, and many at Wardair remembered the success and growth he generated at the company during the years in which he ran the important operation.

Canadian Airlines International evolved out of Pacific Western Airlines, which acquired CP Air in 1986 and was renamed Canadian Airlines International the following year. Executives at Canadian Airlines International in Calgary had high hopes for their business, but their company's potential was not fulfilled in the early and mid-1990s. When recession struck, in 1991 and 1992, the fortunes of Canadian Airlines International faltered. There was a need to solve the problems of high costs and operating losses. Between 1992 and 1994, dramatic alterations occurred in the operations of Canadian Airlines International. Cutthroat competition in the airline industry, together with the firm's internal difficulties, led the firm's president, Edmonton-born Kevin Jenkins, who had received his MBA from Harvard University, to make massive structural adjustments. Of special importance in the company's restructuring was the $200 million share sale to its 16,400 employees, the $246 million share sale to its international service partner American Airlines, and a total of $120 million in loan guarantees from the federal, Alberta, and British Columbia governments.[80]

Under ongoing deregulation, there were further pressures on Jenkins to make structural alterations. Restructuring at Canadian Airlines International continued in the spring of 1996 in the form of a pay cut of seventeen percent for the company's employees, in response to the growing competition it faced with the appearance of two Calgary-based rivals: WestJet Airlines and Greyhound Lines of Canada.[81] Jenkins emphasized the importance of improving Canadian Airlines International's position at home and abroad.

In addition to the financial and operational changes at Canadian Airlines International, its top management was restructured. When he resigned in June 1996, Jenkins was succeeded by Kevin Benson, a South African-born chartered accountant, who remained president of Canadian Airlines International through the company's next phase of restructuring and beyond.[82] The company's growing losses, combined with heightened competition, drove Benson, like Jenkins before him, to focus his attention on trying to get the company's finances into better shape. Like Jenkins, Benson wanted Canadian Airlines International to improve its stature in the national and international business arenas. In November 1996, Benson sought to reduce expenses by asking the company's employees to take an additional pay cut of ten percent.[83] Further, he attempted to rally Canadian Airlines International behind programs to cut administrative and service costs and to achieve greater efficiencies in aircraft operations.[84] Benson's effort to address the company's problems proved an uphill battle, but Canadian Airlines International survived. Indeed, the Calgary-based airline grew under his guidance.

Change in the structure of Alberta firms was an important signpost of the province's evolving business system. Some of the famous big businesses in the province struggled and became insolvent. At few firms was this development more obvious to Albertans than at Eaton's. The history of Eaton's in the difficult years after 1980 dramatized some of the changes that swept across the Alberta business landscape. Eaton's was a successful national corporation that had entered the retail field under Irish-born Timothy Eaton in Toronto in 1869 and become prominent by emerging as a nationwide department store business.[85] From a retailer that began in Alberta by opening a department store in Calgary in 1929, Eaton's had expanded to a network of twelve stores in the province by the mid-1990s.[86] The Toronto-based family enterprise had become a chain of eighty-five stores across Canada.[87]

Eaton's had become a Canadian and Alberta institution, an important part of Canadian and Alberta culture and identity; by the 1990s, it played a mythic role in the identity of the nation and the province, a role carefully fostered by Eaton's advertising over the decades. The success of Eaton's reflected the ability of family executives to command large financial resources to capture leadership in the mass distribution age and to provide secure jobs to thousands of employees. Even Eaton's had to undergo fundamental restructuring in the end, however, to adapt to fierce competition in the retail markets it served.

To George Eaton, president of Eaton's in 1988, the department store business still seemed a promising business opportunity. He wanted Eaton's to maintain its reputation for excellence in retailing and service while it underwent reorganization to adapt to changing conditions in the marketplace. The restructuring that took place at Eaton's included placing a stronger emphasis on medium and high-end fashions and home furnishings.[88] Between 1988 and 1996, however, operating losses came to about $250 million.[89] Eaton's was in worse shape than most of its principal competitors. Once he had a better understanding of the problem, George Eaton recognized that considerable real estate had to go. Eaton's sold off a great deal of real estate in 1996 for $100 million. As a result, Eaton's owned only eleven of its stores; the remaining stores were leased from mall owners.[90]

Even as he scrambled to restructure his company, George Eaton realized that little worked out as well as he had hoped. On 27 February, 1997, after Eaton's had been in business for 127 years, he filed for bankruptcy protection in an Ontario Court, claiming that the company was insolvent.[91] The Court granted Eaton's protection from its creditors, giving the company time to restructure its operations while its stores remained open. "We want to initiate an orderly restructuring of our retail operations in a way that protects, to the extent possible, the interests and future of employees, suppliers, customers, and other stakeholders. Our goal is to emerge with a strong and viable network of stores," said George Eaton.[92]

From George Eaton's discussion with other top executives came a plan for structural adjustments. In this plan, thirty-one of Eaton's eighty-five stores across Canada emerged for review. "Alberta could be hardest hit — seven are under review, almost two of every three stores," observed the *Financial Post*.[93] Eaton's outlets targeted for possible closure in Alberta included its stores at Sunridge Mall and Northland Village Mall in Calgary as well as at West Edmonton Mall. "When we initiated our restructuring process on 27 February, I indicated my expectation that the company could operate through the balance of the year without closing stores. As our negotiations stand now, most of the locations we have to vacate will stop operating as Eaton's stores on 30 June of this year," said George Eaton on 17 March 1997.[94] The basic problem continued to be capital scarcity, but by 11 April Eaton's had attracted support to restructure from two sources: a $101 million loan from Stamford, Connecticut-based General Electric Capital and a $99 million loan from the Royal Bank of Canada, thus putting $200 million in sorely needed cash into Eaton's coffers.[95]

Some of Alberta's big businesses, such as Dome Petroleum, fell by the wayside in the 1980s and 1990s as competition grew.[96] Others faltered as engines of growth and development. The restructuring of businesses occurred in response to the increasing competition they faced. As this situation unfolded, many Albertans looked to small businesses for economic renewal.

■

Small Business and Fresh Opportunities

As part of the restructuring of Alberta's business system, small firms experienced growth in the 1980s and 1990s. As in earlier times, small firms remained a vital part of the province's business system. Between 1992 and 1993, in Alberta, the number of small businesses with fewer than fifty employees rose from 93,713 to 96,198, or by 2.7 percent.[97] Manufacturing was the most important illustration of the growing significance of small business. Between 1985 and 1995, the contribution of manufacturing to Alberta's Gross Domestic Product more than doubled, rising from about $4 billion to $8.2 billion.[98] Much of this increase came from small firms in Alberta.

The history of Barber Industries provides an instructive example of the success of small business in Alberta manufacturing during the last third of the twentieth century. Founded in Longview in 1940 by James Barber, an engineer, Barber Industries was initially involved in repairing oil drilling machinery.[99] Born in Boston and educated at Massachusetts Institute of Technology, Barber worked in the Colorado oil fields before coming to Longview.[100] Once there, Barber purchased a small machine shop to repair

Oilfield products acquired great significance in the Alberta economy in the decades after World War II. Built around 1978, the office machine shop and fabrication plant of Barber Industries in Calgary reinforces our sense of an industrializing society. (Courtesy of Peter S. Grant).

oilfield equipment and he succeeded in his efforts in the next few years. After spending some time seeking a new location for repairing oilfield machinery, Barber moved to Calgary in 1945 to begin anew.[101] Earl Griffiths, a machinist and welder, and Eric Connelly, a chartered accountant, supported Barber's plans and became his partners in Barber Industries. In 1947, while continuing to repair oilfield equipment in its Calgary shop, the firm branched out to Edmonton to open another repair shop there.[102] Around this time, Barber Industries began to receive financial support for its operations in Calgary and Edmonton from the Industrial Development Bank.[103] As the years passed, the Royal Bank of Canada provided some of the needed financing.

In Edmonton, Barber Industries soon moved ahead by starting to manufacture specialty products for niche markets, mainly oilfield wellheads and safety systems. The company entered manufacturing at an auspicious time. The late 1940s and 1950s were years of tremendous expansion for Alberta business, as Alberta became an increasingly industrial and urban province. From a province based on farms and small towns before World War II, Alberta became a province of growing manufacturing businesses and larger cities by the 1950s. A change in ownership at Barber Industries came in 1953, when founding entrepreneur James Barber sold his interest in the firm to Griffiths, Connelly, and three minor shareholders, P. S. Grant, John Johnson, and Archie Campbell.[104] The firm's name, with its promise of continuing to help attract business, remained unchanged. In addition to continuing to repair oilfield machinery in Calgary, around 1960, Barber Industries began to make specialized products for niche markets: compressor packages and drilling rigs.[105]

Although wellheads, safety systems, compressor packages, and drilling rigs were its leading products between the 1960s and 1980s, Barber Industries followed a policy of diversified production and sales.[106] In Calgary, the company also made mining equipment and street light standards.[107] As well, by 1990, the Calgary plant was designing and manufacturing gas separation and filtration equipment.[108] By this time, the Edmonton plant had added valve actuators to its product line.

During the period from the 1950s to the mid-1990s, research was a focus of Barber Industries. Besides exploring what customers desired, executives at Barber Industries encouraged the company's technical personnel in their research efforts.[109] Expenditures for enlarged and improved manufacturing facilities grew in these years. Sales of Barber Industries' high-quality products took place in Alberta and other parts of Canada, as well as in the United States, Mexico, Europe, Australia, New Zealand, China, Hong Kong, India, Pakistan, South America, Central America, Africa, and the Middle East.[110] As time passed, Barber Industries became strong not only at home, but also in foreign markets. The company's service centres at Slave Lake, Grande Prairie, and Brooks helped give it a significant presence in addressing the technical problems of its Alberta customers. Although Barber Industries sold its manufacturing division in Calgary in the early 1990s, the company kept its sales division there and maintained its important manufacturing facilities in Edmonton. By 1996, Barber Industries employed more than 100 men and women, most of whom worked in the Edmonton plant, and enjoyed about $23 million in annual sales.[111]

The growth of the Edmonton Tent & Awning Company also reveals the continuing importance of small business in manufacturing across Alberta. Edmonton Tent & Awning's lineage can be traced back to the firm Edmonton Tent & Mattress formed in 1895.[112] Robert Kenneth, the founding entrepreneur, began manufacturing high-quality tents and mattresses for the local and regional markets. From a tiny concern with little capital in 1895, Edmonton Tent & Mattress became a corporation capitalized at $75,000 in 1906.[113] Headed by Robert Kenneth as president, the company had a handful of employees. Joining him as a director was his wife Agnes.[114] Robert and Agnes Kenneth led their company into a period of substantial growth. In addition to tents and mattresses, the company made pillows and boat and wagon covers.

Robert Kenneth continued to serve as president until he stepped down some time after 1930, and Thomas S. Hollingworth, who had joined Edmonton Tent & Mattress in 1921, became manager in 1933 and took over the company in 1940.[115] The firm changed its name to the Edmonton

Tent & Awning Company.[116] Two high-quality specialty goods, tents and awnings, dominated the company's product line. In 1942, Thomas Hollingsworth's brother Ernest joined the firm as sales manager.[117]

In early 1965, Thomas Hollingsworth thought the time had arrived to retire and, in April, sold Edmonton Tent & Awning to Russ Brown, an experienced tent and awning manufacturer.[118] The company employed about fifteen men and women and was making not only tents and awnings, but also venetian blinds, camper trailers, sleeping bags, and many other camping items. Brown aimed at manufacturing high-quality goods through advanced production methods, whether the products were sleeping bags or awnings. In 1982, at St. Paul, Minnesota, Edmonton Tent & Awning received an international achievement award for one of its products, a retractable awning used for shelter at outdoor functions.[119]

In 1985, Vern Nast, who had started at Edmonton Tent & Awning as a shop hand around 1964, together with two partners, purchased the company.[120] Nast developed a high-quality, specialty product for a niche market, awning signs for businesses across western Canada. By around 1990, the company employed twenty-seven men and women, and awning signs composed about forty-five percent of its sales. Total sales in that year came to $1.5 million.[121] Although awning signs were his leading products, Nast followed a policy of diversified production and sales, manufacturing and selling a wide range of goods including snake- and mosquito-proof hammocks which he exported to oil exploration companies in South America.[122] "Today awnings are trendy, but maybe four years from now sales will peter out. I don't want to count on just one item," explained Nast.[123]

As his company grew, Nast continued to manufacture a diversified range of products, such as tents and other camping equipment, still dominated by specialized products for distinct markets.[124] Awning signs headed the list. In 1995, at Charlotte, North Carolina, Edmonton Tent & Awning was an international achievement award winner for its dramatic awning sign which enhanced visibility by day and night. The market for this awning sign boomed, helping to increase total sales at Edmonton Tent & Awning by sixty per cent.[125]

The experience of the Redcliff Pressed Brick Company, a clay brick manufacturing firm in Medicine Hat, is also an example of how small manufacturing businesses in Alberta prospered in the 1980s and 1990s. By 1991, Medicine Hat was a city of nearly 43,000.[126] Manufacturing helped drive the city's growth. Back in the 1940s, Herbert J. Sissons, the founder of Redcliff Pressed Brick, a family business, had groomed his three sons Gordon, Jack, and Tom for leadership.[127] At Herbert's death in 1949, Gordon, a mining engineer, became general manager. Tom, who had received his B.Sc. in electrical engineering from the University of Alberta,

The Redcliff Pressed Brick Company's trademark, I-XL, became synonymous with top-quality brick products. As the years went on, I-XL Industries was formed and became a subsidiary of the Redcliff Pressed Brick Company. Head office of Redcliff Pressed Brick Company and I-XL Industries at Medicine Hat in 1998. (Courtesy of Gordon S. Sissons).

served as president from 1955 to 1959. Jack, who had graduated with a B. Sc. in mechanical engineering from the University of British Columbia, became president in 1960. When he stepped down in 1963, Jack was succeeded by Gordon, who remained president until 1985. Then Jack assumed the presidency again, holding this position until 1992. During the period from the 1950s to the early 1990s, one of the brothers was always president, while the other two were also executives in top management.

Working closely together and providing reliable service, Gordon, Tom and Jack Sissons succeeded in leading Redcliff Pressed Brick in more than four decades of growth. When Gordon Sissons became general manager in 1949, Redcliff Pressed Brick manufactured and sold its high-quality, specialty products in niche markets in western Canada through two companies, both of which it owned, in Medicine Hat.[128] By the late 1980s, after acquiring Northwest Brick and Tile of Edmonton and Clayburn Industries of Abbotsford, British Columbia, Redcliff Pressed Brick controlled four companies. Redcliff Pressed Brick's growth was funded out of retained earnings and bank credit.[129] The firm had extended itself into distribution abroad, especially in the western United States.

When Jack Sissons retired as Redcliff Pressed Brick's president in 1992, Gordon's son Clayton took the company's helm. Around the same time, sons of Jack and Tom also became executives in top management. Clayton Sissons and the other executives brought a keen desire to expand sales at home and abroad. In 1996, international sales accounted for a significant portion of the firm's consolidated sales, which had reached about

$50 million.[130] Important areas of expansion were the United States and Japan, where increasing prosperity was creating larger clay brick markets. Redcliff Pressed Brick employed 200 men and women.[131] Through scientific research, the company made significant advances in manufacturing efficiency and improved its position in established markets during the last half of the twentieth century.

As in manufacturing, a number of small businesses in Alberta continued to prosper in sales, frequently by adopting the strategy of specialization, even though they faced strong competition from big companies. In addition to still being challenged by department stores and chain stores, independent retailers in Alberta encountered increasing competition from discount stores such as Kmart and Walmart and big-box retailers such as Costco in the 1970s, 1980s, and 1990s. Shopping malls in Alberta cities and towns were also a threat to small retailers, most of whom found their rental fees burdensome. Many small retail businesses, however, survived and grew.

The growth of Duff Layton's Men's Wear shows the ongoing importance of small businesses in retailing across Alberta. Founded in Camrose in 1949 by Duff Layton, it was the first store to specialize in men's wear in town.[132] Layton, who had extensive experience as a men's clothing salesman for Lawrence & Co.'s department store in Camrose, began business with capital of $10,000 in a rented building. In the 1950s and 1960s, Layton's sales efforts proved successful. Work clothes and boots for farmers and oil industry workers accounted for about forty percent of his sales. Other sales consisted largely of suits, shirts, ties, underwear, shoes, and socks. Sales were for cash, but often credit was extended, especially to farmers. Ready-to-wear, high-quality goods were purchased from wholesalers in Winnipeg and Toronto on credit, with payment expected in three months. Layton also offered made-to-measure suits. He had a tailor on the premises to make the suits, and the market for them grew.[133] Layton's personal, dependable service imbued his customers with a sense of confidence that was manifested in their return to his small store to shop year after year.

In the late 1960s, Layton's son Duff Jr., who had entered the family store earlier, took over Duff Layton's Men's Wear. The late 1960s and 1970s were prosperous years for the store, and in the mid-1970s, Duff Layton Jr. brought in Merv Van Slyke as a partner to assist him in running the expanding business. Layton and Van Slyke led their firm into a period of substantial growth. In 1988, Dan Olofson, who had been in the clothing business for twenty-six years, bought out Layton and Van Slyke and became sole owner of the store, keeping the name Duff Layton's Men's Wear.[134]

Dan Olofson's strategy — high-quality goods and personal, reliable service — resulted in an expanding venture in Camrose in the late 1980s and 1990s. By 1991, Camrose was a city of nearly 13,000.[135] Agriculture and trade continued to drive the city's growth. In running his store, Olofson seized on key markets in Camrose and the surrounding region. The clothing he offered appealed to both city and rural customers. The depression of the early 1990s bit into his store's profits, but it successfully weathered these difficult times. Sales continued to grow in the mid-1990s, often spurred by customers' word-of-mouth recommendations. Long-standing customer loyalty to the store was another factor in its continuing success. Olofson enjoyed selling a fortieth-wedding-anniversary-suit to a man who had purchased his original wedding suit at Duff Layton's Men's Wear.[136]

Hutchings & Sharp Clothing in Medicine Hat was also successful in its retail operations in the 1980s and 1990s. Formed as a partnership in 1948, Hutchings & Sharp Clothing was incorporated in 1957 but continued into the 1990s to be run as a small family business.[137] The two partners, Harry Hutchings and James Sharp, both of whom had earlier been connected with the harness and saddlery firm T. Hutchinson Company, got ahead by offering high-quality specialty goods for a distinct market niche — mainly western men's and women's wear — and by providing personal, dependable service. After Harry Hutchings' death in 1963, James Sharp became sole owner of Hutchings & Sharp Clothing.

Headed by James Sharp, Hutchings & Sharp Clothing in downtown Medicine Hat enjoyed $400,000 in annual sales in 1963.[138] Born in Medicine Hat in 1919, Sharp graduated from the local high school, worked for the T. Hutchinson Company, and served overseas with the Canadian Army during World War II. Sharp's return to Medicine Hat after the war brought him good fortune, taking him to the right place at the right time for the kind of business he wanted to develop. An experienced western-wear retailer, by 1963 Sharp was ready to expand his business. He worked to make his western-wear offerings available over a large area between the early 1960s and the late 1970s. Hutchings & Sharp complemented its growing trade in Medicine Hat with increased sales in the surrounding region through its mail-order business. Farmers and residents of small towns who could not easily reach the company's Medicine Hat store selected merchandise from its catalogue and received their goods by railway. In the late 1970s, Hutchings & Sharp sales topped $800,000.[139]

Hutchings & Sharp, however, faced problems. The growth of big retailers in Medicine Hat's suburban shopping malls in the 1970s limited opportunities for Hutchings & Sharp's downtown store sales.[140] Bringing new mobility to Albertans, automobiles increasingly linked farmers to shopping malls in Medicine Hat, thus eroding the importance of Hutchings & Sharp's mail-order business. Although he discontinued his mail-order business in the mid-1970s, Sharp succeeded in keeping his downtown store in good condition.[141] As opportunities for new sales opened up, Sharp took advantage of them. During the 1980s and 1990s, he continued to attract many customers by offering high-quality western men's and women's wear

Hutchings & Sharp was a long-lasting firm that, in the 1990s, still operated a western clothing business. Owner James M. Sharp at the front door of his store at 623 Third Street Southeast, Medicine Hat. (Courtesy of James M. Sharp).

goods and providing personal, reliable service. Sharp's downtown store possessed another key asset — several women clerks known for their willingness to identify closely with the enterprise and ability to satisfy customers.[142]

Just as important as retail-clothing stores in Alberta's small business world in the 1980s and 1990s were retail jewellery stores. Some small retail jewellers found themselves unable to compete with large businesses specializing in jewellery and went out of existence. Others survived and grew. Mitchell & Jewell of Red Deer, for example, competed successfully in jewellery retailing.

As Red Deer grew to a city of more than 58,000 by 1991, Mitchell & Jewell's store in downtown Red Deer prospered, earning a reputation for dependable goods and services.[143] An important turning point in the firm's development occurred in 1955, when A. B. Mitchell died and Robert Jewell became sole owner. Born in Nanton and educated at Crescent Heights High School in Calgary, Robert Jewell served with the Royal Canadian Air Force in the British Commonwealth Air Training Plan during World War II. Hand engraving attracted Jewell. He first studied the subject in St. John, New Brunswick in 1948 and moved to Red Deer the following year to become A. B. Mitchell's junior partner.[144] This preparation for the jewellery business was useful, for Jewell's hand-engraving skills complemented Mitchell's talent in watchmaking.[145]

After he took over Mitchell & Jewell in 1955, Robert Jewell received much of the support from family for developing the firm.[146] Jewell's father and his wife Doris's family provided a great deal of the financing. Robert Jewell assumed responsibility for supervision of the store's daily operations, assisted by Doris. Together Robert and Doris built up the small family jewellery business in the late 1950s, 1960s, and 1970s. Born in Standard, Doris had received her B.Comm. from the University of Alberta and had worked in the Department of National Defence in Ottawa during the war. She performed a variety of tasks, keeping stock fresh, selling high-quality watches, rings, necklaces, and other items, and doing the books. Having hired a watchmaker to repair watches, Robert Jewell focussed his attention on engraving, thus providing an important specialty service. To nurture their store's growth, Robert and Doris took full advantage of opportunities to reach profitable markets for their goods and services in Red Deer and the surrounding region.

The spread of large competitors in the jewellery business in Alberta after World War II, however, challenged small independents such Mitchell & Jewell. In 1971, Robert Jewell sought to meet this challenge by banding together with seven other independent Alberta jewellers in an association — Gemalta — to secure some of the benefits, especially the discounts gained through high-volume purchases, obtained by large businesses. Red Deer was the location of Gemalta's head office. By the late 1980s, over 100 western Canadian jewellery stores belonged to Gemalta. Through Gemalta, Mitchell & Jewell could buy diamonds directly from the association's cutters in Antwerp, Belgium and thus cut costs.[147]

Competition continued to hurt Mitchell & Jewell, however, as the growth of large retailers in Red Deer's suburban Parkland Mall in the 1970s limited sales opportunities for its downtown store. In an effort to offset competition, Doris Jewell diversified by organizing new businesses: Nordic Designs, an enterprise that designed Nordic furniture, and Contrast, a gift store in the Parkland Mall.[148] These businesses were hurt severely by the depression in the early 1980s and, by 1986, had been closed.[149] Setting up branch jewellery stores was a strategy used by some independent jewellers in Alberta to meet competition. For example, Blackburn Jewellers in downtown Pincher Creek devised an additional marketing channel for its goods by opening a branch store in Pincher Creek's Ranchland Mall.[150]

But Mitchell & Jewell did not use this strategy. Instead, the firm ultimately expanded the operations of its jewellery store in downtown Red Deer. Robert and Doris Jewell's son Richard played an important role in taking the downtown store in this direction. Born in Red Deer in 1954, Richard Jewell was educated in a local high school and at Red Deer

Mitchell & Jewell's jewellery store, which appeared on a postcard, was a widely distributed image in Alberta in the 1990s. Like other types of firms, Mitchell & Jewell advertised in many ways. (Courtesy of Richard Jewell).

College. After working on road construction and oil rigs, Richard joined Mitchell & Jewell as a junior partner in 1979.[151]

An energetic man who had worked in the family store from an early age, Richard, like his father and mother, was committed to the downtown store's expansion and acted on the assumption that the market for its goods would grow. Richard proved innovative in hand engraving and flexible in his approach to business. He aimed at offering high-quality watches, rings, pearls, and other items, as well as personal service. The store's sales reached $350,000 by the early 1980s. By 1987, Richard Jewell had taken over Mitchell & Jewell. Under Richard's leadership, the firm invested substantial capital in expansion. Mitchell & Jewell had a large, attractive building on a spacious, new downtown site revamped as part of a new shopping complex and opened for business in October 1994.[152] The firm financed its expansion through retained earnings and bank loans.[153] The store's staff of eight worked hard to develop sales. "The staff makes the place run," observed Richard Jewell. "These people are competent and loyal. For example, Gerda Klanke, the assistant manager, has worked for twenty-three years at Mitchell & Jewell. Much of the staff are better at certain tasks than I am."[154] A risk-taking entrepreneur, Jewell continued to make the investments of money and time necessary for growth. By 1996, Mitchell & Jewell's sales rose to more than $1 million.[155]

In spite of the economic downturns that punctuated the 1980s and 1990s, these decades were a time of tremendous economic growth in Alberta. Like Mitchell & Jewell, other small retail enterprises, such as Rhona and Robyn Mackay's ice cream store in Cochrane, Alan Cornyn's drugstore in Pincher Creek, Ted Thaell's Men's and Ladies' Wear in Fort Macleod, Gerry and Lorraine Maybank's drugstore in Olds, and Ken Chisholm's music store in Medicine Hat, were in the right place at the right time with the right goods to participate in this growth.[156] Internal policies were similar from store to store, most notably, they concentrated on providing high-quality goods and personal service.

As in sales, many small businesses in Alberta continued to flourish in the service industries in the 1980s and 1990s. Big firms, however, became increasingly important in services as the years passed. For instance, in 1993, big chartered banks such as Scotiabank owned assets more than five times as large as those of leading industrial firms such as Canadian Pacific.[157]

Big chartered banks increasingly served small business, giving loans to small retailers, manufacturers, and farmers in Alberta. On 6 June, 1994, John E. Cleghorn, president and chief operating officer of the Royal Bank of Canada, wrote:

> Over the past few years, Royal Bank of Canada, along with the other chartered banks in this country, has been reproached for doing too little to assist in the development, growth and stability of Canada's small and medium-sized businesses. Believe me, this criticism, which is not without foundation, has not gone unnoticed. Although we have many thousands of completely satisfied customers, we recognize that a large number of this country's entrepreneurs and small business owners and managers have felt thwarted in their dealings with Canada's financial institutions. Recently, Royal Bank has been working aggressively to create policies and services that will improve lending practices, eliminate red tape, and provide fast, professional assistance in a variety of ways to our small business customers.[158]

In Alberta, as in the rest of the nation, the Royal Bank increasingly aided small businesses. For instance, between the fourth quarter in 1995 and the third quarter in 1996, Royal Bank loans to small businesses in Alberta rose from $2 billion to $2.3 billion.[159] Lending to agricultural concerns in Alberta, most of which were family farms, was an especially expansive part of the Royal Bank's business from 1993 to 1996.[160]

Other big chartered banks such as the Bank of Montreal also adopted policies designed to spur the development of small businesses in Canada, including those in Alberta. On 20 May, 1994, Matthew W. Barrett, chairman of the board and chief executive officer of the Bank of Montreal, opened the bank's Institute for Small Business as a part of the bank's newly created Institute for Learning in Toronto. "The Institute for Small Business," observed Barrett, "will be a catalyst for practical action. The Bank will sponsor and promote practical initiatives that will have a tangible and meaningful impact on small business, both in Canada and the United States."[161]

Geoff Cannon, appointed the Bank of Montreal's first executive director of the Institute for Small Business, was instrumental in the bank's small business lending efforts. Cannon immediately set an example of leadership. In an address to the bank's human resources division on 1 June, Cannon said:

> Coming from a small business background, as an investor and as an operator of three small businesses, two of which were knowledge-based, turn-around companies, I feel that my practical experience has given us a huge head start. The network of contacts that I already have, in the form of both investors and advisors to small business, has given us an opportunity to identify both the issues and potential initiatives.[162]

As in the rest of the nation, the Bank of Montreal increasingly aided small businesses in Alberta. For example, between the fourth quarter in 1995 and the third quarter in 1996, Bank of Montreal loans to small businesses in Alberta rose from $1.2 billion to $1.3 billion.[163]

Like sales and services, agriculture continued to offer hope to small firms. Natural resources, especially fertile land, continued to play a significant part in the development of farming businesses. Albertans remained the beneficiaries of land capable of sustaining diversified agriculture.

Despite the difficulties small farming businesses had meeting the challenges of the rapidly changing business environment of the 1980s and 1990s, family farms remained important in Alberta's agricultural industry. The dreams of independence and a reasonable income that motivated founders of family farms in the past were still powerful in these decades. Small farmers' ability to react quickly to changes in markets and fluctuations in agricultural prices helped explain their continuing significance.

The development of the Dwelle farm of Nanton was typical of many small businesses in the agricultural industry. Founded in 1918 by Frank Dwelle, the farm was initially simply one of numerous small southern Alberta farms producing grain and livestock for the local and national markets. Born in Kansas, Dwelle moved with his wife Nesta and five children to Nanton and purchased the 640-acre farm complete with buildings for $26 per acre.[164] Dwelle obtained much of the financial support to acquire and develop the farm from the Bank of Nova Scotia and Sun Life Assurance Company of Canada. The profits from farming were large enough in the mid-1920s to allow him to expand by buying an additional 320 acres of farmland.

The next decade was a risky time for Alberta agriculture, a period dominated by a downturn in the business cycle. The Great Depression shut down many family farms in the early and mid-1930s. Dwelle survived the depression, although, by the end of the decade, he was carrying a larger debt load than when he had purchased his farm.[165] Support from his sons John, Frank, and Harry helped his case immensely.

During World War II, relief came when good wheat crops enabled

Dwelle to pay off all his creditors, a move that helped his farm re-establish its prosperity. The venture was again earning profits. In large part, the farm's return to profitability resulted from the economic recovery in Canada and Alberta during the war. Dwelle looked to John for assistance with the farm work, while Harry served with the Royal Canadian Air Force.[166] By 1946, Dwelle had clear title to his farm.

Dwelle's desire to retire brought ownership changes to his farming business.[167] In 1946, sons Harry and John took over the family farm.[168] The business was a well-managed partnership. For the Dwelle brothers, the future was uncertain in 1946, filled with both opportunities and hazards. In the early 1950s, heavy rains meant that the quality of the grain in their fields deteriorated. The main opportunity for Harry and John was still in wheat, but the market for their cattle was also growing. Consequently, in 1951 they set up a feedlot on their farm to fatten their expanding herd of cattle with their own grain for market. Between 1951 and 1955, total annual grain and cattle sales increased from $11,370 to $11,478.[169] Although the growth in sales was modest, the partnership was clearly successful. John and Harry could each support his family from the farm's income.

The Dwelle brothers led their farm into a period of substantial expansion and prosperity. As opportunities for raising and selling more cattle opened up, Harry and John took advantage of them. By 1970, the farm enjoyed $286,000 in annual sales.[170] Of this amount, $256,000 came from cattle. Grain accounted for the remainder.

Harry and John Dwelle lived to see their children become active on the family farm before they terminated their partnership in 1981.[171] The division of the farm and the sale of parts of it was a result of the end of the partnership. Family ties, however, remained of great importance to the development of what remained of the family farm. For instance, Harry assisted his children in financing their farming operations in the 1980s and 1990s in an effort to offset the impact of the economic downswings. Like many young Alberta farmers during these decades, the children looked to their father to stabilize their farming business and make it profitable.

Among successful small farms in Alberta during the 1980s and 1990s was the farm owned and managed by Gordon and Anola Laing at Claresholm. Founded by Gordon's grandfather, Frederick H. Laing, in 1920, the farm originally consisted of 480 acres.[172] Born in Ontario, Frederick Laing focussed on the production of wheat and livestock. His son William began working on the farm at an early age. Upon Frederick's death in 1956, William took over the family farm and expanded the business.[173] By the time of William's death in 1981, the size of the venture had increased to 3,680 acres.[174] In 1960, William had incorporated the family farm as Laing Farms Ltd. with capital of $190,000 and had brought in his wife Ruby and son Gordon as partners.[175] The sixties were years of impressive growth for the farm. As well as expanding their grain operations, the Laings placed fresh emphasis on livestock, setting up a feedlot in 1963 for fattening cattle for local, national, and international markets.

When William retired at fifty, Laing Farms was flourishing.[176] Management succession proceeded smoothly, and by around 1969, Gordon and his wife Anola were running the family farm.[177] After graduating from Olds Agricultural College in 1959, Gordon had learned how to manage the farm from his father. During the 1970s, the farm found its resources fully employed, as Gordon expanded both his cattle and grain operations. In 1980, total sales reached $650,000, with fifty percent coming from grain and fifty percent from cattle.[178]

The early 1980s were notoriously difficult times for Laing Farms. The deep depression of 1981-82 was accompanied by a drop in cattle prices. Unable to escape the worst effects of these harsh economic circumstances, Gordon Laing closed his feedlot in 1983. By 1984, the farm's total sales had fallen to $127,000.[179] Fortunately for Laing Farms, the business was carrying no debt load, and this, together with continuing income from grain, helped it survive. Laing looked to diversification as one way to maintain the farm and, in 1987, opened a seed-cleaning plant on it.[180] Laing was innovative and hard working and his wife Anola was tireless, working long hours on the farm. Much of the reason for Gordon and Anola's success lay in their good management. For Laing Farms, this meant remaining a viable business into the 1990s.

One reason for the success of the Alberta economy was the development of agriculture in the 1980s and 1990s, which helped sustain the growth of urbanization and industrialization. Among many small farms that grew during this period was Hammer Stock Farm at Olds. Founded in 1900 by Louis Hammer, who was born in Missouri, the farm at first consisted of a 160-acre homestead.[181] Hammer grew wheat, barley, and oats and raised dairy cattle, hogs, and sheep. By 1928, with assistance from his seven sons, he had expanded the size of his farm to 2,300 acres. During the Great Depression of the 1930s, Hammer almost went bankrupt. He weathered the depression and, in 1931, even helped his son Louis Leroy start farming on his own in the Olds area.[182]

Louis Leroy Hammer's farm had experienced a fundamental transformation by the 1950s. While he continued to focus on grain and livestock, Louis Leroy embarked on a new path by opening a feedlot on his farm to fatten cattle, mostly Herefords, for the market.[183] By 1978, Louis Leroy's son Garnet, who had been educated at Olds Agricultural College, had taken over part of the family farm. At this point, the name of the business became Hammer Stock Farm.

In order to cope with the growing volume of work at Hammer Stock Farm, three of Garnet's sons were admitted as partners.[184] Garnet

Hammer's commitment to sound bookkeeping was a significant aspect of his entrepreneurship. During the 1980s and 1990s, Hammer Stock Farm owed its important position in the marketplace especially to its successful feedlot operation. By feeding much of the grain they raised to their cattle, mostly Charolais by 1996, Garnet and his sons were able to compete in the broad market.[185] Each year, bank credit allowed them to meet their production expenses. Overall, growth at Hammer Stock Farm came through retained earnings and bank loans, as well as through careful bookkeeping.[186] Between the late 1970s and 1996, the farm's total annual sales rose from $1.3 million to $2 million.[187]

Like agriculture, the newspaper industry provided opportunities for small businesses despite growing competition from big newspaper enterprises such as Bowes Publications in Alberta in the 1980s and 1990s. The history of the *Olds Gazette* illustrates how small weekly newspapers prospered in Alberta during these decades. The paper is one of the oldest, founded in Olds in 1891 as a personal family business by A. J. Samis and A. J. Bush, who initially called it the *Olds Oracle*. In 1904, it changed its name to the *Olds Gazette*. In 1936, the paper was acquired by W. H. Miller, who, with his wife Marian, ran it for ten years.[188]

Miller established the tradition of setting high publishing standards and hiring good help. At the outset, he hired Ron Newsom, who had considerable experience in newspaper work in Alberta.[189] World War II disrupted the routine of the paper, drawing Newsom into the Royal Canadian Air Force. Operating as a small, understaffed paper, it entered the postwar period and struggled to survive. A recovery, initiated by an ailing Miller in March 1945 through hiring his son-in-law Neil Leatherdale, who had also served with the Royal Canadian Air Force, was continued after the war by Miller through rehiring Newsom.[190]

In January 1946, Leatherdale and Newsom bought out Miller.[191] When Newsom and Leatherdale formed their partnership, one of the distinctive features of the *Olds Gazette* was the strong sense of identity at the weekly paper. There was an appreciation of the need to serve the information needs of local and regional readers. Stability in the partnership helped strengthen this sense of identity. Leatherdale and Newsom followed a strategy of accurate reporting and ploughing most of their profits back into their business as the best way to achieve growth. The late 1940s and early 1950s were prosperous years for the *Olds Gazette*. Residents of Olds and farmers in the surrounding region relied on the paper for information, the town's businesspeople required space for advertising, and many organizations and individuals needed commercial printing services. Sales of the paper, advertisements, and commercial printing services increased yearly, rising from $1,000 in 1947 to $6,000 in 1956.[192] During this period, the paper grew from four to eight pages and then to twelve pages and became well known for its high quality. The Heidelberg press, purchased for $10,000 out of profits in the early 1950s, played a significant role in the paper's evolution.

In 1956, after some ten years of partnership, Newsom decided to retire from the paper in order to move to Bashaw, where he acquired the *Bashaw Star*, another small weekly newspaper.[193] To cope with the mounting volume of work at the *Olds Gazette*, Neil Leatherdale asked his wife Norma to assist him in running the business on a part-time basis at first and full-time beginning in 1970. While Neil wrote editorials on local, provincial, and national affairs, Norma looked after the books.[194] The paper was truly a family enterprise, its growth funded mostly through retained earnings but also through bank credit. The *Olds Gazette* went where promising markets led it, including rural areas such as the Hammer district and, in the 1960s, had ten country correspondents, some of whom were farmers' wives.[195] The venture was incorporated in 1976 as Leatherdale Publications but continued to be run as a family business.

After guiding the paper for more than thirty years, in 1987 Neil Leatherdale sold it to his children: Brian, Marilyn, Leslie, and Mary Jane. Under their able leadership, the *Olds Gazette* continued to grow as a high-quality paper. By 1990, the concern stood as an important weekly newspaper running to twenty-four pages and achieving about $1 million in annual sales.[196] Despite tough competition from large newspaper enterprises, Brian, Marilyn, Leslie, and Mary Jane led their small corporation into a period of significant growth and prosperity. By 1997, Leatherdale Publications owned and ran not only the *Olds Gazette*, but also another local paper, the *Mountainview County News*, as well as the *Sundre Roundup*.[197]

Quality was of great importance in Alberta's small weekly newspaper world in the difficult economic climate of the eighties and early nineties. In an era of stiffer competition, quality was a key element to survival as the structure of the newspaper industry continued to change. A number of small, family-owned and -operated weekly papers in Alberta disappeared as big newspaper enterprises increasingly dominated the market.

High-quality family papers remained an enduring feature of the newspaper industry in Alberta in the 1980s and 1990s, as the experience of the *Camrose Booster* revealed. Founded in Camrose in November 1952 by Bill Fowler, the paper was family-owned and -operated.[198] Born in 1917, Fowler began as a delivery boy for the *Edmonton Journal* and later, during World War II, served overseas with the Royal Canadian Air Force.[199] In Camrose, Bill Fowler asked his wife Berdie to join him in the newspaper business. Using their own money and initially assisted by a friend with the artwork, they entered the newspaper industry with the production of a small weekly paper. In addition, they offered commercial printing services. While Bill was responsible for sales, Berdie wrote the editorials. In the 1950s and early 1960s, the *Camrose Booster* successfully broke into established markets in Camrose and the surrounding area. Creative in design, the paper was backed by reliable service. By 1955, the *Camrose Booster* had a weekly circulation of about 3,000 copies.[200]

The *Camrose Booster's* emergence as a weekly paper of local and regional repute during the mid-1960s marked the start of a decade of considerable growth. By 1967, the paper had been incorporated.[201] Bill and Berdie had brought their son Blain into the business as a key member of its sales department in 1964, and he played an important role in the development of the paper. Bill, Berdie, and Blain were equal partners. The paper's weekly circulation topped 8,000 copies in 1976.[202]

As his father reached retirement in 1976, Blain Fowler took over the *Camrose Booster*, while his mother remained as editor of the paper and became an employee.[203] In running his business, Fowler successfully balanced a desire for growth with a quest for excellent products. The strategy of producing a high-quality paper proved to be a helpful formula for success. Blain and Berdie Fowler presided over an expanding and prosperous weekly newspaper. Between 1982 and 1990, total sales increased from $1.7 million to $2.2 million.[204]

The depression in the early 1990s, however, temporarily undermined hopes for further growth. The quality of its products, however, gave the *Camrose Booster* significant control over its market niches in Camrose and the surrounding region.[205] Aided by Berdie as editor, as well as by the other twenty-seven employees, Blain Fowler was still quite successful. As the markets for his sixty-four-page weekly paper and commercial printing services picked up between 1993 and 1995, total sales increased from $2 million to $2.1 million.[206] In 1996, the paper had a weekly circulation of about 12,000 copies. Fowler also devised a new marketing channel abroad for his commercial printing services. The substantial commercial printing job he secured in Ohio provided his small business with important additional income.[207]

■

Growth of Franchising

Despite the fact that the distinction between big firms and smaller businesses in Alberta had become pronounced in numerous fields as the last half of the twentieth century progressed, in franchising there was considerable blurring. It is helpful to view Alberta's business system as a duality, the development of a system comprised of small business in one segment and big business in the other. In franchising, a blurring of the line between small and large firms occurred, because the independence of small business was often more apparent than real.

Many Albertans came to see franchising as a middle ground between large and small firms. In carrying out a strategy of growth, some companies (franchisers) preferred selling to would-be entrepreneurs (franchisees) the right to market their goods or services. In exchange for this initial payment, along with further annual payments based on sales volume, the franchisee received benefits from the parent company. Usually, the franchiser provided training in its business at its regional or head office, as well as the benefits of mass purchasing discounts and national advertising, including a popular trademark. Both could therefore reap benefits: franchisees from the opportunities they associated with small business and the advantages of belonging to big umbrella organizations, and franchisers from the rapid growth of low-cost national or international marketing systems.

Franchising in Alberta developed over almost a century. The International Harvester Company in the United States used franchised dealers in Alberta, such as the Great West Implement Company of Edmonton, to sell its farm machinery before World War I.[208] Building on the International Harvester Company's experiences, American automobile makers and petroleum firms were soon selling cars and gasoline through franchised dealers in the province. By World War II, soft-drink manufacturers, led by Coca-Cola of Atlanta, Georgia, sold their goods through franchised bottlers in Calgary and Edmonton.[209]

After World War II, franchising in Alberta grew at a rapid rate. Many things were being franchised by the 1950s and 1960s, including fast foods, with especially large sales made by the United States-based firms of McDonald's and Kentucky Fried Chicken. By the 1970s and 1980s, there were also Alberta-based franchised food businesses, such as Comac Food Group.[210] With headquarters in Calgary, Comac Food Group controlled ten Grabbajabba coffee stores and twenty Pastel's cafes in Alberta by 1992, as well as twenty-three Company's Coming snack bars across Canada.[211] Acquisitions were very important for Comac Food Group, which grew in 1996 by purchasing Canadian Domino's Pizza chain of 204 outlets.[212]

During the 1980s and 1990s, some Albertans turned to franchise ownership after being caught in corporate restructuring and downsizing. For instance, after serving as an internal auditor with Petro-Canada in Calgary for five years, Barrie Mainwaring lost his job in November 1986 when the company restructured. Mainwaring's careful research led him to take a franchise in Fantastic Sam's, a haircutting salon in Calgary, a year later.[213] Fantastic Sam's, a Memphis-based franchise system, catered to children and middle-income families. Mainwaring was typical of Albertans who found franchise ownership was a solution to their economic problems. "In Alberta, a lot of them are looking to get into something after losing their jobs in the oilpatch, looking for something to invest their severance package in. Franchising, because it has less risk attached to it, is the growing trend," observed Chris McArthur, a Calgary chartered accountant specializing in franchising.[214]

■

New Regulation: Environment Problems

In the last third of the twentieth century, Alberta business owners faced many challenges that had an extraordinary impact on their entire companies. Not least was the problem of how to deal with environmental matters. Environmental issues loomed large across Alberta in the 1970s, 1980s, and 1990s. Public pressures grew for stricter federal and provincial regulation of industrial enterprises whose products hurt the environment.

The role of the federal government remained an important one. As it had from the late nineteenth century, the federal government continued to shape the political climate within which Alberta firms operated and to assist them through developmental economic policies that fostered business opportunities. This assistance was accompanied by federal regulation, and in the decades after 1970, the federal government became heavily involved in new regulatory activity. Major new regulatory initiatives by the government in the areas of environmental protection and occupational health and safety affected the entire Aberta business community.

Prime Minister Pierre Trudeau favoured legislation intended to improve the environment. In 1970, Parliament passed the Government Organization Act to establish the federal department of the environment and, a year later, passed the Clean Air Act.[215] At much the same time that Parliament was churning out environmental laws, the issue received attention in the Alberta legislature. The Alberta government led by Harry Strom acted in 1971, passing legislation creating the Department of the Environment and passing the Clean Air Act and the Clean Water Act to co-operate in trying to solve the problems of air and water pollution at the provincial level.[216] To further protect the health and safety of workers, Parliament passed the Environmental Contaminants Act in 1975.[217] Some businesses in Alberta started to respond to public environmental concerns even before the federal and Alberta governments intervened.

For instance, as early as the 1950s, Imperial Oil in Alberta developed:

...data systems to monitor employee health and to track exposures in the workplace, enabling the company to target prevention programs to specific groups. These programs could involve such simple measures as issuing protective equipment and clothing, redesigning work stations or recommending that materials be handled differently to ensure exposure to toxic substances is appropriately controlled.[218]

Imperial Oil in Alberta "began keeping material safety data sheets in the early 1960s — long before they were required by law — and continually updates information on more than 5,000 substances, including Esso products, to provide employees, customers and regulatory agencies with current information."[219]

These were only some of the many environmental issues Imperial Oil faced in Alberta. In the early 1990s, the company had to deal with the problem of protecting fresh surface water from rivers and lakes it was using at its heavy-oil production facility near Cold Lake. To solve this problem, Imperial Oil developed new procedures designed to greatly reduce the amount of fresh water needed.[220] The company was also aggressive in organizing emergency response crews, such as its efficient crew at the Redwater agricultural chemicals complex, to respond quickly to spills, fires, and accidents.[221] Imperial Oil was concerned about a rising trend in incidents such as fires and spills in 1994 and 1995. Consequently, the company spent increasing sums on environmental controls in Alberta during these years.[222] In these ways, Imperial Oil responded to federal and Alberta environmental laws.

As this example indicates, the new regulations were achieving their goals: the quality of the environment was improved for the benefit of all Albertans. Business generally paid a high price. Corporate executives could no longer choose technological innovations without giving consideration to non-economic factors. The new setting for business activity often made innovation more expensive. Also, the changes in public policy occurred just as the competitive pressures on Alberta corporations were becoming more intense at home and abroad. Many businesses spent considerable sums in an effort to meet society's demands for clean air and water as well as improving their performance in health and safety matters.

■

Alberta Firms' Overseas Expansion

Alberta firms also responded positively to federal government policies to promote overseas expansion. In January 1996, Prime Minister Jean Chretien led a group of Alberta and other Canadian businesspeople and six provincial premiers on a twelve-day trip to India, Pakistan, Indonesia, and Malaysia to explore business opportunities there.[223] As the head of what he called the third Team Canada trade mission, after having led the first such trade mission to China in 1994 and the second to Chile, Argentina, and Brazil in 1995, Chretien urged businesspeople to consider moving more deeply into India, Pakistan, Indonesia, and Malaysia markets. Impressive results came from this mission to South and Southeast Asia. The total value of new business deals signed during this trip was $8.7 billion for Canadian firms. In leading this trade mission, Chretien was keeping one of the promises he had made in his "red book" that appeared in September 1993, during the federal election campaign from which he emerged as Canada's prime minister: "Canadian firms, especially small and medium-sized businesses, must adopt an aggressive trading mentality and a strong outward orientation to take advantage of export markets. More Canadian businesses must become exporters, and government must help them develop the knowledge and skills to make that possible."[224]

Many Alberta businesses, particularly small and medium-sized firms, entered the South and Southeast Asia market during this trip, often through joint ventures.[225] The Asian people proved to be friendly hosts, willing at this time to acquire Alberta business expertise and technology. Albertans recognized that the risks were higher abroad but that the profit opportunities were also greater than in the mature Alberta markets. Using production, distribution, and organizational capabilities first refined in Alberta's home markets, businesses turned their attention overseas and adapted to the demands of overseas cultures.

Among Alberta business leaders who participated in the Team Canada trade mission were representatives of Presson Manufacturing of Nisku, near Edmonton, a company that designs and manufactures natural gas and crude oil processing facilities and plants. Presson Manufacturing signed a $1 million contract with the government agency, Oil and Gas Development Corp. of Pakistan, to supply a gas dehydration plant to Pakistan. Presson Manufacturing expanded its overseas operations by signing a $950,000 contract with Larsen and Toubro of Mumbai, India to supply pressure vessels for the Tapti oil offshore production platform. The Indonesian market proved magnetic for Interprovincial Pipeline International of Edmonton, which entered a joint venture with P. T. Senavangi Wismarta Utama for pipeline development work in central Sumatra, Indonesia.

Other opportunities also bore fruit on the Team Canada trade mission.[226] Sunora Foods of Calgary, a food oil firm specializing in canola oil, signed an $81 million contract with Healthway Food International of Islamabad, Pakistan to supply bottled and bulk canola oil to Pakistan. Alta Terra Ventures Corp. of Slave Lake, an agrifood and environmental products firm, entered a joint venture with Tractors and Farm Equipment of Madras in the state of Tamil Nadu, India to provide that company with technology for manufacturing farm implements and to arrange for the distribution of these implements in Canada.

Albertans made other important overseas investments during Team Canada's visit to South and Southeast Asia.[227] Willoglen Systems of Edmonton, a company specializing in engineering, design and supply of supervisory control and data acquisition systems, and its partner in Malaysia MCB Holdings Berhad signed a $3.8 million contract with the Housing Development Board in Singapore to provide phase four of their supervisory control and data acquisition system. Indo-Canadian Enterprises of Calgary, a firm specializing in retail marketing, consulting and pharmaceutical projects, signed a memorandum of understanding with Anand Pharmaceuticals of Chittorgargh, India to manufacture and sell over-the-counter generic drugs in India, Africa, and the Middle East. In this $5 million joint venture, Indo-Canadian Enterprises undertook to provide funds and technology, as well as management and marketing services. Specializing in distance education consulting and technology, Detac Corp. of Innisfail signed a $170,000 contract with Universiti Kebangsaan Malaysi to supply forty audio-graphic teleconference distance learning systems, to be used in presenting medical courses to students in remote hospitals across Malaysia. All these overseas joint ventures in 1996 allowed Alberta businesses to grow and reap benefits from their technologies.

A major item on Prime Minister Chretien's agenda in January 1997 was to strengthen Canadian firms, especially small and medium-sized businesses, in foreign markets. As the head of the fourth Team Canada trade mission, Chretien led a group of Alberta and other Canadian businesspeople and ten provincial premiers, including Alberta Premier Ralph Klein, on a fourteen-day visit to South Korea, the Philippines, and Thailand to look into marketing possibilities there.[228] Just before leaving Canada on this overseas mission, Chretien observed: "I am confident it will be the highlight of 1997 — Canada's Year of Asia Pacific — which will celebrate and strengthen our longstanding social, cultural and business ties within the Pacific community."[229] As was the case with the previous year's overseas trip, this trade mission to the Asia-Pacific region brought significant results. For Alberta firms alone, it led to a total of $516.2 million in new business deals with South Korea, the Philippines, and Thailand.[230]

South Korean markets had attracted attention from Alberta for many years. As part of its emergence as an increasingly complex industrial province, Alberta stepped up its South Korean sales in the 1980s. Growth in its sales in South Korea led Alberta to set up a trade and investment office in Seoul in 1989. By the end of 1996, three years after Premier Ralph Klein made a trip to South Korea to explore trade expansion, the value of Alberta's annual trade with South Korea had reached between $700 and $800 million.[231] Alberta enjoyed substantial surpluses in commerce with South Korea, with exports significantly larger than imports. While Alberta's leading imports from South Korea included electronic equipment, motor vehicles, and motor vehicle parts, the main exports to South Korea were agrifood, building products, environmental technology, and petrochemicals.

During Team Canada's visit to South Korea in January 1997, the value of new business deals signed came to about $210 million for Alberta firms.[232] Among new deals struck with South Korean partners was an agreement between Chromacolour of Calgary, a major supplier of equipment and materials used in the production of animated film, and the Jung Sung Manufacturing Company. Chromacolour agreed, among other things, to help Jung Sung increase production capacity and improve efficiency at its factory in Taejon. The Polar Bear Water Distillers Manufacturing Company of Pickardville, an Alberta firm specializing in the manufacture of water distillation equipment for residential, commercial, and industrial use, signed a $600,000 contract with Westwood Korea Industries of Seoul to supply that company with Polar Bear products over the next two years. Southern Alberta Cubers of Lethbridge, a marketer of processed forages, entered into agreements with the Korea Silo Company of Inchon and the Seyong Company of Ansong to supply them with Canadian Alfalfa hay cubes.[233]

Asked what he gained from the trip, David Hygaard, president of Hygaard Fine Foods in Sherwood Park, captured the essence of the way in which many small businesses benefited from the visit. "I have four solid business leads to follow up on. I also have a Korean group who is interested in learning more about our automation procedures for food packaging," he observed. "They are coming to Sherwood Park to visit us in the spring. I am confident that at least one of these leads will turn into business for my company." [234]

The Philippines market, which had attracted Alberta businesspeople for many years, also allowed them to increase their presence during the Team Canada visit to the Philippines. The trip to the Philippines led to more than $56.5 million in new business deals for Alberta companies.[235] For example, AltaSpec Communications of Edmonton, a company specializing in advanced telecommunications services and technology, entered a joint venture with the News and Entertainment Network Corporation in Manila to supply technical services to that corporation.[236] Treeline Wood Products of Spruce Grove, a supplier of Canadian lumber and wood poles, signed a memorandum of agreement with the Philreca Trading and Marketing Corporation of Quezon City to make that firm its exclusive distributor of wood poles, crossarms, and anchor logs in the Philippines. Carmacks Construction of Edmonton, a firm involved in various types of construction, consulting and management, signed a $20-million agreement with Pryce Properties Corp. of Manila to manufacture, supply, and install power-saving lighting fixtures for that company.[237]

By the mid-1990s, Thailand had also emerged as a major centre of activity for Alberta businesses. "Between 1994 and 1995, we increased our exports to Thailand by a remarkable thirty-five percent which, in dollars and cents, totals $124 million," observed Premier Ralph Klein.[238] The Team Canada visit to Thailand resulted in $249.7 million in new business deals for Alberta firms.[239] Among Alberta firms involved was Shooting Stars Technologies of Calgary. A marketer of the expertise of the Gimbel Eye Centre in Calgary, Shooting Stars Technologies entered a joint venture with the Asoke Sin Company of Bangkok to build a laser refractive eye surgery centre in association with the Rutnin Eye Hospital in that city.[240]

Polar Bear Water Distillers Manufacturing Company of Picardville signed a $200,000 contract with the Omniact Company of Bangkok, whereby that firm agreed to purchase and distribute Polar Bear water-distribution equipment in Thailand. Challenger Surveys and Services of Edmonton entered into an agreement with the Southeast Asia Technology Company of Bangkok to sell Challenger geomatics technology and expertise through that firm across Thailand and Southeast Asia.[241] "We're getting pro-active. Three years ago my manager decided to focus business development on one core market. Asia's been well-promoted as the No. 1 growth region in the world," said Challenger spokesman Richard Schlachter.[242]

The growth of Alberta interests that federal and Alberta government developmental policies helped bring in the mid-1990s provided opportunities for all these and other Alberta firms to enlarge their overseas business. Using production, marketing, and organizational capabilities first developed in Alberta's home markets, businesses turned their attention abroad; many increased their foreign presence through joint ventures, succeeding in part by adapting to the demands of overseas cultures.

■

Alberta Business at the Close of the Century

Even as they took advantage of overseas opportunities and developed a strong international dimension, Albertans found that their business at home remained central to their efforts. In the 1990s, many business owners wanted their enterprises to improve their stature in the Alberta and international business arenas. An important feature of the plans made for a number of business firms was the aim to look for growth in the future. In these plans, markets at home as well as those abroad emerged as growth areas for Alberta firms.

The stagnant standard of living many Albertans experienced in the early 1990s suggested that the Alberta business system was struggling to meet the changing demands of the marketplace. The rising standard of living that a growing number of people in the province enjoyed in the mid-1990s, however, indicated that the business system was adapting.[243] Some firms, such as Foremost Industries, were dynamic institutions responding to business opportunities.[244] Others, like the Hudson's Bay Company, were improving their position in the Alberta retail world at the beginning of 1997.[245] On the other hand, Eaton's, the Bay's rival in the department-store business, was in serious trouble.[246]

Albertans continued to admire small businesses. As well as creating new jobs, small firms added management opportunities, often for women. Opportunities for small business ownership grew as the Conservative government led by Ralph Klein, committed to reducing substantially the size of Alberta's public sector, privatized government-owned industries such as the Alberta Liquor Control Board stores in 1994.[247] In an increasingly competitive environment, however, many newly formed small businesses were unprofitable and short-lived.

As the business environment changed and competition increased during the 1990s, many Alberta companies adapted. They convincingly demonstrated one of the most important strengths of Alberta's business system: its ability to respond to the forces of change over the long term. After all, within the wide context of organizational change the province's basic business institutions had been transformed twice in the twentieth century: once when the centralized corporation emerged and again when the decentralized firm became the norm among the province's largest companies.

In the 1990s the unstable business environment presented a major challenge for Albertans and sparked a debate about government-business relations and economic policy. For some people in the province, the political economy appeared to offer solutions. This sentiment of Albertans reflected deeply rooted economic and political beliefs, including long-standing public support for government aid for business firms through developmental policies. Turning back to the tradition of government support for enterprises, such as farming and ranching businesses and railways, which began in the Canadian Parliament in the 1870s and 1880s, some Albertans sought to use the federal and Alberta governments to help adjust to competition. They hoped this approach toward business would make it possible for Alberta prosperity to return to the impressive growth rates it had sustained before the early 1980s. Their critics were convinced that a vigorous government program to aid business, besides placing excessive burdens on taxpayers, was stifling private enterprise. The public policy debate showed no consensus among Albertans on economic policy measures aimed at bringing more prosperity to the province and providing individuals and their families with the means of leading secure lives.

By the last decade of the twentieth century, a great deal had changed since Alberta emerged from World War II. The confidence of the generation that developed oil and gas, retail, and farming businesses after the war had given way to a widespread popular anxiety about Alberta's economic future. In the province, the business system itself had been altered significantly after 1945, and even the biggest firms were not untouched by changing global political and economic conditions. Sustained success in the market often came to large corporate concerns whose executives understood the need to combine production, distribution, and financial perspectives in a decentralized organization, while the most successful small businesses frequently were those that possessed enough flexibility to adjust quickly to changes in an increasingly global economy.

Although concerned about their future, Albertans had not lost their sense of optimism in the 1990s. Many businessmen, businesswomen, and government officials saw themselves as part of a society responding to new challenges as the twentieth century drew to a close. Countless business leaders brought renewed energy to their commitment not only to providing new products and new services to new markets, but also to ensuring that those products and services were of the highest possible quality. If they wished to retain a position among successful entrepreneurs and keep pace with their more dynamic and ambitious competitors, they constantly had to meet customer needs. Albertans still had confidence in their business system and still were willing to invest their resources in their traditional strength, small or large business enterprises active in what they viewed as an integrated world economy. As they made plans for the future, Albertans looked to continue to adapt and shape their business firms to take on the challenges of the twenty-first century.

NOTES TO CHAPTER NINE

1. *Calgary Herald*, 24 July 1973.

2. George Radwanski, *Trudeau* (Toronto: Macmillan of Canada, 1978), 280.

3. *Canadian Annual Review for 1972*, 44.

4. *Edmonton Journal*, 25 July 1973.

5. *Calgary Herald*, 27 July 1973.

6. *Edmonton Journal*, 27 July 1973; Canada West Foundation, *A Report on the Western Economic Opportunities Conference* (Calgary, 1973), 1-23.

7. Michael Bliss, *Right Honourable Men: The Descent of Canadian Politics from Macdonald to Mulroney* (Toronto: Harper Collins, 1994), 260.

8. John Herd Thompson and Stephen J. Randall, *Canada and the United States: Ambivalent Allies* (Montreal: McGill-Queen's University Press, 1994), 265-266.

9. Robert L. Mansell and Michael B. Percy, *Strength in Adversity: A Study of the Alberta Economy* (Edmonton: University of Alberta Press, 1990), 17-19.

10. Graham D. Taylor and Peter A. Baskerville, *A Concise History of Business in Canada* Toronto: Oxford University Press, 1994), 468.

11. Peter C. Newman, *The Canadian Revolution, 1985-1995: From Deference to Defiance* (Toronto: Viking, 1995), 313.

12. Roger Gibbins, "National Reconciliation and the Canadian West: Political Management in the Mulroney Era," in Andrew B. Gollner and Daniel Salee, eds., *Canada Under Mulroney: An End-of-Term Report* (Montreal: Vehicle Press, 1988), 90.

13. Howard Palmer with Tamara Palmer, *Alberta: A New History* (Edmonton: Hurtig Publishers, 1990), 354-357.

14. Stephen J. Randall and Herman W. Konrad, "Introduction," in Stephen J.

Randall and Herman W. Konrad, eds., *NAFTA in Transition* (Calgary: University of Calgary Press, 1995), 1-2; Bliss, *Right Honourable Men*, 295, 303.

15. *Financial Post*, 16 October 1993.

16. Alberta Economic Development and Tourism Library, Edmonton, *Alberta's Trade with the United States, 1992-1996.*

17. Ibid.

18. Alberta Economic Development and Tourism Library, *Alberta's Trade with Mexico, 1992-1996.*

19. Ibid.

20. Gulf Canada Resources Archives, Calgary, "Gulf Canada Limited," 1.

21. Ibid., 2.

22. *Edmonton Journal*, 8 January 1929; "Gulf Canada Limited," 3.

23. *Edmonton Journal*, 18 January 1949.

24. "Gulf Canada Limited," 3.

25. Ibid., 4.

26. Ibid.

27. *Edmonton Journal*, 12 April 1960.

28. Gulf Canada Resources Archives, "Gulf Canada Resources Limited — A History," 2.

29. "Gulf Canada Limited," 5.

30. *Calgary Herald*, 21 December 1996.

31. Gulf Canada Resources Archives, Gulf Canada Resources, *Annual Report for 1995*, 2-3.

32. Ibid., 3-7.

33. Ibid., 18-19.

34. Ibid., 21.

35. Canadian Western Natural Gas Company Archives, Calgary, Canadian Western Natural Gas Company, *Annual Report for 1990*, 3.

36. *Lethbridge Herald*, 11 July 1987.

37. Ibid.

38. Ibid.

39. John A. Eagle, *The Canadian Pacific Railway and the Development of Western Canada, 1896-1914* (Montreal: McGill-Queen's University Press, 1989), 249-252; David H. Breen, *Alberta's Petroleum Industry and the Conservation Board* (Edmonton: University of Alberta Press, 1993), 9-15.

40. Alberta Corporate Registry, Canadian Western Natural Gas, Light, Heat and Power Company Ltd. file.

41. *Fort Macleod Gazette*, 7 September 1988.

42. *Calgary Herald*, 15 October 1930.

43. Alberta Corporate Registry, Canadian Western Natural Gas, Light, Heat and Power Company Ltd. file.

44. Fred Stenson, *Waste to Wealth: A History of Gas Processing in Canada* (Calgary: Canadian Gas Processors Association, 1985), 16.

45. Canadian Western Natural Gas Company Archives, Canadian Western Natural Gas, Light, Heat and Power Company, *Annual Report for 1930*, 2.

46. *Lethbridge Herald*, 11 July 1987.

47. Canadian Western Natural Gas Company Archives, Canadian Western Natural Gas Company, *Annual Report for 1960*, 7.

48. Canadian Western Natural Gas Company Archives, Canadian Western Natural Gas Company, *Annual Report for 1970*, 7.

49. Canadian Western Natural Gas Company Archives, Canadian Western Natural Gas Company, *Annual Report for 1980*, 2.

50. *Calgary Herald*, 25 May 1972.

51. Canadian Western Natural Gas Company Archives, Canadian Western Natural Gas Company, *Annual Report for 1980*, 2-3.

52. *Lethbridge Herald*, 11 July 1987.

53. Canadian Western Natural Gas Company Archives, Canadian Western Natural Gas Company, *Annual Report for 1995*, 1-3.

54. Transalta Utilities Corporation Archives, Calgary, Transalta Utilities Corporation, *Annual Report for 1995*, 50-51; "Transalta Utilities: 75 Years of Progress," 46-48.

55. W. E. Hawkins, *Electrifying Calgary: A Century of Public & Private Power* (Calgary: University of Calgary Press, 1987), 95.

56. Ibid., 147.

57. Transalta Utilities Corporation Archives, "Transalta Utilities: 75 Years of Progress," 6.

58. Christopher Armstrong and H. V. Nelles, *Monopoly's Moment: The Organization and Regulation of Canadian Utilities, 1830-1930* (Philadelphia: Temple University Press, 1986), 303.

59. Transalta Utilities Corporation Archives, Calgary Power Company, *Annual Report for 1970*, 2.

60. GAIA, Calgary Power Company Papers, box 3, Calgary Power Company, balance sheets for 1913 and 1920; James H. Gray, *R. B. Bennett: The Calgary Years* (Toronto: University of Toronto Press, 1991), 190-191.

61. Transalta Utilities Corporation Archives, "Transalta Utilities: 75 Years of Progress," 14.

62. *Calgary Herald*, 7 December 1927.

63. Transalta Utilities Corporation Archives, "Transalta Utilities: 75 Years of Progress," 18.

64. Ibid., 28.

65. Transalta Utilities Corporation Archives, Calgary Power Company, *Annual Report for 1950*.

66. "Transalta Utilities: 75 Years of Progress," 36.

67. Transalta Utilities Corporation Archives, Calgary Power Company, *Annual Report for 1956*.

68. Transalta Utilities Corporation Archives, Transalta Utilities Corporation, *Annual Report for 1981*, 2.

69. Ibid., 11-12.

70. Ibid., 10.

71. *Alberta Report*, 18 July 1980.

72. Ibid., 19 February 1996; Transalta Utilities Corporation Archives, Transalta Utilities Corporation, *Annual Report for 1995*, 50-51.

73. Transalta Utilities Corporation Archives, Transalta Utilities Corporation, *Annual Report for 1995*, 50-51.

74. Ibid., 15-17.

75. Ibid., 28-29.

76. Max Ward, *The Max Ward Story: A Bush Pilot in the Bureaucratic Jungle* (Toronto: McClelland & Stewart, 1991), 265.

77. *Edmonton Journal*, 25 January 1978; Ward, *The Max Ward Story*, 254, 277, 293.

78. Ward, *The Max Ward Story*, 303.

79. Ibid., 311.

80. *Calgary Herald*, 2 November 1996.

81. *Calgary Sun*, 7 July 1996; *Calgary Herald*, 23 November 1996.

82. *Calgary Herald*, 29 June 1996.

83. Ibid., 2 November 1996.

84. Ibid., 23 November 1996.

85. Joy L. Santink, *Timothy Eaton and the Rise of his Department Store* (Toronto: University of Toronto Press, 1990).

86. *Albertan*, 28 February 1929; *Calgary Sun*, 28 February 1997.

87. *Financial Post*, 28 February 1997.

88. *Calgary Herald*, 1 March 1997.

89. *Financial Post*, 1 March 1997.

90. Ibid.

91. *Financial Post*, 28 February 1997.

92. *Calgary Sun*, 28 February 1997; *Financial Post*, 28 February 1997.

93. *Financial Post*, 13 March 1997.

94. Ibid., 18 March 1997.

95. *Globe and Mail*, 11 April 1997; *Financial Post*, 11 April 1997.

96. Palmer, *Alberta*, 353; Michael Bliss, *Northern Enterprise: Five Centuries of Canadian Business* (Toronto: McClelland & Stewart, 1987), 548-549; Jim Lyon, *Dome: The Rise and Fall of the House that Jack Built* (Toronto: Avon Books of Canada, 1983).

97. Royal Bank of Canada Archives, Toronto, "Small Business in Canada: A Regional Breakdown," Canadian Bankers Association, 19 April 1994.

98. *Financial Post*, 28 September 1996.

99. Interview by the author with R. Worsley, 3 March 1997.

100. Stenson, *Waste to Wealth*, 69-73.

101. Interview by the author with Peter S. Grant, 18 March 1997.

102. Interviews by the author with Norbert Mann, 3, 4 March 1997.

103. Grant interview, 18 March 1997.

104. Ibid.

105. Mann interviews, 3, 4 March 1997.

106. *Energy Processing Canada*, July-August 1991, 6.

107. Mann interviews, 3,4 March 1997.

108. *Energy Processing Canada*, July-August 1990, 6.

109. Worsley interview, 3 March 1997.

110. Alberta Economic Development and Tourism Library, Canadian Trade Index data.

111. Mann interviews, 3, 4 March 1997; Alberta Economic Development and Tourism Library, Dun & Bradstreet data.

112. *Edmonton Journal*, 28 April 1965.

113. Alberta Corporate Registry, Edmonton Tent & Mattress Ltd. file.

114. Ibid.

115. Ibid., *Edmonton Journal*, 28 April 1965.

116. University of Calgary Library, *Dun & Bradstreet Reference Book*, July 1939, 48.

117. *Edmonton Journal*, 28 April 1965.

118. Ibid.

119. City of Edmonton Archives, Edmonton Tent & Awning clipping file.

120. Ibid.

121. Ibid.

122. Ibid.

123. Ibid.

124. Alberta Economic Development and Tourism Library, Western Industrial Selectory, 1995.

125. *Canadian Textile Journal*, December 1995/January 1996, 43

126. Alberta Municipal Affairs, Edmonton, Alberta Population for 1991.

127. Interview by the author with Gordon and Jack Sissons, 22 May 1996.

128. *Albertan*, 11 August 1956.

129. Sissons interview, 22 May 1996.

130. Ibid.

131. Ibid.

132. Interview by the author with Dan Olofson, 18 May 1996.

133. Ibid.

134. Ibid.

135. Alberta Municipal Affairs, Edmonton, Alberta Population for 1991.

136. Olofson interview, 18 May 1996.

137. Interview by the author with James M. Sharp, 21 May 1996.

138. Ibid.

139. Ibid.

140. *Medicine Hat News*, 24 February 1981.

141. Sharp interview, 21 May 1996.

142. Ibid.

143. Alberta Municipal Affairs, Alberta Population for 1991.

144. Interview by the author with Richard Jewell, 16 May 1996.

145. *Red Deer Advocate*, 27 April 1989.

146. Jewell interview, 16 May 1996.

147. *Red Deer Advocate*, 27 April 1989.

148. *Commerce*, May/June 1994, 31.

149. Jewell interview, 16 May 1996.

150. Interview by the author with Laurie Blackburn, 18 May 1991.

151. Jewell interview, 16 May 1996.

152. *Red Deer Advocate*, 4 November 1994.

153. Jewell interview, 16 May 1996.

154. *Commerce*, May/June 1994, 31.

155. Jewell interview, 16 May 1996.

156. Interview by the author with Rhona Mackay, 11 March 1997; Interview by the author with Alan Cornyn, 23 May 1991; Interview by the author with Ted Thaell, 25 May 1991; Interview by the author with Gerry and Lorraine Maybank, 14 May 1996; Interview by the author with Ken Chisholm, 21 May 1996.

157. Scotiabank Archives, Toronto, Scotiabank, *Annual Report for 1993*, 1; Graham D. Taylor and Peter A. Baskerville, *A Concise History of Business in Canada* (Toronto: Oxford University Press, 1994), 473.

158. Royal Bank of Canada Archives, Toronto, John E. Cleghorn, "Royal Bank Responds: What We Can Do For You," *Royal Bank Business Report: Planning Today for Tomorrow's Challenges*, June 1994, 19.

159. Canadian Bankers Association Statistics, from Bank of Montreal Archives, Calgary.

160. Royal Bank of Canada Archives, Calgary, Royal Bank of Canada Statistics.

161. Bank of Montreal Archives, Toronto, "Creating the Institute for Small Business," *For the Record*, June 1994, 1.

162. Ibid., 1-2.

163. Canadian Bankers Association Statistics, via Bank of Montreal Archives, Calgary.

164. Interview by the author with Harry L. Dwelle, 3 May 1991.

165. Ibid.

166. Ibid.

167. Fort Macleod Court House, Estate of Frank A. Dwelle file, 24 May 1961.

168. Dwelle interview, 3 May 1991.

169. Ibid.

170. Ibid.

171. Ibid.

172. Interview by the author with Gordon and Anola Laing, 11 May 1991.

173. Fort Macleod Court House, Estate of Frederick H. Laing file, 14 June 1956.

174. Laing interview, 11 May 1991.

175. Alberta Corporate Registry, Laing Farms Ltd. file.

176. Laing interview, 11 May 1991.

177. Alberta Corporate Registry, Laing Farms Ltd. file.

178. Laing interview, 11 May 1991.

179. Ibid.

180. Ibid.

181. Interview by the author with Garnet L. Hammer, 14 May 1996.

182. Ibid.

183. Ibid.

184. Ibid.; Olds History Committee, *Olds: A History of Olds and Area* (Olds: Olds History Committee, 1980), 24.

185. Hammer interview, 14 May 1996.

186. Ibid.

187. Ibid.

188. Olds History Committee, *Olds*, 204.

189. Interview by the author with Ron Newsom, 22 March 1977.

190. Interview by the author with Neil Leatherdale, 14 May 1996.

191. Ibid.

192. Ibid.

193. Newsom interview, 22 March 1977.

194. Leatherdale interview, 14 May 1996.

195. Ibid.

196. Ibid.

197. Interview by the author with Brian Leatherdale, 21 March 1997.

198 J. R. Stan Hambly, ed., *A Light into the Past: The History of Camrose* (Camrose: Camrose Historical Society, 1980), 57-58.

199. Interview by the author with Blain Fowler, 18 May 1996.

200. Ibid.

201. Hambly, ed., *A Light into the Past*, 58.

202. Fowler interview, 18 May 1996.

203. Hambly, ed., *A Light into the Past*, 58.

204. Fowler interview, 18 May 1996.

205. *Free Paper Publisher*, December 1994, 12-14.

206. Fowler interview, 18 May 1996.

207. Ibid.

208. Alberta Corporate Registry, Great West Implement Company Ltd. file.

209. *Dun & Bradstreet Reference Book*, July 1939, 17, 47.

210. *Edmonton Sun*, 15 October 1990.

211. *Calgary Herald*, 2 March 1992.

212. *Calgary Sun*, 22 December 1996.

213. *Calgary Herald*, 14 December 1987.

214. Ibid.; *Financial Post*, 16 February 1996.

215. Canada, *Statutes*, 19-20 Elizabeth II, cap. 42, cap. 47.

216. *Statutes of the Province of Alberta*, 1971, cap. 16; cap. 17; cap. 24.

217. Canada, *Statutes*, 23-24 Elizabeth II, cap. 72.

218. Imperial Oil Archives, Toronto, "Imperial Oil — Environment, Health & Safety: Our Commitment, Our Progesss," 6.

219. Ibid., 6.

220. Ibid., 12.

221. Ibid., 16-17.

222. Imperial Oil Archives, Calgary, Imperial Oil Limited, *Annual Report for 1995*, 22-23.

223. Canada, Department of Foreign Affairs and International Trade, Team Canada 1996 press releases, 10-18 January 1996.

224. Liberal Party of Canada Archives, Calgary, *Creating Opportunity: The Liberal Plan for Canada* (Ottawa: Liberal Party of Canada, 1993), 53; *Financial Post*, 16 September, 23 October 1993.

225. Team Canada 1996 press releases, 10-18 January 1996.

226. Ibid.

227. Ibid.

228. Canada, Department of Foreign Affairs and International Trade, Team Canada 1997 press releases, 11 December 1996 - 17 January 1997.

229. Ibid.

230. Alberta, Department of Economic Development and Tourism, news releases, 10-20 January 1997.

231. Ibid.

232. Ibid.

233. Team Canada 1997 press releases, 11 December 1996-17 January 1997.

234. *Alberta Venture*, April 1997, 39.

235. Alberta, Department of Economic Development and Tourism, news releases, 10-20 January 1997.

236. Team Canada 1997 press releases, 11 December 1996-17 January 1997.

237. Ibid.

238. Alberta, Department of Economic Development and Tourism, news releases, 10-20 January 1997.

239. Ibid.

240. Team Canada 1997 press releases, 11 December 1996-17 January 1997.

241. Ibid.

242. *Calgary Herald*, 18 January 1997.

243. Alberta Economic Development and Tourism Library, data on economic changes in Alberta.

244. Foremost Industries Archives, Foremost Industries, corporate fact sheet, 16 September 1996.

245. *Financial Post*, 7 March 1997.

246. Ibid.

247. Gordon Laxer, "The Privatization of Public Life," in Trevor Harrison and Gordon Laxer, eds., *The Trojan Horse: Alberta and the Future of Canada* (Montreal: Black Rose Books, 1995), 101-117.

A Word about the Sources

The primary and secondary sources of this book are contained within the endnotes and the bibliography that follows. But I would like to point out that several have been especially important in stimulating my conceptual approach. In seeking to understand concepts of business, I have often turned for guidance to Michael Bliss, *Northern Enterprise: Five Centuries of Canadian Business* (Toronto, 1987). In arriving at interpretive viewpoints, I also made use of Mansel G. Blackford and K. Austin Kerr, *Business Enterprise in American History*, Third Edition (Borton, 1994); Alfred D. Chandler, Jr., *The Visible Hand: The Managerial Revolution in American Business* (Cambridge, Mass., 1977); and John F. Wilson, *British Business History, 1720-1994* (Manchester, 1995).

Primary Sources

Manuscript Collections

Alberta Corporate Registry, Edmonton

       Alberta Foundry & Machine Company Ltd. file.

       Alberta Grain Company Ltd. file.

       Antelope Butte Ranch Ltd. file.

       ATCO Industries Ltd. file.

       Calgary Iron Works Ltd. file.

       Canadian Foremost Ltd. file.

       Canadian Western Natural Gas, Light, Heat and Power Company Ltd. file.

       Company's Coming Publishing Ltd. file.

       Dunlap Drug Company Ltd. file.

       Edmonton Tent & Mattress Ltd. file.

       Gainers Ltd. file.

       Great West Implement Company Ltd. file.

       Groceteria Stores Company Ltd. file.

       Home Hardware Stores Ltd. file.

       Imperial Oil Ltd. file.

       Imperial Women's Wear Ltd. file.

       John Sommerville & Sons Ltd. file.

       John Tynan & Company Ltd. file.

       Johnstone Walker Ltd. file.

Kenny & Allin Company Ltd. file.

Laing Farms Ltd. file.

Link Hardware Company Ltd. file.

Louie Petrie Ltd. file.

McDougall & Secord Ltd. file.

P. Burns & Company Ltd. file.

Reach & Co. Ltd. file.

R. J. Welsh Ltd. file.

Ross Bros. Ltd. file.

Standen's Ltd. file.

Stokes Drug Company Ltd. file.

T. Hutchinson Company Ltd. file.

Tynan Furniture Ltd. file.

Alberta Economic Development and Tourism Library

Alberta Industry and Resources, 1990.

Alberta's Trade with Mexico, 1992-1996.

Alberta's Trade with the United States, 1992-1996.

Canadian Trade Index data.

Data on Economic Changes in Alberta.

Dun & Bradstreet data.

Western Industrial Selectory, 1995.

Alberta Machinery Company Archives, Camrose

The Alberta Machinery Report, January 1989.

Alberta Municipal Affairs Archives, Edmonton

Alberta Census for 1991.

Alberta Treasury Branches Head Office Library, Edmonton

Annual Report for 1968-1969.

Financial Statements for the years 1947-1997.

Bank of Montreal Archives, Calgary

Canadian Bankers Association Statistics.

Bank of Montreal Archives, Toronto

"Creating the Institute for Small Business," *For the Record*, June 1994.

Calgary Court House, Records

Estate of Frederick D. Blake file.

Calgary Land Titles Office

Mortgage Records.

Canada Safeway Archives, Calgary

Canada Safeway Records.

Canadian Federation of Independent Business Library, Toronto

Ted Mallett, "Small Business: Banking on Job Creation, Results of 1994 CFIB Survey on Banking Issues."

Pat Thompson, "Small Business and Job Creation in Alberta 1991."

Canadian Pacific Railway Corporate Archives, Montreal

Canadian Pacific Railway Letterbook, 1910.

Canadian Western Natural Gas Company Archives, Calgary

Canadian Western Natural Gas Company, Annual Reports for 1960, 1970, 1980, 1990, 1995.

Canadian Western Natural Gas, Light, Heat and Power Company, *Annual Report for 1930.*

Canbra Foods Archives, Lethbridge

Canbra Foods Ltd., Annual Reports, 1985, 1990, 1995.

*Canbra Foods Ltd. 25*th *Anniversary Sept.13, 1982.*

City of Edmonton Archives

Edmonton Tent & Awning clipping file.

Gainers clipping file.

Lafleche Bros. clipping file.

Imperial Oil Ltd. clipping file.

James A. Powell & Company clipping file.

John A. McDougall & Co., Stock Book, 1884-1885.

Johnstone Walker clipping file.

Richard Secord Papers, Daily Journal for 1891.

Ross Bros. clipping file.

Sommerville Hardware Company clipping file.

Tax Revisions file.

Welsh's Saddlery clipping file.

W. W. Arcade Ltd. clipping file.

Foremost Industries Archives, Calgary

Canadian Foremost Ltd., Annual reports, 1989, 1990, 1991, 1992, 1994, 1995.

Foremost Industries, Corporate Fact Sheet, 16 September 1996.

Fort Macleod Court House, Records.

Estate of William Berry file.

Estate of Frank A. Dwelle file.

Estate of George M. Godley file.

Estate of Frederick H. Laing file.

Estate of Pearl Reach file.

Glenbow-Alberta Institute Archives, (GAIA)

Bruce Nodwell Papers.

Calgary Brewing and Malting Company Papers.

Calgary Power Company Papers.

Cyril Standen Papers.

George G. Coote Papers.

Frank Lynch-Staunton Papers.

Godsal Family Papers.

Great West Saddlery Company Papers.

Interview by Charles Ursenbach with Cyril Standen, 15 March 1979.

Interview by Charles Ursenbach with Ronald Henry Jenkins, September 1975.

Jenkins Grocerteria Ltd. Papers.

Reminiscences of Bruce Nodwell, Calgary, 1971.

Wesley F. Orr Letterpress Books.

Gulf Canada Resources Archives, Calgary

"Gulf Canada Limited."

Gulf Canada Resources, *Annual Report for 1995.*

"Gulf Canada Resources Limited — a history."

Gulf Oil Canada ... Proud Past, Exciting Future. Toronto: Gulf Oil Canada, 1969.

Imperial Oil Archives, Calgary

Imperial Oil Limited, *Annual Report for 1995.*

Imperial Oil Archives, Toronto

The Story of Imperial Oil. Toronto: Imperial Oil Limited, 1991.

"Imperial Oil — Environment, Health & Safety: Our Commitment Our Progress."

I-XL Industries Archives, Medicine Hat

W. Jack Sissons, "The History of Redcliff Pressed Brick Company Limited," Medicine Hat: typescript copy, 1995.

Lethbridge Court House, Records.

Estate of Ernest B. Stokes file.

Liberal Party of Canada Archives, Calgary

Creating Opportunity: The Liberal Plan for Canada. Ottawa: Liberal Party of Canada, 1993.

Provincial Archives of Alberta

Report of the Commissioner on Banking and Credit with Respect to the Industry of Agriculture in the Province of Alberta, 1922.

Red Deer and District Museum and Archives

Clippings file.

R. J. Welsh Ltd. Archives, Edmonton

"A Brief History of R. J. Welsh Ltd."

Royal Bank of Canada Archives, Calgary

  Royal Bank of Canada Statistics.

Royal Bank of Canada Archives, Toronto

  John E. Cleghorn, "Royal Bank Responds: What Can We Do For You," *Royal Bank Business Report: Planning Today for Tomorrow's Challenges,"* June 1994.

  "Small Business in Canada: A Regional Breakdown," Canadian Bankers Association, 19 April 1994.

Scotiabank Archives, Toronto

  Scotiabank, *Annual Report for 1993.*

Transalta Utilities Corporation Archives, Calgary

  Calgary Power Company, Annual reports for 1956, 1970.

  Transalta Utilities Corporation, Annual reports for 1981, 1995.

  "Transalta Utilities: 75 Years of Progress."

Interviews by the Author

Laurie Blackburn, 18 May 1991.

Donald F. Blake, 2 May 1991.

Andrew Carmichael, 9 July 1976.

Art Chesney, 26 September 1975; 2 August 1996.

Ken Chisholm, 21 May 1996.

Alan Cornyn, 23 May 1991.

Gordon W. Denoon, 9 March, 12 December 1991.

Mary Dover, 29 October 1973.

Stuart W. Dunlap, 20 May 1996.

Harry L. Dwelle, 3 May 1996.

Blain Fowler, 18 May 1996.

Maurice Francoeur, 18 May 1996.

Geoffrey Godley, 18 May 1991.

Peter S. Grant, 18 March 1997.

Garnet L. Hammer, 14 May 1996.

Tom Hoskin, 17 May 1996.

Emily Isley, 3 March 1997.

Frances Jean, 2, 13 February 1997.

Ronald H. Jenkins, 8 November 1973.

Richard Jewell, 16 May1996.

Gordon and Anola Laing, 11 May 1991.

Brian Leatherdale, 21 March 1997.

Neil Leatherdale, 14 May 1996.

Hugh Lynch-Staunton, 24 May 1991.

Rhona Mackay, 11 March 1997.

Norbert Mann, 3, 4 March 1997.

Gerry and Lorraine Maybank, 14 May 1996.

John A. McBride, 28 June 1994.

Ron Newsom, 22 March 1977.

Jack Nodwell, 8 December 1996.

Dan Olofson, 18 May 1996.

Jean Pare, 4 July 1996.

Charles G. Reach, 22 May 1991.

James Rouse, 17 May 1996.

James M. Sharp, 21 May 1996.

Gordon and Jack Sissons, 22 May 1996.

George W. Skene, 28 September 1974.

Cyril Standen, 11 November 1991.

John Stevenson, 23 May 1974.

Jack Stokes, 25 May 1991.

Sam Stone, 22 May 1996.

William E. Suitor, 22 April 1975.

Mel Svendsen, 9, 17 December 1996.

Ted Thaell, 25 May 1991.

William J. Tynan, 18 November 1991.

Donald G. Wilson, 25 May 1991.

R. Worsley, 3 March 1997.

University of Calgary Library
Dun & Bradstreet Reference Books.
Mackenzie King Diaries, Transcripts 21, 50, 52.

Newspapers
Albertan
Calgary Herald
Calgary Sun
Claresholm Advertiser
Edmonton Bulletin
Edmonton Capital
Edmonton Free Press
Edmonton Journal

Edmonton Sun.

Financial Post

Financial Times of Canada

Free Paper Publisher

Globe and Mail

High River Times

Lambton Observer and Western Advertiser

Lethbridge Herald

Macleod Gazette

Medicine Hat News

Nanton News

Red Deer Advocate

Stettler Independent

Strathcona Plaindealer

Business Magazines

Alberta Business

Alberta Report

Alberta Venture

Business Press

Calgary Commerce

Canadian Cattlemen

Canadian Grocer

Canadian Machinery & Metalworking

Canadian Textile Journal

Commerce

Energy Processing Canada

Food in Canada

Imperial Oil Review

Logging & Sawmillling Journal

Report on Business Magazine

Research

The United Farmer

Trade and Commerce

Western Business & Industry

Government Documents

Alberta, Department of Business Development and Tourism, Annual reports for 1976-77, 1979.

Alberta, Department of Economic Development and Tourism, news releases, 10-20 January 1997.

Canada, Department of Foreign Affairs and International Trade, Team Canada 1996 press releases, 10-18 January 1996; Team Canada 1997 press releases, 11 December-17 January 1997.

Canada, Department of Labour, *Report of Commissioner on investigation under the Combines Investigation Act into an alleged combine in the distribution of Tobacco Products in the Province of Alberta and elsewhere in Canada*, 31 August 1938.

Canada, *House of Commons Debates*, 1922-1935.

Canada, *Sessional Papers*, 1895, no. 30, *Report of the Railway Rates Commission*, 7 May 1895.

Canada, *Sessional Papers*, 1920, vol. 10, no. 37, *Report of the Deputy Minister of Labour for the year 1919*.

Canada, *Sessional Papers*, 1920, vol. 20, no. 36a, *Report of the Registrar of Boards of Conciliation and Investigation for the year ending 31 March 1916*, Proceedings, 1907-08.

Canada, *Statutes*, 1889, 1910, 1923, 1935.

Canada Year Book.

Canadian Annual Review.

Census of Canada, 1931.

Census of Canada, 1941.

Census of the Northwest Provinces, 1906.

Fourth Report of the Board of Railway Commissioners for Canada for 1909.

Fifth Report of the Board of Railway Commissioners for Canada for 1910.

Industry Canada, "Quarterly Report on Small- and Medium-Sized Enterprises, June 1994."

Industry Canada, "Reference Handbook on Small Business Statistics for 1994."

Industry Canada, "Regional Extension of the Reference Handbook on Small Business Statistics for 1992."

Industry Canada, "Small Business in Canada: A Statistical Overview, December 1993."

Journals of the Legislative Assembly of the Province of Canada, vol. 13, 1854-55, Appendix (Y.Y.).

Journals of the House of Commons, 1906-07, Appendix no. 6, Proceedings of the Select Committee Appointed for the Purpose of Inquiring into the Prices Charged for Lumber in the Provinces of Manitoba, Alberta, and Saskatchewan.

Labour Gazette, 1906,1947.

Ernest C. Manning, "A White Paper on Human Resources Development," March 1967.

Northwest Territories, Legislative Assembly, Debates, 1893.

Report of the Royal Commission on Price Spreads. Ottawa: King's Printer, 1935.

Pamphlets and Directories

Henderson's Calgary City Directory, 1908-1949.

Henderson's Edmonton Directory, 1908-1949.

Edmonton Directory for 1996.

Books

Alberta Law Reports, 1908.

Armstrong, Christopher, and H. V. Nelles, Monopoly's Moment: The Organization and Regulation of Canadian Utilities, 1830-1930. Philadelphia: Temple University Press, 1986.

Babcock, D. R., A Gentleman of Strathcona: Alexander Cameron Rutherford. Calgary: University of Calgary Press, 1989.

Bautier, Robert-Henri, The Economic Development of Medieval Europe. New York: Harcourt, Brace, Jovanovich, 1971.

Bennett, Richard E., A House of Quality It Has Ever Been: History of the Great-West Life Assurance Company. Winnipeg: The Great-West Life Assurance Company, 1992.

Bercuson, David Jay, ed., Alberta's Coal Industry, 1919. Historical Society of Alberta, Vol. 2, Calgary: Historical Society of Alberta, 1978.

Berton, Pierre, The National Dream: The Great Railway, 1871-1881. Toronto: McClelland & Stewart, 1970.

Berton, Pierre, The Last Spike: The Great Railway, 1881-1885. Toronto: McClelland & Stewart, 1971.

Blackford, Mansel G., and K. Austin Kerr, Business Enterprise in American History, Third Edition. Boston, Mass.: Houghton Mifflin Company, 1994.

Bliss, Michael, Northern Enterprise: Five Centuries of Canadian Business. Toronto: McClelland & Stewart, 1990.

Bliss, Michael, Right Honourable Men: The Descent of Canadian Politics from Macdonald to Mulroney. Toronto: Harper Collins Publishers, 1994.

Breen, David H., Alberta's Petroleum Industry and the Conservation Board. Edmonton: University of Alberta Press, 1993.

Breen, David H., The Canadian Prairie West and the Ranching Frontier, 1874-1924. Toronto: University of Toronto Press, 1983.

Breen, David H., ed., William Stewart Herron: Father of the Petroleum Industry in Alberta. Introduced and Edited by David H. Breen. Calgary: Alberta Records Publication Board, Historical Society of Alberta, 1984.

Brown, Craig, ed., The Illustrated History of Canada. Toronto: Lester Publishing, 1991.

Brown, Robert Craig, Robert Laird Borden: A Biography, Volume I: 1854-1914. Toronto: MacMillan Canada, 1975.

Brown, Robert Craig, and Ramsay Cook, Canada 1896-1921: A Nation Transformed. Toronto: McClelland & Stewart, 1974.

Byfield, Ted, ed., The Birth of the Province 1900-1910: Alberta in the Twentieth Century Volume 2. Edmonton: United Western Communications, 1992.

Byfield, Ted, ed., The Boom and the Bust 1910-1914: Alberta in the Twentieth Century, Volume 3. Edmonton: United Western Communications, 1994.

Byfield, Ted, ed., *The Great War and its Consequences 1914-1920: Alberta in the Twentieth Century*, Volume 4. Edmonton: United Western Communications, 1994.

Calgary, Alberta. Calgary, 1911.

Calgary Alberta Merchants and Manufacturers Record: The Manufacturing, Jobbing and Commercial Center of the Canadian West. Calgary: Jennings Publishing Company, 1911.

Canada West Foundation, *A Report on the Western Economic Opportunities Conference.* Calgary, 1973.

Chandler, Alfred D., Jr., *Scale and Scope: The Dynamics of Industrial Capitalism.* Cambridge, Mass.: Harvard University Press, 1990.

Chandler, Alfred D., Jr., *Strategy and Structure: Chapters in the History of the American Industrial Enterprise.* Cambridge, Mass.: MIT Press, 1962.

Chandler, Alfred D., Jr., *The Visible Hand: The Managerial Revolution in American Business.* Cambridge, Mass.: Harvard University Press, 1977.

Clark, E. Ritchie, *The IDB: A History of Canada's Industrial Development Bank.* Toronto: University of Toronto Press, 1985.

Craven, Paul, *An Impartial Umpire: Industrial Relations and the Canadian State, 1900-1911.* Toronto: University of Toronto Press, 1980.

Cruickshank, Ken, *Close Ties: Railways, Government, and the Board of Railway Commissioners, 1851-1933.* Montreal: McGill-Queen's University Press, 1991.

Dawson, R. MacGregor, *William Lyon Mackenzie King: A Political Biography, 1874-1923*, Volume One. Toronto: University of Toronto Press, 1958.

Dempsey, Hugh A., ed., *The CPR West: The Iron Road and the Making of a Nation.* Vancouver: Douglas & McIntyre, 1984.

den Otter, A. A., *Civilizing the West: The Galts and the Development of Western Canada.* Edmonton: University of Alberta Press, 1982.

Dominion Law Reports, 1917.

Eagle, John A., *The Canadian Pacific Railway and the Development of Western Canada.* Monteal: McGill-Queen's University Press, 1989.

Evans, Simon M., *Prince Charming Goes West: The Story of the E. P. Ranch.* Calgary, University of Calgary Press, 1993.

Finkel, Alvin, *The Social Credit Phenomenon in Alberta.* Toronto: University of Toronto Press, 1989.

Foran, Max, and Heather MacEwan Foran, *Calgary: Canada's Frontier Metropolis.* Toronto: Windsor Publications, 1982.

Fort Macleod History Book Committee, *Fort Macleod — Our Colourful Past: A History of the Town of Fort Macleod, from 1874 to 1924.* Fort Macleod: Fort Macleod History Book Committee, 1977.

Fullerton, Douglas H., *Graham Towers and his Times: A Biography.* Toronto: McClelland & Stewart, 1986.

George, Peter James, *Government Subsidies and the Construction of the Canadian Pacific Railway.* New York: Arno Press, 1981.

Glassford, Larry A., *Reaction & Reform: The Politics of the Conservative Party under R.B. Bennett, 1927-1938.* Toronto: University of Toronto Press, 1992.

Gray, James H., *R. B. Bennett: The Calgary Years*. Toronto: University of Toronto Press, 1991.

Hambly, J. R. Stan, ed., *A Light into the Past: The History of Camrose*. Camrose: Camrose Historical Society, 1980.

Hawkins, W. E., *Electrifying Calgary: A Century of Public & Private Power*. Calgary: University of Calgary Press, 1987.

Hesketh, Bob, and Frances Swyripa, eds., *Edmonton: The Life of a City*. Edmonton: NeWest Publishers, 1995.

Innis, Harold A., *A History of the Canadian Pacific Railway*. Toronto: University of Toronto Press, 1971.

Jamieson, Stuart, *Times of Trouble: Labour Unrest and Industrial Conflict in Canada, 1900-66*. Ottawa: Information Canada, 1968.

Johnston, Alex, John E. Stokes, Irma Dogterom, J. A. Sherman, and Carlton R. Stewart, *Lethbridge: Its Medical Doctors, Dentists, and Drug Stores*. Lethbridge: Lethbridge Historical Society, 1991.

Jones, David C., *Empire of Dust: Settling and Abandoning the Prairie Dry Belt*. Edmonton: University of Alberta Press, 1987.

Lambrecht, Kirk N., *The Administration of Dominion Lands, 1870-1930*. Regina: Great Plains Research Center, 1991.

Leonard, David, John E. McIsaac, and Sheilagh Jameson, *A Builder of the Northwest: The Life and Times of Richard Secord, 1860-1935*. Edmonton: Richard Y. Secord, 1981.

Levine, Allan, *The Exchange: 100 Years of Trading Grain in Winnipeg*. Winnipeg: Peguis Publishers, 1987.

Lyon, Jim, *Dome: The Rise and Fall of the House that Jack Built*. Toronto: Avon Books of Canada, 1983.

MacEwan, Grant, *Charles Noble: Guardian of the Soil*. Saskatoon: Western Producer Prairie Books, 1983.

MacEwan, Grant, *Frederick Haultain: Frontier Statesman of the Canadian Northwest*. Saskatoon: Western Producer Prairie Books, 1985.

MacEwan, Grant, *Pat Burns: Cattle King*. Saskatoon: Western Producer Prairie Books, 1979.

MacGregor, James G., *Edmonton Trader: The Story of John A. McDougall*. Toronto: McClelland & Stewart, 1963.

Macleod, R.C., *The North-West Mounted Police and Law Enforcement, 1873-1905*. Toronto: University of Toronto Press, 1976.

Mallory, J.R., *Social Credit and the Federal Power of Canada*. Toronto: University of Toronto Press, 1954.

Mansell, Robert L., and Michael B. Percy, *Strength in Adversity: A Study of the Alberta Economy*. Edmonton: University of Alberta Press, 1990.

McDowall, Duncan, *Quick to the Frontier: Canada's Royal Bank*. Toronto: McClelland & Stewart, 1993.

McIntosh, Robert, *Different Drummers: Banking and Politics in Canada*. Toronto: MacMillan of Canada, 1991.

McKenzie-Brown, Peter, Gordon Jaremko, and David Finch, *The Great Oil Age: The*

Petroleum Industry in Canada. Calgary: Detselig Enterprise, 1993.

Miller, Ruth Suitor, *Some Suitor Families of Canada and of the United States of America.* Asheville, North Carolina: Ward Publishing Company, 1987.

Miquelon, Dale, *Dugard of Rouen: French Trade to Canada and the West Indies, 1729-1770.* Montreal: McGill-Queen's University Press, 1978.

Morris, William E., *Chosen Instrument A History of the Canadian Wheat Board: The McIvor Years.* Winnipeg: The Canadian Wheat Board, 1987.

Morton, Desmond, *Ministers and Generals: Politics and the Canadian Militia, 1868-1904.* Toronto: University of Toronto Press, 1970.

Morton, W. L., *The Kingdom of Canada: A General History From Earliest Times,* Second Edition. Toronto: McClelland & Stewart, 1969.

Morton, W. L., *The Progressive Party in Canada.* Toronto: University of Toronto Press, 1950.

Nanton and District Historical Society, *Mosquito Creek Roundup.* Nanton: Nanton and District Historical Society, 1975.

Neatby, H. Blair, *William Lyon Mackenzie King, Volume II, 1924-1932.* Toronto: University of Toronto Press, 1963.

Newman, Peter C., *The Canadian Revolution, 1985-1995: From Deference to Defiance.* Toronto: Oxford University Press, 1995.

Olds History Committee, *Olds: A History of Olds and Area.* Olds: Olds History Committee, 1980.

Palmer, Howard, with Tamara Palmer, *Alberta: A New History.* Edmonton: Hurtig Publishers, 1990.

Radwanski, George, *Trudeau.* Toronto: MacMillan of Canada, 1978.

Randall, Stephen J., and Herman W. Konrad, eds., *NAFTA in Transition.* Calgary: University of Calgary Press, 1995.

Rasporich, A. W., ed., *The Making of the Modern West: Western Canada Since 1945.* Calgary: University of Calgary Press, 1984.

Regehr, T.D., *The Canadian Northern Railway: Pioneer Road of the Northern Prairies, 1895-1918.* Toronto: MacMillan of Canada, 1976.

Reynolds, Lloyd G., *The Control of Competition in Canada.* Cambridge, Mass.: Harvard University Press, 1940.

Richards, John, and Larry Pratt, *Prairie Capitalism: Power and Influence in the New West.* Toronto: McClelland & Stewart, 1979.

Rolph, William Kirby, *Henry Wisewood of Alberta.* Toronto: University of Toronto Press, 1950.

Santink, Joy L., *Timothy Eaton and the Rise of his Department Store.* Toronto: University of Toronto Press, 1990.

Schneider, Ena, *Ribbons of Steel: The Story of Northern Alberta Railways.* Calgary: Detselig Enterprises, 1989.

Stenson, Fred, *Waste to Wealth: A History of Gas Processing in Canada.* Calgary: Canadian Gas Processors Association, 1985.

Taylor, Graham D., and Peter A. Baskerville, *A Concise History of Business in Canada.* Toronto: Oxford University Press, 1994.

Thomas, Lewis G., *The Liberal Party in Alberta: A History of Politics in the Province of Alberta, 1905-1921*. Toronto: University of Toronto Press, 1959.

Thomas, Lewis H., *The North-West Territories 1870-1905*, The Canadian Historical Association Booklet No. 26. Ottawa: The Canadian Historical Association, 1970.

Thomas, Lewis H., ed., *William Aberhart and Social Credit in Alberta*. Toronto: Copp Clark Publishing, 1977.

Thompson, John Herd, and Stephen J. Randall, *Canada and the United States: Ambivalent Allies*. Montreal: McGill-Queen's University Press, 1994.

Traves, Tom, *The State and Enterprise: Canadian Manufacturers and the Federal Government, 1917-1931*. Toronto: University of Toronto Press, 1979.

Voisey, Paul, *Vulcan: The Making of a Prairie Community*. Toronto: University of Toronto Press, 1988.

Waite, Peter B., *Canada 1874-1896: Arduous Destiny*. Toronto: McClelland & Stewart, 1971.

Waite, P. B., *The Loner: Three Sketches of the Personal Life and Ideas of R. B. Bennett, 1870-1947*. Toronto: University of Toronto Press, 1992.

Ward, Max, *The Max Ward Story: A Bush Pilot in the Bureaucratic Jungle*. Toronto: McClelland & Stewart, 1991.

Watkins, Ernest, *The Golden Province: A Political History of Alberta*. Calgary: Sandstone Publishing, 1980.

Wetherell, Donald G., and Irene R. A. Kmet, *Town Life: Main Street and the Evolution of Small Town Alberta, 1880-1947*. Edmonton: University of Alberta Press, 1995.

Wilkins, Mira, *The Maturing of Multinational Enterprise: American Business Abroad from 1914 to 1970*. Cambridge, Mass.: Harvard University Press, 1974.

Wilkins, Mira, and Frank Ernest Hill, *American Business Abroad: Ford on Six Continents*. Detroit: Wayne State University Press, 1964.

Wilton, Carol, ed., *Beyond the Law: Lawyers and Business in Canada 1830 to 1930*. Toronto: The Osgoode Society, 1990.

Wood, David G., *The Lougheed Legacy*. Toronto: Key Porter Books, 1985.

Articles

Bliss, Michael, "Another Anti-Trust Tradition: Canadian Anti-Combines Policy, 1889-1910," *Business History Review* 47 (Summer 1973), 177-188.

Elofson, W.M., "Adapting to the Frontier Environment: The Ranching Industry in Western Canada, 1881-1914," in Donald H. Akenson, ed., *Canadian Papers in Rural History, Volume VIII*. Gananoque, Ontario: Langdale Press, 1992.

Foran, Max, "Calgary, Calgarians and the Northern Movement of the Oil Frontier, 1950-1970, in A. W. Rasporich, ed., *The Making of the Modern West: Western Canada Since 1945*. Calgary: University of Calgary Press, 1984.

Gibbins, Roger, "National Reconciliation and the Canadian West: Political Management in the Mulroney Era," in Andrew B. Gollner and Daniel Salee, eds., *Canada Under Mulroney: An End-of-Term Report*. Montreal: Vehicule Press, 1988.

Klassen, Henry C., "Canadian Bank of Commerce and Charles Rowley," *Alberta History* 39 (Summer 1991), 9-20.

Klassen, Henry C., "Cowdry Brothers: Private Bankers in Southwestern Alberta, 1886-1905," *Alberta History 37* (Winter 1989), 9-22.

Klassen, Henry C., "Entrepreneurship in the Canadian West: The Enterprises of A. E. Cross, 1886-1920," *Western Historical Quarterly 22* (August 1991), 313-333.

Klassen, Henry C., "Family Businesses in Calgary to 1939," in Max Foran and Sheilagh Jameson, eds., *Citymakers: Calgarians after the Frontier.* Calgary: The Historical Society of Alberta, Chinook Country Chapter, 1987, 303-319.

Klassen, Henry C., "I. G. Baker and Company in Calgary, 1875-1884," *Montana The Magazine of Western History 35* (Summer 1985), 40-55.

Klassen, Henry C., "Lawyers, Finance, and Economic Development in Southwestern Alberta, 1884-1920," in Carol Wilton, ed., *Beyond the Law: Lawyers and Business in Canada, 1830-1930.* Toronto: The Osgoode Society, 1990, 299-319.

Klassen, Henry C., "Private Banking in the West," *Canadian Banker 97* (September-October 1990), 52-56.

Klassen, Henry C., "R. G. Dun & Co.'s Early Years in Alberta, 1880-1900," *Alberta History 44* (Spring 1996), 11-18.

Klassen, Henry C., "The Bay and Calgary, 1874-1995," Short History of the Hudson's Bay Company in Calgary. Calgary: Hudson's Bay Company, 1995.

Klassen, Henry C., "The George F. Downes Firm and the Development of Edmonton and its Region, 1903-1930," in Carol Wilton, ed., *Inside the Law.* Canadian Law Firms in Historical Perspective. Toronto: University of Toronto Press, 1996.

Klassen, "The Hudson's Bay Company in Southwestern Alberta, 1874-1905," in Jennifer S. H. Brown, W. J. Eccles and Donald P. Heldman, eds., *The Fur Trade Revisited: Selected Papers of the Sixth North American Fur Trade Conference, Mackinac Island, Michigan, 1991.* East Lansing: Michigan State University Press, 1994, 393-408.

Klassen, Henry C., "The Role of Life Insurance Companies in the Economic Growth of Early Alberta," unpublished paper presented at Project 2005: An Alberta History Workshop, 12-14 May 1988, Red Deer College, Red Deer.

Knafla, Louis A., "Richard Bonfire Bennett: The Legal Practice of a Prairie Corporate Lawyer, 1898 to 1913," in Carol Wilton, ed., *Beyond the Law: Lawyers and Business in Canada, 1830 to 1930.* Toronto: The Osgoode Society, 1990.

Laxer, Gordon, "The Privatization of Public Life," in Trevor Harrison and Gordon Laxer, eds., *The Trojan Horse: Alberta and the Future of Canada.* Montreal: Black Rose Books, 1995.

Pratt, Larry, "The Political Economy of Province-Building: Alberta's Development Strategy, 1971-1981," in David Leadbeater, ed., *Essays on the Political Economy of Alberta.* Toronto: New Hogtown Press, 1985.

Taylor, Graham D., "From Branch Operation to Integrated Subsidiary: The Reorganization of Imperial Oil under Walter Teagle, 1911-1917," *Business History 34* (July 1992), 49-68.

Theses

Gordon, Stanley Bruce, "R. B. Bennett, M.L.A., 1897-1905: The Years of Apprenticeship," M. A. thesis, University of Calgary, 1975.

INDEX